CHILD MAINTENANCE –
THE CHILD SUPPORT ACT 1991

CHILD MAINTENANCE –
THE CHILD SUPPORT ACT 1991

Roger Bird LLB

District Judge, Bristol County Court and District Registry

with a contribution on Scottish law from

Joseph Thomson
Regius Professor of Law
University of Glasgow

FAMILY LAW
1993

Published by
Family Law, a publishing
imprint of Jordan Publishing Limited
21 St Thomas Street
Bristol BS1 6JS

© Jordan Publishing Limited 1993

British Library Cataloguing-in-Publication Data

A catalogue record for this book is available
from the British Library.

ISBN 0-85308-189-1

Cover illustration by Lesley Gwyther, aged 11

Photoset by Rowland Phototypesetting Ltd, Bury St Edmunds, Suffolk
Printed in Great Britain by Henry Ling Ltd, The Dorset Press, Dorchester

FOREWORD

The first edition of this book, published in 1991, provided a clear and sure guide to the provisions of the Child Support Act 1991. The necessary delegated legislation has now been enacted, and on 5 April the Act will be in force. District Judge Bird's book provides a comprehensive account of the new system of law which will have a vital impact on the family and the law – and on those who have to give advice.

The underlying message of the legislation is that the old law, administered by lawyers and the courts, was unnecessarily fragmented, uncertain in its results, slow and ineffective, and few would deny that there was scope for improvement. It has – certainly since the report of the Finer Committee nearly twenty years ago – been widely believed that there could be great advantage in allowing many issues about financial support levels to be settled by administrative means; but the extent to which the courts have been marginalised by the Child Support Act marks a bold – some may think a rash – assertion of the effectiveness of the new procedures.

Perhaps unfortunately, this change of direction does not mean that lawyers and the courts can leave everything to the officials of the Child Support Agency. Quite the contrary. It seems clear that in every divorce case in which there are children the court will need to know precisely what the – actual or potential – liability of the parties under the Child Support Act will be because that liability will be a financial obligation to which the court is bound, by the provisions of the Matrimonial Causes Act, to have regard; and the right of the parent with care to apply to the Agency for a Child Support assessment against the absent parent is equally obviously a resource to be taken into account. Moreover, there will be many cases in which lawyers will need to advise clients both on liability – is the father habitually resident in this country, and is he indeed the father, for example – and on the Act's procedures – is a person who has information about an absent parent entitled or bound to disclose it to the Agency, for example.

Although the Agency has published much very helpful explanatory material designed both for advisers and consumers, there is a self-evident need for an authoritative independent text such as is provided by this book. In the light of the House of Lords' decision in *Pepper v Hart* the quotations from government spokesmen made during the passage of the legislation through Parliament may be particularly helpful.

STEPHEN CRETNEY
February 1993

PREFACE

When the Child Support Act 1991 became law in the summer of 1991 it was known that it was intended to come fully into force in April 1993 and that much detail remained to be settled by statutory instrument. The regulations have now been made and April 1993 is nearly upon us, and so a second edition of this book has become necessary; it includes all the up-to-date material and, it is hoped, all that is necessary for the interested inquirer.

As before, I must thank Professor Stephen Cretney for reading the manuscript and for kindly agreeing once again to write a foreword. Readers of the first edition will remember that the cover design was taken from the winning entry in a competition among the pupils of SS Joseph and Teresa's Primary School, Wells, Somerset for a painting entitled 'Parent and child'; the Publishers and I were so pleased with the result that we have decided to retain it for this edition.

Finally, as the book goes to press, we learn that amendment regulations are to be laid before Parliament at some stage before April 1993. The probable effects of some of these amendments are predicted in the appropriate places in the text. It can confidently be predicted that these amendments will not be the last.

ROGER BIRD
February 1993

CONTENTS

APPENDICES

Table of Cases

References in the right-hand column are to paragraph numbers

Table of Statutes

References in the right-hand column are to paragraph numbers

Table of Statutory Instruments

References in the right-hand column are to paragraph numbers

List of Abbreviations

CS(AIAMA)Regs 1992	Child Support (Arrears, Interest and Adjustment of Maintenance Assessments) Regulations 1992
CSAT(P)Regs 1992	Child Support Appeal Tribunals (Procedure) Regulations 1992
CS(CE)Regs 1992	Child Support (Collection and Enforcement) Regulations 1992
CS(CEOFM)Regs 1992	Child Support (Collection and Enforcement of other Forms of Maintenance Regulations 1992
CSC(P)Regs 1992	Child Support Commissioners (Procedure) Regulations 1992
CS(IED)Regs 1992	Child Support (Information, Evidence and Disclosure) Regulations 1992
CS(MAJ)Regs 1992	Child Support (Maintenance Arrangements and Jurisdiction) Regulations 1992
CS(MAP)Regs 1992	Child Support (Maintenance Assessment Procedure) Regulations 1992
CS(MASC)Regs 1992	Child Support (Maintenance Assessments and Special Cases) Regulations 1992
CSAT	Child Support Appeal Tribunals
CSEG	Child Support Evaluation Group
CSO	Child Support Officer
DPMCA	Domestic Proceedings and Magistrates' Courts Act 1978
DSS	Department of Social Security
FPR	Family Proceedings Rules 1991
HFEA	Human Fertilisation and Embryology Act 1990
MCA 1973	Matrimonial Causes Act 1973
MCA 1980	Magistrates' Courts Act 1980
NFCA	National Foster Care Association
SSAC	Social Security Advisory Committee
SSAT	Social Security Appeal Tribunals

CHAPTER ONE

The Law before the
Child Support Act 1991

1. Introduction

1.1   Before 1990 it would not have occurred to most lawyers or members of
the public that the courts were not the appropriate forum for decisions as to
child maintenance when the parents could not agree. Maintenance of children
was regarded as merely one aspect of the family jurisdiction of the courts, and
there would have been few who would have thought that this aspect should be
removed from the courts and dealt with as a free-standing subject.

Nevertheless, this is precisely what has been achieved by the Child Support
Act 1991, the principles and provisions of which will be considered in Chapter 3
and the remainder of this book. In this chapter the powers of the courts and
the rights of parties before the coming into force of the Act must be considered.
There are two reasons for this.

First, the changes brought about by the Act can only be understood if what
went before is clear; as will be seen, the Act does not repeal any of the pre-existing
statutes nor establish new rules of law to be followed. Section 8, for example,
which in effect ousts the jurisdiction of the courts, does not change the pre-
existing law as such; it merely provides that in cases to which the Act applies 'no
court shall exercise any power which it would otherwise have'. The powers of the
court are not abolished; the effect is merely that they may not be exercised.

Secondly, the courts retain jurisdiction in respect of children who are not
'qualifying children', that is to say the natural or adopted children of both
parents. When the position of non-qualifying children, for example stepchildren, is considered in Chapter 8 it will be necessary to refer back to this
chapter for guidance as to the law which is applicable.

1.2   The coming into force of the Children Act 1989 introduced some order
into what had been a somewhat confusing system of overlapping jurisdictions.
Areas of the old law such as affiliation proceedings and the various Guardianship of Minors Acts have now gone and a clearer picture has emerged.

It is unfortunate, perhaps, that the Children Act did not introduce into the
field of child maintenance the degree of rationalisation and standardisation
which it might have done, but at least the system today is more rational than
it was.

Immediately before the coming into force of the 1991 Act, the position could be summarised using the following categories:

(a)   powers of the court in matrimonial proceedings under the Matrimonial Causes Act 1973;
(b)   powers of the court in domestic proceedings in magistrates' courts;
(c)   the position of married and unmarried parents under the Children Act 1989;
(d)   public law cases in respect of children.

These categories will now be considered in turn, with one further word of introduction. The Children Act 1989 introduced new 'private law' remedies and procedures relating to financial support of children which appear, on the face of the statute, to be all embracing and to be applicable in all cases no matter what the status of the parents or the context in which the proceedings are being brought. At the same time, it failed to repeal or amend certain statutes governing the same subject matter, notably the Matrimonial Causes Act 1973. The wording of the two statutes is different in minor but potentially significant respects and there could therefore be argument in a particular case as to whether the 'guidelines' in the 1973 Act or the 1989 Act should apply.

The view to be adopted in this book is that, despite appearances, the position is clear and that in applications under the 1973 Act, the 1978 Act (in the magistrates' courts) or the 1989 Act the court must follow the guidelines laid down by the Act under which the application is brought. Applications under different Acts will therefore be treated in (theoretically) different ways, but at least there will be no scope for confusion during the application itself.

2.   Powers of the Court in Matrimonial Proceedings

1.3   For the purpose of this section, 'matrimonial proceedings' means proceedings brought in a county court or the High Court under the Matrimonial Causes Act 1973.

Section 23 of the 1973 Act provides as follows:

'(1)   On granting a decree of divorce, a decree of nullity or a decree of judicial separation or at any time thereafter (whether in the case of a decree of divorce or of nullity of marriage, before or after the decree is made absolute) the court may make one or more of the following orders, that is to say . . .'

Various classes of orders as between spouses are then listed, before the following:

'(d)   an order that a party to the marriage shall make to such person as may be specified in the order for the benefit of a child of the family, or to such a child, such periodical payments, for such term, as may be specified;

> (e) an order that a party to the marriage shall secure to such person as may be so specified for the benefit of such a child or to such a child, to the satisfaction of the court, such periodical payments, for such term, as may be so specified;
>
> (f) an order that a party to the marriage shall pay to such person as may be so specified for the benefit of such a child, or to such a child, such lump sum as may be so specified;
>
> subject, however, in the case of an order under paragraph (d), (e) or (f) above, to the restrictions imposed by section 29(1) and (3) below, on the making of financial provision orders in favour of children who have attained the age of eighteen.
>
> (2) The court may also, subject to those restrictions, make any one or more of the orders mentioned in subsection (1)(d), (e) and (f) above –
>
> (a) In any proceedings for divorce, nullity of marriage or judicial separation, before granting such a decree; and
>
> (b) where any such proceedings are dismissed after the beginning of the trial, either forthwith or within a reasonable period after the dismissal.
>
> (3) Without prejudice to the generality of subsection (1) . . . (f) above –
>
> (a) . . .
>
> (b) an order under this section for the payment of a lump sum to or for the benefit of a child of the family may be made for the purpose of enabling any liabilities or expenses reasonably incurred by or for the benefit of that child before the making of an application for an order under this section in his favour to be met;
>
> (4) The power of the court under subsection (1) or (2)(a) above to make an order in favour of a child of the family shall be exercisable from time to time; and where the court makes an order in favour of a child under subsection (2)(b) above, it may from time to time, subject to the restrictions mentioned in subsection (1) above, make a further order in his favour of any of the kinds mentioned in subsection (1)(d), (e) or (f) above.'

1.4 Section 23 therefore sets out the classes of orders which the court may make in respect of children, namely orders for periodical payments, secured periodical payments, and a lump sum. 'Interim lump sum orders' under s 23(3)(b), while on the face of it a very useful way of obtaining interim relief, are, for some reason, almost completely ignored and the legal profession appears to be unaware of this subsection; it will not, therefore, be considered further here.

1.5 The 1973 Act imposes certain limits on the duration of children's orders and the age beyond which applications cannot be made. The general position is that no financial provision order or transfer of property order may be made in favour of a child who has attained the age of eighteen (s 29(1)) and the term to be specified in an order for periodical payments or secured periodical payments shall not in the first instance extend beyond the date of the child's birthday next following the school-leaving age (ie at present not beyond seventeen) unless the court considers that it should be so extended, and in any event must not extend beyond eighteen (s 29(2)(a) and (b)). However, by s 29(3), the court has discretion to waive these limits if the child is, or would be if an order were made, receiving instruction at an educational establishment or undergoing training for a trade, profession or vocation, whether or not he is also in gainful employment, or there are special circumstances which justify the making of an order without complying with these provisions.

The wording of the standard form of order for or to a child provides that the periodical payments shall continue until the child 'attains the age of seventeen or ceases full-time education, whichever be the later, or further order' (Practice Direction dated 10 July 1987 [1987] 2 All ER 1084) and this reflects the thinking behind the Act but, as has been seen, the court has wide discretion to do what is just in the circumstances.

1.6　Section 25 of the 1973 Act sets out 'guidelines' or statutory criteria to which the court must have regard when making any orders for financial relief under the Act; it has been said on occasions too frequent to enumerate that the provisions of s 25 are all that the court should consider and that reports of decided cases are of little importance in comparison.

Section 25(1) begins with the general requirement that it is the duty of the court to have regard to 'all the circumstances of the case, first consideration being given to the welfare while a minor of any child of the family who has not attained the age of eighteen'.

Section 25(2) sets out various matters to which the court must have regard as between parties to the marriage and s 25(3) continues as follows:

'(3)　as regards the exercise of the powers of the court . . . in relation to a child of the family, the court shall in particular have regard to the following matters –
(a)　the financial needs of the child;
(b)　the income, earning capacity (if any), property and other financial resources of the child;
(c)　any physical or mental disability of the child;
(d)　the manner in which he was being and in which the parties expected him to be educated or trained;
(e)　the considerations mentioned in relation to the parties to the marriage in paragraphs (a), (b), (c) and (e) of subsection (2) above.'

By virtue of s 25(2)(e) it is therefore necessary to refer back to s 25(2), the relevant considerations of which are as follows:

'(a)　the income, earning capacity, property and other financial resources which each of the parties to the marriage has or is likely to have in the foreseeable future, including in the case of earning capacity any increase in that capacity which it would, in the opinion of the court, be reasonable to expect a party to the marriage to take steps to acquire;

(b)   the financial needs, obligations and responsibilities which each of the parties to the marriage has or is likely to have in the foreseeable future;

(c)   the standard of living enjoyed by the family before the breakdown of the marriage;

(d)   any physical or mental disability of either of the parties to the marriage.'

Finally, s 25(4) deals with the position as regards the exercise of the powers of the court against a party to the marriage in favour of a child of the family who is not the child of that party. The significance of the term 'child of the family' in such circumstances will be considered further below at para **1.9** but for the moment it should be noted that s 25(4) provides that:

'. . . the court shall also have regard –

(a)   to whether that party assumed any responsibility for the child's maintenance and, if so, to the extent to which, and the basis upon which, that party assumed such responsibility and to the length of time for which that party discharged such responsibility;

(b)   to whether in assuming and discharging such responsibility that party did so knowing that the child was not his or her own;

(c)   to the liability of any other person to maintain the child.'

1.7   Although the statute provides for property adjustment orders and lump sum orders in favour of children, such orders are rare and applications for them have found little favour with the courts. In *Lord Lilford v Glyn* [1979] 1 WLR 78 (an application for a settlement of property), Orr LJ said that 'a father, even the richest father, ought not to be regarded as under financial obligations or responsibilities to provide funds for the purpose of such settlements as are envisaged in this case on children who are under no disability and whose maintenance and education are secure'. Likewise, in *Kiely v Kiely* [1985] 1 FLR 248, Booth J observed that 'lump sum orders in favour of children whose parents are of limited means, are rare' and later, disapproving the order which had been made in the lower court, she said that 'there was no evidence of need on the part of the children, or special circumstances which called for capital provisions to be made for their benefit'.

Accordingly, in the overwhelming majority of cases, financial relief for children has been limited to periodical payments and there has been little authority concerning the level of such periodical payments. In virtually all the reported cases (eg *Peacock v Peacock* [1984] 1 WLR 532, *Stockford v Stockford* [1982] 12 Fam Law 30, and *S v S* [1976] 3 WLR 775, the approach has been to consider the needs of the custodial parent and the family as a whole and to balance such needs against the ability of the non-custodial parent to pay. In reality there are few cases where the needs of the child can be considered in isolation from the needs of the caring parent who has to provide a home not only for the child or children but for herself.

In so far as any 'guidelines' have emerged, the practice of the courts has been to use two sets of figures as points of reference for the amount of children's orders. The first of these is the DSS income support allowances, which have fixed weekly amounts for children of various ages. These represent subsistence levels and show the amount which it is thought is needed to maintain a child at an adequate though fairly basic standard of living.

The second set of figures is that produced annually by the National Foster Care Association. These are, in effect, recommendations to local authorities by the NFCA, which is a voluntary organisation representing the interests of foster parents, and give the sums which the NFCA calculates are needed to cover the cost of looking after a foster child. These figures are much higher (sometimes three times greater) than the DSS allowances and are not adopted by all local authorities. Their use in the matrimonial jurisdiction is limited by the fact that few parents could afford to pay orders of that size. Nevertheless, they represent something akin to the 'upper limit', whereas the DSS figures represent basic needs.

These two sets of figures have therefore come to be used as the margins between which an order may be calculated whenever it has been necessary to consider a child's maintenance in isolation from that of its custodial parent.

Against this, of course, it is necessary to weigh the ability of the non-custodial parent to pay, and here the DSS figures have been frequently used again to calculate what might be called that parent's 'protected earnings' ie the level below which his income cannot be allowed to fall, calculated by reference to his housing needs, and his need to provide for himself and any new responsibilities, such as a wife or cohabitee and children or stepchildren, which he may have acquired.

1.8   A complicating factor in these calculations has been the disposition of the former matrimonial home. The 1973 Act contains wide powers to adjust the property rights of the parties to the marriage and to transfer property of either or both of them from one to the other. These will be considered in more detail in Chapter 2 as factors leading to the 1991 Act, but here it may be said that courts have accepted that where, for example, a husband has been deprived of his interest in a matrimonial home to provide security for his former wife and his children, it is not only necessary to recognise that he will incur considerable housing costs in 'starting again' but also some allowance should be made for the fact that he has been deprived, on paper at least, of his 'investment'. Given that orders for periodical payments are usually assessed on a global basis for the family as a whole, this has been one weight in the balance which has led to some very low orders for children.

1.9   Reference was made above to 'the child of the family' and the meaning of this term must now be considered. It will be seen later that the 1991 Act deals only with 'natural' children, ie the 'biological' or adopted children of both parents, and excludes stepchildren so that the latter will continue to be dealt with under the 'old law'.

By s 52(1) of the 1973 Act, 'child of the family' in relation to the parties to a marriage means:

'(a) a child of both those parties; and
(b) any other child, not being a child who has been boarded out with those parties by a local authority or voluntary organisation, who has been treated by both those parties as a child of their family.'

(As will be seen later, s 105(1) of the Children Act 1989 employs very similar wording.)

Where, therefore, a child is the natural child of one party to the marriage only (and has not been adopted) the non-parent's liability to maintain the child will depend on whether he and the natural parent have treated the child as a child of their family. There must be 'a family'; in *M v M* [1981] 2 FLR 39, where the parties separated before the birth of a child and never lived together during the lifetime of the child, it was held that the child was not a child of the family. However, once the parties live together with the child a very short period indeed may be taken as indication that they have treated the child as a child of the family; see *W v W* [1984] FLR 796 (two weeks), *Teeling v Teeling* [1984] FLR 808 (six months).

1.10 A child may be a child of more than one family. Moreover, more than one 'father' may be liable to maintain him; for example, where a husband and wife have treated the wife's child of a previous union as a child of their family, the husband will be liable to maintain the child but this does not relieve the natural father of his liability. Section 25(4) of the 1973 Act (see para **1.6**) provides some additional guidelines to be taken into account in such cases.

1.11 For the sake of completeness it should be noted that the 1973 Act provides a further remedy in respect of the maintenance of (inter alia) children, namely orders based on failure to provide reasonable maintenance. Section 27 of the 1973 Act provides that:

'(1) Either party to a marriage may apply to the court for an order under this section on the ground that the other party to the marriage (in this section referred to as the respondent) –
(a) has failed to provide reasonable maintenance for the applicant, or
(b) has failed to provide, or to make a reasonable contribution towards reasonable maintenance for any child of the family.'

The guidelines as to the exercise of the court's powers are similar to those set out above, and the orders which may be made are for periodical payments or a lump sum.

Section 27 might have been thought to provide a useful 'halfway house' remedy, enabling a parent to avoid the magistrates' court and go straight to the county court without making it necessary to start divorce, nullity or judicial separation proceedings. In fact, this remedy is very little used and there seems no point in further elaborating on it.

3   Powers of the Court in Domestic Proceedings in Magistrates' Courts

1.12   It is intended in this section to deal only with remedies under the Domestic Proceedings and Magistrates' Courts Act 1978, which applies where the parents are married. The position where the parents are not married is governed by the Children Act 1989 and will be considered below (see paras **1.16** to **1.22**).

By s 1 of the 1978 Act, an applicant may seek a financial order on the ground that the other party has failed to provide or make proper contribution towards reasonable maintenance for any child of the family. By s 8, 'child of the family' is defined in very similar terms to those contained in s 52(1) of the 1973 Act (set out at para **1.9** above). The case-law under the 1973 Act is equally applicable to the use of the phrase in the 1978 Act.

1.13   The other grounds for making an order under the 1978 Act apply as between husband and wife and need not be considered further. An application made in respect of a child will therefore turn on whether or not there has been failure to provide 'reasonable maintenance'. What is 'reasonable maintenance' is a matter of degree in each case and there is nothing in the Act to guide the courts on this point.

The law as developed in county courts and the High Court under the divorce jurisdiction is relevant to some extent and is frequently referred to; however there is one important difference, namely that in those courts the presumption is that the marriage has broken down and that the separation is permanent, whereas this may not always be the case in magistrates' courts proceedings.

Nevertheless, the guidelines as to the needs of the child, based on the DSS and NFCA figures (see para **1.7** above) are frequently used, and in deciding whether a parent has failed to provide reasonable maintenance his ability to pay must be a relevant factor. Accordingly his means and obligations will have to be considered by the court.

1.14   There are certain limited bars to the making of any order under the 1978 Act. First, s 26(1) requires a court hearing an application to consider whether there is any possibility of a reconciliation between the parties to the marriage and if at any stage, it considers that there is a reasonable possibility of such reconciliation, the court may adjourn the proceedings to enable reconciliation attempts to be made.

Secondly, by virtue of s 127 of the Magistrates' Courts Act 1980, the application must be made with six months of the date when the cause of complaint arose. However, failure to provide reasonable maintenance is almost invariably a continuing situation so it is unlikely that this would cause any difficulty in most cases.

1.15   Once the court finds the complaint that the respondent has failed to provide reasonable maintenance to be proved, it has to consider what order to make and on what basis it should be made. There are two orders which may be made under s 2 of the 1978 Act, namely:

(a)   an order that the other party shall make to the applicant such periodical payments in respect of a child of the family as may be specified in the order

(b)   an order for payment of a lump sum (not exceeding £1000) to or for the benefit of each child of the family.

For the reasons given in para **1.7** above, lump sum orders in favour of children are comparatively rare although it must be noted that the 1978 Act contemplates only very modest lump sums and such an order could be made, for example, to provide a school uniform, the cost of a minor operation or a school trip.

Nevertheless, the order which is most likely to be made is an order for periodical payments. The guidelines to be observed by the court in the exercise of its discretion are set out at s 3(1) and (2) of the 1978 Act; they are substantially similar to those contained in s 25 of the 1973 Act (see para **1.6** above) and need not be repeated here. The principles to be observed by magistrates' courts are therefore the same as in the courts above.

4.   Applications under the Children Act 1989

1.16   The Children Act 1989 is an important piece of legislation designed to embody all statutory provisions giving the court powers to make orders relating to the upbringing of children both in public and private law. It contains provisions relating to financial applications for children which, taken at their face value, seem to apply to all financial applications relating to children. However, as was explained at para **1.2** above, the Children Act does not repeal other statutory provisions such as the 1973 Act which also relate to this subject and it must therefore still be possible to make applications under those provisions.

This much is clear also from the Family Proceedings Rules 1991 which came into force on 14 October 1991, the same day as the Children Act. These rules clearly provide for applications for financial relief for children to be made either in the course of the matrimonial proceedings (in which case the 1973 Act would apply) or under the Children Act (in which case that Act would apply). The position is therefore that the applicant may have a choice of which statute to pray in aid, and that choice will determine the form of the application.

1.17   The powers of the court in relation to financial provision for children are set out in Sch 1 to the Children Act. Paragraph 1(1) defines the persons who may apply for an order against a parent of a child as:

(a)   a parent,
(b)   a guardian,
(c)   any person in whose favour a residence order is in force.

The meaning of 'parent' is not defined in the Children Act; its primary meaning is one who is, either in a biological sense or by virtue of an adoption order, the father or mother of the child. However, further considerations arise in cases to which ss 27 and 28 of the Human Fertilisation and Embryology Act 1990 apply; this subject is considered further at para **3.4**. Furthermore, as will be seen at para **1.23** below, orders may be made against a person who is not the mother or father of the child. The Children Act itself does not define the term 'child of the family' as does the 1973 Act (see para **1.9** above) but it must be taken that 'parent' in the Children Act includes someone, such as a step parent, who has treated a child as a child of the family and acquired 'parental responsibility'.

'Guardian' is defined by reference to s 5. Any individual may apply to the court to be appointed guardian of a child if either that child has no parent with parental responsibility for him or a residence order has been made in favour of a parent or guardian who has died.

A residence order may be made in favour of any person with whom the child lives, including a local authority in whose care the child is.

1.18   The financial provision orders which the court may make pursuant to Sch 1, para 1 are as follows:

'(a)   an order requiring either or both of the parents of a child –
   (i)   to make to the applicant for the benefit of the child; or
   (ii)   to make to the child himself,
   such periodical payments, for such term, as may be specified in the order;
(b)   an order requiring either or both parents of a child –
   (i)   to secure to the applicant for the benefit of the child; or
   (ii)   to secure to the child himself,
   such periodical payments, for such term, as may be so specified;
(c)   an order requiring either or both parents of a child –
   (i)   to pay to the applicant for the benefit of the child; or
   (ii)   to pay to the child himself,
   such lump sum as may be so specified;
(d)   an order requiring a settlement to be made for the benefit of the child, and to the satisfaction of the court of property –
   (i)   to which either parent is entitled (either in possession or in reversion); and
   (ii)   which is specified in the order;
(e)   an order requiring either or both parents of a child –
   (i)   to transfer to the applicant for the benefit of the child; or

(ii)   to transfer to the child himself,
such property to which the child is, or the parents are, entitled (either in possession or reversion) as may be specified in the order.'

Application for any of the orders mentioned above may be made to the High Court or a county court. Applications to a magistrates' court are limited to orders under (a) and (c).

1.19   The power conferred by para 1 of Sch 1 set out above may be exercised at any time (para 1(3)). However, the powers under the Matrimonial Causes Act 1973 to order a lump sum or transfer of property have been interpreted as meaning one lump sum and one transfer of property only and presumably this would be the case in relation to the Children Act powers. Periodical payments, as a continuing matter, may be varied or discharged at any time and para 1(4) specifically provides for this.

Without prejudice to the power of the court to order payment of a lump sum, para 5(1) provides that an order for

'payment of a lump sum may be made for the purpose of enabling any liabilities or expenses:
(a)   incurred in connection with the birth of a child or in maintaining the child; and
(b)   reasonably incurred before the making of the order, to be met.'

The power of a magistrates' court to order payment of a lump sum is limited to £1000 or such sum as may be fixed by statutory instrument.

1.20   By para 2, a person aged 18 or over may apply for the orders requiring either or both of his parents to pay to him periodical payments or to pay him a lump sum if:

(a)   he is, will be or (if an order were made) would be receiving instruction at an educational establishment or undergoing training for a trade, profession or vocation, whether or not while in gainful employment; or
(b)   there are special circumstances which justify the making of an order.

There are, however, two restrictions on this provision. First, an application may not be made by any person if, immediately before he reached the age of sixteen, a periodical payments order (as defined by para 2(6)) was in force with respect to him. Secondly, no order may be made at a time when the parents of the applicant are living together in the same household.

1.21   The provisions as to duration of children's orders, contained in para 3 of Sch 1, are virtually identical to those contained in s 29 of the 1973 Act (see para **1.5** above) and need not be repeated here. Paragraph 4 sets out the matters to which the court is to have regard in making orders for financial relief. These are as follows:

'(a)   the income, earning capacity, property and other financial resources which each person mentioned in subparagraph (4) has or is likely to have in the foreseeable future;

(b)   the financial needs, obligations and responsibilities which each person mentioned in subparagraph (4) has or is likely to have in the foreseeable future;
(c)   the financial needs of the child;
(d)   the income, earning capacity (if any), property and other financial resources of the child;
(e)   any physical or mental disability of the child;
(f)   the manner in which the child was being, or was expected to be, educated or trained.'

Subparagraph (4) states that the persons mentioned in subparagraph (1) are:

'(a)   in relation to a decision whether to exercise its powers under paragraph 1 [ie any of the orders set out at para **1.18** above], any parent of the child;
(b)   in relation to a decision whether to exercise its powers under paragraph 2 [ie applications by a person aged eighteen or over], the mother and father of the child;
(c)   the applicant for the order;
(d)   any other person in whose favour the court proposes to make the order.'

1.22   The guidelines set out above are very similar to those contained in s 25 of the 1973 Act (see para **1.6** above). However, there are two differences. First, the 1973 Act requires the court to have regard to any increase in the earning capacity of either party to the marriage which it would, in the opinion of the court, be reasonable to expect a party to the marriage to take steps to acquire. Secondly, by s 25(2)(c), the court must have regard to the standard of living enjoyed by the family before the breakdown of the marriage. Neither of these factors is mentioned in para 4 of Sch 1.

In *K v K (Minors: Property Transfer)* [1992] 2 FLR 220, CA, the court considered an application for the transfer of a council house tenancy from the unmarried father to the mother 'for the benefit of the children'. The application was brought under ss 11B(2)(d) and 12A of the Guardianship of Minors Act 1971, the provisions of which are very similar to those in the Children Act. It was held that the benefit referred to in s 11B was not confined to a financial benefit, nor does the child have to be given a financial interest in the property. It was also held that the judge's failure to apply the statutory checklist contained in s 12A was a fatal error.

1.23   Paragraph 4(2) of Sch 1 provides that:

'in deciding whether to exercise its powers under paragraph 1 against a person who is not the mother or father of the child, and if so in what manner, the court shall, in addition [to the matters set out in para 4(1)] have regard to –
    (a)   whether that person had assumed responsibility for the maintenance of the child and, if so, the extent to which and basis on

which he assumed that responsibility and the length of the period during which he met that responsibility;

(b) whether he did so knowing that the child was not his child;

(c) the liability of any other person to maintain the child.'

By para 4(3), where the court makes an order against a person who is not the mother or father of the child it shall record in the order that the order is made on the basis that the person against whom the order is made is not the child's father.

The practice of the courts in assessing the amount of child maintenance in applications under the 1973 Act (see para **1.7** above) would be equally applicable to cases decided under the Children Act.

5. Procedure in 'Private Law' Cases

1.24 The term 'private law' is used here to distinguish all the classes of case already discussed from the public law cases (which are dealt with at para **1.25** ff below). As has already been said, the powers conferred by various statutes overlap and the procedure to be adopted will depend on the statute which is chosen.

The position can be summarised as follows:

(a) *Application to magistrates' court under Domestic Proceedings and Magistrates' Courts Act 1978.* An application for a financial provision order under s 2 is made in Form 1, which is prescribed by the Family Proceedings Courts (Matrimonial Proceedings etc) Rules 1991. An application for a consent order is made in Form 2. Within 14 days of service of the application the respondent must file and serve an answer in the appropriate form.

(b) *Application to magistrates' court or county court under Children Act 1989.* This is governed by Part IV of the Family Proceedings Rules 1991. By r 4.4(1)(a), an application in respect of each child must be made in the appropriate form, specified in Appendix 1; the appropriate form is CHA 13. The form may be adapted so as to be used in whichever forum, magistrates' court or county court, the applicant chooses. Within 14 days of service of the application the respondent must file and serve an answer in Form CHA 13A. A directions appointment will then normally be given.

(c) *Application under Matrimonial Causes Act 1973.* This is governed by Part II of the Family Proceedings Rules 1991. Pursuant to r 2.55, applications for ancillary relief in respect of children are made in Form M 11 in the court in which the divorce suit is pending. By r 2.58 (2) and (3) the applicant must file an affidavit in support of the application and the respondent must file an affidavit in answer within 28 days after service. There will then be either a directions appointment or a hearing of the application.

6. The Public Law Aspect of Child Maintenance

1.25 It has always been a source of potential confusion that in addition to the whole system of 'private law' which has been considered so far in this chapter there existed also a body of social security law which might be invoked against a person who, under the 1991 Act, would be called an absent parent. The development of this law leading up to the 1991 changes will be considered further in Chapter 2 but the general principles may be considered here.

1.26 By s 24 of the Social Security Act 1986 (now embodied in the Social Security Administration Act 1992), the Secretary of State for Social Security may make a complaint to a magistrates' court where income support is claimed by or in respect of a person whom another person is liable to maintain. The court hearing the complaint has the power to order the liable person to pay such sum as it considers appropriate. By these means the DSS is able to enforce the liability to maintain.

The existence of a maintenance order or an order dismissing the right to maintenance made in other proceedings is in itself no bar to the magistrates considering the matter *de novo*. The possibility therefore existed (and still exists) that one court might decide that no maintenance was payable and, at the same time, another court might order a liable person to pay maintenance.

1.27 Until 1990 such clashes of jurisdiction were comparatively rare and the DSS normally accepted whatever the courts dealing with the private law aspect of the case ordered. However, this was changed by the insertion of a new s 24A into the Social Security Act 1986 (as now incorporated in the 1992 Act) and the introduction of the Income Support (Liable Relatives) Regulations 1990 and the Magistrates' Courts (Social Security Act 1986) (Transfer of Orders to Maintain and Enforcement of Maintenance Orders) Rules 1990.

The combined effect of these provisions may be summarised as follows:

(a) With the introduction of s 24A, the DSS obtained the power to transfer its own s 24 orders to the claimant when income support ceases. If the claimant is again in receipt of income support, the DSS will transfer back all rights previously transferred to the claimant. The only exception to this is that an order in respect of a personal allowance element cannot be transferred and is suspended until such time as a repeat claim is made.

(b) Section 24A allowed the DSS to seek recovery of the claimant's income support personal allowance (ie the sum payable by the DSS for the support of the claimant) in addition to the allowances for dependent children. The personal allowance element can only be recovered where the claimant is divorced from or was never married to the liable relative and applies only to 'lone parents' (ie not claims from couples or grandparents). Recovery will cease when the child is aged 16.

(c) The amounts which the court may order a liable relative to pay are the following:

  (i)   the income support personal allowance for each child the liable relative is liable to maintain;
  (ii) the family premium;
  (iii) the lone parent premium;
  (iv) the disabled child premium;
  (v)   any carer premium payable in respect of a disabled child for whom the liable relative is liable;
  (vi) all or some of the claimant's personal allowance.

1.28 The liabilities set out above are potentially substantial and herald the arrival of the 1991 Act. The changes came into effect on 15 October 1990. The advent of the 1991 Act may mean that that Act will be relied upon and that the 1990 changes to the 1986 Act and regulations will have only a short life.

1.29 Further sanctions continue to exist by virtue of s 26 of the 1986 Act, under which a person who persistently neglects or refuses to maintain himself or any person whom he is liable to maintain is guilty of an offence and is liable to imprisonment or a fine or both. This provision applies only where income support is being paid to the person who is not being maintained.

CHAPTER TWO

The Background to the Child Support Act 1991

1. Introduction

2.1 The Child Support Act 1991 has radically changed the law and procedure as to the determination and recovery of child maintenance throughout the United Kingdom. A remarkable feature of these changes has been the speed with which they have been introduced. The Children Act 1989 was a major piece of legislation which was intended to encompass all necessary provisions relating to children, and, as part of these provisions, contained a lengthy and elaborate schedule dealing with child maintenance. That Act completed its legislative passage in 1989 and was brought into force on 14 October 1991; however, even before it had come into force, the Child Support Act had been introduced, completed all its legislative stages and received Royal Assent. The result is that, even before it came into force, that part of the Children Act which deals with child maintenance was reduced to the status of transitional provision as it related to most children.

2.2 The purpose of this chapter is to provide an outline of the milestones in the events leading up to the passage of the Act. The present author is not a social historian, and is not therefore qualified to deal in detail with the question of whether there was popular pressure for the reform of the old system. A more limited task must be undertaken, and it is intended to set out what seems to have been the sequence of events leading up to the government of the day indicating its support for reform in 1990.

This account of events begins in about 1986, but it may be remembered that in 1974 the Finer Report recommended that maintenance for children and spouses should be assessed by administrative means and enforced by civil servants, without reference to the courts; one of the principal innovations in the Act has, therefore, its roots in the early 1970s, although whether the philosophy of Finer was an influence acknowledged by the proponents of the Act is debatable.

2.   The Australian System

2.3   It is generally agreed that the changes to the child maintenance system in Australia which began in 1986 have had a significant influence on the thinking of those responsible for the changes in the United Kingdom. Accordingly, a fairly detailed examination of the Australian provisions will assist in tracing the development of the 1991 legislation and in highlighting the differences between the two systems.

In 1986 the Australian Government circulated a discussion paper entitled *Child Support: A Discussion Paper on Child Maintenance* (Australian Government Publishing Service, Canberra, 1986). This drew attention to the fact that the majority of non-custodial parents did not make regular payments of maintenance and that where payment was made it was generally at low levels; the result was poverty among single parent families and high government expenditure on social security payments. The government of Australia set out its broad aims as follows:

'(a)   that non-custodial parents should share the cost of supporting their children according to their capacity to pay;

(b)   that adequate support be available for children of separate parents;

(c)   that commonwealth [government] expenditure be limited to what is necessary to ensure that those needs are met;

(d)   to ensure that neither parent is discouraged from participating in the work force; and

(e)   that the overall arrangements should be simple, flexible, efficient and respect personal privacy.'

2.4   The Australian government decided that the new scheme should be based on the use of a statutory formula for the administrative assessment of maintenance; that all persons and not only social security cases should be covered by the scheme; that taxation and other government information not available to the general public could be used in locating non-custodial parents and providing information about their income and other resources, and that deduction from earnings would be used where possible as a means of collecting maintenance.

Accordingly the Child Support Act 1988 was enacted, followed by the Child Support (Assessment) Act 1989. Although the scheme was conceived as a whole it was introduced in two stages. Stage 1, introduced in 1988, provided for the collection of maintenance orders and registered agreements through a Child Support Agency. Stage 2, which came into effect on 1 October 1989, provided for the administrative assessment of the amount of child support by means of the application of the statutory formula together with the collection by the Agency of the amounts so assessed. Stage 2 was not retrospective and applied only to parents who separated after 1 October 1989 or had a child on or after that date. Accordingly, a large number of families remain permanently outside stage 2.

Under stage 2 the function of assessing child maintenance was transferred from the courts to the Agency in all but a few unusual cases. It also allows parents to register their private agreements with the Agency.

In social security cases an element of compulsion exists in that any 'sole parent pensioner' with an order or agreement made after 1 June 1985 is compelled to register it with the Agency and a 'pensioner' is obliged to apply for assessment.

2.5 The Australian legislation is complicated and the statutes contain many provisions of a kind which will be included in statutory instruments here. In September 1989 the then Australian Minister for Social Security established the Child Support Evaluation Group (CSEG) whose terms of reference were to monitor the level of orders made by or registered with courts for maintenance of those children excluded from the assessment process under stage 2; to compare the levels of such orders with the levels of support obtainable under the stage 2 formula in comparable circumstances; and to monitor procedures to maximize the child support received by sole pensioners and ensure that the level of that support was adequate.

CSEG submitted its report in August 1990, and its findings can be briefly summarised as follows:

(a) The average level of court orders registered under stage 1 had increased substantially since the coming into force of the child support scheme; however, this average level still fell short of the administrative assessments made under stage 2.

(b) The real value of stage 1 orders and agreements declined every year because of inflation whereas stage 2 provided for automatic updating.

(c) In the year 1988/89, there were 8 cancellations of social security support for failure to 'take reasonable action for maintenance'; in the following year there were 35. However, the report observes that: 'this is not an adequate measure of the effect that the reasonable action requirement has had on sole pensioner numbers, but the other possible consequences are not easily estimated. For example there may be some people who will not have applied or not have proceeded with an application for sole parent pension because of reluctance to take maintenance action. More likely, there will be some sole parent pensioners who have voluntarily surrendered their pension or, when their entitlement has been reviewed, failed to return their review form rather than take the required action.'

(d) Approximately 1% of liable parents remain untraceable.

The recommendations of the CSEG were as follows:

(a) that the eligibility provisions of the 1989 Act be widened to include all children, including those at present restricted to stage 1.

(b) that, for the additional cases included by this widening of eligibility, application for administrative assessment under the Act be optional at the discretion of the custodial parent; and

(c) that the non-custodial parent who might be brought into stage 2 as a result of the widening of eligibility be entitled to object to administrative assessment; and that the grounds for objection include unfairness having regard to prior financial arrangements made between the parents, present obligations to other persons, and other relevant matters. Such objections should be dealt with by the courts.

2.6 It has been shown above that the Australian scheme is different in some respects from the United Kingdom scheme, notably in the two-stage system and in the ability to register orders and agreements with the Agency; there is also an important difference in the fact that in Australia if an absent parent foregoes his interest in a former matrimonial home in favour of the caring parent, the equity which he forgoes is converted into weekly sums and deducted from the formula maintenance payments. However, the scheme is very similar in structure and philosophy. One advantage (in terms of economic efficiency) which the Australian system has over its British counterpart is its use of the tax system to enforce payment.

The clear impression is that the introduction of the child support scheme in Australia has resulted in a much more efficient means of enforcing payment of reasonable maintenance by non-custodial parents.

3.   The Child Maintenance Review

2.7 On 18 July 1990 the then Prime Minister made an announcement in the House of Commons regarding changes in the child maintenance system. This followed a period during which concern had been expressed in various quarters about the shortcomings of the existing system. This concern seemed to have been directed at three main areas. First, the fact that there were many cases where children were born to young single mothers and no effort was made to recover maintenance from the father. Secondly, the demands on the social security budget caused by the increasing rate of marriage breakdown and financial settlements involving former matrimonial homes, under which absent parents were not required to pay realistic child maintenance. Thirdly, it was suggested by some that in adjudicating on marital financial disputes the courts had lost sight of the public interest element; in short, 'the taxpayer' was ignored. Some thought the high-water mark of this approach was the decision of the Court of Appeal in *Delaney v Delaney* [1990] 2 FLR 457, where the welfare benefits to which the wife was entitled played a major part in the Court's decision.

In her announcement on 18 July 1990, the Prime Minister declared the government's intention to:

'set up a new Child Support Agency which will have access to the information necessary to trace absent parents and make them accept their financial obligations . . . [and to] . . . move to assessing maintenance through a standard administrative formula which will take account of the parents' ability to pay, of the cost of bringing up a child – and the right of that child to share in their parents' rising living standards. Complicated cases may still have to be referred to the courts but the existence of the formula will help in these cases too.'

2.8 Following that announcement a discussion paper entitled *Child Mainten-ance Review* was published and circulated to interested bodies, making it clear that a White Paper was to be published in the Autumn. Among the objectives of the new proposals, it was said that:

'the needs of children should take priority over the interests of the parents in any financial or property arrangements and that the child's right to support should continue irrespective of the relations between the parents. It follows that as a matter of law the financial and property provisions for the child should be settled first, with issues about such provisions between the parents being limited to the residue of family income and assets.'

It is not clear whether that statement was intended to represent the govern-ment's interpretation of the law as it was in 1990 or as it was intended to be with the enactment of the proposed legislation.

The views of interested parties on the proposals were sought.

4. *Children Come First*

2.9 In October 1990 the government published a White Paper containing its proposals as to maintenance of children entitled *Children Come First*. This was in two parts, the first of which contained the proposals themselves and the second the statistical data on which the assertions made in the first part were based.

The case for change was succinctly set out in the summary (at vol I/i) in the following terms:

'The present system of maintenance is unnecessarily fragmented, uncertain in its results, slow and ineffective. It is based largely on discretion. The system is operated through the High and county courts, the magistrates' courts, the Court of Session and the sheriff courts in Scotland and the Offices of the Department of Social Security. The cumulative effect is uncertainty and inconsistent decisions about how much maintenance should be paid. In a great many instances, the maintenance awarded is not paid, or the payments fall into arrears and take weeks to re-establish. Only 30% of lone mothers and 3% of lone fathers receive regular maintenance for their children. More than 750,000 lone parents depend on income support. Many lone mothers want to go out to work but do not feel able to do so.'

The summary of the data in volume II itself made the following points (vol II/i):

(a)   Lone parent families in Great Britain have grown from under 600,000 in 1971 to over one million in 1986; they now form 14% of all families with children.

(b)   Lone parent families have become more dependent on social security benefits and have become less likely to receive maintenance.

(c)   Child maintenance is normally an issue for 13 to 16 years of a child's life.

(d)   There was great inconsistency in the amounts ordered by the courts, and also in the 'processing times' of the courts.

(e)   About 40% of cases experienced at least one period where the absent parent had failed to pay maintenance; 80% of arrears in DSS cases were not recovered.

2.10   The White Paper therefore proposed a new system for child maintenance. The assessment of maintenance would be based on a formula, the essential parts of which were a maintenance bill, exempt income of parents, a deduction rate of 50% from assessable income and a protected level of income. A Child Support Agency would be created. Where caring parents were receiving income support or family credit, they would be required to make a claim for maintenance to the Agency. The jurisdiction of the courts would be excluded. Caring parents in receipt of state benefits would not have the first £15 of maintenance taken into account in calculating their income.

A number of examples were given in the White Paper to show how the proposed system would work (some of these will be mentioned in later chapters as illustrations).

2.11   Comments were invited, to arrive not later than 14 December 1990. Many organisations and individuals did in fact comment and some of the positions which were reflected later in the parliamentary debates were foreshadowed. For example, one writer after commenting that 'few would dispute the government's contention that the present system of child maintenance is a shambles' went on:

'there is considerable cynicism about the government's motives for reforming child maintenance and fears about the consequences of some of the proposals. While conceding that the child maintenance system is due for reform the Child Poverty Action Group rejects government claims that the proposals are in the interests of either children or single parents. "We are worried" says Carey Oppenheim "that the prime motivation is saving money. Poverty will increase in families where women won't cooperate with the DSS. If their benefits are cut it is the children who will suffer."' (Anne Grossfurth, 10 *Legal Action*, December 1990.)

The article concluded:

'There is a need for a more rational basis for calculating maintenance payments. The formula proposed by the White Paper may even prove to be an effective solution. Transfer of responsibility for assessing, collecting and enforcing maintenance from the courts to an administrative agency may help to end delay and inconsistency. But underlying the proposals is the more objectionable aim of cutting benefits to one parent families. It is important that the government does not allow its commitment to the Treasury to take precedence over the financial wellbeing and physical safety of women and children.'

Nevertheless, when the government's bill was published on 15 February 1991, it was virtually identical with the proposals in *Children Come First*.

5.   The Maintenance Enforcement Act 1991

2.12   In the meantime, between the publication of *Children Come First* and the closing date for submissions, the government introduced a Maintenance Enforcement Bill in the House of Lords. This Bill was intended to deal with the problem that courts making maintenance orders were unable to specify detailed methods of payments; for example it was not possible to make an attachment of earnings order until arrears had accrued.

The provisions of the Bill can be summarised as follows:

(a)   The High Court and county courts are given the power, when making or dealing with orders for periodical payments, to specify the method of payment. Henceforth these courts will be able to order payment by eg standing order. The Bill also confers on the High Court and county court the power to make an attachment of earnings order immediately rather than having to wait for arrears to accrue.

(b)   Magistrates' courts are required to specify the method of payment of a maintenance order, for example by direct payment through the court, by standing order or by attachment of earnings order.

2.13   Moving the second reading of the Bill on 29 November 1990, Earl Ferrers referred to *Children Come First* and explained the government's proposals to reform the law relating to child maintenance. He continued:

'However, the Child Support Agency, if it has Parliament's approval, will not be fully operational until the mid 1990s and we cannot ignore until then the problems which lone parents face in collecting and enforcing mainte-nance for themselves and for their children. That is why we have introduced this Bill today.'

The Bill went through the usual legislative process and passed into law.

6.   The Child Support Bill

2.14   The Bill which became the Child Support Act was published on 15 February 1991 and received Royal Assent on 25 July 1991. The entire process, initial announcement by the Prime Minister, consultation paper, White Paper and Bill going through all its legislative stages, thus took almost exactly one year, a tribute to the commitment of the proponents of the legislation.

The explanatory and financial memorandum accompanying the Bill stated that:

'it introduces a new method of conducting maintenance by a non-discretionary formula. The formula is designed to produce a level of maintenance that reflects the day to day living costs of raising a child but takes account of the essential living expenses of both the person with care and the absent parent.

The Bill makes provision for the Secretary of State to trace absent parents and assess, collect and enforce maintenance payments. In large measure it removes from the courts the responsibility for assessing claims for child maintenance and varying existing orders.'

The financial effects of the Bill were as follows:

'When fully implemented, the additional cost to the Department of Social Security of the administrative arrangements required for the purposes of the Bill is an estimated £35 million per year. Costs will eventually be reduced, to some extent, by the reduction of work connected with the existing terms of maintenance. The improved arrangements for the assessment and payment of maintenance which are provided by the Bill are expected to provide a reduction of an estimated £400 million per year in social security expenditure from the Consolidated Fund.

As a necessary adjunct to the measures in the Bill, Cm 1264 *Children Come First* announced benefit changes affecting family credit, housing benefit and community charge benefit designed to assist parents who wish to work. After the transitional period, these changes will cost £63 million (net) per year at 1990/91 prices.

From April 1993 the Child Support Agency will require approximately 4,700 staff. Some 2,500 posts currently allocated within the Department of Social Security to work relating to maintenance will be subsumed within that figure.'

2.15   The scene was thus set for some lively Parliamentary debates. In this section it is intended to record briefly some of the arguments for and against the Bill in the debates in the House of Lords (the Commons debates, though full, were on more partisan lines and failed to demonstrate the expertise shown in the Lords and the Commons own social security committee).

Moving the second reading of the Bill, the Lord Chancellor reminded the House of the Children Act 1989:

'That Act brings together in a single coherent code the law on the physical care and upbringing of children. This Bill, in achieving a similar result for the duty to maintain children, is a natural adjunct to it. Like the Children Act and the rest of the review of the family law it is informed by two central principles or objectives, namely the giving of priority to the welfare of the child and the primary responsibility of parents for securing that welfare even where the parents' own relationship has broken down . . .

One consequence of the technical nature of the Bill is that it contains . . . a rather larger than usual number of regulation-making powers. The principles and intentions of the scheme are quite clear on the face of the Bill. However, the great variety of situations to which the scheme is to be applied requires that the detailed provisions are better left to be dealt with by secondary legislation. This controlled use of regulations allows a valuable flexibility within the scheme.' (*House of Lords, Official Report*, 25 February 1991, col 773 and 778).

Replying, Lord Mishcon referred to the Bill as a 'legislative skeleton' and commented:

'. . . under the Bill there will fall to be made 94 regulations. Of that figure, if your Lordships examine clause 38 of the Bill, 12 only are subject to the affirmative resolution of Parliament. That is very distressing; it is constitutionally objectionable.' (col 780).

The Bishop of Gloucester said that he believed 'that the creation of a single, powerful and well publicised Child Support Agency could be significant of the nation's will to grapple with the problem of the children who are at risk and suffering as a result of family breakdown.' (col 808).

2.16 Outright and forthright opposition to the Bill was expressed by Lord Houghton of Sowerby:

'This Bill is not a Child Support Bill; it is a taxing Bill. I am surprised that the Chancellor of the Exchequer has not certified it as a Money Bill and included it as a schedule in the Finance Bill. It imposes a form of taxation upon an identifiable section of the community who will be mostly men; there are to be inspectors who will assess what they shall pay, determine the method and the order in which they shall pay it, and they have the power to enforce it. In short this tax is PAYT, pay as you are told. It is levied by a separate arm of the bureaucracy which is to be specially created for the task. The Bill reflects the outburst of the former Prime Minister, Mrs Thatcher, whose concern for children came second to not allowing absentee fathers to get away with non-payment of maintenance. It is a middle class approach to the conventional obligations of men towards their children.' (col 812).

This was merely the first of many critical contributions by Lord Houghton at all stages of the Bill's passage through the Upper House. Similarly, the speech of Lord Simon of Glaisdale, a former Solicitor General, President of the then Probate Divorce and Admiralty Division and Lord of Appeal in Ordinary foreshadowed his contribution to many of the debates to come.

Lord Simon drew attention to the 'extraordinary nature' of the formula:

'I ask your Lordships, how many maintenance debtors or creditors, how many citizens' advice bureaux, can possibly make head or tail of what it means? It is just as incomprehensible as the ancient Egyptian hieroglyphs must have been to an illiterate peasant in the Nile Delta. It would not matter so much if the background of the Bill were less bureaucratic . . . so what we have is a bureaucratic formula which is to be administered, as has been pointed out, by a considerable bureaucracy; 4,700 people, of whom 2,200 are to be newly recruited and added to our existing bureaucracy. Is that what we want?' (col 817).

2.17   The battle-lines were drawn, and the debate continued throughout the Bill's passage. Possibly the most acrimonious exchanges (if that term can be used when referring to the civilised and courteous debate in the House of Lords) came during the committee stage on 19 March 1991 when clause 22 was being debated. Clause 22 provided for a partial disallowance of benefit for a caring parent who fails to co-operate with the Child Support Agency and reappears in the Act as s 46.

Moving an amendment to the clause, Earl Russell pointed out that income support:

'is a subsistence benefit. I am not convinced by the argument that it is possible to live on 20% of it. The right to social security benefit is part of the nexus of obligations which make up citizenship. It goes with the obligations to pay taxes and the right to vote. For a long time it has been a basic principle of English law that allegiance carries with it the right to protection. In this day and age I do not think that we can interpret the right to protection as meaning simply the right to protection from violent crime or external aggression. It also means protection from deprivation. I do not see any good reason for depriving people of benefit to the point where they get below subsistence level.' (*House of Lords, Official Report*, 19 March 1991 col 535).

The contrary view was put by Lord Coleraine:

'It cannot be right for the single mother to refuse to name the parent of her illegitimate child so that the state, rather than the parent, who is probably working, bears the cost of the maintenance. That means that the maintenance is paid by the taxpayer.' (col 540).

The matter went to a division where the government suffered a defeat and clause 22 was amended in such a way as to delete its punitive aspect. However, this was to be a shortlived victory for the opponents of the clause; it was re-introduced in the House of Commons and was part of the Bill which finally received Royal Assent.

2.18   The whole parliamentary passage of the Bill cannot be chronicled here. Further extracts from speeches in the debates are set out, where appropriate, in later chapters. It is fair to say that it was a controversial measure, particularly in the House of Lords, and that tempers were sometimes frayed. Eventually, however, it received Royal Assent and is now in force, fully as from 5 April 1993.

7. The Regulations

2.19 One of the distinctive features of the Act was the large amount of detail which was left to be determined by regulation. Until these regulations were published it was not possible to predict accurately the overall effect of the provisions of the Act (see, for example, the first edition of this book).

Sets of regulations were laid before Parliament and eventually made on various dates beginning with 20 July 1992, to come into force on 5 April 1993. These were the Child Support (Maintenance Assessment Procedure) Regulations 1992; the Child Support (Information, Evidence and Disclosure) Regulations 1992; the Child Support (Arrears, Interest and Adjustment of Maintenance Assessments) Regulations 1992; the Child Support (Maintenance Assessments and Special Cases) Regulations 1992; the Child Support (Collection and Enforcement Regulations 1992; the Child Support (Collection and Enforcement of other Forms of Maintenance) Regulations 1992; the Child Support Appeal Tribunals (Procedure) Regulations 1992; the Child Support Commissioners (Procedure) Regulations 1992; the Child Support Fees Regulations 1992; and the Child Support (Maintenance Arrangements and Jurisdiction) Regulations 1992. These sets of regulations emanated from the Department of Social Security. At the same time, various orders and sets of rules came from the Lord Chancellor's Department. These dealt with such matters as consent orders and applications for declaration as to parentage and details will be found in the appropriate chapters. Finally, the Child Support Act 1991 (Commencement No 3 and Transitional Provisions) Order 1992 was made.

Particulars of the acronyms used to describe these various sets of regulations throughout this book will be found in the List of Abbreviations, at page xxv.

CHAPTER THREE

The General Principles and Characteristics of the Act

1. Introduction

3.1 The long title of the Act is 'An Act to make provision for the assessment, collection and enforcement of periodical maintenance payable by certain parents with respect to children of theirs who are not in their care; for the collection and enforcement of certain other kinds of maintenance; and for connected purposes'.

In earlier chapters the background and purposes of the Act, and its relationship to the 'old law' have been considered; in later chapters the detail of the Act and the way in which it is intended to work will be examined. Here, it is intended to set out in outline the general scheme of the Act, to consider its basic principles and to examine some of its key terms and concepts. It will be seen that some terms (eg 'parent') have a different meaning under this Act from that adopted in other legislation, even legislation as close in time and subject matter as the Children Act 1989.

2. The Duty to Maintain

3.2 Section 1 of the Act sets out the basic principle underlying the whole Act, namely that parents have an obligation to maintain their children, and then deals with how that obligation may be discharged. By s 1(1):

'. . . each parent of a qualifying child is responsible for maintaining him.'

This defines the obligation in general terms. Section 1(2) then goes on to provide that for the purposes of the Act:

'. . . an absent parent shall be taken to have met his responsibility to maintain any qualifying child of his by making periodical payments of maintenance with respect to the child of such amount, and at such intervals, as may be determined in accordance with the provisions of this Act.'

In other words, once the obligations imposed by the Act have been discharged, no further liability under the Act exists.

Section 1(3) introduces the concept of the 'maintenance assessment'; and provides that:

'where a maintenance assessment made under this Act requires the making of periodical payments, it shall be the duty of the absent parent with respect to whom the assessment was made to make those payments.'

In s 1, therefore, are found the statutory obligations to maintain (s 1(1)), and to pay the maintenance assessment (s 1(3)) and, in s 1(2), a statement of the sufficiency of making payments under the Act.

3.3   Section 1 introduces the terms 'qualifying child', 'absent parent' and 'maintenance assessment'. These are all terms new to English law, as are 'person with care', and 'child support maintenance', which appear in s 3. These terms are central to the philosophy of the Act and their meaning must be considered in detail.

Section 3 is a definition section and sets out the meaning of certain terms of the Act, as follows.

By s 3(1), a child is a 'qualifying child' if:

'(a)   one of his parents is, in relation to him, an absent parent; or
(b)   both of his parents are, in relation to him, absent parents.'

Section 3(2) defines an absent parent as follows:

'The parent of any child is an "absent parent", in relation to him, if:
(a)   that parent is not living in the same household with the child; and
(b)   the child has his home with a person who is, in relation to him, a person with care.'

This definition leads on to the definition of 'person with care'. By s 3(3) a person is a 'person with care' if he is a person:

(a)   with whom the child has his home;
(b)   who usually provides day to day care for the child (whether exclusively or in conjunction with any other person); and
(c)   who does not fall within a prescribed category of person.'

Paragraphs (a) and (b) are clear enough, but (c) requires further clarification. The Act supplies a part of this by the negative provisions of s 3(4). This sets out a list of people whom the Secretary of State may not prescribe as a category under s 3(3)(c).

The result of this combination of double negatives is therefore as follows. By s 3(3)(c) the Secretary of State may prescribe categories of persons who are not capable of being a person with care and who are thus unable to apply for a 'maintenance assessment'). Since they may not include the persons set out in s 3(4), those persons are always capable of being 'a person with care'.

Section 3(4) provides that the Secretary of State:

'. . . shall not, under subsection (3)(c), prescribe as a category:
(a) parents;
(b) guardians;
(c) persons in whose favour residence orders under section 8 of the Children Act 1989 are in force;
(d) in Scotland, persons having the right to custody of a child.'

By reg 51(1) of the CS(MAP)Regs 1992 the prescribed persons who may not be persons with care are:

(a) a local authority;
(b) a person with whom a child who is looked after by a local authority is placed by that authority under the provision of the Children Act 1989;
(c) in Scotland, a person with whom a child is boarded out by a local authority under the provisions of s 21 of the Social Work (Scotland) Act 1968.

By s 3(5), for the purposes of the Act, there may be more than one person with care in relation to the same qualifying child.

3.4 It should be noted here that the term a 'person with care' has a greater significance than its subsidiary role in 'qualifying child' and 'absent parent'. A 'person with care' is one of the classes of person who may apply for a maintenance assessment under s 4(1).

At this stage, before considering the general principle of the Act, one further term must be defined, namely that of 'parent', and for this it is necessary to turn to s 54, the general interpretation section. 'Parent', in relation to any child 'means any person who is in law the mother or father of the child'. To be 'a parent' therefore it is necessary to be either the natural father or mother of the child (unless the child is subsequently adopted) or to be treated in law as parent by virtue of an adoption order. However, even the term 'natural mother or father' is now subject to qualifications because of modern scientific advances in 'artificial' means of procreation. The position is governed both by common law and ss 27 and 28 of the Human Fertilisation and Embryology Act 1990, the combined effect of which is as follows:

(a) a woman who bears a child will, at the child's birth, always be regarded as the legal mother (HFEA, s 27(1));
(b) in principle, the father of a child is the person who provides the sperm which leads to conception. However, this is subject to the following exceptions;
    (i) the husband of a woman who is artificially inseminated is treated as the father of the child, unless it is proved that he did not consent to the treatment (HFEA, s 28(2));
    (ii) where a woman has been artificially inseminated in the course of treatment provided for her and a man under the licensing

procedure established by HFEA then the man is treated as the
father (HFEA, s 28(3));

(c) a donor of sperm for the purposes of 'treatment services' provided
under the HFEA is not to be treated as the child's father;

(d) at common law, a number of presumptions arise, all of which are
capable of being rebutted, eg the husband of a married woman is the
father of the child and a man whose name is entered as father in the
Register of Births is the father.

The concept of 'child of the family' does not appear in the Child Support Act;
a stepchild, or child who has been treated as a child of the family, is not capable
of being a 'qualifying child' as regards the step parent. However, such a child,
or his parent, does not lose his right to be maintained under the 'old law' and
this is considered further in Chapter 8 (see para **8.5**). In passing, it may be said
that henceforth a husband or wife whose spouse has children of a previous
union will have a positive disincentive to seek to adopt those children.

The general principle of the Act may therefore be stated as follows: the Act
imposes obligations upon the parents of children where:

(a) the parents are or are presumed to be the natural or adoptive parents of the
child;

(b) one or both parents do not live in the same household as the child;

(c) the child lives with a person with care who provides for the child.

3.5 Section 1(3) above refers to a 'maintenance assessment', which, by s 54, is
defined as 'an assessment of maintenance made under this Act'. There is no
further definition in the Act but the meaning is clear in the context of the Act,
since, as will be seen, a maintenance assessment can only be made by a child
support officer. Section 3(6) provides that 'periodical payments which are
required to be paid in accordance with a maintenance assessment are referred
to in this Act as "child support maintenance"'.

The manner in which child support maintenance is determined is considered
further below (see paras **3.10** to **3.13**).

3.   The Welfare of the Children

3.6 The marginal note to s 2 of the Act describes that section as 'welfare of the
children: the general principle'. Section 2 itself provides that:

'Where, in any case which falls to be dealt with under this Act, the Secretary
of State or any child support officer is considering the exercise of any
discretionary power conferred by this Act, he shall have regard to the welfare
of any child likely to be affected by his decision.'

Section 2 was not included in the original Bill and so represents the result of
further thought on the part of the government. In considering what this
provision will mean it may be useful to begin with a comparison with two other
statutory provisions in related fields.

Section 1(1) of the Children Act 1989 repeats a principle contained in earlier statutes, namely that in proceedings concerned with the upbringing of a child or the administration of a child's property or the application of any income arising from it:

'the child's welfare shall be the court's paramount consideration.'

Section 25(1) of the Matrimonial Causes Act 1973 was amended in 1984 to include the provision that, when considering any application for financial relief, whether for the parties to a marriage or their child, it is the duty of the court to have regard to all the circumstances of the case:

'first consideration being given to the welfare while a minor of any child of the family who has not attained the age of eighteen.'

Section 2 of the 1991 Act differs from its predecessors in three important respects. First, it imposes obligations on the Secretary of State and the child support officers, reflecting the fact that it is they rather than the courts who will be making decisions affecting children. This will be significant when the question of remedies for breach of the statutory obligations is considered.

Secondly, it does not make the welfare of children the first or paramount consideration; it merely says that regard is to be had to such welfare. It therefore carries less force than the other provisions.

Thirdly, s 2 has a wider ambit than the other provisions in that it directs attention to the welfare of any child likely to be affected by the decision. The other statutes require regard to be had to the welfare of a child who is directly involved in the litigation; the reference to 'any child' goes very much further than this as will be seen at para **3.8**.

3.7 There are many occasions on which the Secretary of State or child support officer will have to have regard to s 2. The occasions on which discretion will be exercised are numerous, but the most important may be summarised as follows.

(a)   The decision as to whether to arrange for the collection and enforcement of maintenance (s 4(2) and (3)).

(b)   The decision whether to require a person with care to give the authorisation to apply for a maintenance assessment (s 6(2)).

(c)   The decision as to whether to make an interim assessment (s 12(1)).

(d)   The decision as to whether to make a fresh assessment (s 19).

(e)   The decision as to whether to arrange for the collection of child support maintenance (s 29(1)).

(f)   The decision as to whether to collect and enforce other forms of maintenance, and how sums should be allocated (s 30(1) and (3)(c)).

(g)   The decision as to whether to make a deduction from earnings order (s 31(2)).

(h)   The decision as to whether to apply to magistrates for a liability order (s 32(2)).

(i)   The decision whether to enforce a liability order by distress (s 35(1)).

(j)   The decision whether to apply to magistrates for commitment to prison (s 40).

(k)   The decision whether to give a reduced benefit direction (s 46(5)).

3.8   When making any of these decisions the Secretary of State or child support officer must 'have regard to' the welfare of any child. What does this mean? As has been seen, the welfare of children is not the first or paramount consideration. Would the production of a completed checklist showing that the officer concerned had gone through a prescribed procedure and applied his mind to the welfare of children be sufficient?

Only a tentative answer can be given to such questions. It is suggested that, where it could be shown that the consequences of any decision would be detrimental to the welfare of any child in question, it could then fairly be argued that the officer concerned had not had regard to the welfare of that child. It might be thought that the areas which are most likely to produce a challenge to the discretionary powers of the child support officer are reduced benefit directions, liability orders and distress.

The requirement to have regard to the welfare of any child likely to be affected by the decision is a wide one. It clearly includes not only the children in respect of whom maintenance assessments are being made or enforced but also the children in the home of the absent parent for whom that parent provides. The possibility might then arise of a conflict of interest between the child whose maintenance assessment was not being paid, and whose needs were therefore not being provided for, and the child of the absent parent who would suffer deprivation if the absent parent were forced to pay money which he could not afford or were committed to prison.

3.9   What is the remedy of a person who considers that the Secretary of State or child support officer has failed to observe the statutory duty imposed by s 2? In principle the answer is an application for judicial review. This is considered further in Chapter 6 (see para **6.37** et seq) and will not be discussed in detail here, save to say that judicial review is concerned with the propriety of the decision-making process rather than the merits of the decision itself, and that judicial review would not be appropriate where the structure of the Act itself contained a right of appeal.

4.   The Child Support Officer and the Agency

3.10   Moving the second reading of the Child Support Bill on 25 February 1991 the Lord Chancellor said:

'. . . a Child Support Agency will be established as a next steps agency under the authority of . . . the Secretary of State for Social Security. The agency will trace absent parents, investigate the parents' means and assess, collect and enforce payments of child maintenance . . . [A]s a next steps agency, the agency will have no independent existence in statute. The powers that it will need to do its work are, therefore, expressed as powers of . . . the Secretary of State for Social Security.'

Although in reality the Child Support Agency looms large in any consideration of the new law and procedure it is nowhere mentioned in the Act, for the reason given above by the Lord Chancellor. Instead, the Act confers all the powers to be exercised by the Agency on 'the child support officer', to be appointed under s 13.

By s 13, the Secretary of State (wherever reference is made to 'the Secretary of State' it is a reference to the Secretary of State for Social Security) must appoint child support officers for the purpose of exercising functions conferred on them by the Act or by any other enactment, or functions assigned to them by the Secretary of State. Section 13(2) provides that a child support officer may be appointed to perform only such functions as may be specified in his instrument of appointment. Whatever the functions of an individual officer may be, the general intention is clear.

When procedure is considered in Chapter 4, it will be seen that, under s 4(1), applications for child support maintenance ('a maintenance assessment') must be made to the Secretary of State, on whom s 4 imposes certain obligations. Not surprisingly, the Secretary of State will not carry out these obligations personally; instead, under s 11, he must refer any application for a maintenance assessment to a child support officer 'whose duty it shall be to deal with the application in accordance with the provision made by or under this Act'. It will therefore be the function of the child support officer to consider the application, to obtain such information as he requires, to make the assessment and, if necessary, to take steps to enforce it. Further, when appeals are considered in Chapter 6, it will be seen that when a person is dissatisfied by a maintenance assessment his first step is to apply to the Secretary of State for a review, whereupon, by s 18(7), the Secretary of State will 'arrange a review . . . to be conducted by a child support officer who played no part in taking the decision which is to be reviewed'. Initially, therefore, one child support officer will review the decision of another, a procedure familiar to social security law.

3.11 It is provided that a chief child support officer shall be appointed under s 13(3), whose duty shall be to:

'(a)   advise child support officers on the discharge of their functions in relation to making, reviewing or cancelling maintenance assessments;

 (b)   keep under review the operation of the provision made by or under this Act with respect to making, reviewing or cancelling maintenance assessments; and

(c) report to the Secretary of State annually, in writing, on the matters with
which the Chief Child Support Officer is concerned.'

The only comment which needs to be made is that this is a fairly common
arrangement in social security legislation.

The other significant personnel to feature in the Agency's work will be the
inspectors. By s 15(1), the Secretary of State may appoint inspectors where he
'considers it appropriate to do so for the purpose of acquiring information . . .
for purposes of this Act'. Their powers will be considered further in Chapter 4,
but here it may be noted that they have wide powers of investigation and
entry.

5. The Formula

3.12 We must now consider how assessments are to be made and what
principles are to be employed.

Section 11(2) and (3) provide as follows:

'(2) The amount of child support maintenance to be fixed by any maintenance assessment shall be determined in accordance with the provisions of Part I of Schedule 1.

(3) Part II of Schedule 1 makes further provision with respect to maintenance assessments.'

Schedule 1 will be considered in detail in Chapter 5. Here, it is necessary
only to note the vital fact that it contains a formula, or series of formulae, for the
determination of maintenance assessments. The formula consists of four basic
elements, namely:

(a) The maintenance requirement, ie an amount, calculated by reference to
the income support rates, which represents the basic cost of maintaining
the children who qualify for a formula award.

(b) The assessable income, ie the sum left from the parent's net income (ie
after deduction of tax and national insurance contributions) after deducting 'exempt income' or income which is considered necessary for the
parents' essential day to day expenses.

(c) The deduction rate, ie the percentage of the parent's assessable income to
be taken to meet the maintenance requirement, subject to a top limit.

(d) Protected income, ie the income level below which no absent parent's
income will be allowed to fall.

This process therefore involves a series of calculations, the formula being
applied to the facts of any particular situation. The intention is that no element
of discretion should be involved, so that there will be a 'correct' decision in
every case, provided the formula has been properly applied.

3.13 The belief that proper application of the formula will give an un-
challengeable answer is given as the reason why the role of the courts has been

rendered unnecessary (as to which see paras **3.14** and **3.15** below) and explains the thinking behind the system of review and appeals. The child support officer will apply the formula to the facts of a particular case as if he were calculating a benefit such as income support. It is likely that computers will be used for this process, as they are in family credit applications. When one party is aggrieved the first step is review by another child support officer who checks to make sure that the formula has been correctly applied. Further appeal is to a tribunal whose role will be to ensure that the rules have been correctly applied. No element of discretion will be allowed; the formula alone will rule. Since no element of discretion is involved, the welfare of the child or children cannot be invoked by a person dissatisfied by an assessment.

6. The Exclusion of the Court

3.14 One of the most novel features of the new child support law is the virtual total exclusion of the jurisdiction of the courts. Even the residual 'topping up' function left to the courts can only be embarked upon after a full formula assessment has been made by the child support officer.

Section 8 applies where a child support officer would have jurisdiction to make a maintenance assessment with respect to a qualifying child and an absent parent of his on an application duly made by a person entitled to apply (s 8(1)). The section applies, and the jurisdiction of the court is excluded, even where the circumstances of the case are such that the child support officer would not make an assessment if it were applied for (s 8(2)); this means that, for example, if the result of the formula calculation is that no assessment should be made, there is no alternative remedy available to the person with care. Section 8(3) provides:

'In any case where subsection (1) applies, no court shall exercise any power which it would otherwise have to make, vary or revise any maintenance order in relation to the child and absent parent concerned.'

In other words, where a person entitled to apply for a maintenance assessment in respect of a qualifying child and an absent parent wishes to apply for maintenance, it must be done by means of an application to the Secretary of State and not to the courts. The jurisdiction of the courts is completely excluded. Some of the possible reasons for this have already been discussed. Whatever the reason may be, the intention of the legislation is clear. Child maintenance is assessed by means of the formula which is certain and un-changeable. To permit the courts to become involved, whether in making the assessment or in reviewing assessments, would be to introduce an element of discretion which might result in departures from the formula. This cannot be contemplated; hence the exclusion of the role of the courts.

3.15 It follows from this that (subject to the transitional provisions, as to which see Chapter 9) parents who wish to make formal arrangements for the payment of maintenance have the choice of either a voluntary agreement, which can be legally binding and be sued upon like any other civil debt (this will be considered further in Chapter 8) or an application to the Secretary of State for a maintenance assessment. In the latter case they must accept the formula award whether they like it or not. The position of persons with care who are in receipt of state benefits is even more closely regulated and is dealt with at para **3.16** below.

In the context of breakdown of marriage, there are further implications. For example, a court dealing with an application for a property adjustment order pursuant to s 23 of the Matrimonial Causes Act 1973 will not be able to make an order in respect of the children of the marriage as part of its overall disposition; moreover, a parent with care who is, or will at any time in the future be, in receipt of benefit will not be able to contract out of the right to receive or the duty to pay child maintenance as part of a larger 'package deal'. Insofar as they can, the parties and the court will have to predict what the liability of the absent parent is likely to be and bear that in mind when negotiating or ordering that part of the financial and other obligations and liabilities with which the court can deal.

The courts retain jurisdiction in respect of non-qualifying children such as stepchildren. In respect of qualifying children, the role of the court is limited to three cases. First, where a maintenance assessment is in force, the court may make an order for additional amounts to be paid. Secondly, the court may make orders limited to periodical payments for some or all of the expenses incurred in the provision of instruction or training or to meet some or all of any expenses of a disabled child which are attributable to that disability. These possibilities are considered further in Chapter 8. Finally, by s 8(4), it is provided that the prohibition of the intervention of the court contained in s 8(3) does not prevent a court from revoking a maintenance order.

7.   The Link with State Benefits

3.16   The fact that the new child support system is the creature of the Department of Social Security has never been concealed. The Secretary of State responsible is the Secretary of State for Social Security. The system of child support officers, Chief Child Support Officer, inspectors, and tribunals is modelled on the social security system and the amounts of maintenance assessments are based on social security rates of payment. However, there are further provisions in the Act which impose particular obligations on a person with care of a qualifying child who is in receipt of benefit. Section 6 provides:

'(1)   Where income support, family credit or any other benefit of a pre-scribed kind is claimed by or in respect of, or paid to or in respect of, the parent of a qualifying child she shall, if:
(a)   she is a person with care of the child; and
(b)   she is required to do so by the Secretary of State,
authorise the Secretary of State to take action under this Act to recover child support maintenance from the absent parent.

(5)   That authorisation shall be given, without unreasonable delay, by completing and returning to the Secretary of State an application . . .'

The remainder of the section will be considered in detail in Chapter 4 but the extract given above sets out the basic principle. It should also be noted at this stage that s 6(9) imposes on the parent an obligation to give such information as may be necessary to enable the absent parent to be traced.

3.17   Many details of the system established by the Act were left to be determined by statutory instrument. The principle is clear: a parent (normally a mother) who is in receipt of benefit must apply for a maintenance assessment. The specific benefits cited are of a non-contributory nature and so the Department of Social Security would gain from the making of a maintenance assessment by an appropriate reduction in the maintenance recovered. The other benefits which the Secretary of State has prescribed are of the same nature and do not include contributory benefits such as unemployment benefit or sickness benefit.

The duty to give information means that the mother has to name the father and give all necessary information to enable him to be traced. It may be noted at this stage that, under s 6(10), the Secretary of State may prescribe by statutory instrument circumstances in which the obligation to provide information shall not apply and may also waive the obligation in prescribed circumstances, and such regulations have been made. These will be considered in more detail later, but one obvious example of where this would be appropriate would be where the mother was in genuine fear of physical violence at the hands of the father. There is, of course, nothing new about the DSS taking an assignment of an order for periodical payments where the receiving parent is in receipt of benefit. Such orders have normally been made in, or, if made elsewhere, registered in, a magistrates' court. For about 20 years it has not been the practice of the DSS to seek to compel a parent to take action against a father, so there is a new element in this legislation, and the statutory obligation to provide information is also new.

The new system is tailor-made for the parent on benefit; the whole organisation of assessment and enforcement will make it easier and more effective for such a parent (or, more accurately, the DSS, to which in fact the financial gain will accrue) to recoup money from an absent parent. However, a distinctive feature of the new system is that the parent who is not in receipt of benefit has to go through exactly the same system, if maintenance is to be recovered other than by voluntary agreement.

8.   The Role of Delegated Legislation

3.18   During the parliamentary debates on the Bill, one criticism frequently made was that so much remained to be determined by statutory instrument. On dozens of occasions, power is conferred on the Secretary of State to make regulations to govern a particular implementation of the Act. The result was that it was sometimes difficult to predict exactly how the Act was going to work, although it must be said that some of the regulation-making powers are quite specific about what the regulations may provide (for example the regulations as to protected income provided for under Sch 1, para 6).

3.19 Whatever the reasons or justification for this state of affairs, it is a fact that the complete picture of how the Act works only emerged when all the regulations were made and published. This process is now complete and the regulations will be discussed in detail in the appropriate places in this book.

9. Tax Relief

3.20 Under the 'old law', parents who made payments of maintenance to a spouse or former spouse for the benefit of a child or children are entitled to tax relief on the payments up to a maximum limit of the difference between the single person's and married couple's personal allowance. By s 62(1) of the Finance (No 2) Act 1992 this has been extended to payments of child support made under the child support scheme.

10. General Summary

3.21 The outline of the general principles and characteristics of the legislation given above shows that the whole system of assessment and recovery of financial support for children has very radically changed. Detailed consideration of how the new system will work in practice will be given later. At this stage, however, the following general observations may be made.

The system of child maintenance under which parents pursue their remedies through the courts is almost completely abolished. Subject to limited exceptions and transitional provisions the only way to recover maintenance is to apply to an organ of the state which will assess maintenance according to a predetermined formula with no scope for discretion. This state agency also has powers of investigation for the purposes of obtaining information for the assessment and is charged with the task of enforcing and recovering the money due under its assessment. Parents in receipt of state benefits are compelled to apply for assessments and subject to statutory obligations to provide information to the agency.

This clearly represents a major extension of the role and powers of the state into what has hitherto been regarded as an area of private law. The detailed implications of this will be explored in the remainder of this book.

CHAPTER FOUR

Procedure for Obtaining Assessment

1. Introduction

4.1 A person with care of a qualifying child who decides to apply for an assessment of maintenance will probably do so for one of three reasons. First, she may have no choice; if she is in receipt of state benefits the Act imposes a positive obligation on her to do so (see para **4.9** below). Secondly, the absent parent may be paying nothing or, even if he is paying, the person with care may consider the payment to be insufficient; in other words, the parents have reached no agreement on what is a suitable amount. Thirdly, the parents may have agreed a figure but the parent with care requires the protection of a formal arrangement.

4.2 As has been seen in Chapter 1, the Australian scheme for child support, on which the Act was largely based, permits parents to register an agreement with the authorities and the agreement can then be enforced under the statutory provisions. There is no such provision in the Act. By s 9(2), nothing in the Act shall be taken to prevent any person from entering into a maintenance agreement (defined, by s 9(1), as 'any agreement for the making, or for securing the making, of periodical payments by way of maintenance, or in Scotland aliment, to or for the benefit of any child'. Anyone therefore, even a parent with care in receipt of income support, may make a maintenance agreement.

However, there are two important factors which restrict this right. In the first place, s 9(3) provides that the existence of a maintenance agreement shall not prevent any party to the agreement, or any other person, from applying for a maintenance assessment with respect to any child to or for whose benefit periodical payments are to be made or secured under the agreement. Secondly, s 9(4) provides that a provision in an agreement which purports to restrict the right of any person to apply for a maintenance assessment shall be void. It is therefore impossible to contract out of the child support system (except, to a limited extent, under the transitional provisions, as to which see Chapter 9).

It should also be borne in mind that a parent with care, with or without the benefit of a maintenance agreement, who applies for an assessment, has no say in what the result would be. Therefore, a parent with the benefit of an agreement would not be able to request an assessment in an agreed sum; the system allows no such flexibility. The assessment would be that dictated by the formula, nothing more nor less. (Limited scope exists for consent orders: see para **8.34**.)

The Act contains separate provisions for persons with care who are in receipt of state benefits and those who are not; a clear two-tier system is established. A person not in receipt of benefits has the choices set out in the preceding paragraph. These choices are not available to someone in receipt of benefits who, as will be seen, may be compelled to apply for an assessment and will be subject to sanction if she does not do so.

2.   Jurisdiction

4.3   The first point to be established in any particular case is whether the child support officer has jurisdiction to make an assessment. Section 44(1) provides that he only has jurisdiction:

> with respect to a person who is:
> (a)   a person with care;
> (b)   an absent parent; or
> (c)   a qualifying child;
> if that person is habitually resident in the United Kingdom.

It is therefore necessary for all three persons mentioned above to be habitually resident; if any of them is not, the child support officer will not have jurisdiction. The term 'habitually resident' is not defined in the Act, but it occurs in other statutes, for example Domicile and Matrimonial Proceedings Act 1973, s 5(2)(b), and has been considered in several cases, for example *R v Barnet London Borough Council, ex parte Shah* [1985] 2 AC 309 and *Kapur v Kapur* [1984] FLR 920. Habitual residence does not require continued presence in a place but involves the establishment of a sufficient degree of settled residence in a country to justify the court, or in this case the child support officer, assuming jurisdiction.

Where the person with care is not an individual, it is not necessary to show habitual residence of that person.

By s 44(3), regulations may provide for the cancellation of any assessment where any of the three persons mentioned above ceases to be habitually resident.

Although there appears to be no specific regulation governing this point, the position also seems to be covered by para 16(5)(a) of Sch 1 to the Act which enables a child support officer to cancel an assessment where he would no longer have jurisdiction to make an assessment if it were to be applied for at that time; reg 52 of the CS(MAP)Regs 1992 sets out the procedure to be followed in such cases (see further para **4.56**).

3. Is the Child a Qualifying Child?

4.4 The first question to be asked is that set out above; if the child is not a qualifying child it will be necessary to make application to the courts and this is dealt with in Chapter 8. The meaning of 'qualifying child' was considered in Chapter 3 at paras **3.3** and **3.4** and need not be considered further here. However, it is essential that the qualifying child be a child; s 55 deals with the meaning of 'child'.

By s 55(1), a person is a child if:

'(a) he is under the age of 16;
 (b) he is under the age of 19 and receiving full-time education (which is not advanced education):
   (i) by attendance at a recognised educational establishment; or
   (ii) elsewhere, if the education is recognised by the Secretary of State;
 (c) he does not fall within paragraph (a) or (b) but:
   (i) he is under the age of 18, and
   (ii) prescribed conditions are satisfied with respect to him.

Section 55(4) provides that the Secretary of State may recognise education provided otherwise than at a recognised educational establishment only if he is satisfied that education was being provided for the child immediately before the age of 16; s 55(6) provides that, in determining whether a person falls within s 55(1)(b), no account shall be taken of such interruptions in his education as may be prescribed.

By these provisions, therefore, there is no doubt as to the eligibility of a person aged under 16. Likewise a person aged 19 and over is excluded from the definition of child; a 'child' at university therefore will normally not fall within the Act and, if maintenance is sought for such a 'child', it will be necessary to apply to the courts.

The 16 to 18-year-old is in an intermediate position. If he receives 'advanced education', he is excluded; 'advanced education' is defined as 'education of a prescribed kind'. The term 'recognised educational establishment' contained in s 55(1)(b)(i) means 'an establishment recognised by the Secretary of State for the purposes of this section as being, or as comparable to, a university, college or school'.

4.5 The position of 16 to 18-year-old children only becomes clear when the regulations are considered, and the position is governed by Sch 1 to the CS(MAP)Regs 1992. By para 2 'advanced education', for the purposes of s 55, is defined as a course in preparation for a degree, a diploma of higher education, HND or HNC, or a teaching qualification, plus any other course which is of a standard above ordinary national diploma, national diploma or national certificate of the Business and Technician Education Council or the Scottish Vocational Educational Council, SCE A level or Scottish Higher level or certificate of sixth-form studies.

Anyone involved in any such course, therefore, is not a 'child' for the purposes of the Act. This does not, of course, mean that no maintenance is recoverable for such a child, since the jurisdiction of the court would not be excluded.

Paragraph 1 of Sch 1 deals with 16 and 17-year-olds who are not in full-time non-advanced education ('non-advanced education' is a term first encountered in the regulations, but it is introduced to tie up with the definition in s 55(1)(b) set out above); para 1 deals in effect with young people who are on training schemes.

A person of 16 or 17 who is not in full-time non-advanced education can only be a child within the meaning of s 55(1)(c) if four conditions are fulfilled. These conditions may be summarised as follows:

(a)   he is registered to work or for training under youth training with the Department of Employment, or the Ministry of Defence, or a local education authority (in England and Wales), or an education authority (in Scotland) or a corresponding body in another member state of the EC;

(b)   he is not engaged in remunerative work, other than work of a temporary nature that is due to cease before the end of the extension period which applies to him;

(c)   the extension period has not expired;

(d)   immediately before the extension period begins he is a child for the purposes of the Act without regard to this paragraph.

Para 2 contains the detail about 'extension periods' and need not be set out here. It is important to note that a person may not be a child for the purposes of the Act if he is engaged on training under Youth Training or if he is entitled to income support.

A 16 to 18-year-old who has left school and is not engaged in education of any sort will be excluded from the definition of child.

Finally, it should be noted that para 3 of Sch 1 defines what is 'full-time education'. Essentially, the course must comprise more than 12 hours' instruction, tuition, project, etc per week. There are quite elaborate provisions for dealing with interruptions of full-time education which need not be set out here and will be found in the regulations themselves at Appendix 2.

4.6   For the purposes of the Act, a person is not a child if he:

'(a)   is or has been married;

(b)   has celebrated a marriage which is void; or

(c)   has celebrated a marriage in respect of which a decree of nullity has been granted.'

The excluding factor is therefore the participation in a ceremony of marriage, whether or not this was a valid ceremony. Presumably, a person aged under 16 who had taken part in a ceremony of marriage (which would be void *ab initio*) would be excluded from the provisions of the Act. 'Marriage' is not defined in the Act.

4. Who May Apply?

4.7 Having established that the child is a qualifying child and that there is in existence an absent parent (as defined in s 3(2) – see Chapter 3, para **3.3**), it must next be ascertained whether a person intending to make a claim for an assessment is entitled to do so. Section 4(1) provides that either the person with care or the absent parent may apply to the Secretary of State for a maintenance assessment; however, s 4(9) provides that no application may be made under s 4 if there is in force a maintenance assessment made in response to an application under s 6. 'Person with care' is defined by section 3(3) and is discussed at Chapter 3, para **3.3** above.

More than one person may be a person with care in relation to a qualifying child (s 3(5)); in such cases, where more than one application for an assessment is made the Act provides that regulations may provide for two or more applications to be treated as a single application and for the replacement of a maintenance assessment made on the application of one person by a later application made on the application of that or any other person (Sch 1, Part II, para 14).

4.8 These regulations are to be found in reg 4 and Sch 2 of the CS(MAP)Regs 1992. Schedule 2 sets out the permutations which may apply. They appear complicated at first sight, but may be summarised as follows.

(a) Where a person with care or an absent parent makes an effective application for a maintenance assessment (or, in Scotland, a child makes such an application) and, before the assessment is made, makes another application in respect of the same absent parent or person with care, as the case may be, the applications will be treated as a single application (Sch 2, paras 1 and 2).

(b) Applications by different persons. The table below shows how multiple applications will be dealt with. It should be noted that in all these cases, where the applications are not in respect of identical qualifying children, the application with which the child support officer proceeds will be treated as a single application in respect of all the qualifying children with respect to whom applications have been made (para 3(13)). However, where the child support officer is satisfied that the same person with care does not provide the principal day-to-day care for all such qualifying children, he must make separate assessments in relation to each person with care providing such principal day-to-day care (para 3(14)).

Applications made by	Applications to be proceeded with
1. Person with care and absent parent	Person with care (para 3(2))
2. (In Scotland only) The child and either parent	The parent (para 3(31))
The child and both parents	The parent with care (para 3(4))
The child and the parents, and a person with parental responsibility	The parent with care (para 3(4))
More than one qualifying child	The eldest child (para 3(5))
3. Two persons, both treated as absent parents	To be dealt with as one application (para 3(7))
4. The parent with care and a person having parental responsibility	The parent with care (para 3(8))
5. More than one person with care, both having parental responsibility, one of whom falls to be treated as an absent parent	The one who is not to be treated as an absent parent (para 3(9))
6. As 5, but where there is more than one person who does not fall to be dealt with as an absent parent	As in 7
7. More than one person with care, neither having parental responsibility	The application of the principal provider of day-to-day care, as determined in accordance with para 3(12)

Note

Sub-para (12) may be summarised as follows. Where the child support officer can establish with which person the child spends the greater part of its time (or, in the case of more than one child, the greatest proportion of their time, taking account of the time each child spends with each person with care), the application of that person will proceed. Where he cannot so determine, and child benefit is paid to one person with care but not both, the application of the person receiving child benefit will proceed. Where all else fails, the application of the applicant 'who in the opinion of the child support officer is the principal provider of day-to-day care . . .' will proceed.

Where there is more than one person with care of a qualifying child and one or more, but not all, of them have parental responsibility for (in Scotland, parental rights over) the child, only those persons with parental responsibility (rights) may apply (s 5(1)). 'Parental responsibility' is defined by s 3 of the Children Act 1989 as 'all the rights, duties, powers, responsibilities and authority which by law a parent of a child has in relation to the child and his property'.

5. Applications by Parents Receiving Benefit

4.9   The Act distinguishes between those parents with care who are in receipt of benefit and those who are not. Since the former class of persons is, it may be argued, the group for whom the structure of the new system is designed, they will be considered first.

As has been seen above, any parent or person with care, whether or not in receipt of benefit, may apply for an assessment under s 4, and that right to apply ceases to apply only when a maintenance assessment under s 6 is in force. However, for the purposes of this discussion, it will be assumed that an assessment under s 6 will be required in all cases where benefit is payable.

Section 6(1) provides that:

'Where income support, family credit or any other benefit of a prescribed kind is claimed by or in respect of, or paid to or in respect of, the parent of a qualifying child she shall if:
(a)   she is a person with care of the child; and
(b)   she is required to do so by the Secretary of State, authorise the Secretary of State to take action under this Act to recover child support maintenance from the absent parent.'

Three initial points should be noted. First, s 6(8) provides that subsection (1) has effect regardless of whether any of the benefits mentioned is payable with respect to any qualifying child. Accordingly, payment of benefit of a prescribed kind of any amount or nature empowers the Secretary of State to make this requirement. Secondly, although s 6(1) refers to the Secretary of State taking action, it is clear from the general context of the section that when he takes action he does so on behalf of the parent with care; he is not entitled to make an application on his own behalf. Thirdly, s 6 refers to a 'parent' whereas s 4 refers to a 'person'. The difference is significant. Only a person with care who is a parent may be compelled to take action pursuant to s 6. Therefore, a person with care who was not a parent and was in receipt of benefit could make an application for an assessment under s 4 but could not be compelled to do so under s 6.

The only benefit, payment of which imposes the requirement under 6(1) to be prescribed by the regulations is disability working allowance (CS(MAP) Regs 1992, reg 34); that benefit, together with income support and family credit, are therefore the three classes of benefit which trigger off the section.

4.10   Section 6 nowhere defines how the Secretary of State is to require the parent with care to give the authorisation. Clearly, until he has so required the person with care, no obligation exists. However, regulations provide for the manner in which the requirement is to be notified to some extent.

Regulation 2(2) of the CS(MAP)Regs 1992 provides that maintenance application forms provided by the Secretary of State under s 6 shall be supplied without charge. Apart from this, there is no reference in any regulation to the procedure. However, it is clearly envisaged that the Secretary of State will provide a parent with care receiving benefit with a maintenance application form; the application form has been published and will be found at Appendix 3. This is a form which covers both s 4 and s 6 applications; where it is known that the person with care is in receipt of benefit – a shorter version of the form, which omits much of the detail about the applicant's means (these being already known to the DSS) will be provided if the applicant wishes.

With the application form the applicant will receive document CSA 1 which is the 'child support maintenance application pack'. This document is 35 pages long (the longer form itself is 36 pages) and explains the child support system, including the obligation to authorise the Secretary of State to proceed.

If the form is adequately completed and returned no further obligation arises. Once the Secretary of State has required the parent with care to give the authorisation, the remainder of s 6 comes into force. The authorisation must extend to all the children of the absent parent in relation to whom the proposed applicant is a person with care (s 6(4)).

4.11   The manner of giving the authorisation as prescribed by the Act is to be on the maintenance application form which is provided to the person with care by the Secretary of State (s 6(6)). Section 6(7) provides that a maintenance application form shall indicate in general terms the effect of completing and returning it and, as has been seen in para **4.10**, this is done by means of the 'child support application pack'.

From the foregoing it is clear that the form will consist of the following:

(a)   an application for the making of a maintenance assessment with respect to a qualifying child or qualifying children; and
(b)   authority for the Secretary of State to take action under the Act to recover, on behalf of the person with care, the amount of child support maintenance so assessed.

4.12   The Secretary of State will therefore notify his requirement by requiring the parent with care to complete and return the maintenance application form, which will explain to the parent with care what is to happen next. By s 6(5), the authorisation must be given 'without unreasonable delay'. However, without the necessary information from the parent with care the form will be of little use, so s 6 goes on to make provision for the giving of information by the person with care. This is a part of the legislation which caused some heated controversy during its passage through parliament.

Under s 6(9), a person who is under the duty imposed by subsection (1) (ie to authorise the Secretary of State to take action):

'shall, so far as she reasonably can, comply with such regulations as may be made by the Secretary of State with a view to the Secretary of State or the child support officer being provided with the information which is required to enable –

(a)   the absent parent to be traced;

    (b)   the amount of child support maintenance payable by the absent
          parent to be assessed; and

    (c)   that amount to be recovered from the absent parent.'

The information which may be required is set out in reg 3(2) of the CS(IED) Regs 1992. It includes the following:

    (a)   the habitual residence and name and address of the absent parent;

    (b)   the name and address of any current or recent employer of an absent
          parent;

    (c)   persons living in same household as absent parent.

In addition, of course, information about the applicant and the child must be supplied.

This section raises few problems in the context of marriage breakdown since there is normally no doubt as to the identity of the absent parent. However, difficulties might arise in the case of a single mother. Criticisms of these provisions were made sharper by the fact that, by s 46 (see below), sanctions may be imposed on a person with care who is in breach of the obligation to give the prescribed information.

Critics pointed out that they constitute an unwarranted intrusion into the private life of the parent with care. She might not know the name of the absent parent; if she does, she might be in fear of him because of violence. She might not want to reopen a painful relationship.

It was also said that there might be problems of verification. A parent with care of a child might say, for example, that the father was a man she had met once and never seen again, or that he was a member of the Royal Family. It was suggested that the child support officer would have severe problems in such cases.

In answer, the simple point made was that 'it cannot be right for the single mother to refuse to name the parent of her illegitimate (sic) child so that the state, rather than the parent, who is probably working, bears the cost of maintenance. That means that the maintenance is paid by the taxpayer' (Lord Coleraine, *House of Lords, Official Report*, 19 March 1991, col 540).

In the event, the clause permitting sanctions was defeated in the House of Lords but restored by the Commons.

4.13   There are two subsections in s 6 which are designed to deal with the problem of the parent with care who does not wish to give information. First, s 6(2) provides:

'The Secretary of State shall [ie must] not require a person ("the parent") to give him the authorisation mentioned in subsection (1) if he considers that there are reasonable grounds for believing that –

    (a)   if the parent were to be required to give that authorisation; or

    (b)   if she were to give it,

there would be a risk of her, or of any child living with her, suffering harm or undue distress as a result.'

It will therefore be open to the parent with care to make representations to show that she might suffer harm or distress if the assessment were to be made. Section 6(3) provides that subsection (2) shall not apply if the parent requests the Secretary of State to disregard it; such occasions may be quite few.

If these representations are not accepted and the requirement to give the authorisation is insisted upon, it would be necessary to turn to the next safeguard, subsection (10), which deals with the requirement on the parent with care to provide information to enable the absent parent to be traced and his means to be ascertained.

Subsection (10) provides that the obligation to provide information:

'(a) shall not apply in such circumstances as may be prescribed; and
(b) may, in such circumstances as may be prescribed, be waived by the Secretary of State.'

The child support officer would therefore be able to release the parent with care from the obligation to supply information in certain prescribed circumstances, were such circumstances to be prescribed. In fact, no prescribed circumstances are contained in the regulations so the possibility does not arise at present. What the regulations do contain is a new provision for review of a reduced benefit direction (see para **6.15**, below).

In the House of Lords debate (*Official Report*, 14 March 1991, col 386), Lord Henley expressed the following views, which may be an indication of the general approach to be adopted:

'Without good cause is the key. We have always recognised that there will be circumstances in which it would not be right to require the caring parent to cooperate in obtaining maintenance. We have already said that we will make exception where rape and incest is involved. There has been much concern that violence should be accepted as good cause. The SSAC [Social Security Advisory Committee], for example, said that while accepting the threat of violence may be difficult to prove, a woman could be put in the position of having to choose between the risk of violence and a benefit reduction which would lower her living standards.

We have given careful thought to what has been said on this issue. Our proposals are aimed at putting the interests of children first, and their interests are not served if risk of violence to the caring parent is increased. So we agree that if on the evidence before us we are satisfied that there has been a history of violence in a case or the parent has well-founded fear that seeking maintenance will put her or the child at risk of violence that will be accepted as good cause . . . A detailed and rigid list is neither possible nor sensible. We do not want to add to risk by spelling out just what an absent parent needs to say or do or threaten to avoid maintenance.'

4.14 The fact remains that in cases which fall outside whatever guidelines are to be laid down, a parent with care who fails to give the necessary information may incur a sanction under s 46. Section 46(1) states that the section applies where any person on whom s 6(1) imposes an obligation (ie the parent with care receiving benefit who is required to authorise the Secretary of State):

(a)   fails to comply with that obligation; or
(b)   fails to comply with any regulation made under section 6(9).

In effect, therefore, s 46 will bite when either the person with care refuses to make an application or to give information or gives information about which the child support officer is suspicious.

By s 46(2), a child support officer may serve written notice on the parent:

'requiring her, before the end of the specified period, either to comply or to give him her reasons for failing to do so.'

This is implemented by reg 35 of the CS(MAP)Regs 1992 which provides that where the Secretary of State considers that a parent has failed to comply with the obligation under s 6 he shall serve written notice on that parent that, unless she complies with the obligation, he intends to refer the case to a child support officer for action under s 46. The notice will state that the case will not be referred to a child support officer prior to the expiry of six weeks from the date of service of the notice.

When the case is referred to the child support officer and a s 46(2) notice is served, the period to be specified in the notice is 14 days. The total time which the parent with care will have in which to consider her position is eight weeks.

Presumably, if the required information is supplied, s 46 will cease to apply and the child support officer will proceed with the assessment. The reasons given by the person with care may be in writing or orally (s 46(10)). If the information is not supplied, subsection (3) will apply. This provides that:

'When the specified period has expired, the child support officer shall consider whether, having regard to any reasons given by the parent, there are reasonable grounds for believing that, if she were to be required to comply, there would be a risk of her or of any children living with her suffering harm or undue distress as a result of complying.'

It will be noted that the test to be applied by the child support officer is the same as in s 6(2) (see para **4.13** above). It should be noted also that the child support officer can form this conclusion only on the basis of reasons given by the parent; he would need to know something new.

The child support officer then has two choices. If he considers that there are reasonable grounds under subsection (3), he must take no further action under s 46 in relation to the failure in question and notify the parent in writing accordingly (s 46(4)). If he considers that there are no such reasonable grounds, he may give a reduced benefit direction with respect to the parent (s 46(5)).

4.15   The first question to be addressed by the child support officer is whether the parent with care has in fact failed to comply with any requirement or any regulation; 'comply' means to comply with the requirement or the regulation in question (s 46(11)).

There can be no doubt that what is foreseen, and what the section seeks to prevent, is that parents may refuse to say who the absent parent (inevitably the father) is or where he may be found.

When the mother refuses to complete the maintenance application form at all, or plainly refuses to name the father there will be little doubt about the failure to comply. Again, if the name of the father were given as, for example the President of the United States, the Archbishop of Canterbury or the Secretary of State himself, the official view might well be that this was so inherently improbable as to justify the belief that there was no compliance with the regulations and requirements.

In any event, it is submitted, the child support officer should start with the presumption that any information given is true, and only form the impression that the parent has failed to comply if there is evidence to justify such a conclusion. Only when that conclusion has been reached can the child support officer go on to consider whether a notice should be served under s 46(2). On receipt of any reasons for non-compliance within the specified period, he then has to make a decision as to whether reasonable grounds for non-compliance are shown; here the onus will be on the parent.

'Reasonable grounds' will have the same meaning here as in s 6 (see para **4.13** above) and need not be considered further here.

4.16   If the child support officer is satisfied that reasonable grounds are not shown, he may give a reduced benefit direction. This is the sanction which the Act imposes.

'Reduced benefit direction' is defined (s 46(11)) as:

'a direction, binding on the adjudication officer, that the amount payable by way of any relevant benefit to, or in respect of, the parent concerned be reduced by such amount, and for such period, as may be prescribed.'

'Relevant benefit' means 'income support, family credit or any other benefit of a kind prescribed for the purposes of section 6' (at the moment, only disability working allowance).

The direction must therefore deal with the amount of the reduction of benefit and the period of time for which it will last. As to amount, s 46(11) merely provides that the amount of the reduction and the period shall be such amount as may be prescribed. From the parliamentary debates it was clear that the proportion which the Secretary of State had in mind was 20% of the parent's allowance; a figure sometimes mentioned in the debates was £7.35 per week. The government had to weigh up the undoubted hardship which would be caused to the parent and family against the wish to have a realistic sanction.

In another social security field (disqualification from unemployment benefit after voluntarily giving up employment), the period of disqualification is 26 weeks. However, that is a total disqualification from benefit. In some of the parliamentary debates the period of 18 months was mentioned as a possible disqualification period. As was pointed out, if the period were too low it would be tempting for an absent parent to 'buy off' the parent with care.

4.17 In the event, the detail is contained in reg 36 of the CS(MAP)Regs 1992. There is to be a two-stage reduction. The first, which lasts for 26 weeks, is equal to $0.2 \times B$ where B is the weekly amount in the applicable amounts schedule; that is to say, it is 20% of the weekly personal allowance of the parent. In the year 1993/4 the allowance for a lone parent aged 18 or over is £44 per week so the deduction from that figure would be £8.80 per week. This is to be followed by a reduction for a period of 52 weeks of a sum equivalent to $0.1 \times B$, that is 10% of the benefit (£4.40 per week on current figures). The total period of reduced benefit will therefore be 18 months. The direction will come into operation on the first day of the second benefit week following the review.

Regulation 36(8) provides that only one direction in relation to a parent shall be in force at any one time. It is also provided that where a direction has been in operation for the full 18-month period, no further direction shall be given with respect to the same parent on account of that parent's failure to comply with the s 6 obligations in relation to any child in relation to whom the direction that has been in operation for the full period was given (reg 36(9)). In other words, once a parent has been punished in full for a breach of the obligation, she may not be punished again. However, if she has another child and again is found to be in breach of the s 6 obligation, another reduced benefit direction could be given. Furthermore, in theory at any rate, there would seem to be nothing to prevent a child support officer successively penalising a mother of more than one child of different fathers who refused to name any of the fathers. A slightly different situation seems to be contemplated by reg 47 which deals with the position where a reduced benefit direction is in operation and a child support officer gives a further direction with respect to the same parent on account of that parent failing to comply with the obligation, imposed by s 6 in relation to an additional qualifying child of whom she is a person with care. 'Additional qualifying child' is defined as a qualifying child of whom the parent concerned is a person with care and who was either not such a qualifying child at the time the earlier direction was given or had not been born at the time the earlier direction was given (reg 47(8)).

Regulation 47(1) provides that the earlier direction will cease immediately before the new direction comes into force; there would, of course, be nothing to prevent the child support officer from waiting to the end of the first reduced benefit period before giving notice under reg 35.

4.18 As will be seen below, provision is made for reduced benefit directions to be terminated or suspended under regs 38 (benefit ceasing to be payable), 41 (compliance with the s 6 obligations) and 42 (successful application for review). Regulation 47 has to deal with these possibilities which may complicate the smooth running of the successive periods of reduced benefit imposed by reg 47(1), and does so as follows.

First, where a direction has ceased to be in force by virtue of reg 38(2) and a further direction is given, no further direction may be given in relation to the child or children in relation to whom the direction that has ceased to be in force was given; in other words, once the further direction is given the earlier direction is dead and may not be revived.

Regulation 47(4) deals with the position where a further direction is given in accordance with reg 47(1) and this further direction would then cease to be in force because of the parent either complying with the s 6 obligations (reg 41) or successfully applying for a review (reg 42). What then happens to the earlier direction which terminated before the coming into force of the further direction? The answer is that the later direction does not in fact cease to be in force, but continues for a period known as the 'extended period', calculated under reg 47(5).

This extended period is $(78–F–S)$ weeks where F is the number of weeks for which the earlier direction was in operation and S is the number of weeks for which the later direction has been in operation. It will be seen that the result of this is that the total period of reduced benefit direction before and after the further direction will be 18 months.

4.19 There are a number of modifications of the principle imposing the reduced benefit direction. The first, contained in reg 37, provides that where, as a result of a reduced benefit direction, benefit payable would be nil or less than the minimum amount of the relevant benefit payable as determined:

(a) in the case of income support, by reg 26(4) of the Social Security (Claims and Payment) Regulations 1987, or

(b) in the case of family credit and disability working allowance, by reg 27(2) of those regulations, the amount of the reduction shall be decreased to such extent as to raise the amount of the benefit to the minimum amount payable.

Secondly, by reg 40, where the applicable amount of benefit is calculated by the regulations relating to persons in residential care and nursing homes, patients or persons in residential accommodations, any reduced benefit is suspended for such period or for 52 weeks, whichever period is the shorter.

4.20 Regulation 38 provides for suspension of a reduced benefit direction when the relevant benefit ceases to be payable. The suspension is for a period of 52 weeks from the date the relevant benefit ceased to be payable, and at the end of that period, if no relevant benefit is then payable, the reduced benefit direction will cease to be in force. Where relevant benefit again becomes payable before the expiry of 52 weeks, the reduced benefit direction will be in force for the balance of the reduction period. This could lead to careful calculations. To take an example, a parent in respect of whom a reduced benefit direction had been made who ceased to be eligible for benefit four months thereafter and who would be eligible for benefit seven months thereafter might have to weigh up whether she should wait for another month before applying for benefit so as to escape the resumption of the reduced benefit direction period.

Finally, the regulations provide for termination of a reduced benefit direction. By reg 41, where a parent with care complies with her obligations under s 6, the direction will cease to be in force on the last day of the benefit week in which she has so complied.

For the position in Scotland where a child applies for a maintenance assessment while a reduced benefit direction is in force see Chapter 10.

A reduced benefit direction is terminated when the absent parent himself comes forward and applies for a maintenance assessment in respect of all the qualifying children and an assessment is made in response to that application (reg 44).

Section 46(7) provides that any person who is aggrieved by a reduced benefit direction may appeal to a child support appeal tribunal against that decision. Appeals are considered in more detail in Chapter 6.

Furthermore, reg 42 provides a new remedy for the parent with care in the form of the right to apply for review of the reduced benefit direction. This is also dealt with in Chapter 6 at para **6.0**.

4.21   Where a parent with care who has been in receipt of benefits ceases to receive them, she may allow the assessment to remain in force, in which case the payments would continue to be collected from the absent father. By s 6(11), a person with care who has authorised the Secretary of State under subsection (1) but who subsequently ceases to fall within that subsection may request the Secretary of State to cease to act. The Secretary of State is under a duty to comply with such a request, subject to any regulations made under subsection (13) which are to make 'incidental or transitional provision' (s 6(12)). The assessment itself will of course continue until terminated (see paras **4.54** to **4.57** below).

6.   Applications by Persons Not Receiving Benefit

4.22   A person with care who is not receiving benefit is in a different position from that of a parent receiving benefit in that there is no compulsion on her to take or authorise action, nor is there any sanction, other than the abandoning of the claim, if she fails to supply the necessary information. Nevertheless, the procedure for applying for an assessment is broadly similar and the result will be exactly the same; furthermore, of course, if she chooses not to avail herself of the services of the child support agency there is no other way of obtaining money from an absent parent who is unwilling to pay.

As has been seen in para **4.7** above, either the person with care or the absent parent may apply to the Secretary of State for a maintenance assessment. There will be a series of regional offices for the Child Support Agency, and application should be made to the office nearest to the applicant. Fees will be payable, on a scale to be prescribed, as to which see para **4.58**.

4.23   Clearly, the applicant will have to give the Secretary of State the necessary information to proceed with the assessment; as the application is voluntary there should be no problem as to this. Nevertheless, s 4(4) provides that a person who applies for an assessment:

shall, so far as that person reasonably can, comply with such regulations as may be made by the Secretary of State with a view to the Secretary of State or the child support officer being provided with the information which is required to enable –

'(a)   the absent parent to be traced (where that is necessary);

(b)   the amount of child support maintenance payable by the absent parent to be assessed; and

(c)   that amount to be recovered from the absent parent.'

Section 4(7) provides that the obligation to provide information:

(a)   shall not apply in such circumstances as may be prescribed; and

(b)   may, in such circumstances as may be prescribed, be waived by the Secretary of State.

This is identical to the provision applying to persons in receipt of benefit but it is difficult to see its purpose here. Unlike a person receiving benefit, a person not receiving benefit is only going to recover any money if the absent parent can be traced and a proper assessment carried out. It is not immediately obvious what information might be waived, particularly when it is remembered that one of the purposes of the Child Support Agency is to act as a buffer between the parties and that there need be no direct contact between them.

The procedure for the application is that the application must be made on a maintenance application form provided by the Secretary of State (CS(MAP)Regs 1992, reg 2(1)). These forms are to be supplied without charge (reg 2(2)). For details of the form see para **4.10** above.

The application will be an effective application provided it is made on the maintenance application form and is completed in accordance with the Secretary of State's instructions (reg 2(4)). Where the application is not effective (presumably where the Secretary of State considers that the application has not been completed in accordance with his instructions), the Secretary of State may either return the form to the applicant, with, if he thinks appropriate, a fresh maintenance application form and request that the application be resubmitted, or request the applicant to provide such additional information or evidence as the Secretary of State specifies (reg 2(5)).

An effective application may be amended by notice in writing to the Secretary of State at any time before a maintenance assessment is made, but no amendment may relate to any change of circumstances arising after the effective date of a maintenance assessment resulting from an effective application (reg 2(6) and (7)).

The information which the Secretary of State may require is the same as that on an application under s 6 (as to which see para **4.12**, above).

4.24   A person who has applied to the Secretary of State for an assessment may at any time request him to cease acting (s 4(5)), and it shall be the duty of the Secretary of State to comply with this request, subject to regulations of an incidental, supplemental or transitional nature (s (4)(6)).

The making of the assessment is dealt with below. However, it may be noted here that where a maintenance assessment has been made, the person with care or the absent parent may apply to the Secretary of State for him to arrange the collection of the child support maintenance and the enforcement of the obligation to pay; the Secretary of State may agree to arrange this, but it seems that this is entirely at his discretion (s 4(2)).

7.   The Assessment

4.25   The principles for calculation of the assessment are set out in Chapter 5 and need not be considered here; this chapter is concerned with procedure only.

By s 11(1), any application for a maintenance assessment (whether or not the person with care is receiving benefit) received by the Secretary of State shall be referred to a child support officer whose duty it shall be to deal with the application in accordance with the Act. Child support officers are to be appointed under s 13(1) for the purpose of exercising functions conferred on them by the Act or assigned to them by the Secretary of State; a child support officer may be appointed to perform only such functions as may be specified in his instrument of appointment (s 13(2)).

All child support officers will be officers of the Agency and, as such, (quasi) civil servants. However, in applying the formula to make decisions about maintenance assessments, it is intended that they will be acting under the statutory authority of the Act; just as decisions are made in the benefit system by independent adjudication officers, it is intended that in the child support system decisions will be made by statutorily independent child support officers.

4.26   Once the child support officer has all the information he needs, the assessment will be made in accordance with the formula. In order to make an assessment, the child support officer will need information from the person with care and from the absent parent. The obligation of the former to supply information has already been considered at paras **4.12** (benefit cases) and **4.22** (non-benefit cases). As to information from or about the absent parent, s 14(1) provides that the Secretary of State may make regulations requiring any information or evidence needed for the determination of any application under the Act or any question arising in connection with such an application to be furnished by such person as may be prescribed by regulations and in accordance with the regulations.

Regulation 5(1) of the CS(MAP)Regs 1992 provides that when an effective application for a maintenance assessment has been made, the Secretary of State shall, as soon as is reasonably practicable, give notice in writing of that application to the relevant persons other than the applicant; 'relevant persons' for this purpose includes the absent parent (reg 1(2)). Any person to whom notice is given must also be given a 'maintenance enquiry form' and a written request that the form be completed and returned (reg 4(2)). A notice to an absent parent must also specify the effective date of the maintenance assessment if one is to be made and set out in general terms the provisions relating to interim maintenance assessments (reg 4(3)); these topics will be further considered at para **4.38**, but it will be noted that the clear intention is to warn the absent parent of the consequences of delay.

The CS(IED)Regs 1992 contain provisions which overlap with the CS(MAP)Regs 1992, relating to the information which the Secretary of State may require to be given. The general duty to give information is set out in reg 2(1); it covers many possibilities and in this context may be summarised as providing that where an application for a maintenance assessment has been received a 'relevant person' (in this context, the absent parent or a person who is alleged to be the parent of a qualifying child) shall (ie must) furnish such information or evidence as is required by the Secretary of State, and which is needed to enable a determination to be made in relation to one or more of the matters listed in reg 3(1). Those matters, again in the present context, are to enable:

(a)   a decision to be made as to whether, in relation to an application for a maintenance assessment, there exists a qualifying child, an absent parent and a person with care;

(b)   a decision to be made as to whether a child support officer has jurisdiction to make a maintenance assessment under s 44 of the Act;

(f)   the amount of child support maintenance payable by an absent parent to be assessed.

4.27   By reg 3(2) the information or evidence to be furnished may in particular include information and evidence as to (inter alia) the following:

(g)   the name and address of any current or recent employer of an absent parent;

(h)   the address from which an absent parent who is self-employed carries on his trade or business, the trading name, and the gross receipts and expenses and other outgoings of the trade or business;

(i)   any other income of an absent parent;

(m)   income of persons living in the same household as the absent parent;

(p)   housing costs;

(q)   the identifying details of any bank, building society or similar account held in the name of the absent parent and statements relating to any such account.

The maintenance enquiry form will contain questions designed to elicit all this information.

Regulation 6(1) of the CS(MAP)Regs 1992 provides that a person who has received a maintenance enquiry form must complete the form in accordance with the Secretary of State's instructions and return it within 14 days of its having been given or sent. The information given may be amended in writing at any time before a maintenance assessment is made. However, no amendment may relate to any change of circumstances arising after the effective date of any maintenance assessment (reg 7(3)).

4.28 In addition to the information which he obtains from the person with care and the absent parent, the Secretary of State may also obtain information from other persons. First, the records of other government departments may be examined and used.

Section 14(2) provides that the Secretary of State may make use of any information in his possession which was acquired by him in connection with his functions under any of the benefit Acts. It was frequently said during the passage of the Bill that information gained for the purpose of making a maintenance assessment would be confidential and subject to strict rules about disclosure; given that the principle of confidentiality in respect of information obtained in other fields of social security has now been breached it remains to be seen how long it will remain intact in the field of child support; for example it seems highly probable that information contained in a maintenance application form about an applicant's cohabitee will be available to the child support officer if the mother of the cohabitee's child applies for an assessment in respect of that child.

Indeed, reg 10 of the CS(IED)Regs 1992 provides that a child support officer may disclose any information held by him for the purposes of the Act to, and as required by, the Secretary of State for use in connection with the functions of the Secretary of State under any of the benefit Acts.

4.29 However, the clearest departures from the principle of confidentiality in government records occur in Sch 2 which provide for provision of information to the Secretary of State from Inland Revenue records and local authority records.

Paragraph 1 of Sch 2 applies where the Secretary of State requires information for the purpose of tracing the current address of an absent parent or the current employer of an absent parent. Paragraph 1(2) states:

'In such a case, no obligation as to secrecy imposed by statute or otherwise on a person employed in relation to the Inland Revenue shall prevent any information obtained or held in connection with the assessment or collection of income tax from being disclosed to –

(a)   the Secretary of State;

(b)   the Department of Health and Social Services for Northern Ireland; or

(c)   an officer of either of them authorised to receive such information in connection with the operation of this Act or of any corresponding Northern Ireland legislation.'

It will be seen, therefore, that the obligation as to secrecy may be waived only if the current address or current employer of an absent parent is not known. Where the address or employer is known no application to the Inland Revenue may be made. However, Sch 2 imposes no limit as to the information which may be disclosed once it is established that information may be given; para 1(2) refers to 'any information obtained in connection with the assessment or collection of income tax'. This obviously includes details of the absent parent's earnings and entitlement to allowances and it would appear that all of this may be disclosed once the obligation as to secrecy is removed. Accordingly, the Secretary of State may well be able to obtain all the information he needs for the purpose of making a maintenance assessment in addition to tracing the absent parent or his employer.

Paragraph 1 extends only to disclosure by or under the authority of the Commissioners of Inland Revenue (para 1(3)); presumably the Commissioners will delegate this power to senior officers.

4.30 Paragraph 2 of Schedule 2 deals with local authority records and applies where:

(a) the Secretary of State requires relevant information in connection with the discharge by him, or by any child support officer, of functions under the Act; or
(b) the Department of Health and Social Services for Northern Ireland requires relevant information in connection with the discharge of any functions under any corresponding Northern Ireland legislation.

When the above conditions are satisfied the Secretary of State may give a direction to the appropriate authority requiring them to give him such relevant information in connection with housing benefit or community charge benefit to which an absent parent or person with care is entitled as the Secretary of State considers necessary in connection with his determination of:

'(a) that person's income of any kind;
 (b) the amount of housing costs to be taken into account in determining that person's income of any kind; or
 (c) the amount of that person's protected income.'

Under para 2(4), 'appropriate authority' means, in relation to housing benefit, the housing or local authority concerned, and, in relation to community charge benefit, the charging authority or, in Scotland, the levying authority; 'relevant information' means information of such a description as may be prescribed.

As a kind of quid pro quo, reg 9 of the CS(IED)Regs 1992 provides that the Secretary of State or a child support officer may disclose information held by him for the purposes of the Act to, and as required by, an appropriate authority for use in the exercise of its functions relating to housing benefit or council tax benefit. The Child Support Agency and local authorities are therefore entitled to exchange and pool information in their possession for the purpose of enforcing child support and the council tax.

4.31 Given the very wide power to collect information from a variety of sources it is not surprising that the Act contains sanctions to discourage the unauthorised disclosure of information (although it has to be said that these provisions were not contained in the original Bill). Section 50 applies to any person who is, or has been, employed in employment as:

(a)   the chief child support officer;
(b)   any other child support officer;
(c)   any clerk to, or other officer of, a child support appeal tribunal;
(d)   any member of the staff of such a tribunal;
(e)   a civil servant in connection with the carrying out of any functions under the Act; and
(f)   employment of any other kind which is prescribed for the purposes of the section.

This list is extended by reg 11 of the CS(IED)Regs 1992 which prescribes the following kinds of employment in addition to those specified in s 50(a) to (e):

(a)   the Controller and Auditor General;
(b)   the Parliamentary Commissioner for Administration;
(c)   the Health Service Commissioner for England;
(d)   the Health Service Commissioner for Wales;
(e)   the Health Service Commissioner for Scotland;
(f)   any member of the staff of the National Audit Office;
(g)   any other person who carries out the administrative work of that office, or who provides, or is employed in the provision of services to it;
(h)   any officer of any of the commissioners referred to in paragraphs (b) to (e) above; and
(i)   any person who provides, or is employed in the provision of services to the DSS.

Any such person is guilty of an offence if, without lawful authority, he discloses any information which:

(a)   was acquired by him in the course of that employment; and
(b)   relates to a particular person.

A person guilty of an offence under s 50 is liable on conviction on indictment to imprisonment for a term not exceeding two years or a fine or both, and on summary conviction to imprisonment for a term not exceeding six months or a fine not exceeding the statutory maximum or both (s 50(4)).

It is not an offence to disclose information in the form of a summary or collection of information so framed as not to enable information relating to any particular person to be ascertained from it, or to disclose information which has previously been disclosed to the public with lawful authority (s 50(2)). This would protect an officer who was giving a report on his activities.

Section 50(3) provides a statutory defence to a prosecution under the section; it is a defence to prove that at the time of the alleged offence:

(a)   the officer believed that he was making the disclosure in question with lawful authority and had no reasonable cause to believe otherwise; or

(b) he believed that the information in question had previously been disclosed to the public with lawful authority and had no reasonable cause to believe otherwise.

The question of lawful authority is obviously central to the section, and is defined by subsection (6). A disclosure is to be regarded as made with lawful authority if, and only if, it is made:

'(a) by a civil servant in accordance with his official duty; or
(b) by any other person either –
   (i) for the purposes of the function in the exercise of which he holds the information and without contravening any restriction duly imposed by the responsible person; or
   (ii) to, or in accordance with an authorisation duly given by, the responsible person;
(c) in accordance with any enactment or order of a court;
(d) for the purpose of instituting, or otherwise for the purposes of, any proceedings before a court or before any tribunal or other body or person mentioned in the Act; or
(e) with the consent of the appropriate person.'

Section 50(7) defines the 'responsible person' as the Secretary of State, the Lord Chancellor, any person authorised by them or any prescribed person. 'The appropriate person' is defined by s 50(8) as the person to whom the information relates, or in certain cases the specified classes of receiver or attorney dealing with his affairs.

Regulation 8 of the CS(IED)Regs 1992 extends the ability of the Secretary of State to disclose, and provides that the Secretary of State or a child support officer may disclose any information held by them for the purposes of the Act to:

(a) a court;
(b) any tribunal or other body or person mentioned in the Act;
(c) any tribunal established under the benefit Acts

where such disclosure is made for the purposes of any proceedings before any of those bodies relating to this Act or to the benefit Acts.

4.32 The Secretary of State has therefore wide powers to obtain information from other public bodies. However, his powers do not end there because he also has powers to require different classes of persons to furnish information or evidence. As to the purposes for which such information or evidence may be required, reg 3(1) of the CS(IED)Regs 1992 provides that the information or evidence may only be required if needed to enable certain decisions to be made or purposes to be fulfilled. These are set out in full in the regulation but may be summarised as decisions as to whether to proceed or whether there is jurisdiction on which application should proceed, identification and tracing of absent parents, assessing and enforcing child support maintenance and identifying related proceedings.

The persons who may be required to furnish information or evidence are listed in reg 2(2), but it must be noted that different classes of person may be required to give the information or evidence if it is required for certain specific purposes; not all the matters set out in reg 3(1) apply to all such persons.

4.33 'The relevant person' (ie a person with care, an absent parent, a person treated as an absent parent and a child who applies under s 7) is so required for all the purposes set out in reg 3(1).

A person who is alleged to be the parent of a child but who denies this is so required for the purpose of reg 3(1)(b) (a decision to be made as to whether a child support officer has jurisdiction) and 3(1)(d) (an absent parent to be identified).

A current or recent employer of either parent is so required for the purposes of identifying or tracing an absent parent, assessing and recovering child support maintenance, and enforcing court orders.

A local authority in whose area either parent lives is so required for the purpose of making a decision as to whether there exists a qualifying child, an absent parent and a person with care.

Finally, in any case where, in relation to the qualifying child or children, or the absent parent there is or has been a relevant court order, or there have been or are pending related proceedings before a court, certain information or evidence may be required from the senior district judge of the Principal Registry, the district judge of a district registry, the proper officer of a county court, a clerk to the justices or (in Scotland) the deputy principal clerk of session or the sheriff clerk, as the case may be. This requirement is limited to cases where the information or evidence is required for the purpose of ascertaining the amount payable under a relevant court order, recovering the same from an absent parent or identifying any related proceedings. By reg 1(2) 'related proceedings' are defined as proceedings in which a relevant court order is or was being sought and 'relevant court order' means an order as to periodical or capital provision or variation of property rights made under an enactment set out in s 8(11) (eg Matrimonial Causes Act 1973, Domestic Proceedings and Magistrates' Courts Act 1978, Children Act 1989) in relation to a qualifying child or a relevant person; similar provisions apply to Scotland.

4.34 As to the nature of the information or evidence to be furnished, reg 3(2) sets out a very detailed list of particular matters. Before summarising these matters it should perhaps be said that the purpose of the regulations is to compel the persons listed in reg 2(2) to give this information as evidence to the Secretary of State or child support officer for any of the purposes appropriate to those persons as defined in reg 3(1).

The information or evidence listed in reg 3(2) includes such matters as the habitual residence of the parents or child, their marital status, where the child spends its time, matters relevant to disputes as to parentage, names and addresses of employers, gross and net earning of parents, amounts payable under court orders, persons living in the same household as parents of a child and details of their incomes, benefits payable, housing costs, details of bank or building society accounts. A complete list will be found in the regulation which is set out in full at Appendix 2.

4.35 Child support officers, using the powers of the Secretary of State, will have wide powers enabling them to gather information from many sources. Interim assessments and inspectors are dealt with below. Here it may merely be said that once all the information is available the child support officer will make the assessment which 'shall be made in such form and contain such information as the Secretary of State may direct' (Sch 1, para 12).

As to the date from which the assessment will run, para 11 provides that a maintenance assessment 'shall take effect on such date as may be determined in accordance with regulations made by the Secretary of State' and that 'that date may be earlier than the date on which the assessment is made'; in other words it may be backdated and provide for payment of arrears.

The regulations are now contained in the CS(MAP)Regs 1992, reg 30, which defines the effective dates of new maintenance assessments ('effective date' having been defined in reg 1(1) as the date on which a maintenance assessment takes effect for the purposes of the Act).

Where no maintenance assessment is in force with respect to the person with care or the absent parent the effective date of a new assessment will depend on who made the application. Where the application was made by a person with care or (in Scotland) a child under s 7 the effective date is the date on which a maintenance enquiry form was given or sent to the absent parent. Time therefore starts to run from the date of the sending or giving of the form and as reg 30(3) provides that reg 1(6)(b) (which provides that any document sent to any person by the Secretary of State shall be treated as having been given or sent on the second day after posting) does not apply to these provisions, this must mean the date of posting.

4.36 Where the application is made by an absent parent or is an application made under reg 3 (application on termination of an earlier maintenance assessment) the effective date is the date on which an effective maintenance application form is received by the Secretary of State.

Regulation 30(4) provides that where a child support officer is satisfied that an absent parent has deliberately avoided receipt of a maintenance enquiry form he may determine the date on which the form would have been sent or given but for such avoidance.

By reg 33(1), child support maintenance is calculated at a weekly rate and will be in respect of successive maintenance periods, each of seven days. The first maintenance period will commence on the effective date (reg 33(2)).

Given that the absent parent has 14 days in which to respond to notification of the application (reg 6(1)) and it may take a little time after that for the assessment to be made it seems inevitable that every maintenance assessment will have to provide for the payment of some arrears. The provisions as to arrears are dealt with in more detail in Chapter 7; here it may be noted that reg 4(1) of the CS(CE)Regs 1992 provides that the Secretary of State shall specify the day and interval by reference to which the payments of child support maintenance are to be made by the liable person and may from time to time vary such day or interval.

Paragraph 15 provides that an assessment may provide for different amounts for different periods.

4.37 Schedule 1 also makes provision for consolidated assessments and applications (para 14). The possibility may arise that a person with care has children of more than one father and it may also be that an absent parent has children in the care of different people. Applications could therefore overlap in one way or another; it is therefore provided that regulations may provide:

(a) for two or more applications for maintenance assessments to be treated, in prescribed circumstances, as a single application; and

(b) for the replacement, in prescribed circumstances, of a maintenance assessment made on the application of one person by a later maintenance assessment made on the application of that or any other person.

The regulations have now been made and are to be found in Sch 2 of the CS(MAP)Regs 1992, the effect having been summarised at para **4.8**, above.

8. Interim Assessments

4.38 It is, of course, always possible that, even with the very wide powers conferred on him by the Act, the child support officer may find that he still has insufficient information about the means of the absent parent to make a final assessment. In these circumstances, s 12(1) provides that, where it appears to the child support officer that he does not have sufficient information to enable him to make an assessment in accordance with the provision made under the Act, he may make an interim maintenance assessment. It is intended that such an assessment will be of a fairly robust nature, designed to encourage the absent parent to co-operate and to reveal whatever information remains to be revealed. The enforcement provisions contained later in the Act refer to 'any child maintenance assessment' and this must include an interim assessment so that a recalcitrant absent parent may find that a substantial sum, exceeding the likely amount of a final assessment, is being deducted from his earnings.

4.39 The making of interim assessments is governed by regulations, which, by s 12(3) provide for the procedure to be followed and the basis on which the amount of an interim assessment is to be calculated.

Section 12(4) provides that before making any interim assessment a child support officer shall, if it is reasonably practicable to do so, give written notice of his intention to make an interim assessment to the absent parent, the person with care and, where the application is made under s 7 (under which, in Scotland, the child may apply for an assessment), the child concerned. The child support officer may not make the assessment until the end of the period of such notice (s 12(5)).

The detail is to be found in Part III (regs 8 and 9) of the CS(MAP)Regs 1992. By reg 8(1), where a child support officer serves notice under s 12(4) of his intention to make an interim assessment, he may not make the interim assessment before the end of a period of 14 days commencing with the date that notice was given or sent. The absent parent therefore has 14 days in which to disclose all the information that the child support officer is trying to obtain.

By reg 8(2) the amount of child support maintenance fixed by an interim assessment shall be 1.5 multiplied by the maintenance requirement in respect of the qualifying child or children concerned. The method of calculation of the maintenance requirement is dealt with in detail in Chapter 5; here it will suffice to say that it is the aggregate of the income support allowances for the children and the parent, less child benefit.

4.40   To take an example, suppose that the parent with care has two children aged 13 and 14. The maintenance requirement (based on social security rates for 1993/4) would be as follows:

lone parent	£44.00 per week
1st child	22.15
2nd child	22.15
Family premium	9.65
lone parent premium	4.90
	102.85
less child benefit	18.10
Maintenance requirement	£84.75 per week.

Regulation 8(2) provides that paras 2 to 9 of Sch 1 of the Act shall not apply to interim assessment, so no account is taken of the income of the parent with care or protected income of the absent parent.

The maintenance requirement multiplied by 1.5 would be £127.12 per week, which would be the amount of the interim assessment. The effective date of the assessment (as to which see para **4.35** above) will be not earlier than the first and not later than the 7th day following the expiry of the 14 days' notice. However, reg 8(4) provides that where a maintenance assessment is made after an interim maintenance assessment has been in force, it will be payable in respect of the period preceding that during which the interim assessment was in force. The reason for this is that the effective date of a maintenance assessment can be as early as the date on which the maintenance enquiry form was first sent (see para **4.35** above). Since an interim assessment cannot be made for at least 14 days thereafter, and probably longer, an absent parent who only provides the necessary information for the making of a proper mainte-nance assessment after an interim assessment is made cannot thereby escape liability for the period from the effective date to the date of the interim assessment.

4.41   An interim assessment can be enforced in exactly the same way as any other maintenance assessment (by s 54 'maintenance assessment' includes an interim assessment except in prescribed circumstances). The powers of the child support officer to make, eg, deductions from earnings orders therefore apply to interim assessments.

The child support officer is therefore in a position to make and enforce an interim assessment which may well be in excess of anything the absent parent can afford to pay, and this interim assessment will continue to be enforceable until stopped by the operation of provisions in the regulations. There are only three ways in which an interim assessment may be terminated, some of which overlap.

First, by reg 8(6) a child support officer may cancel an interim maintenance assessment where he is satisfied that there was unavoidable delay by the absent parent in completing and returning the maintenance enquiry form or in providing information or evidence required by the Secretary of State. However, the interim maintenance assessment may not be cancelled with effect from a date earlier than that on which the provisions of reg 6(1) (which require the absent parent to return the maintenance enquiry form within 14 days) could have been complied with (reg 8(7)).

Secondly, by reg 8(9), an interim assessment shall cease to have effect on the first day of the maintenance period during which the Secretary of State receives the information which enables a child support officer to make a maintenance assessment. In other words, once the absent parent gives the required information the interim assessment will cease. This does not have a retrospective effect, so that if the maintenance assessment is less than the interim assessment the 'extra' sums paid under the interim assessment will not be recoverable unless the absent parent is able to take advantage of some other provision in the regulations, such as reg 8(6) set out above. However, the effect of reg 8(10) is that where a maintenance assessment is made following an interim assessment, and the assessment is for a higher figure than the interim assessment, the amount payable shall be the higher figure throughout and not the lower figure.

4.42   Thirdly, an absent parent may apply to a child support officer under reg 9(1) for the interim assessment to be cancelled. Such an application must be in writing and must include a statement of the grounds for the application. The onus is therefore on the absent parent to take some positive action in this way.

By reg 9(3), where the child support officer receives the application to cancel the interim assessment he must do three things, as follows.

(a)   Decide whether the interim assessment is to be cancelled and if so the date from which it is to be cancelled. He will presumably not decide that it should be cancelled unless he either has all the information to enable him to make an assessment or he decides that no assessment should be made because of, eg, lack of jurisdiction. As to the date from which it should be cancelled, presumably this will be the start of the maintenance period during which the necessary information is supplied unless the absent parent can take advantage of reg 8(6).

(b)   In any case where he does cancel an interim assessment, decide whether it is appropriate for a maintenance assessment to be made.

(c)   Where it is appropriate, make the assessment. When the child support officer has made his decision, he must immediately notify the absent parent and give him reasons in writing (reg 9(4)).

Regulation 8(8) provides that the child support maintenance payable under an interim assessment shall not be adjusted following the making of an interim assessment except where regs 8(6) (child support officer satisfied as to unavoidable delay) and 8(10) (where the maintenance is increased from that payable under the interim assessment) apply.

The absent parent has no right to apply for a review of the interim assessment under ss 17 (reviews on change of circumstances) or 18 (the general right of review by another child support officer) (reg 8(11)). However, by reg 9(6), an absent parent may apply to the Secretary of State for review of a decision made by a child support officer in respect of an application to cancel an interim assessment under reg 9(1) and this will be dealt with as a s 18 review (ie the first stage of an appeal).

9.   Inspectors

4.43   The final weapon in the child support officer's armoury is the use of inspectors; this is a novel element in family law but not, of course, in the field of social security. Inspectors are designed to be able to get out and about and make the investigations which the child support officer himself cannot make.

Inspectors are appointed under the authority contained in s 15(1); every inspector must be furnished with a certificate of his appointment which he must, if so required, produce on applying for admission to any premises (s 15(2) and (8)). The powers of the inspector are to enter, to question and to require information.

4.44   The general purpose of an inspector's appointment is 'the purpose of acquiring information'.

Under s 15(4) an inspector shall have power:

'(a)   to enter at all reasonable times –
   (i)   any specified premises, other than premises used solely as a dwelling house; and
   (ii) any premises which are not specified but which are used by any specified person for the purpose of carrying on any trade, profession, vocation or business; and
(b)   to make such examination and enquiry there as he considers appropriate'.

Section 15(10) provides that 'specified' means specified in the certificate of appointment. Two points flow from this. First, it seems that the certificate of appointment will be limited to a particular case and will refer to particular premises. Secondly, the child support officer will presumably specify the premises which he authorises the inspector to enter. In addition, the inspector has the power to make his own decision as to whether or not to enter premises on which a person specified in his certificate of appointment appears to be working. The only premises which may not be entered are those used wholly as a dwelling house.

Once an inspector is inside premises, he may make such examination and enquiry as he thinks fit; this presumably includes the power to inspect any documents which he finds there and to question any person.

Although it is anticipated that premises specified will be premises where it is thought an absent parent is or has been working, there is no reason on the face of the statute why this should be so; strictly speaking the child support officer could specify a solicitor's office or a bank.

By reg 7 of the CS(IED)Regs 1992, subject to Her Majesty not being in residence, an inspector may enter any Crown premises for the purpose of exercising any powers conferred on him by that section. No guidance is given as to how the inspector should satisfy himself as to the absence of the sovereign.

4.45 The inspector may, therefore, require entry to certain premises. Once there he is empowered to question any person aged 18 or over whom he finds on the premises (s 15(5)); he may therefore question anyone he meets there. It is not provided that the inspector must produce his certificate as evidence of his right to ask questions but no doubt it will be prudent for him to do so.

Section 15(6) goes into more detail about the obligation of persons questioned to answer questions put to them and to supply documents. The obligation is laid on any person who is or has been:

'(a) an occupier of the premises in question;
 (b) an employer or an employee working at or from those premises;
 (c) carrying on at or from those premises any trade, profession, vocation or business;
 (d) an employee or agent of any person mentioned in paragraphs (a) to (c).'

The definition is a wide one. Anyone who has occupied or worked at that place of work seems to be contained within it. Section 15(6) goes on to provide that, if required to do so by an inspector exercising his powers, any person who is or has been within the definition above 'shall furnish to the inspector all such information and documents as the inspector may reasonably require'.

4.46 Anyone who fails to co-operate with the inspector will find himself in trouble. Although s 15(7) provides that no person shall be required under s 15 to answer any question or give any evidence tending to incriminate himself or, in the case of a person who is married, his or her spouse; 'incriminate' means render himself liable to criminal proceedings; an absent parent who did not wish to give evidence of his means would not be able to avail himself of this provision. Subject to this exception, under s 15(9), if any person:

'(a)   intentionally delays or obstructs any inspector exercising his powers; or

(b)   without reasonable excuse, refuses or neglects to answer any question or furnish any information or to produce any document when required to do so under this section, he shall be guilty of an offence and liable on summary conviction to a fine not exceeding level 3 on the standard scale.'

Once the identity of the inspector is made known, and subject to subsection (7), it is difficult to see what might amount to 'reasonable excuse'.

4.47   The wide powers conferred on inspectors attracted some adverse comments during the parliamentary debates. One of the more measured criticisms came from Lord Simon of Glaisdale, a former Solicitor General, President of the Probate, Divorce and Admiralty Division and Lord of Appeal in Ordinary. Lord Simon made clear that he had:

'. . . no sympathy for fathers who default on their duty to maintain their children. I hope that I made plain my view that it is entirely reasonable that steps should be taken to re-imburse the general body of taxpayers on whom the liabilities are thrown. However, there must be a limit to what one will do in pursuit of those aims. It is no good having enormous paving stones of good intentions. What is done in this clause goes far beyond what is permissible in any decent system of civil liberties.

I should be perfectly content if the Draconian powers were allowed on a magistrate's warrant. However even that safeguard is not vouched safe . . . I hope that [the Lord Chancellor] who is the embodiment of the law, as Gilbert said, will recognize that an important principle of the rule is at stake.' (*House of Lords, Official Report*, 19 March 1992, col 588).

In reply the Lord Chancellor pointed out that Lord Simon had said that:

'it is no good having a paving stone system of good intentions. I say that it is no good having an intention to enable children to be properly maintained by their parents without giving the necessary powers to those who are to make that effective. Having pious thoughts and supporting the principle of the Bill without giving the necessary powers to those charged with the responsibility of collecting the maintenance is not to support the principle of the Bill at all.' (ibid).

10.   Periodical Reviews and Reviews on Changes of Circumstances

4.48   The Act contains provision for reviews of assessments. Some of these are by way of appeal and are dealt with in Chapter 6 below. Here it is necessary to consider reviews which may take place not because of any challenge to the validity of the original assessment but because of the passage of time or some change in circumstances.

4.49   Clearly, once an assessment is made it will not last for ever. Children get older and cost more to keep, the means of parents wax and wane and, most significantly perhaps, social security allowances normally increase every year in step with retail prices. Section 16 of the Act therefore requires the Secretary of State to:

'make such arrangements as he considers necessary to secure that, where any maintenance assessment has been in force for a prescribed period, the amount of child support maintenance fixed by that assessment ("the original assessment") is reviewed by a child support officer under this section as soon as is reasonably practicable after the end of that prescribed period.'

These arrangements are contained in Part V of the CS(MAP)Regs 1992, reg 17(1) of which provides that a maintenance assessment which has been in place for 52 weeks shall be reviewed by a child support officer under s 16. There is therefore a compulsory annual review of any maintenance assessment; however, by reg 17(3) a child support officer may decide not to conduct such a review if any fresh maintenance assessment would cease to have effect within 28 days of the effective date of the fresh assessment.

The child support officer must give 14 days' notice of the proposed review to the relevant persons (normally the person with care and the absent parent) and request such persons to provide such information or evidence as to their current circumstances as may be specified (unless they are in receipt of income support) (reg 17(4)–(6)). However, the requirement to request information or evidence as to means does not apply to a relevant person where:

(a)   the case is a special case (see para **5.47**);

(b)   there has been a review under s 16 or 17 in relation to another maintenance assessment in force relating to the person;

(c)   the child support officer has notified that person of the assessments following that review within the preceding 13 weeks;

(d)   the child support officer has no reason to believe that there has been a change in that person's circumstances (reg 17(7)).

4.50   Section 16(3) provides that a review shall be conducted 'as if a fresh application for a maintenance assessment had been made by the person in whose favour the original assessment was made'; the whole matter is therefore considered *de novo*. This means that all the powers of investigation employed in the first assessment may be used again. On completing any review under s 16, the child support officer must 'make a fresh maintenance assessment, unless he is satisfied that the original assessment has ceased to have effect or should be brought to an end' (s 16(4)). Even if the amount of the assessment is exactly the same as before, it will therefore be necessary to issue a fresh assessment. Any fresh assessment made shall take effect either on the day immediately after the end of the prescribed period mentioned in s 16(1) (ie at the end of the prescribed period after which the child support officer must carry out a review), or:

'in such circumstances as may be prescribed, on such later date as may be determined in accordance with regulations made by the Secretary of State.'

By reg 31(1) of the CS(MAP)Regs 1992, where a fresh assessment is made following a review under s 16, the effective date of that assessment shall be 52 weeks after the effective date of the previous assessment. Some backdating may therefore be involved.

4.51   Section 17 provides for reviews on a different basis from the preceding paragraphs; this basis is analogous to variations under the old law. Section 17(1) provides that where a maintenance assessment is in force:

'(a)   the absent parent or person with care with respect to whom it was made; or

(b)   where the application for the assessment was made under section 7 [right of child in Scotland to apply for assessment], either of them or the child concerned, may apply to the Secretary of State for the amount of child support maintenance fixed by that assessment ("the original assessment") to be reviewed under this section.'

An application under s 17 may be made only:

'on the ground that, by reason of a change of circumstances since the original assessment was made, the amount of child support maintenance payable by the absent parent would be significantly different if it were to be fixed by a maintenance assessment made by reference to the circumstances of the case as at the date of the application'.

The method of application is not stated but no doubt it should be in writing.

Although it is provided that an application 'may be made only' on the ground given, there is clearly nothing that can be done to prevent an application, however unpromising, from being made if it purports to rely on that ground. However, to forestall applications which are clearly doomed to failure, s 17(3) provides that:

'The child support officer to whom an application under this section has been referred shall not proceed unless, on the information before him, he considers that it is likely that he will be required by subsection (6) to make a fresh maintenance assessment if he conducts the review applied for.'

The making of an assessment, or a fresh assessment, is a formal step. The intention of this subsection seems to be that if, after making the necessary calculations, the child support officer considers that the original assessment would be unchanged, he may merely reject the application and not issue a fresh assessment identical with the first one.

The procedure for a review under s 17 is contained in Part VI of the CS(MAP)Regs 1992, reg 19(1) which provides that where a child support officer proposes to conduct a review under s 17 he must give 14 days' notice to the relevant persons (normally the person with care and the absent parent). As with a s 16 review, the child support officer will request those persons to provide, within 14 days, evidence and information as to their current circumstances unless they are in receipt of income support (reg 19(2) and (3)). By reg 19(4) where an application for a s 17 review is made at the time that a s 16 review is being conducted, the child support officer may proceed with the s 17 review, notwithstanding that he has not requested information or evidence as to means if, in his opinion, compliance with that requirement is not required in the particular circumstances of the case.

Regulation 19(5) provides, in effect, for certain applications for maintenance assessments to be deemed to be s 17 applications. It is provided that where a maintenance assessment is in force and the parent with care authorises the Secretary of State to take action to recover child support maintenance from the same absent parent in respect of an additional child of whom he is the parent, that authorisation shall be treated by the Secretary of State as an application for a review under s 17.

The result of the review itself, if the application is not refused, will turn on whether a 'significantly different' result will be achieved. This term is not defined and there is no provision in s 17 for the making of regulations to prescribe a definition (although there is a general power, under s 51(2)(a)(iii), to make regulations about reviews). In the absence of regulations this would have to be defined on normal principles using the plain sense of the English language; however, what is significant for one person may not be significant for another. For this reason, 'significantly different' will have to be interpreted only in the light of the limits specified under s 17(6)(b) (see para **4.52** below).

4.52 Section 17(4) and (5) contain provisions as to notice to the parties and the basis of the fresh assessment similar to those contained in s 16(2) and (3) (see paras **4.49** and **4.50** above). Section 17(6) then provides that, on completing any reviews under s 17, the child support officer concerned:

'shall make a fresh maintenance assessment unless –
(a) he is satisfied that the original assessment has ceased to have effect or should be brought to an end, or
(b) the difference between the amount of child support maintenance fixed by the original assessment and the amount that would be fixed if a fresh assessment were to be made as a result of this review is less than such amount as may be prescribed.'

These prescribed amounts are contained in reg 20 of the CS(MAP)Regs 1992. It should first be noted that there are no restrictions in respect of a s 16 review; here a fresh assessment may be made no matter how small a change is involved.

The position is different for s 17 reviews. By reg 20(1) a child support officer may not make a fresh assessment after a s 17 review if the difference between the assessment in force and the fresh assessment would be less than £10 per week. Therefore, if the child support maintenance as a result of the fresh assessment would be £9.99 per week more or less than that payable on the current assessment, there would be no change until the anniversary of the original assessment when a s 16 review would be carried out.

However, this is subject to, and must be read with, reg 20(2) which applies where, as a result of a fresh assessment, the circumstances of the absent parent are such that the provisions of para 6 of Sch 1 to the Act would apply to the assessment; that is to say, payment by the absent parent of the amount so assessed would reduce his disposable income below his protected income level. In such a case, the child support officer may not make a fresh assessment if the difference between the original assessment and the fresh assessment would be less than £1 per week.

4.53   It must be said that the combination of these two provisions produces a potentially obscure result. Regulation 20(1) is clear enough, but reg 20(2) seems not to regard the protected income calculations as part of 'the assessment'.

Be that as it may, it seems that the intended result of these provisions is that calculations are to be carried out. In the first calculation the protected income level is ignored and the assessment remains unchanged if the difference is less than £10 per week. The second calculation only applies if the assessment is less than it would normally be by virtue of the protected earnings level and here it may not change unless the change is more than £1 per week. It can only be said that this result does not emerge as clearly from these provisions as it might have done.

Regulation 20(3) provides that were a fresh assessment to be made after a s 17 review the children concerned would not be identical with the children in respect of when the original assessment was made, the child support officer may not make a fresh assessment if the difference between the original and fresh assessment would be less than £1 per week.

Finally there are certain similar provisions in regs 21, 22 and 23, relating to special cases.

11.   Termination of Assessments

4.54   Paragraph 16 of Schedule 1 prescribes the circumstances in which a maintenance assessment may be terminated. An assessment shall cease to have effect '(a)   on the death of the absent parent or of the person with care . . .'; this requires no amplification. It would also cease to have effect '(b)   on there no longer being any qualifying child with respect to whom it would have effect'; this might apply if the qualifying child died, attained the age of 16 and ceased full time education, attained the age of 18 and prescribed conditions ceased to apply or attained the age of 19. The assessment also ceases to have effect:

'(c)   on the absent parent with respect to whom it was made ceasing to be a parent of –
 (i)   the qualifying child with respect to whom it was made; or
 (ii)   where it was made with respect to more than one qualifying child, all of the qualifying children with respect to whom it was made.'

'Parent' means any person who is in law the mother or father of the child. A person could therefore cease to be a parent if an adoption order were made in respect of the child. A declaration of a court that an absent father was not the natural father of the child would not of itself cause a termination under this subparagraph, but it would lead to the review of the assessment under other provisions of the Act.

Under para 16(1)(d), where the absent parent and the person with care in respect to whom an assessment was made have been living together for six months, the assessment will cease to have effect. Resumption of cohabitation is not in itself a ground for termination of the assessment, although presumably it would be a ground for a review under s 17(1). It is necessary to live together for six months. However, this does not apply where the parties jointly seek a termination as it is provided that the assessment will cease:

'(a) where a new maintenance assessment is made with respect to any qualifying child with respect to whom the assessment in question was in force immediately before the making of the new assessment.'

4.55 Paragraph 16(2) of Schedule 1 provides that a maintenance assessment made in response to an application under s 4 or 7 (ie where the person with care is not receiving benefit) must be cancelled by a child support officer if the person on whose application the assessment was made asks him to do so.

However, for obvious reasons, this does not apply to persons with care who are receiving benefit. By para 16(3), a maintenance assessment made in response to an application under s 6 shall be cancelled by a child support officer if:

'(a) the person on whose application the assessment was made ("the applicant") asks him to do so; and
(b) he is satisfied that the applicant has ceased to fall within subsection (1) of that section' [ie has ceased to receive benefits].

Regulation 32 of the CS(MAP)Regs 1992 provides that where a child support officer cancels a maintenance assessment under para 16(2) or (3) of Sch 1 to the Act the assessment shall cease to have effect from the date of receipt of the request for cancellation of the assessment or from such later date as the child support officer may determine.

4.56 Clearly, where a person in whose favour a maintenance assessment has been made ceases to be the person with care in relation to the qualifying child, or any of the qualifying children, the assessment must be terminated. Paragraph 16(4) therefore permits the child support officer to cancel the assessment where he is satisfied that this is the case.

Paragraph 16(5) deals with the position where a maintenance assessment is in force 'but a child support officer would no longer have jurisdiction to make it if it were to be applied for at that time'. Jurisdiction is considered at para **4.3** above. It provides that where the child support officer would no longer have jurisdiction, and:

'(b) the assessment has not been cancelled, or has not ceased to have effect, under or by virtue of any other provision made by or under this Act, it shall be taken to have continuing effect until cancelled by a child support officer in accordance with such prescribed provision (including provision as to the effective date of cancellation) as the Secretary of State considers it appropriate to make.'

The assessment will therefore continue until cancelled.

4.57 Paragraph 16(6) provides that, where both the absent parent and the person with care with respect to whom a maintenance assessment was made request a child support officer to cancel the assessment, he may do so if he is satisfied that they are living together. This seems to apply only to benefit cases, although it is not stated to be limited in this way, because in non-benefit cases the child support officer must cancel, under para 16(2), if the person with care asks him to do so.

12. Fees

4.58 By the Child Support Fees Regulations 1992 the Secretary of State is entitled to charge fees for the use of the Child Support Agency. The overall power is contained in reg 2 which provides that where a maintenance assessment is made following an application under s 4, 6 or 7, fees shall be payable in accordance with regs 3 and 4.

4.59 Regulation 3 deals with the persons liable to pay fees, who are the person with care and the absent parent with respect to when the assessment was made. However, some categories of person are exempt from paying fees. They are:

(a) any person receiving income support, family credit or disability allowance;

(b) any person under 16, or under 19 and receiving full-time education which is not advanced education;

(c) any person whose assessable income is nil;

(d) an absent parent whose protected income effects a reduction in any assessment.

The regulations do not specify which of the parents is to pay the fee. However, presumably the applicant person with care will pay initially and the absent parent against whom an assessment is made will be required to repay it. The fact that one party is exempt from fees does not mean that the other party is also exempt.

4.60 Regulation 4 sets out the services for which fees are payable. These are:

(a) an assessment fee, ie for carrying out the assessment; and

(b) a collection fee, ie for the Secretary of State arranging collection and for enforcement.

The assessment fee is £44 and the collection fee is £34; no doubt these will be periodically updated. An assessment fee is payable on assessment and thereafter on each anniversary of that date. A collection fee is payable on the date the Secretary of State arranged collection and thereafter whenever an assessment fee is charged.

Fees are payable 14 days after an invoice is sent.

CHAPTER FIVE

How Child Maintenance is Assessed

1. Introduction

5.1 As has already been pointed out, the Act introduces a remarkable innovation in English family law in the shape of a 'maintenance formula' which prescribes the method of calculating the maintenance payable in any particular case and which cannot be departed from. This formula is administered by an administrative agency, the powers of the courts having been excluded, and any appeal relates solely to whether the formula has been correctly applied and not to any other merits or hardships involved in the case. The clear intention of the Act is that the formula should be sufficiently flexible to permit justice to be done in all cases, while retaining the desired element of certainty and consistency which were considered to be missing before the implementation of the Act.

5.2 The formula consists of four key elements, namely

(a)   the maintenance requirement;
(b)   the parents' assessable income;
(c)   the deduction rate; and
(d)   the protected income.

These elements will be considered in turn. At the outset, however, it must be said that the detailed provisions relating to the formula which are contained in the Sch 1 to the Act are initially baffling and certainly not 'reader friendly'. It may be helpful to give an initial overall picture of how the whole system will work.

The examples are taken from the Child Support Agency's *Notes for Advisers* published in 1992; the figures used in the examples are taken from 1992/93 social security rates and so are not completely up to date.

First, an example is given of how the maintenance requirement will be calculated for a lone-parent family with two children aged 9 and 12. The maintenance requirement is as follows;

child aged 9	£14.55
child aged 12	21.40
family premium	9.30
lone-parent premium	4.75

adult allowance	42.45
sub total	92.45
less child benefit	17.45
Total maintenance requirement	75.00

Next the assessable incomes of the parents are calculated, and in the next relevant example the given facts are that the father, Peter, has an assessable income of £140 per week whereas the mother, Sally, does not work and has no assessable income. (Peter's assessable income will have been calculated by deducting from his net earnings the single adult personal allowance and his housing costs).

The maintenance requirement if £75. Peter is required to pay one half of his assessable income, namely £70 per week. He cannot afford the full maintenance requirement of £75 per week.

5.3 In the next example the parents are Len and Eileen. The maintenance requirement is still £75 per week. Len's assessable income is £120 per week and Eileen has assessable income of £20 per week, a total of £140 per week between them. Half this figure is £70 per week which is less than the maintenance requirement. As the maintenance requirement is not fully met Len will pay half his assessable income, i.e. £60 per week.

5.4 The examples given are of the most basic kind but they illustrate the working of the Formula. Further examples given in *Notes for Advisers* deal with housing costs, the effect of remarriage and so on. The final stage of the calculation is concerned with the protected level of income. The method of calculating this is explained in *Notes for Advisers* and need not be set out here since it is explained in detail at para **5.38** et seq below; the purpose is to provide that an absent parent retains enough income after paying maintenance to meet his or her day to day needs and that of any second family.

In the example in *Notes for Advisers*, Archibald is an absent parent and has been assessed to pay maintenance of £40 per week. He has a wife, Edwina and a baby, Winston. Edwina's daughter aged 7 also lives with them. The family's disposable income (from all sources) is £230 per week and the protected income level is £200.

The assessed maintenance is therefore reduced to £30, this being the maximum maintenance he can pay and still be left with his protected income level of £200.

If Edwina had income of her own, whether maintenance for the children or her own earnings, this would be added to the income of the household and would reduce the level of protected income. In the example given, additional income for Edwina of £30 per week would have been enough to result in no reduction of the formula award of maintenance for Archibald's first family.

It will be noted that the social security figures are taken throughout as the determining factor; no allowance is made for such matters as the cost of

Michael travelling to work, his buying a car, or any loan repayments on furniture for the new home.

2.   The Maintenance Requirement (MR)

5.5   While *Children Come First* and, it is hoped, the examples given above give an intelligible account of how the new system would work, it was the task of the parliamentary draftsman to translate this into a watertight formula for inclusion in the Act. This has been done by means of a set of mathematical formulae, not unknown in revenue legislation but novel in this field.

Section 11(2) and (3) of the Act provide as follows:

'(2)   The amount of child support maintenance to be fixed by any maintenance assessment shall be determined in accordance with the provisions of Part I of Schedule 1.

(3)   Part II of Schedule 1 makes further provision with respect to maintenance assessments.'

Schedule 1 begins by defining the 'maintenance requirement' as:

'the amount, calculated in accordance with the formula set out in subparagraph (2), which is to be taken as the minimum amount necessary for the maintenance of the qualifying child or, where there is more than one qualifying child, all of them.' (para 1(1)).

Paragraph 1(2) defines the formula as:

$$MR = AG - CB$$

MR is the maintenance requirement.
AG (an abbreviation of 'aggregate') is the aggregate of the amounts to be taken into account under para 1(3).
CB is the child benefit which is payable for the child or children in question, or which would be payable if the person with care were an individual (ie credit will still be given for child benefit when the child is in the care of a local authority). It is to be assumed that child benefit is payable for any qualifying child at the basic rate (para 1(4)). It is further provided that 'basic rate' has the meaning for the time being prescribed, and the term is in fact defined by reg 4 of the CS(MASC)Regs 1992 as 'the rate of child benefit which is specified in reg 2 (i) of the Child Benefit and Social Security (Fixing and Adjustment of Rates) Regulations 1976 (rates of child benefit) applicable to the child in question'. It therefore includes the enhanced rate for the first child.

5.6   Paragraph 1(3) sets out the factors to be taken into account for the purpose of calculating AG. Once again, the actual amounts are determined by delegated legislation and para 1(3) merely contains very broad categories, in the following terms:

'(a)   such amount or amounts (if any), with respect to each qualifying child, as may be prescribed;

(b)   such amount or amounts (if any), with respect to the person with care of the qualifying child or qualifying children, as may be prescribed; and

(c)   such further amount or amounts (if any) as may be prescribed.'

The detailed provisions are contained in the CS(MASC)Regs 1992, reg 3 which provides that the amounts to be taken into account for the purposes of calculating AG in the formula are:

(a)   with respect to each qualifying child, the income support allowance for child or young person;

(b)   with respect to a person with care of a qualifying child aged less than 16 the income support personal allowance for a single claimant aged not less than 25;

(c)   income support family premium;

(d)   where the person with care of the qualifying child or children has no partners, the income support lone parent premium.

'Partner' is defined by reg 1(1) as;

(a)   in relation to a member of a married or unmarried couple who are living together, the other member of that couple;

(b)   in relation to a member of a polygamous marriage, any other member of that marriage with whom he lives.

It will be seen, therefore, that the predictions contained in *Children Come First* (and the examples at paras **5.2** et seq) have been broadly confirmed. The only difference is that once a child is 16 the 'parent as carer' allowance is no longer taken into account.

5.7   The shape of MR is therefore reasonably clear. AG is the total income support entitlement (ignoring housing costs) of the caring parent. Child benefit at the 'basic rate' is deducted. The resulting sum is MR.

Under the law prior to the Act's implementation, maintenance of a child or children is assessed in respect of each child and an award is made in respect of each child separately. Under the Act, the family unit which contains the qualifying children is assessed as a whole, and there is one maintenance requirement to cover them all. This is a new departure.

5.8   Having calculated MR, the next stage is to calculate the contribution of the parents to that sum. The reality is that the share to be borne by the absent parent must be calculated. At the outset it will be useful to underline another basic concept of the Act. When the absent parent's income is such that, after making all the allowances to which he is entitled, MR is equal to not more than a prescribed proportion (half) of his assessable income, he will pay no more than MR. This is known as the basic element (BE). However, it is intended that children of wealthier parents should not be confined to income support rates and accordingly, when the absent parent's income exceeds a certain level, a basic element (BE) and an additional element (AE) will be payable. This has the effect of creating a 'two-tier' system.

The example given in *Notes for Advisers* is that of Len and Eileen who were considered at Para **5.3** above. Eileen has had a pay rise increasing her assessable income to £50 per week. Len still has assessable income of £120 per week, making a total joint assessable income of £170 per week. Half of this is £85, which exceeds the maintenance requirement of £75.

Notes for Advisers states that the lower deduction rate to be applied to the balance of assessable income after the maintenance requirement is met is 25 per cent. This will be applied under the formula until the maximum amount of maintenance is reached.

Applying this to Len's case, the fraction to calculate his share is

$$£75 \times \frac{£120}{(£120 + £50)} = £52.94$$

The additional element is calculated as follows;

Len's assessable income	£120
less Already used up at 50% deduction rate	£105.88
Balance	14.12
AE payable at 25%	£3.53

The maximum amount payable under the formula will be the aggregate of the income support allowance for the child and the family premium multiplied by three.

When the formulae are considered in greater detail at Para **5.29** et seq it will be seen that the calculations are complex and involved. The simplified version set out above may serve as a useful aide-mémoire when considering those calculations.

3. Assessable Income

5.9 Certain further terms are defined by Sch 1 and must be considered in some detail, as follows.

The assessable incomes of the absent parent and the parent with care first fall to be calculated. The former is described in Sch 1 as 'A' and the latter as 'C'.

Paragraph 5(1) provides that:

$$A = N - E$$

N is defined as 'the amount of that [the absent] parent's net income, calculated or estimated in accordance with regulations made by the Secretary of State for the purpose of this sub-paragraph'. These regulations are in fact contained in reg 7 and Sch 1 of the CS(MASC)Regs 1992; reg 7 sets out the classes of income which are then defined in the schedule. The result is that N (and indeed M, the income of the person with care, for the same criteria apply to both; the term 'parent' rather than 'absent parent' is therefore used in the text) consists of the aggregate of the following amounts (A) to (E), below.

(A)   Earnings of the parent

In the case of employment as an employed earner this means any remuneration or profit derived from that employment and includes a list of detailed items in para 1(1) of Sch 1, Part 1 such as bonus or commission, holiday pay, retainer, expenses not wholly, exclusively and necessarily incurred in the performance of the duties of the employment, compensation for unfair dismissal, sick pay, maternity pay and payment in lieu of notice.

'Earnings' does not include expenses wholly, exclusively and necessarily incurred in the performance of duties of the employment, occupational pension, advances of earnings or loans or payments in kind. The full lists of both classes of income are in the schedule set out in Appendix 2.

By para 1(3) the earnings to be taken into account are gross earnings less:

(a)   any amount deducted by way of income tax or primary Class 1 contributions; and
(b)   one-half of any sums paid by the parent towards an occupational or personal pension scheme.

Paragraph 2 contains detailed provision for calculating weekly earnings. For weekly-paid earners the last five weeks' earnings will be divided by five; for monthly paid earners the last two months' earnings will be multiplied by 6 and divided by 52; for earners paid in some other way the past three months' earnings will be multiplied by 4 and divided by 52.

5.10   Chapter 2 of Sch 1, Part 1 deals with the earnings of a self-employed earner. By para 3(1) 'earnings' means the gross receipts of the employment. From this is to be deducted:

(a)   expenses reasonably incurred and wholly and exclusively defrayed for the purposes of the owner's business;
(b)   VAT;
(c)   income tax;
(d)   national insurance contributions;
(e)   one-half of any premium paid in respect of a retirement annuity contract or a personal pension scheme.

There are the detailed provisions as to how the various sums are to be calculated, which will be found in full at Appendix 2. However, what has been said already sets out the generall overall effect of the provisions. Clearly, the child support officer will be greatly assisted when the absent parent can produce up-to-date accounts, and para 5(2) provides that where a self-employed earner provides a profit and loss account and, where appropriate, a trading account or a balance sheet or both, and the profit and loss account is in respect of a period of at least 6 months but not exceeding 15 months and that period terminates within the 12 months immediately preceding the effective date, the amount of his earnings shall be determined by reference to the average of the earnings over the period to which the profit and loss account relates, and such earnings shall include receipts relevant to that period whether or not received in that period.

A self-employed earner should therefore ensure that he has proper accounts for a period terminating not more than one year before the assessment is made. It may be mentioned in passing that a self-employed absent parent is going to have an advantage over an employed earner insofar as his motoring and/or travel expenses will normally be deductible for his gross earnings to arrive at his net profit whereas there is no provision anywhere (even in the protected income calculations) for the necessary travelling expenses of an employed earner to be taken into account.

Clearly, one difficulty which the child support officer will face is that many self-employed earners do not have properly audited up-to-date accounts; some persons with care may feel that they are prejudiced by the fact that the means of such an absent parent cannot be investigated with all the rigour of the procedures adopted by courts.

It is likely that this problem will lead to many appeals to the Child Support Appeal Tribunal. As will be seen at para **6.23** et seq the Tribunal will have wide powers to order discovery of documents and to compel the attendance of witnesses and it may well be that, while the child support officer must do his best on the information available to him, the only forum in which the issue can be satisfactorily determined will be the Tribunal.

(B)   Benefit payments under the Social Security Contributions and Benefits Act 1992 paid to or in respect of the parent
5.11   'Benefit payments' means any payment made under the Act except those specifically excluded by Sch 2 (as to which see para **5.16** below). It normally includes family credit. Once again, the detailed provisions are complex and will be found at Appendix 2.

(C)   Any other income of the parent
5.12   This includes pension or other benefit under an occupational or personal pension scheme or retirement annuity contract or other such scheme for the provision of income in retirement. By para 11 of Sch 1, it includes a student grant or student loan (but not those sums attributable to, eg, fees, additional residence costs, books or travel costs), except where the grant or student loan is the only source of the student's income (reg 7(3)(b)).

'Other income' includes interest or dividends and maintenance payments in respect of a parent (para 14), since, as will be seen below, the method of calculating M (person with care's assessable income) is identical with that for N. It is interesting to note that any maintenance paid by an absent parent to the person with care for herself will be regarded as part of the person with care's income, but there is nowhere any provision for the deduction of such maintenance from the absent parent's income.

(D)   Any income of a relevant child which is treated as the income of the parent

5.13   By reg 1(1) a 'relevant child' is a child of an absent parent or parent with care who is a member of the same family as that parent, 'family' being defined to mean living together. Paragraph 18 of Sch 1 provides that where a child is a member of the family of his parent (whether or not he is a qualifying child in relation to that parent) the relevant income of that child shall be treated as the income of his parent.

Where child support maintenance is being assessed for the support of only one qualifying child, that child's relevant income is treated as the income of the parent with care; however, where there is more than one qualifying child the relevant income of each qualifying child is treated as the income of the parent with care only to the extent that it does not exceed the aggregate of:

(a)   (i)   the income support personal allowance for that child, and
      (ii)   the total of such of the various other amounts applicable under reg 3(1)(b) or (d), that is to say adult income support allowance, family premium and lone parent premium as are applicable to the case in question, divided by the number of children for whom child support maintenance is being calculated, less the basic rate of child benefit for the child in question; and
(b)   three times the total of the income support allowance for that child and the family premium (Sch 1, paras 19 and 20).

The position where there is only one child is clear enough; his relevant income is regarded as that of the parent with care with whom he lives.

5.14   An example taken from *Notes for Advisers* with the figures updated to 1993/94 levels may illustrate the position where there are several children.

There are two children, Avril aged 12 and Sarah aged 14 who live with their mother, Jennifer. Sarah has a net income of £40 per week from capital in a building society. The maximum amount of maintenance payable for Sarah under the formula is worked out as follows;

Personal allowance	£22.15
Half of adult allowance	£22.00
Half of family premium	4.83
Half of lone parent premium	2.45
Additional maintenance	
i.e. 3 × (£22.15 + £9.30)	94.35
sub total	145.78
less child benefit	10.00
	£135.78

Sarah's income of £40 is less than the maximum amount for her and so all of it is added to Jennifer's net income.

The position is different where the child in question is not a child in respect of whom child support maintenance is being assessed. Here, by reg 21, his income is regarded as the income of his parent to the extent that it does not exceed the figure in reg 9(1)(g), that is to say the income support personal allowance for that child (the position is slightly different where the child is disabled).

The regulations do not define what is the 'relevant income' of the child. However, reg 23 defines what is not to be regarded as the relevant income of the child; relevant income does not include:

(a)   any earnings of the child;

(b)   payments by an absent parent in respect of the child for whom maintenance is being assessed;

(c)   where the class of persons who are capable of benefiting from a discretionary trust include the child in question, payments from that trust except in so far as they are made to provide for food, ordinary clothing and footwear, gas, electricity or fuel charges or housing costs (in which case they would be regarded as the child's relevant income); or

(d)   any interest payable on arrears of child support maintenance for that child.

Finally, para 24 of Sch 1 provides that the amount of the income of a child which is treated as the income of the parent shall be determined in the same way as if such income were the income of the parent. Given that earnings (whether on an employed or self-employed basis) cannot be regarded as 'relevant income', this can only mean that Parts II (benefits), III (any other income) and V (amounts treated as income) are to be used in determining the amount of the child's income; these classes of income are dealt with elsewhere in this chapter when considering the income of the parent per se.

(E)   Any amount which is treated as the income of the parent
5.15   The criteria for this are set out in Part V of Sch 1 and fall into two broad classes, as follows.

(a)   Non-remunerative services, ie where a person has performed a service for no remuneration or remuneration which is less than that normally paid for the service, for another person who is not a member of the same family or a body which is neither a charity nor a voluntary organisation, and the child support officer is satisfied that the service was performed for a person or body able to pay remuneration at the normal rate, that the principal purpose of the exercise is to reduce the parent's assessable earnings and that any remuneration forgone would have fallen to be taken into account as earnings.

(b)   Income or capital intentionally forgone, ie where the child support officer is satisfied that a person has intentionally deprived himself of any income or capital which would otherwise be a source of income, or any income or capital which it would be reasonable to expect would be secured by him, with a view to reducing his assessable income, the child support officer may estimate the income so forgone and include it as part of the parent's income. However, by para 28, unemployment benefit or a payment from a discretionary trust or a trust derived from a payment made in consequence of a personal injury may not be treated as income for this purpose.

When the child support officer determines that a parent has intentionally deprived himself of capital he will treat the interest which might have been earned on that capital as weekly income of the parent. This will last for 52 weeks and then, by the operation of para 30, the 'capital' will be reduced over a period of the succeeding 52 weeks by the weekly amount of income deemed to be earned on it during the preceding 52 weeks.

5.16   Having determined what is or may be the income of the parent, the regulations also provide, in Sch 2, a list of items which must be disregarded; that is to say they may not be regarded as income of the parent. The complete list is set out in Sch 2, to be found at Appendix 2; it is much too lengthy to be set out here. However, the following may be noted (the paragraph numbers are those in the schedule).

2.   Income tax applicable to the income in question.
5.   Compensation for personal injury and payment from a trust fund set up for the purpose.
8.   Disability living allowance or mobility supplement.
9.   (a) Attendance allowance.
10.   Pensioners' Christmas bonus.
11.   Any social fund payment.
16.   Child benefit not exceeding the basic rate.
18.   War disablement pension and war widows' pension not exceeding £10.
28.   In the calculation of the income of the parent with care any payments made by the absent parent in respect of his qualifying child.
29.   Foster-care payments or their equivalent.
35.   Any contribution to the expenses of maintaining a household which is made by a non-dependent member of the household.
41.   Payments made to a holder of the Victoria Cross or George Cross.
45.   Where following a divorce or separation:
    (a) capital is divided between the parent and the person who was his partner before the divorce or separation; and
    (b) that capital is intended to be used to acquire a new home for that parent or to acquire furnishings for a home of his, income derived from the investment of that capital for one year following the date on which that capital became available to the parent.
46.   Payments in kind.

Finally, by reg 7(3), where a parent's income consists only of a YTS allowance, or, in the case of a student, only of grant and/or student loan or only of prisoner's pay, such sums shall be disregarded.

5.17 E is defined by para 5(1) as 'that [the absent] parent's exempt income, calculated or estimated in accordance with regulations made by the Secretary of State'. Before considering how E is likely to be calculated, it is perhaps prudent to recall that E should not be confused with 'protected income'. E is the figure deducted to arrive at A (assessable income), a proportion of which is the maintenance assessment; the protected income is the final safety net and the method of calculating it will certainly differ from that used in calculating E.

The regulations governing the determination of E are contained in reg 9 of the CS(MASC)Regs 1992. E is the aggregate of the following:

(a) income support personal allowance for a single claimant aged not less than 25;

(b) housing costs (as to which, see paras **5.18** to **5.25** below);

(c) where the absent parent is the parent of a relevant child (ie a child living with him in his family) lone parent premium where appropriate;

(d) a sum equivalent to income support disability premium, where the parent would be entitled to this;

(e) sums equivalent to income support severe disability premiums and income support carer premiums where the parent would be entitled to these;

(f) income support family premium, where appropriate (or half that sum where reg 9(2) applies, as to which see para **5.26** below);

(g) the income support allowance for each relevant child (as defined in (c) above) (or half that sum where reg 9(2) applies, as to which see para **5.26** below);

(h) where the parent in question or his partner is living in accommodation provided under Part III of the National Assistance Act 1948 or under paras 1 and 2 of Sch 8 to the National Health Service Act 1977, or in a nursing home or residential home, the amount of the fees paid in respect of such occupation.

5.18 Two matters arising out of this list need to be considered further, namely housing costs and the effect on the calculation of a partner or cohabitee.

As has been seen, the housing costs of a parent are a necessary part of any exempt income, but not all housing costs are allowable; some limit has to be placed on what a parent spends on his own accommodation.

Paragraph 8 of Sch 1 to the Act provides that where regulations require a child support officer to take account of the housing costs of any person in calculating or estimating his assessable income or disposable income, those regulations may make provision:

'(a)   as to the costs which are to be treated as housing costs for the purpose of the regulations;

(b)   for the apportionment of housing costs; and

(c)   for the amount of housing costs to be taken into account for prescribed purposes not to exceed such amount (if any) as may be prescribed by, or determined in accordance with, the regulations.'

The rules for determining housing costs are contained in regs 14 to 18 of the CS(MASC)Regs 1992 and Sch 3.

5.19   Schedule 3 contains the classification of the types of housing costs which are allowable. Paragraph 1 sets out a list which contains all the usual kinds of housing costs such as rent, mortgage interest payments, hire-purchase agreement to buy a home, interest payments on loans for repairs and improvements, and so on. Absent parents who take to the hills will be pleased to see that where the home is a tent, payments in respect of the tent and the site on which it stands are eligible. The list also includes mooring charges for a houseboat and payments to an almshouse. It does not include community charge or council tax, these being included in the protected income calculation.

Paragraph 2 deals in more detail with loans for repairs and improvements. 'Repairs and improvements' are defined as major repairs necessary to maintain the fabric of the home and any of a list of measure undertaken with a view to improving its fitness for occupation. These measures are the provision or improvement of:

(a)   bath, shower, wash basin or lavatory;

(b)   damp proofing;

(c)   ventilation or natural lighting;

(d)   electric lighting and sockets;

(e)   drainage facilities;

(f)   structural condition of house;

(g)   facilities for storing, preparation and cooking of food;

(h)   heating, including central heating;

(i)   storage facilities for fuel and refuse;

(j)   insulation;

(k)   other improvements which the child support officer considers reasonable.

5.20   Paragraph 3 of Sch 3 contains some additional provisions. Where the protected income level of an absent parent is considered at paras **5.38** et seq, below, it will be seen that it will again be necessary to refer to Sch 3 to determine the absent parent's housing costs on a separate calculation. However, para 3 is stated to apply only for the purpose of calculating exempt income. The general effect of para 3 is that when mortgage payments include payments in reduction of capital or payments of premiums on an endowment mortgage such payments may be considered as housing costs. However, payments of mortgage arrears, or payments towards a second or subsequent mortgage incurred because of arrears, are not so eligible and will be disregarded.

By para 4, housing costs are only eligible if they are incurred in relation to the parent's home and the parent or a member of his family is responsible for them. It is also provided that costs are only eligible if the liability to meet those costs is to a person other than a member of the same household. Thus, where an absent parent lives with a new partner in her accommodation, payment of her housing costs, being the cost of both their accommodation, would be allowable. However, if she had no accommodation costs it would not be permissible for the absent parent to pay rent to her and then seek to include this as housing costs.

5.21 Having established the kinds of payments which may be considered as housing costs it is now necessary to turn to regs 15 and 18 which deal with the amount of such costs. The general principle is contained in reg 15(1); 'a parent's housing costs shall be the aggregate of the eligible housing costs payable in respect of his home'.

Most of these regulations are taken up with setting out the position when there are other persons in the same household. By reg 15(3), where a parent has eligible housing costs and another person who is not a member of his family (family being defined as a married or unmarried couple and any children living with them for whom one of them cares) is also liable to make payments in respect of the home, the amount of the parent's housing costs shall be his share of those costs.

The remainder of reg 15 is taken up with the position of non-dependants who live in the same household; broadly speaking, non-dependants are those who would be classified as such for the purpose of the housing benefit regulations. The general effect of the regulation is that the housing costs are reduced by such amounts as would be applicable if housing benefit were payable. No deduction will be made where the non-dependant normally resides elsewhere, is in receipt of a training allowance under YTS or equivalent, is a student, is aged under 25 and receives income support, or is a prisoner or patient.

By reg 15(10) a parent shall be treated as having no housing costs where he is a non-dependent member of a household and is not responsible for meeting housing costs except to another member or members of that household.

5.22 Regulation 17 deals with the apportionment of housing costs for the purpose of exempt income only (not for the protected income level). First, where a parent does not have a partner, the amount of his housing costs is the whole amount of such costs. However, where he has a partner it is necessary to apply one of two mathematical formulae, depending on whether or not the relationship is a polygamous marriage.

Where the parent is not a member of a polygamous marriage (which will be the most common situation), the housing costs must be multiplied by:

$$\frac{0.75 \times (A \times 0.2)}{1.00 \times (B \times 0.2)}$$

where A is the number of relevant children (if any) and B is the number of children in that parent's family (if any).

The implications of this must be considered. First, where there are no children at all in the household, the parts of the formula in brackets will have no value so that the proportion of housing costs allowable will be 75%.

'Relevant child' means a child of the absent parent or parent with care who is a member of the same family (ie household) of that parent. Therefore, if there were, for example, two children of the parent in question in that household but no other children the proportion would be:

$$\frac{0.75 + (2 \times 0.2)}{1.00 + (2 \times 0.2)} = 0.82$$

However, if there were a total of four children in the family, two of whom were not relevant children, the proportion would be:

$$\frac{0.75 + (2 \times 0.2)}{1.00 + (4 \times 0.2)} = 0.63$$

5.23 Where the parent is a member of a polygamous marriage, the formula is as follows:

$$\frac{0.75 + (A \times 0.2)}{1.00 + (X \times 0.25) + (B \times 0.2)}$$

It will be seen that the new element which has been introduced is $(X \times 0.25)$ and X is defined as 'the number which is one less than the number of partners'. (The important question therefore is not how many wives a man has but how many of them are sharing his household.) To take an example, if a man were living in the same household as four wives, but the facts were the same as in the second example given above, the equation would be:

$$\frac{0.75 \times (2 \times 0.2)}{1.00 + (3 \times 0.25) + (4 \times 0.2)}$$

$$= 0.45$$

5.24 Finally, reg 18 provides for limits on excessive housing costs. Subject to the qualifications set out below, the amount of housing costs may not exceed the greater of £80 or half the amount of N. In other words, where the parent's net income is £160 or less the housing costs may not exceed either £80 or one-half of net earnings (for the purposes of the Act), whichever be the lesser. Where the net earnings exceed £160 the housing costs may not exceed £80 or one-half of the earnings, whichever be the greater. (A slightly different formula applies when the protected income level is being considered.)

However, by reg 18(2), this restriction does not apply in the following classes of case:

(a)   where the absent parent has been awarded housing benefit (or is awaiting the outcome of a claim to that benefit), has the day-to-day care of any child or would be entitled to disability premium if entitled to income support;

(b)   the parent in question, following a divorce from, or the breakdown of his relationship with his former partner, remains in the house he previously occupied with his former partner; a parent who continues to live in the 'former matrimonial home' or its equivalent will therefore not be subject to the restrictions in reg 18(1);

(c)   the parent is responsible for making payments in respect of housing costs which are higher than they would be otherwise because of the unavailability of his share of the equity of the property formerly occupied with his partner and which remains occupied by that former partner.

5.25   This last class is likely to be quite common in cases where the parents have been married and the parent with care continues to occupy the former matrimonial home. Presumably, 'unavailability of his share of the equity' will include cases where that share has been transferred to the parent with care. Once the child support officer has satisfied himself that the share of equity is not available and that in consequence the absent parent's housing costs are higher than they would otherwise be (which would normally be almost a necessary inference), the restriction in reg 18(1) disappears and the absent parent may incur such housing costs as he chooses with no risk of their being considered excessive.

5.26   The other factor affecting N is the operation of reg 9(2). This part of the regulation applies where the parent in question has a partner, and the parent and the partner are parents of the same relevant child (ie their child, living with them, for whom they care), and the income of the partner (calculated under reg 7(1) as if the partner were an absent parent) exceeds the aggregate of:

(a)   income support personal allowance for a single claimant aged not less than 25;

(b)   half the income support personal allowance to the child;

(c)   half of any income support disabled premium in respect of that child;

(d)   half the income support family premium except where it is payable irrespective of that child;

(e)   the amount by which the housing costs of the absent parent, calculated under the regulations, has been reduced by an apportionment under reg 17 (as to which see para **5.22** above; this means that for this calculation the reduction under reg 17 is notionally 'paid back').

What reg 9(2) means in effect therefore is that the partner may earn enough to keep herself (based on the income support rates) and half the sum needed to support the child of the parent and herself before any account need to be taken of her income for certain specified purposes.

However, when that sum is exceeded, her income is relevant, and its effect is seen in the operation of reg 9(1)(f) and (g) which sets out the calculation of exempt income; provision is made there for the income support personal allowances for a relevant child to be included in the aggregate of exempt income. However, where reg 9(2) applies, only one half of such allowances may be included.

5.27 The assessable income of a parent who has care of the qualifying child or children is described as 'C' and must now be considered. C is defined as:

$$C = M - F$$

M is defined in exactly the same terms as N and F is defined exactly as is E. Clearly, it was possible that, by virtue of the provision made by the regulations defining them, N might differ from M and E from F; otherwise there would have been no point in separate letters of identification. However, by regs 8 and 10 of the CS(MASC)Regs 1992, it is provided respectively that M and F are to be calculated in exactly the same way as N and E, as if references to the absent parent were references to the parent with care. It should finally be noted that 'C' is defined by para 2(1) as the assessable income of the parent who is not the absent parent, where that parent is the person with care 'and otherwise has such value (if any) as may be prescribed'. The possibility exists therefore that regulations might attribute a notional income to a parent with care even where she has no actual income. However, reg 5 of the CS(MASC)Regs 1992 provides that the value of C, otherwise than in a case where the other parent is the person with care, is nil. There is therefore no minimum value for C.

4. The Maintenance Assessment

5.28 Once the maintenance requirement and the assessable incomes of the parents have been established, the maintenance assessment may be calculated. Paragraph 2(1) of Sch 1 to the Act provides as follows:

'In order to determine the amount of any maintenance assessment, first calculate –

$$(A + C) \times P'$$

The meanings of A and C (the assessable incomes of the absent parent and the parent with care respectively) have been discussed above and need no further elaboration. P is defined as 'such number greater than zero but less than 1 as may be prescribed'. P is, in effect, the fraction which will be applied to the joint assessable incomes. In *Children Come First* and the parliamentary debates it was taken that the figure would be 0.5, or 50% and this is in fact the value which is now prescribed by reg 5(b) of the CS(MASC)Regs 1992.

5.29 The first step in calculating the maintenance assessment is to aggregate the assessable incomes (A and C) of the two parents and divide by two. What happens next will depend on whether the result is more or less than MR (the maintenance requirement). As has been pointed out already, there is a 'two-tier system' in that when half the assessable income does not exceed MR, the absent parent's liability is limited to one half of A. However, where the result of (A + C) × P is more than MR, a further liability may be incurred.

Paragraph 2(2) of Sch 1 to the Act provides that where the result of (A + C) × P is an amount which is equal to, or less than, MR, the amount of maintenance payable by the absent parent shall be an amount equal to A × P, i e one half of the absent parent's assessable income. An example may help here. Assume that MR = £60, A = £100 and C = £20. Half of MR is £60, so that the absent parent's liability will be limited to half of A, namely £50. However, if either A or C increases, one half of the total will exceed MR and so it would be necessary to consider the additional element.

5.30 Paragraph 2(3) provides that, where the result of (A + C) × P is more than MR:

'the amount of maintenance payable by the absent parent for that child or those children shall consist of –
(a) a basic element calculated in accordance with the provisions of paragraph 3; and
(b) an additional element calculated in accordance with the provisions of paragraph 4.'

The basic element is described as BE and the additional element as AE.

It should be borne in mind, therefore, that once it has been established that (A + C) × P exceeds MR, that calculation is abandoned; BE and AE are calculated and together replace it. The purpose of the calculations is to provide an extra 25% of the balance of assessable income remaining after the maintenance requirement is met.

5.31 Before proceeding to consider the method of calculating BE, it is necessary to define one of its constituent elements 'G'. By para 3(2), the value of G is determined by applying the formula:

$$G = \frac{MR}{(A + C) \times P}$$

Returning to the example given above, if MR had remained at £60 and the result of (A + C) × P was £75, G would be 60/75 or 0.8. Clearly, G is a variable figure which will be different in every calculation.

It is now possible to approach BE. Paragraph 3(1) provides that BE is calculated by applying the formula:

$$A \times G \times P$$

Assume, for the sake of illustration, that A = £130, G = 0.8, and P = 0.5. In this case the basic element (BE) will be:

$$£130 \times 0.8 \times 0.5 = £52$$

It will be noted that this is, in fact, less than MR. This is because it was assumed that A = £130 and C = £20. Had A been £150 and C nil, BE would have risen to £60. In other words, where (A + C) × P exceeds MR because of the caring parent's income, the position is adjusted in favour of the absent parent at this stage.

5.32 Calculation of AE is complicated by the fact that it is necessary to consider two alternative formulae, and then to settle for the lower of two figures. The first calculation to be performed is as follows:

$$AE = (1 - G) \times A \times R$$

In the example given above, G was 0.8, so in that case the result of $(1 - G)$ would be 0.2. 'A' continues to represent the absent parent's assessable income. 'R' is defined as 'such number greater than zero but less than 1 as may be prescribed', but by reg 6(1) of the CS(MASC)Regs 1992 the value of R is 0.25. It may be helpful to have another example here:

Assume that A = £200, C = nil, and MR = £60
G is therefore $\dfrac{60}{200 \times 0.5}$ = 0.6

AE would therefore be 0.4 (ie 1.00 – 0.6) × £200 × 0.25 = £20.

5.33 However, it is always necessary to calculate the alternative formula in case that provides a lower amount for AE. Paragraph 4(2) of Sch 1 provides that:

'Where applying the alternative formula set out in sub-paragraph (3) would result in a lower amount for the additional element, that formula shall be applied in place of the formula set out in sub-paragraph (1).'

Before considering the alternative formula, the reason for this provision should be briefly considered. If the general intention of the calculation of the additional element under para 4(1) was to provide an additional slice of the absent parent's income for the child, this could, in the case of a very rich parent, provide a completely disproportionate amount of maintenance for the child. The purpose of the alternative formula is therefore to produce a maximum figure or ceiling above which child maintenance cannot go. Any application for further maintenance could then be dealt with by an application to a court under s 8(6) (see Chapter 8).

Paragraph 4(3) introduces two new elements, namely Z and Q. Z is defined as such number as may be prescribed and this is now contained in reg 6(2)(a) of the CS(MASC)Regs 1992, which gives the value of Z as 3. Q is the aggregate of:

'(a) any amount taken into account by virtue of paragraph 1(3)(a) in calculating the maintenance requirement; and
(b) any amount which is both taken into account by virtue of paragraph 1(3)(c) in making that calculation and is an amount prescribed for the purposes of this paragraph.'

Paragraph 1(3)(a) comprises in effect the income support allowances for the children. By reg 6(2)(b) of the CS(MASC)Regs 1992 the amount for the purpose of para (b) above is the same as the income support family premium in respect of each qualifying child (at present, on 1993/4 figures, the family premium is £9.65).

5.34 The alternative formula is calculated as follows:

$$AE = Z \times Q \times \frac{A}{A + C}$$

Applying the same figures as used in the first alternative formula, the result would be as follows; first it would be necessary to calculate Q. Assume there are two children aged between 11 and 15. Using 1993/4 income support rates, Q would consist of:

2 × 22.15	=	44.30
2 × 9.65	=	19.30
		£63.60

$$Z \times Q \times \frac{A}{A + C} = 3 \times 63.60 \times \frac{200}{200}$$
$$= £190.80$$

This is so much greater than the result of the first calculation that there is no doubt that the first calculation would prevail and the difference appears almost absurd. It is possible from this, however, to see approximately what the upper limit will be. A/A + C is not an important part of the calculation; it merely provides for some apportionment between the parents.

On present figures, the result of Z × Q for a child aged under 11 is £24.70 and for a child aged 11 to 15 is £31.80. Three times those figures are £74.10 and £95.40, respectively. That is the kind of sum per child which, added to the basic calculation of MR(BE), will be the maximum which can be assessed under this scheme.

Explaining the 'alternative formula' in the House of Lords debate, Lord Henley said that the government had been guided by three considerations in devising a formula for a 'cut off point':

'First, it should reflect the number and age of children to whom the maintenance requirement applies – the more children, and the older the children, the higher the cut off point. Secondly the cut off point should rise over time to match rises in income and prices, and we do not want to have to amend primary legislation to change the level of the ceiling. Finally, it is right to take account of the caring parent's ability to support the child when looking at the cut off point for that child . . . we believe that the amendment secures our aim. It ensures that the total maintenance payable by both parents depends upon the maintenance requirement plus some multiple (named Z in the formula) of the aggregate Q of the amounts used in calculating the maintenance requirement and which are paid for the child or children and is therefore linked to the number and age of children' (*House of Lords Official Report*, 22 July 1991, col 591).

5.35   The provision in para 5(4) to Sch 1 of the Act that a parent in receipt of income support or any other prescribed benefit is to be taken to have no assessable income has already been noted (see para **5.23**). Paragraph 5(3) provides that where the result of the relevant calculations is that a person's assessable income is a negative amount his assessable income shall be taken to be nil.

It is also provided, however, that the Secretary of State may prescribe a minimum amount of child support maintenance (para 7(1)). Where, but for para 7, the amount of child maintenance which would be fixed by a maintenance assessment would be nil, or less than the prescribed minimum amount, the amount to be fixed by the assessment is to be the prescribed minimum amount (para 7(2)). By reg 13(1) of the CS(MASC)Regs 1992 the minimum amount is prescribed as 5% of the income support personal allowance for single claimants aged not less than 25. On 1993/4 figures this is £44 so the minimum amount would be £2.20. This will be the minimum amount to be enforced except in two broad classes of case.

First, a 'special case' under the Act is created by reg 26 and Sch 4 of the CS(MASC)Regs 1992. Where reg 26 applies, the case is treated as a special case for the purpose of the Act, the minimum amount shall not apply and the amount of the child support maintenance to be fixed by the assessment will be nil. Regulation 26 applies when any one of the following conditions are satisfied.

(a)   The income of the absent parent includes (or would in principle, if all the relevant conditions were satisfied, include) one or more of the payments or awards specified in Sch 4. Schedule 4 contains 23 such payments or awards, ranging from sickness benefit, invalidity pension, attendance allowance, maternity allowance and analogous payments to disablement pensions under, eg, the Royal Warrant of 21 December 1964 (service in the home guard before 1945; however, it is unlikely that the ranks of absent parents will include many ageing Captain Mainwarings!).

(b)   The protected income of the absent parent includes a sum equivalent to the family premium.

(c)   The absent parent is a child within the meaning of s 55 of the Act.

(d)   The absent parent is a prisoner.

(e)   The absent parent is a person in respect of whom N is less than the minimum amount (ie it is conceded that where his net income is less than the minimum amount he cannot be expected to pay the minimum amount).

Secondly, para 7(3) of Sch 1 provides that this is not to be the case where s 43 applies although, as will be seen, s 43 does not in fact operate to remove the need to make the minimum payment.

5.36   Section 43 applies where an absent parent is, by virtue of para 5(4) of Sch 1, taken for the purposes of Sch 1 to have no assessable income and 'such conditions as may be prescribed for the purposes of this section are satisfied'. These prescribed conditions are contained in reg 28 of the CS(MASC)Regs 1992, and are as follows:

(a) the absent parent is aged 18 or over (and is in receipt of income support);
(b) he is not entitled to the family premium (ie has no children living with him in his family);
(c) he is not entitled to any of the payments or awards set out in Sch 4 (see above).

In such cases the prescribed amount to be deducted from his benefits will be the minimum amount. Where s 43 applies, the power of the Secretary of State to make regulations under s 51(1)(r) of the Social Security Act 1986 (deductions from benefits) may be exercised:

'with a view to securing that –
(a) payments of prescribed amounts are made with respect to qualifying children in place of payments of child support maintenance; and
(b) arrears of child support maintenance are recovered.'

Clearly it is now provided that an absent parent in receipt of benefits may have sums of money deducted from those benefits as maintenance for his children.

Where this is not the case, but the absent parent's income is such that the assessment is either nil or less than the prescribed amount, he will have to pay the prescribed amount of £2.20 per week. It may be asked why a person whose income is so low that he is either in receipt of income support or assessed as being liable to pay nothing should have to pay anything at all. When this point was made in the House of Lords debate (*Official Report*, 29 April 1981, cols 593 and 594) Lord Henley, on behalf of the government, replied as follows:

'. . . there is an important point of principle here. The legal and moral obligations on parents who are in receipt of income support are exactly the same as those on other parents. They are responsible for maintaining their children. It is important that the responsibility for maintenance should be established straight away, not least so that liability can be clearly established in readiness for if and when circumstances change. In principle all parents should make some contribution to their child's maintenance. Perhaps I may put the picture straight and remind the House of exactly who on income support will be liable to have some small deduction made. We are talking about a small deduction of about £2 a week at 1991 rates. Parents who are sick or disabled and are unable to work will be zero rated. Those who have dependent children for whom they are also claiming income support will have their liability established but their contributions in maintenance will again be zero rated so that no deduction from income support will be made in their case. In other words, we are dealing with those who are able and fit to work but have no dependent children.'

5.37 Finally, para 9 of Sch 1 makes provision for regulations about income and capital. These regulations, eg as to income of a child being treated as that of the parent, are dealt with elsewhere in this book in the appropriate places (see, for example, para **5.13**), in accord with existing Department of Social Security regulations which refer to 'notional capital'. Notional capital covers the position where a person has:

(a)   deprived himself of capital,
(b)   abstained from claiming capital to which he is entitled,
(c)   arranged for capital to be paid to a third party, or
(d)   has assets in a limited company or trust fund.

The other matters in respect of which regulations under para 9 may make provision are for capital or income which a person does possess to be disregarded (para 9(d)); for income to be treated as capital (para 9(e)); and for capital to be treated as income (para 9(f)). Again, this is all dealt with elsewhere in this book at paras **5.15** et seq.

5.   Protected Income

5.38 The calculation of protected income is the final stage of the whole process of maintenance assessment. The concept of protected earnings is of course a familiar one in other areas, particularly in respect of attachment of earnings orders, and has long been used by the courts when making maintenance orders so as to provide a safety net to ensure that the paying party has enough money left to remain above subsistence level. It will be seen that some liabilities which an absent parent may have incurred but which are not included in his exempt income for the purpose of calculating assessable income may be eligible for inclusion when calculating protected income.

5.39 Paragraph 6 of Sch 1 contains the relevant provisions, and applies (para 6(1)) where:

'(a)   one or more maintenance assessments have been made with respect to an absent parent; and
(b)   payment by him of the amount, or the aggregate of the amounts, so assessed would otherwise reduce his disposable income below his protected income level.'

'Protected income level', as defined by para 6(6), means an amount of income calculated by reference to the circumstances of a particular absent parent in accordance with regulations.
    The general rule is then contained in para 6(2):

'The amount of the assessment, or (as the case may be) of each assessment, shall be adjusted in accordance with such provisions as may be prescribed with a view to securing so far as is reasonably practicable that payment by the absent parent of the amount or (as the case may be) aggregate of the amounts, so assessed will not reduce his disposable income below his protected income level.'

It should be remembered that there is one maintenance assessment for each family unit so that when the statute refers to more than one assessment it means more than one family.

Paragraph 6 goes on to provide that any adjustment made under these provisions shall not reduce the assessment to less than the prescribed minimum amount (para 6(3)); this has already been discussed at para **5.35** above and no further elaboration is needed here.

The meaning of 'disposable income' is determined by regulations (para 6(4)), and such regulations may in particular (para 6(5)):

'provide that in such circumstances and to such extent as may be prescribed –

(a)   income of any child who is living in the same household with the absent parent; and

(b)   where the absent parent is living together in the same household with another adult of the opposite sex (regardless of whether or not they are married), income of that other adult, is to be treated as the parent's income for the purposes of calculating his disposable income.'

Presumably an absent parent who was living in a homosexual relationship would have an advantage here.

5.40   The regulations applicable to protected income are the CS(MASC)Regs 1992, reg 11(1), which provides that subject to subparas (3) and (4) thereof (as to which see para **5.42**, below) the protected income level of an absent parent shall be the aggregate of the following.

(a)   The income support personal allowance for a single claimant aged not less than 25 years or, where he has a partner, the income support personal allowance for a couple where both members are aged not less than 18; where the absent parent is a member of a polygamous marriage he is entitled to the allowance for one of his partners and himself as a couple, plus in respect of each additional partner a sum equivalent to the difference between the single allowance and the couple's allowance.

(b)   An amount in respect of his housing costs. This is determined in exactly the same way as the housing costs when calculating exempt income under regs 14, 15, 16 and 18 (see para **5.21**, above). Where he has no housing costs (see reg 15(10)(a)), his housing costs are taken to be the non-dependent amount which would be calculated in respect of him under reg 15(5) (ie the non-dependent deduction under the housing benefit regulations).

(c)   Lone parent premium, where appropriate.

(d)   Disability premium, where appropriate.

(e)   Severe disability and carer premiums, where appropriate.

(f)   Family premium, where appropriate.
(g)   Income support allowance for each child who is a member of the family of the absent parent, plus, where appropriate, disabled child premium.
(h)   Any other income support premium to which the parent would be entitled if he were a claimant.
(i)   Where the absent parent or his partner is living in:
    (i)   accommodation provided under Part III of the National Assistance Act 1948;
    (ii)   accommodation provided under paras 1 and 2 and Sch 8 of the National Health Service Act 1974; or
    (iii) a nursing home or residential care home,
    the amount of the fees paid for such accommodation.
(j)   The amount of council tax which the absent parent in question or his partner is liable to pay in respect of the home for which housing costs are included under (h) above, less any council tax benefit.
(k)   An amount of £8.
(l)   Where the income of:
    (i)   the absent parent;
    (ii)   any partner; and
    (iii) any child or children for whom an amount is included under g(i) above exceeds the sum of the amount in such paras (a) to (k),
    10% of the excess.

5.41   'Income', for the purposes of (l) above, is defined by reg 11(2). The income of the absent parent or any partner is defined in the same way as N (net income of absent parent), except that child benefit and any maintenance paid in respect of a child of the absent parent's family are added, and maintenance paid by the absent parent or his partner under a maintenance order is deducted where an application for a maintenance assessment could not have been made in respect of that child.

The income of any child of the absent parent is taken to be the excess of that child's income over the sum allowed for him under (g) above.

5.42   As indicated above, this definition of protected income is subject to reg 11(3) and (4), and this deals with the position where the absent parent has day-to-day care of a child (whether or not a relevant child) for fewer than seven nights a week. ('Day-to-day care' is defined by reg 1(2) as care of not less than two nights a week on average during the 12-month period ending with the relevant week, or such other period, ending with the relevant week, as in the opinion of the child support officer is more representative of the current arrangements for the care of the child in question.) In such circumstances the lone parent premium, family premium and personal allowances for the children are in effect multiplied by X/7 where X would be the average number of nights in question. (This is the author's own fraction, not yet another formula created by the Act.)

5.43 Having calculated the protected income, the disposable income must then be calculated under reg 12. Disposable income is defined as the aggregate of the income of the absent parent and any member of his family 'calculated in like manner as under reg 11(2)' (see above, para **5.41**). Regulation 12(2) and (3) repeats, in effect, para 6(2) of Sch 1 of the Act.

5.44 *Children Come First* gave an example of how the protected income calculation would work (see also para **5.3** above).

However, in view of the slight differences in the formula which emerge in the regulations and the fact that income support rates have been increased it may be helpful to modify and update this example as follows: Michael has a net income of £195 per week and assessable income of £130 per week. He has a maintenance assessment of 50% of the latter sum, namely £65 per week, which leaves him with £130 per week for himself.

He has remarried and has two stepchildren. His wife does not work. His protected income (based on 1993/4 figures) is as follows:

	£
Children's allowance	30.10
Couple's allowance	69.00
Family premium	9.65
Housing costs	60.00
Margin	8.00
Council tax	10.00
	186.75

Note the 10% difference under reg 11(1)(1) does not apply in this case. If the assessment were to be unchanged the income of the household would be £130 per week (ie £195 less £65 assessment), plus child benefit of £18.10, making a total of £148.10. This figure would be £30.65 below the protected level of income so that the maintenance assessment is reduced from £65 to £34.35.

5.45 The example given above demonstrates how the system will work and it is possible to see how it might be varied. For example, if Michael's new wife receives maintenance from the father of her children, this sum would be part of the income of the household and narrow or wipe out the margin between protected income and actual income. If Michael's wife works, her income will be taken as part of the family income and will have the same effect.

It had been predicted that the cost of travelling to work would be a proper expense for consideration at the protected income level stage; it was normally the practice of the courts to allow such deductions when considering maintenance applications.

The cost of travel to work can vary a great deal. An absent parent living in the Home Counties and working in London would naturally expect that the cost of his season ticket would be allowed. A man who lives in the country with no access to public transport and who works some miles from his home would argue that he had to have a car. He would claim that an allowance should be made for the cost of petrol, road tax, insurance and perhaps the cost of buying the car. Using the example of Michael given above, it will be seen that he is left with £178.45 per week for the support of his new family and that £60 of this goes on housing costs, leaving him with £118.45 per week for all other expenditure. If he were to buy a car for £8,000 with the aid of a loan, this might well cost him up to half of his remaining income. If no allowance were made for this expense, he would have the choice of either not working or working but suffering severe deprivation. However, this is what is going to happen since the regulations in fact make no provision for the allowance of the cost of travel to work. The reason for this is not clear; protected income levels are based on income support rates, but people in receipt of income support do not have the cost of travelling to work. Nevertheless, the position is now clear; travel costs will not be allowed (except in the case of self-employed people who can, of course, set off motoring costs against income as a business expense).

The cost of setting up a new home has also sometimes been allowed by the courts, which recognise that, where a man leaves his first family (not necessarily by his own choice), he frequently takes nothing with him, and may have to obtain a loan for simple furniture and household effects. However, the regulations make no provision for this.

6. Possible Model for Calculation

5.46   The following model is suggested as a useful way of calculating maintenance assessments and the liability of parents. It contains figures based on the 1993/4 income support rates; these should be updated annually.

In the majority of cases it should be possible to produce an accurate calculation by these means. However, it is important to note that it has been assumed:

(a)   that *no* apportionment is required under reg 11(3) and (4) of the CS(MASC)Regs 1992 (ie in relation to protected income, child with parent for fewer than seven nights per week); and

(b)   that this is *not* a special case (see Part III, CS(MASC)Regs 1992).

In either case further adjustments would be needed.

Stage One: The Maintenance Requirement

Number of child(ren)	Aged		*Scale allowance*
	0–11	£15.05 each	£
	11–15	£22.15 each	£
	16–17	£26.45 each	£
Total =			£
add Allowance for parent with care			£44.00
Family premium			£9.65
is parent with care a lone parent? YES/NO			

If YES *add* £4.90

      Total =   £

deduct

    £10.00 for 1st child
+ £8.10 for each subsequent child
                         =   £
    Maintenance Requirement =   £   = MR

Stage Two: Assessable Incomes

A. Parent with care:
1. Is she receiving income
    support   YES/NO
    If YES, assessable income = nil
    If NO, proceed to 2

2. Gross earnings   £   per week
deduct
    Income tax   £
    National insurance   £
    50% superannuation   £

                       £
    Net earnings =   £
add
    Other income
    (a) of parent with care from Appendix 1 =
    (b) of child(ren) from Appendix 2   =
    Total income   =   £   = M

3. Exempt income
His/her children living with him/her

		Scale allowance	
aged 0–11 at	£15.05	£	
11–15	£22.15	£	
16+	£26.45	£	

Parent   £44.00
Family premium   £9.65
Lone parent   £4.90
Housing costs
(b/f from Appendix 3) = £
Total = £
Is he/she a lone parent?

YES/NO

If YES   Proceed to B

If NO

(a)   *deduct*   £4.90

(b)   Is partner a parent of any child living with them?

YES/NO

If NO proceed to 4

If YES

   (i)   What is partner's net income?

      £

  (ii)   What is half the scale allowance
for the child(ren) of whom he is
the parent?

      £

 (iii)   Add figure result from
Appendix 2

 (iv)   Add £44.00
     + £4.83   £48.83

  (v)   Does (ii) + (iii) + (iv)
exceed (i)?

YES/NO

If YES proceed to 4

If NO

deduct half-scale
allowance for child(ren)
of whom he is parent = £   plus £4.83= £

Exempt income = £   = F

4.   M b/f from 2 = £   = £
deduct   F   = £
  Assessable income   = £   = C

B.   Absent parent

1.   Is he receiving income
support?   YES/NO
If YES proceed to stage 5
If NO proceed to 2

2.   Gross earnings   £

deduct

  Income tax   £

  National insurance   £

  50% superannuation   £   £

  Net earnings =   £

add other income

(a)   of absent parent
from Appendix 1 =
(b)   of child(ren)
living with him
from Appendix 2 =
Total income =   £   = N

3.   Exempt income
His/her children living with him/her

		Scale allowance	
aged 0–11 at	£15.05	£
11–15	£22.15	£
16+	£26.45	£

Parent   £44.00
Family premium   £9.65
Lone parent   £4.90
Housing costs
(b/f from Appendix 3) = £
Total = £

Is he/she a lone parent?
  YES/NO
  If YES   Proceed to B
  If NO
  (a)   *deduct*   £4.90
  (b)   Is partner a parent of
        any child living with them?
        YES/NO
        If NO proceed to 4
        If YES
        (i)   What is partner's net income?
                  £
        (ii)   What is half the scale allowance
                for the child(ren) of whom he is the parent?
                  £
        (iii)   Add figure result from
                Appendix 2
        (iv)   Add £44.00
                  + £4.83   £48.83
        (v)   Does (ii) + (iii) + (iv)
                exceed (i)?
                YES/NO
                If YES proceed to 4
                If NO
                Deduct half-scale
                allowance for child(ren)

of whom he is parent = £   plus £4.83 =£

Exempt income = £   = F

4.   N (b/f from 2) = £

deduct E   = £

Assessable income = £   = A

Stage Three: The Maintenance Assessment

1.   C (b/f from *Stage 2* A4) =   £

Add A (b/f from *Stage 2* B4) =   £

   Total =   £.   = (A + C)

Divide by 2 =

2.   Does result of calculation of 1

   exceed MR?   YES/NO

   If NO, the maintenance

   assessment = one-half of

   A = £

   Proceed to stage 4

   If YES proceed to 3

3.   (a)   MR (from *Stage 1*)   =   £

   (b) $\dfrac{(A + C)}{2}$ (from *Stage 3* para 1)   =   £

   Divide (a) by (b)   =   £   = G

   (c)   A (from *Stage 2*)   =   £

          Multiply G by A   =   £

          Divide by 2   =   £   = BE

                                                         (c/f to 6)

4.   (a)   G (c/f from 3(b))   =   £

   (b)   Deduct G from 1   =   £

   (c)   A (from *Stage 2*)   =   £

   (d)   Multiply result of (b) by A   =   £

   (e)   Multiply result of (d) by 0.25   =   £

5.   (a)   Allowances for the qualifying children   =   £

          (taken from *Stage 1*)

          Add

          Number of qualifying children ×

          £9.30 =   £

          _____

          Total = £   =   Q

   (b)   A (taken from *Stage 2*)   =   £

          C (taken from *Stage 2*)   =   £

          Total = £   =   (A + C)

   (c)   Divide A by (A + C)   =   £

    (d)   Multiply result by Q
         Result   =   £
    (e)   Multiply result of (iv) by 3   =   £

6.   Select the lower result of
    4 or 5
       = £
    add BE
       (from 3) = £
    Total = £   = Assessment

Stage Four: Protected Income

1.   Has absent parent a partner?   YES/NO
    If NO, c/f £44.00 to 5
    If YES, c/f £69.00 to 5

2.   Is absent parent a member of a
    polygamous marriage   YES/NO
    If NO, proceed to 5
    If YES, multiply £24.15 by
    number of partners less one = £
    c/f to 5

3.   Has absent parent children living
    with him?   YES/NO
    If NO, proceed to 5
    If YES, *add*
    child(ren) aged 0–10 at £15.05 each =
    child(ren) aged 11–15 at £22.15 each =
    child(ren) aged 16 or 17 at £26.45 each =
      Family premium   £9.65
    Is any child disabled?   YES/NO
    If YES, add disabled child premium   £
    If NO
        Total =   £
          c/f to 5

4.   Is absent parent a lone parent?
      YES/NO
    If YES, c/f £4.90 to 5
    If NO, proceed to 5

5.   *Add*
    (a)   Figures b/f from 1–4 above =   £
         Housing costs (from Appendix 3)   £
         Council tax (annual sum divided by 52)   £
         Prescribed amount   £8
                               —————
        Total =   £

(b) *add*
      net income of parent (N)   £
      income of partner   £
      income of any child(ren) mentioned in 3   £
      child benefit received   £
      maintenance received   £
           Total =   £
      less maintenance paid allowable under
      reg 11(2)(a)(ii)   £
      Result =   £
(c) Does result of (b) exceed result of (a)?
     YES/NO
     If YES, *deduct* result of (a) from (b)
     result =   £
10% of result =   £
Add this to result of (a) =
c/f to 6
If NO, c/f result of (a) to 6

6. Result of calculation under 5(b) =   £
    deduct Maintenance assessment
        (c/f from Stage 3, para 6) =   £
        Result =   £
    Does result exceed result of 5?   YES/NO
    If YES, maintenance assessment is unchanged
    If NO, *deduct* result from result of 5
    Result =   £
    Deduct this sum from maintenance assessment
    Maintenance assessment =   £

Stage Five – Minimum Requirement

Is either the assessment or the adjusted assessment less than £2.20?   YES/NO

If NO, assessment remains unchanged
If YES, are any of the following conditions satisfied?
(a) absent parent entitled to one of the payments
     or awards set out in Sch 4, CS(MASC)Regs 1992;
(b) absent parent entitled to family premium;
(c) absent parent a child;
(d) absent parent a prisoner;
(e) N less than £2.20 per week.

If YES, assessment = nil
If NO, assessment unchanged

Appendix One   Other income of parent

1. Has parent any other income?   YES/NO
    If YES, what is the figure?   £

2. Do any of the matters in Part V, CS(MASC)Regs 1992 apply?
    (Amounts treated as income of parent)
    YES/NO
    If YES, what are the sums involved (if not stated at 1)?   £

3. Should any income of any child be treated as income of parent under Part
    IV, CS(MASC)Regs 1992?
    YES/NO
    If YES, what are the sums involved?   £

4. Are any of the sums set out above included in Sch 2, CS(MASC)Regs
    1992?
    YES/NO
    If YES, delete and disregard

5. Subject to 4, what is total of
    1, 2 + 3? = £
    Carry back to calculation

Appendix Two   Income of child

1. Does the child live with the parent whose income is under
    consideration?   YES/NO
    If NO, this part does not apply. Return to calculation.

2. If YES, has the child any income?   YES/NO
    If YES, what is the nature of the income and how much is it?

3. (a) Is child support maintenance being assessed for the child in
        question?   YES/NO
    (b) If NO, does income exceed the personal allowance for that child
        under reg 9(1)(g)?   YES/NO
        If NO, disregard

4. If answer to 3(a) is YES, is the child the only child in respect of whom a
    maintenance assessment is to be made?   YES/NO
    If YES, treat the whole income as parent's income subject to 5 and 6

5. If NO, how many qualifying children are there?
    Does the child's income exceed the sum as calculated under para 20 to Sch
    1, CS(MASC)Regs 1992? If NO, disregard.
    If YES, treat the excess as parent's income

6. Does any income of the child come within para 23 to Sch 1, CS(MASC)
    Regs 1992 or Sch 2?   YES/NO
    If YES, disregard

Appendix Three   Housing costs

1. Should the parent be treated as having no housing costs within the meaning of reg 5(10), CS(MASC)Regs 1992?
    YES/NO. If YES, return to calculations;
    housing costs nil

2. If NO, what are the housing costs?
    Do they fall within any of the classes in Sch 3?

3. If YES, is housing benefit paid to parent?
    YES/NO. If YES, deduct from housing costs

4. If NO (to 3) is any person who is not a member of parent's family liable to make payments in respect of the home?
    YES/NO
    If YES, calculate parent's share of the housing costs and only consider that sum

5. Are there any non-dependants in the parent's household?
    YES/NO
    If YES, calculate non-dependent amounts under reg 15(5) to (9) and *deduct* from parent's housing costs

6. *In respect of exempt income only,*
    ie *Not protected income,*
    has parent a partner?   YES/NO
    If NO, treat whole housing costs as eligible, subject to 7 below.

    If YES, take A to be number of relevant children (if any) and B the number of children in the parent's family (if any) and multiply housing costs by

    $$\frac{0.75 + (A \times 0.2)}{1.00 + (B \times 0.2)}$$

    if parent is member of polygamous marriage treat X as number of partners less one and multiply housing costs by

    $$\frac{0.75 + (A \times 0.2)}{1.00 + (X \times 0.25) + (B \times 0.2)}$$

7. Does any part of reg 18(2) apply to the parent?   YES/NO
    If YES, disregard remainder of this paragraph.
    If NO:
    (a) in respect of exempt income only do housing costs exceed the greater of £80 or one-half of N?   YES/NO
    If NO, no adjustment needed
    If YES, restrict to that sum
    (b) in respect of protected income only do housing costs exceed the greater of £80 or one-half of the aggregate sum at *Stage 4, para 5(c)*?
    If NO, no adjustment needed
    If YES, restrict to that sum

7. Special Cases

5.47 It may be that any of the provisions affecting maintenance assessments will be waived or varied in certain 'special cases'. Section 42(1) provides that the Secretary of State may by regulations provide that in prescribed circumstances a case is to be treated as a special case for the purpose of the Act. The effect of this will be that those cases will be treated in a different way from the normal cases.

Some guidance as to what this will mean is contained in s 42(2), which provides as follows:

'Those regulations may, for example, provide for the following to be special cases –
- (a) each parent of a child is an absent parent in relation to the child;
- (b) there is more than one person who is a person with care in relation to the same child;
- (c) there is more than one qualifying child in relation to the same absent parent but the person who is the person with care in relation to one of those children is not the person who is the person with care in relation to all of them;
- (d) a person is an absent parent in relation to more than one child and the other parent of each of those children is not the same person;
- (e) the person with care has care of more than one qualifying child and there is more than one absent parent in relation to those children;
- (f) a qualifying child has his home in two or more separate households.'

By s 42(4), regulations may in particular:
- '(a) modify any provision made by or under this Act, in its application to any special case or any special case falling within a prescribed category.
- (b) make new provision for any such case; or
- (c) provide for any prescribed provision made by or under this Act not to apply to any such case.'

5.48 Clearly the intention is to provide in detail for cases which are out of the ordinary. The whole new child support system is to be governed by statute and rule, and there is to be no room for discretion; hence the need to prescribe for every eventuality. The detailed rules are contained in Part III of the CS(MASC) Regs 1992. Since all these special cases will be somewhat unusual, and the regulations speak for themselves, the detailed effect of the regulations will not be summarised here. Instead, the broad classes of special case will be set out and the reader is referred to the regulations themselves (set out in Appendix 2), if further enquiry is needed.

5.49 The special cases are as follows.

Regulation 19 Both parents are absent
Clearly where there is not a parent with care the standard formula cannot be applied.

Regulation 20   Persons treated as absent parents
This arises where two or more persons at least one of whom is a parent who
do not live in the same household each provide day-to-day care for a child;
one of them has to be treated as an absent parent and the regulations provide
a procedure for ascertaining who this is to be and the formula for maintenance assessments to be adopted.
Regulation 21   One parent is absent and one is treated as absent
This applies where one parent is treated as an absent parent under the
previous regulation and the other parent is an absent parent.
Regulation 22   Multiple applications in relation to an absent parent
This governs the position where two or more applications for a maintenance
assessment have been made in respect of the same absent parent which relate
to different children (presumably made by different parents with care).
Regulation 23   Person caring for children of more than one absent parent
The formula clearly has to be adjusted.
Regulation 24   Persons with part-time care – not including a person treated
as an absent parent
This governs the position where two or more persons, neither of whom is
eligible to be treated as an absent parent and who do not live together, each
provide day-to-day care.
Regulation 25   Care provided in part by a local authority
This applies where a local authority and a person each provide day-to-day
care.
Regulation 26   Cases where child support maintenance is not to be payable
This applies where the minimum amount would normally be payable and
sets out a list of cases where it is not to be payable. This has already been
considered at para **5.35** et seq.
Regulation 27   Child who is a boarder or in-patient.
Regulation 28   Amount payable where absent parent is in receipt of income
support or other prescribed benefit. This has already been dealt with at para
5.35 et seq.

8.   Provision above the Formula Amounts

5.50   Finally, and for the sake of completeness, it should be remembered that,
once the maximum sum due under the formula has been reached, application
may be made to the courts for a 'top up', or for 'one-off' capital sums. This is
considered further in Chapter 8.

CHAPTER SIX

Disputes as to Parentage, Reviews and Appeals

1. Introduction

6.1 This chapter is concerned with the various ways in which a challenge to the operation of the system of child support maintenance may be mounted.

The most obvious way for an absent father to challenge the system is to deny paternity, since only a 'natural' father or one who has assumed obligations by adoption is liable under the Act. In addition, a person with care or an absent parent may apply for a review of a child support officer's decision, and a child support officer may himself review a decision of his own volition if he considers it defective. If any party is dissatisfied by a review, there is a right of appeal to a tribunal and from there to a Child Support Commissioner, and there is a right of appeal from a Commissioner to the Court of Appeal. Finally, although the Act itself does not provide for it, the possibility of judicial review cannot be excluded and this will be considered briefly.

Reviews on the ground of change of circumstances, where no error in the original decision is alleged, are not considered here but are dealt with in Chapter 4.

2. Disputes as to Parentage

6.2 Only an absent parent can be required to pay a maintenance assessment under the provisions of the Act; 'parent' is defined by s 54, in relation to any child, as 'any person who is in law the mother or father of the child'.

A person may become in law the mother or father of a child by an adoption order of the court. Apart from that, a woman is in law the mother of a child only if she has given birth to it, and a man is the father only if he is the natural father in a biological sense (but see para **3.4** above for the effect of the Human Fertilisation and Embryology Act 1990). Since only such persons can be liable under the Act, a dispute as to parentage is therefore of greater importance under the Act than it is elsewhere in the law of child maintenance. In matrimonial proceedings for example, a person may be liable for maintenance if he or she has treated a child as a child of the family even though there is no biological connection. (This liability will continue but outside the ambit of the child support system.)

Inevitably we are here concerned almost exclusively with the position of a man who denies that he is the father of a child. This is not because of any particular prejudice but rather for the simple reason that there is rarely any doubt as to whether a woman has given birth to a child. It is not impossible that a mother who is an absent parent will raise a similar claim, but it would be unusual and will not be considered further here.

6.3 Detailed provisions as to disputes about parentage are contained in ss 26 and 27 of the Act. The overall rule is that a child support officer may not make a maintenance assessment when parentage is in dispute unless the case falls within a specified class. The child support officer or the person with care may refer any other case to a court for a decision, but unless the issue is decided in favour of the child support officer he cannot proceed.

6.4 Section 26(1) provides that where an alleged parent (presumably an absent parent) denies that he is one of the child's parents 'the child support officer concerned shall not make a maintenance assessment on the assumption that the alleged parent is one of the child's parents unless the case falls within one of those set out in subsection (2)'.

The effect of this is that where the alleged parent falls within one of the cases set out in subsection (2) his protests will be of no avail and the assessment will be made.

It is implied by the wording of the statute that once an assessment has been made an alleged parent who denies parentage will be in a different position from one who denies parentage before an assessment is made. Presumably in the former case it would be for the alleged parent to make his own application to the courts and the assessment will continue to run until his application was determined in his favour.

6.5 Section 26(2) sets out the cases where it is permissible for a child support officer to act as follows:

'CASE A
Where the alleged parent is a parent of the child in question by virtue of having adopted him.'

This requires little comment. The production of the adoption order would be conclusive. By s 26(3), 'adopted' means adopted within the meaning of Part IV of the Adoption Act 1976 or, in relation to Scotland, Part IV of the Adoption (Scotland) Act 1978.

'CASE B
Where the alleged parent is a parent of the child in question by virtue of an order under section 30 of the Human Fertilisation and Embryology Act 1990 (parental orders in favour of gamete donors).'

The general effect of the 1990 Act has already been considered at para **3.4** above. Section 30 enables a married couple who have provided the genetic material which has led to a child's conception to apply to a court for a so called 'parental order' which will provide for the child to be treated in law as their child.

'CASE C

Where –
(a) either –
  (i) a declaration that the alleged parent is a parent of the child in question (or a declaration which has that effect) is in force under section 56 of the Family Law Act 1986 (declarations of parentage); or
  (ii) a declarator by a court in Scotland that the alleged parent is a parent of the child in question (or a declarator which has that effect) is in force; and
(b) the child has not subsequently been adopted.'

It should be remembered that s 56 of the 1986 Act (substituted by s 22 of the Family Law Reform Act 1987) deals with the right of an individual to apply to the court for a declaration that a named person is or was his parent or that he is the legitimate child of his parents. No one other than the 'child' can make the application; a parent cannot apply for a declaration in respect of his child. Although a person under the age of 18 could make such an application, acting by a next friend, it is envisaged that the majority of such applications would be made by adults with a view to inheritance or to prove nationality. It will therefore be unusual for Case C to apply.

'CASE D

Where –
(a) a declaration to the effect that the alleged parent is one of the parents of the child in question has been made under section 27; and
(b) the child has not subsequently been adopted.'

Section 25 will be considered below. The effect of Case D is that once a declaration has been made under s 27 the alleged parent cannot reopen the matter.

'CASE E

Where –
(a) the child is habitually resident in Scotland;
(b) the child support officer is satisfied that one or other of the presumptions set out in s 5(1) of the Law Reform (Parent and Child) (Scotland) Act 1986 applies; and
(c) the child has not subsequently been adopted.'

'CASE F

Where –
(a) the alleged parent has been found, or adjudged, to be the father of the child in question –

(i)   in proceedings before any court in England and Wales which are
      relevant proceedings for the purposes of section 12 of the Civil
      Evidence Act 1968; or
(ii) in affiliation proceedings before any court in the United Kingdom,
      (whether or not he offered any defence to the allegation of paternity)
      and that finding or adjudication still subsists; and
(b)   the child has not subsequently been adopted.'

Section 12(1)(b) of the Civil Evidence Act 1968 provides as follows:

'The fact that a person has been found to be the father of a child in relevant
proceedings before any court in England and Wales or has been adjudged to
be the father of a child in affiliation proceedings before any court in the
United Kingdom shall . . . be admissible in evidence for the purpose of
proving, where to do so is relevant to any issue in those civil proceedings,
that he . . . is (or was) the father of that child, whether or not he offered any
defence to the allegation of paternity and whether or not he is a party to the
civil proceedings; but no findings or adjudication other than a subsisting one
shall be admissible in evidence by virtue of this section.'

(The definition of 'relevant proceedings' in the 1968 Act has been extended
by the Courts and Legal Services Act 1990, Sch 16, para 2.)

6.6   From the list set out above it will be seen that the cases in which a parent
is, in effect, estopped from denying that he is the father of a child are all cases
where, in one way or another, a court has adjudicated on the question and a
declaration or order to the effect that the person concerned is the father of the
child has been made; the issue might be said to be *res judicata*. If one of these
cases applies, it would seem that the alleged parent's only method of taking the
matter further would be by way of appeal.

This, however, leaves a grey area where, for example, the 'parents' have
been divorced and there has been the usual declaration that a child 'is or may be
a child of the family'. 'Child of the family' is not the same as 'child of the
parties'. It remains to be seen whether, for the purposes of the Act, a man who
has been married and divorced and has never raised the question of paternity
will be able to deny paternity once an application is made for a child
maintenance assessment. It may be that the child support officer would be
entitled to take the view that the order or finding of the court remained in effect
and valid until a different order was made and that he was entitled to proceed
with the assessment.

6.7   Section 27 deals with the procedure where there is a denial of parentage.
By s 27(1) where:

'(a)   a child support officer is considering whether to make a maintenance
       assessment with respect to a person who is alleged to be a parent of the
       child, or one of the children, in question ("the alleged parent");

(b)   the alleged parent denies that he is one of the child's parents; and

(c)   the child support officer is not satisfied that the case falls within one of those set out in section 26(2),

the Secretary of State or the person with care may apply to the court for a declaration as to whether or not the alleged parent is one of the child's parents.'

It will therefore be for the Secretary of State or the person with care to take the initiative in applying to the court, and until this application is adjudicated upon the assessment cannot proceed. It is important to note that the application would be brought under this section and not by virtue of any other statute.

6.8   If, on hearing any application under s 27, the court is satisfied that the alleged parent is, or is not, a parent of the child in question, it shall make a declaration to that effect (s 27(2)); a declaration under s 27 has effect only for the purposes of the Act (s 27(3)).

Section 27(4) provides that, subject to any provision under Sch 11 to the Children Act 1989, 'court' means the High Court, a county court or a magistrates' court. Schedule 11 to the 1989 Act empowers the Lord Chancellor to make orders specifying proceedings which may be commenced in a specified level of court or which must be transferred to such a level of court. This order is contained in the Children (Allocation of Proceedings) (Amendment) Order 1992 which provides that references to courts for declarations as to parentage are to be dealt with in exactly the same way as public law cases under the Children Act 1989; that is to say, that reference or application will commence in a magistrates' court, but may be transferred by the magistrates, to a county court (and from there to the High Court) in cases of complexity.

6.9   Section 27 does not apply to Scotland, the position within that jurisdiction being dealt with under s 28. This provides a procedure broadly similar to that established by s 27, save that it is provided that the Secretary of State may bring an action for declarator of parentage under s 7 of the Law Reform (Parent and Child) (Scotland) Act 1986 and that the Secretary of State may defend an action for declarator of non-parentage or illegitimacy brought by a person named as the alleged parent in an application for a maintenance assessment.

3.   Reviews at Instigation of Child Support Officers

6.10   Although s 19, which governs this topic, follows the section dealing with reviews on the applications of the parties, it seems logical to deal with it first so as to allow the material on applications for review by the parties to precede the next step for them, namely appeals.

Section 19 applies where a child support officer is not conducting a review under s 16, 17 or 18 (those sections dealing with periodical reviews, reviews on changes of circumstances and reviews at the request of one or both of the parents):

> 'but is nevertheless satisfied that a maintenance assessment which is in force is defective by reason of –
> (a) having been made in ignorance of a material fact;
> (b) having been based on a mistake as to a material fact; or
> (c) being wrong in law' (s 19(1)).

In these circumstances he may make a fresh maintenance assessment on the assumption that the person in whose favour the original assessment was made has made a fresh application for a maintenance assessment.

6.11 Clearly, s 19(1) applies where the child support officer was unaware of some material fact at the time of the assessment, or was in error as to some relevant provision of law. In such a case he may put the matter right under the subsection. However, s 19(2) goes on to provide a distinct but overlapping power of review. Where a child support officer is not conducting a review under section 16, 17 or 18, but is nevertheless satisfied that if an application were to be made under s 17 or 18 it would be appropriate to make a fresh maintenance assessment, he may do so. Section 17, which has already been considered in Chapter 4, para **4.51**, deals with reviews on change of circumstances. Section 18 will be considered at para **6.13** below and deals with applications for review; these applications amount to the first stage of an appeal by one of the parties involved.

Section 19(2) therefore allows the child support officer to pre-empt any such appeal if he thinks it appropriate and to make a fresh assessment of his own volition.

6.12 It is provided that, before making a fresh assessment under any part of s 19, the child support officer must give 'to such persons as may be prescribed, such notice of his proposal to make a fresh assessment as may be prescribed' (s 19(3)). Regulation 23 of the CS(MAP)Regs 1992 provides, in effect, that a review under s 19 shall be conducted as if an application for a review under s 17 had been made; that is to say, regs 20, 21 and 22 apply (as to which see para **4.52** et seq).

4. Applications for Review by Person with Care or Absent Parent

6.13 Section 17, which deals with reviews on change of circumstances, has already been considered in Chapter 4, para **4.51**. Here, it is intended to consider s 18, which is, in effect, the first step where either a person with care or an absent parent wishes to challenge any decision of a child support officer on the ground that it was wrong. These reviews fall under five heads, and these will be considered in turn.

6.14   However, before considering the various types of review which may be carried out, it may be helpful to deal with the question of time-limits, and the associated factor of grounds for the application for review.

The original Bill provided that if application under s 18 was made within a period of 28 days beginning with the date on which notice of the decision in question was given to the applicant, the applicant could require a review as of right and was not required to state any ground for seeking the review. This was changed, and s 18(11) now provides that the Secretary of State may make regulations to govern the manner in which applications are to be made and the procedure to be followed. There is no mention of time in the section.

However, the relevant provisions are now contained in reg 24(1) of the CS(MAP)Regs 1992, which provides that an application for review shall not be referred to a child support officer unless that application is received by the Secretary of State within 28 days of the date of notification to the applicant of the decision whose review he seeks. Nevertheless, by reg 24(2) the Secretary of State may refer a late application if he is satisfied that there was unavoidable delay in making the application.

Any application for a review under s 18 must be made in writing and must give the applicant's reasons for making it (s 18(5)). The illiterate aggrieved person will therefore be at some disadvantage.

Under s 18(6), the Secretary of State must refer to a child support officer any application under s 18 which is duly made (ie made in writing and setting out reasons)

> 'and the child support officer shall conduct the review applied for unless in his opinion there are no reasonable grounds for supposing that the refusal, assessment or cancellation in question –
> (a)   was made in ignorance of a material fact;
> (b)   was based on a mistake as to a material fact;
> (c)   was wrong in law.'

Exactly how the child support officer will make such a decision without carrying out a review is unclear, but the intention of this is that he may reject *ad limine* an application which is clearly frivolous or vexatious. This does not affect the aggrieved person's appeal rights since, as will be seen, an appeal may lie against the child support officer's refusal to review.

6.15   The various types of review may now be considered. First, there are special rules relating to reduced benefit directions. By s 46(7) a person who is aggrieved by a reduced benefit direction may leapfrog the review procedure and appeal direct to a child support appeal tribunal. In addition to this, however, a new procedure which is distinct from the other review provisions has now been introduced by reg 42 of the CS(MAP)Regs 1992. No time-limits are imposed on this procedure, which may be adopted at any time during the currency of the reduced benefit direction.

The general nature and effect of reduced benefit directions has already been considered in detail at para **4.12** et seq. Regulations 42(1) and (2) provide that where a person with care with respect to whom a direction is in force gives the Secretary of State reasons:

(a) additional to any reasons given by her in response to the notice served on her under s 45(2) for having failed to comply with the obligations imposed by s 6; or

(b) as to why she should no longer be required to comply with the obligations imposed by s 6,

the Secretary of State shall refer the matter to a child support officer who shall conduct a review of the direction to determine whether the direction is to continue or to cease to be in force; the child support officer is then required to carry out the review and he may not be the same child support officer who gave the original direction.

6.16 It will be seen that the reference to the child support officer, and the review, are mandatory; it would seem that the Secretary of State and child support officer have no power to refuse to carry out the review and that s 18(6) of the Act (see above) does not apply.

Regulation 42(4) provides that where the child support officer who is conducting the review considers that the person concerned is no longer to be required to comply with the obligations imposed by s 6, the direction shall cease to be in force on the last day of the benefit week during the course of which the parent gave the reasons. Clearly, the child support officer will either uphold or discharge the direction. The regulation does not state to what matters he should address his mind when making this decision. However, he would presumably have to satisfy himself either that the person with care had now fulfilled her obligations under s 6 or that the ground set out in s 46(3) (as to which see para **4.14**) applied.

6.17 The remaining classes of review derive from s 18.

Secondly, under s 18(1), a review may be called for:

'Where –

(a) an application for a maintenance assessment is refused; or

(b) an application, under section 17, for the review of a maintenance assessment which is in force is refused,

the person who made that application may apply to the Secretary of State for the refusal to be reviewed.'

The first category is clear enough, although it should be borne in mind that the child support officer may not decline to make a maintenance assessment on the ground that the assessment would be nil (Sch 1, para 13) so that the kind of refusal contemplated by this provision would be a refusal to make any assessment, for example on the ground that the child was not a qualifying child, or that the absent parent was not the father.

Section 17 deals with reviews on change of circumstances so it is that class of case which is contemplated in s 18(1)(b).

6.18   Thirdly, under s 18(2), where a maintenance assessment is in force the absent parent or person with care may apply to the Secretary of State for the assessment to be reviewed. (It also provides for such an application where an assessment is made in response to an application under s 7; s 7 is confined to Scotland and provides that a child may apply for an assessment).

This is likely to be the most commonly used method of application for review. It will be the one relied on where it is alleged that the assessment is insufficient or excessive. It will also be used in relation to disputes as to housing costs, whether the correct amount of protected earnings had been allowed, and whether the correct income figures had been used. An application under this subsection could be of the 'can't pay – won't pay' variety, but, in such a case, the child support officer could refuse to carry out the review under the authority of s 18(6).

6.19   Fourthly, where a maintenance assessment is cancelled, the appropriate person may apply under s 18(3) for the cancellation to be reviewed. The types of cancellation provided for in para 16 of Sch 1 are dealt with in Chapter 4, para **4.54**. 'Appropriate person' means the absent parent or person with care with respect to whom the maintenance assessment in question was, or remains, in force (s 18(12)).

Finally, where an application for the cancellation of a maintenance assessment is refused, the appropriate person may apply to the Secretary of State for the refusal to be reviewed (s 18(4)). The type of decision which will be challenged under this ground is where both the absent parent and the person with care have requested cancellation of the assessment on the ground that they are living together. Presumably the Secretary of State might refuse to cancel an assessment where he was not satisfied of the truth of the reasons given.

6.20   Having dealt with the types of review which may be sought under s 18, the procedure for review must now be considered. Section 18(7) provides that the Secretary of State shall arrange for a review to be conducted by a child support officer who played no part in taking the decision which is to be reviewed; in other words, it is an internal review at the same level of decision-making.

This arrangement attracted some adverse comment during the legislative passage of the Bill. One noble Lord conjured up the picture 'of a colleague walking over to another colleague in the same room, or possibly the next room, and saying "You have been asked to review this matter. I shall explain to you briefly why I made my decision. Do you mind initialling this paper to say you approve of what I did and said?"' (Lord Mishcon, *House of Lords, Official Report*, 29 April 1991, col 548). In reply, it was said that the Secretary of State would make arrangements to secure that the matter was independently considered by a different child support officer but that it was important that the procedure should be carried out promptly.

A precedent for this procedure already exists in the Social Security Act 1986. Section 34(1) of the 1986 Act (now s 66 of the Social Security Administration Act 1992) provides that a social fund officer shall review any determination by himself or another social fund officer if an application for review is made. The social fund directions issued by the Secretary of State for Social Services under the 1986 Act provide for a decision to be reviewed on broadly similar grounds to those set out in s 18(6) of the 1991 Act and give directions to the persons carrying out the review. In particular, the Secretary of State directs that full regard must be had to whether: (i) the decision is sustainable on the evidence; (ii) all relevant considerations were taken into account and irrelevant considerations were not taken into account; (iii) the law and the Secretary of State's directions were interpreted correctly; (iv) the officer acted fairly and exercised his discretion to arrive at a conclusion which was reasonable in the circumstances; and (v) the required procedural steps were followed, with the applicant having sufficient opportunity to put his case and without bias. In *R v Social Fund Inspector and Secretary of State for Social Services, ex parte Roberts* (1990) Crown Office Digest 288, it was said that the directions required a two stage process, the first being akin to judicial review and the second involving the examination of new evidence and changes of circumstances.

6.21 Section 18(11) of the 1991 Act provides that the Secretary of State may make regulations as to the manner in which applications are to be made and the procedure to be followed and these regulations are now contained in regs 24 to 27 of the CS(MAP)Regs 1992. Regulation 24, which deals with time-limits, has already been considered above.

Regulation 25(1) and (2) provides that the child support officer must give 14 days' notice of the proposed review to 'the relevant persons' (normally the absent parent and the person with care). He must send to the relevant persons the applicant's reasons for making the application, together with the information which was included under reg 10(1) when notification of the assessment was given. He must also invite representations, either in person or writing, from the relevant persons 'on any matter relating to the review'.

The notice must also inform the relevant persons of the provision of reg 25(3), namely that if no representations are received within 14 days he may proceed to complete the review (this time-limit may be extended for 'good reason for failure to keep an appointment').

Regulation 25(6) provides that except where written permission is given, any document sent in connection with a review shall not contain any person's address or other information which might lead to a person being located (by the other party) nor any information the use of which might reasonably be expected to lead to any person other than a qualifying child or relevant person being identified.

As to the manner of applying for a review, it has already been seen that s 18(5) stipulates that any application shall give the applicant's reasons in writing; there will therefore be no provision for anything other than a written application.

6.22   If the child support officer conducting the review is satisfied that a maintenance assessment or (as the case may be) a fresh maintenance assessment should be made 'he shall proceed accordingly' (s 18(9)). In making such a maintenance assessment a child support officer must, if he is aware of any material change of circumstances since the decision being reviewed was taken, take account of that change of circumstances in making the assessment (s 18(10)).

By para 11(1) of Sch 1, a maintenance assessment (which includes a fresh assessment) shall take effect on such date as may be determined by regulations, and para 11(2) provides, in effect, that such an assessment may be backdated.

By reg 10(1) and (2) of the CS(MAP)Regs 1992, notification of the result of a review must be given in the same way as notification of an assessment.

It should be noted that regulation 20 (as to which see para **4.52**) applies to s 18 reviews. If any party is dissatisfied by the result of the review it will be necessary to proceed to appeal to a tribunal; such appeals are dealt with below.

5.   Appeals to Child Support Tribunals

6.23   As has been seen s 18 provides that the first step of an absent parent or person with care who is aggrieved by a maintenance assessment, or refusal or cancellation, is to apply for a review by another child support officer. It is intended that such a review should be quick and as informal as possible. The next stage in the procedure for a person who remains aggrieved is to appeal to a child support appeal tribunal.

Here, perhaps, a general point may be made about reviews. It is not difficult to envisage that disputed issues of fact will arise on reviews; these disputes could be between the child support officer and the parents or between the parents themselves. An example of a potential area of dispute might be whether or not either parent was cohabiting with, and receiving financial support from, another person.

It is difficult to see how the child support officer will evaluate the evidence in such disputes. The regulations clearly contemplate that the child support officer will conduct interviews but there seems to be no opportunity for one parent directly to challenge the evidence of the other. It seems, therefore, that the only place to make such a challenge will be at the tribunal.

The provisions for the child support appeal tribunals (CSAT) bear a striking resemblance to those applicable to social security appeal tribunals (SSAT), and in fact it may confidently be predicted that the CSAT will consist of largely the same individuals as those who sit on and service the SSAT and will sit in the same rooms. Indeed, in the eyes of the public, the two bodies may be indistinguishable from each other.

Section 21(1) provides that there shall be tribunals known as CSATs which shall, subject to any order made under s 45, hear and determine appeals under s 20; s 45 is dealt with at para **6.38** below, and s 20, which deals with grounds etc. for appeals, is considered at para **6.26** below.

By s 20(4), Schedule 3 has effect with respect to CSATs; not all the provisions of that Schedule need be considered here, but the following matters are worthy of note.

A CSAT will consist of a chairman and two other persons; the chairman and the other members must not all be of the same sex, unless the chairman rules that it is not reasonably practicable to comply with that requirement in those proceedings (para 2(1) to (3)).

Chairmen of CSATs will be nominated by the President of the CSATs (who combines this position with that of President of the SSATs and other tribunals) from a panel appointed under s 7 of the Tribunals and Inquiries Act 1971 or from among those appointed under the Social Security Act 1975 to act as full-time chairmen of SSATs; alternatively, under para 4 of Sch 3, full-time chairmen of CSATs may be appointed. It appears likely that many full-time or part-time chairmen of SSATs will combine that position with that of full-time or part-time chairman of a CSAT.

A part-time chairman must hold a five-year general qualification (within the meaning of the Courts and Legal Services Act 1990) or, in Scotland, be an advocate or solicitor of five years' standing. In the case of a full-time chairman, the period in each case is seven years. Retirement age is normally 72 but this may be extended to 75.

Members of a CSAT other than the chairmen (lay members) will be drawn from an appropriate panel constituted under para 5. By para 5(3), the panel 'shall be composed of persons appearing to the President to have knowledge or experience of conditions in the area and to be representative of persons living or working in the area'.

Each CSAT will be serviced by a clerk.

6.24   The structure of a CSAT, with a legally qualified chairman, two lay members and a clerk, is a familiar one and is identical with that of a SSAT. Procedure is to be governed by regulations made under s 21(2). Under s 18(3), such regulations may in particular make provision for the following.

(a)   Procedure.

(b)   Striking out appeals for want of prosecution.

(c)   The persons entitled to appear and be heard on behalf of any of the parties.

(d)   Requiring persons to attend and give evidence or produce documents. Regulations about powers to compel attendance, whether by order, witness summons, or otherwise, have no equivalent in relation to SSATs.

(e)   Evidence and the administration of oaths.   It is most likely that evidence will be given unsworn as is now the case in most tribunals. The power to administer oaths will probably be a 'back-up' provision.

(f)   Confidentiality.

(g)   Notification of the result.

6.25 Regulations have now been made, pursuant to s 18(3), and are contained in the CSAT(P)Regs 1992. The most important part of these regulations may be summarised as follows.

(a) *The notice* Appeal must be by notice in writing signed by the person making it (or his representative where it appears to a chairman that he was unable to sign personally) or by a barrister, advocate or solicitor on his behalf (reg 3(1)); a notice of appeal must contain sufficient particulars of the decision under appeal to enable it to be identified (reg 3(9)); any notice of appeal or application other than for an extension of time must state the grounds on which it is made (reg 3(10)); a chairman may direct an appellant or applicant to provide such particulars as the chairman may reasonably require (reg 3(11)).

(b) *Service of notice* The notice must be sent or delivered to the clerk to the tribunal at the Central Office of Child Support Appeal Tribunals, whose address is Anchorage Two, Anchorage Quay, Salford Quays, Manchester M5 2YN (reg 3(21)).

(c) *Time-limits* An appeal under s 20(1) shall be brought within 28 days beginning with the date on which notification of the decision in question was given or sent to the appellant (reg 3(3)); an application under reg 15 (as to which, see below) must be made within three months beginning with the date when a copy of the record of the decision was given or sent (reg 3(4)); the date of the appeal will be taken to be the date on which notice is actually received by the clerk to the tribunal (reg 2(1)).

(d) *Extension of time* A chairman may extend time for appeal or application for special reasons (reg 3(6)); where an application for an extension of time does not include reasons for delay the chairman may give the appellant or applicant a reasonable opportunity to provide reasons (reg 3(7)); an application for an extension of time which has been refused may not be renewed, but any chairman may set aside a refusal under reg 15(1) (see below).

(e) *Lack of jurisdiction* Where a chairman is satisfied that the tribunal does not have jurisdiction he may make a declaration to that effect; this will dispose of the purported appeal (reg 4).

(f) *Directions* At any stage a chairman may give directions. This may be either:
  (i) of his own motion; or
  (ii) on a written application made to the clerk of the tribunal by any party to the proceedings.
These directions may be such as the chairman considers necessary or desirable for the just, effective and efficient conduct of the proceedings. In particular, any party may be directed to provide such further particulars or to produce such documents, as may be reasonably required (reg 5). This power, in effect, to order discovery of documents is likely to be of crucial importance in cases where the means of either parent are in dispute.

(g) *Striking out* Where any party fails to comply with a direction or to reply to an enquiry from the clerk about availability to attend a hearing, a chairman may order that the appeal or application shall be struck out, either of his own motion or on the application of a party. However, before doing so, he must send notice of his intention to all parties to the proceedings, giving each a reasonable opportunity to show cause why the order should not be made (reg 6(1) and (2)). Where an appeal or application is struck out, a chairman may give leave to reinstate, providing application is made within one year from the order (reg 6(3)).

(h) *Representation* Any party may be accompanied at the hearing. Whether or not he attends he may be represented by anyone he chooses (reg 9).

(i) *Witness summons* A chairman may, by summons, require any person in Great Britain to attend as a witness and produce documents, provided not less than 10 days' notice is given and the necessary expenses of attendance are paid. No person may be compelled to give evidence or produce documents which he could not be compelled to give or produce in a court. In exercising his powers the chairman must take into account the need to protect any matter relating to intimate personal or financial circumstances, that is commercially sensitive, consists of information communicated or obtained in confidence, or concerns national security. Any person summoned may apply to the chairman to vary or set aside the summons (reg 10). Where a party wishes to require a witness to attend, he should personally apply in writing to the chairman for a direction under reg 5.

(j) *The hearing* The hearing will be oral, on 10 days' notice to all parties. Any party is entitled to be present and to address the tribunal, give evidence, call witnesses and cross-examine any witness or the representative of the child support officer. A tribunal may require any witness to give evidence on oath or affirmation (reg 11(1)–(5)).

(k) *Decisions* Decisions are taken by a majority of all the tribunal, and both the majority decision and the minority decision must be stated in writing (reg 13(1) and (2)). This is exactly the same as procedure in a SSAT.

(l) *Power to set aside* By regulation 15, any tribunal may set aside any decision of itself or any other tribunal where it appears just to do so on the ground of:
   (i)   non-receipt of documents; or
   (ii)   non-attendance of a party or his representative; or
   (iii) some procedural irregularity or mishap.

6.26 Having considered the structure of tribunals and the pattern of how they will operate, the reader is now in a better position to consider s 20 which deals with the right to appeal and the grounds for appeal. The right to appeal arises only in relation to reviews under s 18, under which the person with care or the absent parent will have sought review of an assessment, cancellation or refusal (see paras **6.13** to **6.22** above). By s 20(1), any person who is aggrieved by the decision of a child support officer on a review under s 18 or by his decision to refuse an application for such a review may appeal to a CSAT against that decision. In the original version of the Bill it was stipulated that an appeal could only be brought on a specified ground, namely:

'that the decision in question

(a) was made in ignorance of a material fact;
(b) was made on a mistake as to a material fact;
(c) was wrong in law.'

This provision was amended at a later stage, the Lord Chancellor informing the House that this area would now be covered by regulations. The regulations set out at para **6.25**, above, do not in fact contain any further provisions as to the specified ground for appealing, so that the tribunal may not decline to entertain an appeal which seems doomed to failure provided the grounds for the appeal are stated. The tribunal's powers in this respect are limited to the chairman's power to declare that the tribunal has no jurisdiction under reg 4. However, this could not extend to rejecting an appeal *ad limine* because it seemed hopeless.

Although appeals to a CSAT under s 20 are limited to the matters discussed above, it should be recalled that a person with care who is aggrieved by a reduced benefit direction has a right of appeal direct to a CSAT under s 46(7) without going through the review procedure. Section 46(8) provides that s 20(2) to (4) and s 21 apply to such appeals. This means that the procedure will be as for a s 20 appeal and in particular it will be necessary to give notice of appeal within 28 days of the reduced benefit direction.

6.27 Under s 20(3), when an appeal is allowed, the tribunal must remit the case to the Secretary of State who must arrange for it to be dealt with by a child support officer. By s 20(4), the CSAT may, in remitting the case, give such directions as it considers appropriate. This might include correcting some aspect of the original decision and directing the child support officer to recalculate the assessment.

6. Appeals to Child Support Commissioners

6.28 Assuming that one or other party does not accept the decision of a CSAT, the next step is an appeal to a Child Support Commissioner; as will be seen, such appeals are limited to points of law.

By s 22(1), the Crown may appoint a Chief Child Support Commissioner and such number of other Child Support Commissioners as may be thought fit; the qualification is a 10-year general qualification (within the meaning of the Courts and Legal Services Act 1990) or, in Scotland, 10 years' standing as an advocate or solicitor.

The general provisions as to child support commissioners are contained in Sch 4; it is unnecessary to recite all the provisions here but it may be noted that, by para 5(1), if it appears to the Chief Child Support Commissioner that an appeal falling to be heard by one of the Child Support Commissioners involves a question of law of special difficulty, he may direct that the appeal be dealt with by a tribunal consisting of any three of the Child Support Commissioners. It appears that the position of Child Support Commissioner will be combined with that of Social Security Commissioner, so that the same individual will combine both roles.

6.29   The right to appeal to the Commissioners is contained in s 24(1), which provides that any person who is aggrieved by a decision of a CSAT, and any child support officer, may appeal to a Child Support Commissioner on a question of law. Therefore, either the person with care, the absent parent or the child support officer has this right of appeal, but only on a point of law.

There is a further restriction on the right of appeal, contained in s 24(6), which provides that no appeal lies within s 24 (ie no appeal may be made to the Commissioner) without the leave:

(a)   of the person who was the chairman of the CSAT when the decision appealed against was given or of such other chairman of a CSAT as may be determined in accordance with regulations made by the Lord Chancellor; or

(b)   subject to and in accordance with regulations so made, of a Child Support Commissioner.

Clearly, if the chairman of the CSAT which gave the decision grants leave, the appeal may be brought. There are also circumstances in which the chairman concerned may not be available to grant leave and in such cases regulations will provide for another chairman to consider the application for leave. In the alternative, the Commissioners will be free, subject to regulations, to grant leave in suitable cases.

6.30   Section 24(7) contains power for the Lord Chancellor to make regulations as to the manner in which and the time within which appeals under s 24 are to be brought and applications for leave are to be made.

These regulations are contained in the CSC(P)Regs 1992, the most important features of which are as follows.

(a)   *Time-limits for applications for leave*   An application for leave to appeal must be made:
   (i)   in the case of application to an appeal chairman, within three months from the date on which notice of decision was sent to the applicant; or
   (ii)   in the case of application to a commissioner, within 42 days of the date of sending notice of chairman's refusal of leave (reg 2(1)), see also (b), below.

(b)   *To whom is application made?*   Application may only be made to a commissioner where the applicant has been refused leave to appeal by a chairman (reg 2(3)). However, where there has been a failure to apply to a chairman, within three months or at all, an application for leave may be made to a commissioner who may accept and consider an application if he thinks fit for special reasons (reg 2(4)). In such a case, the application may be accepted outside the normal time-limit if the commissioner thinks fit for special reasons (reg 2(5)).

(c) *The notice* Application for leave to appeal must be by notice in writing to the clerk to the tribunal at the Central Office (for address see para **6.25**). It must contain:

(i) the name and address of the applicant;

(ii) the ground on which the applicant intends to apply;

(iii) applicant's address for service;

(iv) when the applicant is to be represented by a person who is not a barrister, advocate or solicitor, the written authority of the applicant for that person to represent him. It must have annexed to it a copy of the decision against which leave to appeal is sought. Where a chairman has refused leave, a copy of that decision must be annexed also, and the date on which notice of refusal was given must be stated. In the case of a late application, the reasons for delay must be stated (reg 3).

(d) *Determination of application* A chairman will give a written determination which will be served on all parties (reg 4(1)). When a commissioner grants leave he may, with the consent of all parties, treat and determine any question arising as though it were a question arising on an appeal (reg 4(3)). As to oral hearings, see (h), below.

(e) *Notice of appeal* (It is now assumed that leave to appeal has been granted.) The appeal is by way of notice to a commissioner, and the notice must contain:

(i) the name and address of the appellant;

(ii) the date on which leave to appeal was granted;

(iii) the ground on which the appellant intends to reply;

(iv) appellant's address for service.

The notice must have annexed to it a copy of the determination granting leave to appeal and a copy of the decision appealed against (reg 5).

(f) *Time-limit for appeal* Forty-two days from the date on which the applicant was given notice in writing that leave to appeal was granted (reg 6(2)). However, a commissioner may accept a notice of appeal served after the expiry of 42 days if for special reasons he thinks fit (reg 6(2)).

(g) *Directions* As soon as practicable after receipt of notice of appeal a commissioner must give such directions as appear necessary, specifying:

(i) the parties who are to be respondents to the appeal; and

(ii) the order in which and the time (not less than 30 days) within which any party is to be allowed to make written observations.

Where two or more parties appeal the commissioner will direct which of these is to be treated as appellant (reg 7). At any stage a commissioner of his own motion, or on application, may require any party to furnish such further particulars as may be reasonably required, or give such directions as may be necessary for the efficient and effective dispatch of the proceedings. He may also direct any party to make such written observations as may seem necessary. A party seeking a direction must do so in writing to the commissioner (reg 10).

(h) *Oral hearings* A commissioner may determine any appeal, or application for leave to appeal, without an oral hearing (reg 11(1)). However, any party may request an oral hearing, and the commissioner must grant such request unless he is satisfied that he can properly determine the appeal or application without a hearing. In that event he must inform the party concerned in writing that the request for a hearing has been refused. He may then determine the matter. He may direct an oral hearing of his own motion (reg 11). Oral hearings are in public (unless otherwise directed), and all parties may attend and address the commissioner. With the leave of the commissioner, but not otherwise, they may give evidence, call witnesses and question other witnesses (reg 13). A commissioner may summon any person to attend or produce documents on not less than seven days' notice (reg 14).

(i) *Decisions* Decisions of commissioners are in writing. They may be set aside, under reg 20, on grounds similar to those in reg 15 (see para **6.25** above, at (l)).

6.31 Similar provisions to those set out above exist in respect of social security appeals, the ground for appeal there being that 'the decision of the tribunal was erroneous in point of law' (s 101 of the Social Security Act 1975). That section also provides that leave of the chairman of a tribunal or of a Commissioner must be given.

The tests for determining whether an appeal will lie are well established. In *R (A) 1/72*, it was held that a decision would be wrong in law if:

(a) it contained a false proposition of law on its face;
(b) it was supported by no evidence, or
(c) the facts found were such that no person acting judicially and properly instructed as to the relevant law could have come to the determination in question.

Another decision, *CSB 29/81*, cites *R (1) 14/75* as adding further grounds, namely breach of the requirements of natural justice, and failure to state adequate reasons.

6.32 Section 24(2) provides that where, on an appeal under s 22, a Child Support Commissioner holds that the decision appealed against was wrong in law he shall set it aside. If the decision is set aside, the Commissioner may take one of the three courses of action set out in s 24(3):

'(a) if he can do so without making fresh or further findings of fact, give the decision which he considers should have been given by the child support appeal tribunal;

(b) if he considers it expedient, make such findings and give such decisions as he considers appropriate in the light of those findings; or

(c) refer the case, with directions for its determination, to a child support officer or, if he considers it appropriate, to a child support appeal tribunal.'

If all the facts are clear, therefore, he may merely substitute his own decision for that of the CSAT and, in effect, make the assessment, cancellation, or refusal, as the case may be. Alternatively he can send it back to either of the levels below for redetermination in the light of his findings.

When the reference back is to a child support officer, this must, subject to any direction of the Commissioner, be to an officer who has taken no part in the decision originally appealed against (s 24(4)), and when the matter is referred back to a CSAT, then subject to any such direction, the tribunal shall consist of persons who were not members of the tribunal which gave the decision which has been appealed against (s 24(5)).

7. Appeal from Child Support Commissioner

6.33 The final stage of the appeal procedure provided by the Act lies from a Child Support Commissioner, on a point of law only.

Section 25(1) provides that an appeal on a question of law shall lie to the appropriate court from any decision of a Child Support Commissioner; the meaning of 'question of law' has already been considered at para **6.31** above. 'Appropriate court' is defined by s 25(4) as:

'the Court of Appeal unless in a particular case the Child Support Commissioner to whom the application for leave is made directs that, having regard to the circumstances of the case, and in particular the convenience of the persons who may be parties to the appeal, the appropriate court is the Court of Session.'

By s 25(2), no appeal may be brought except:

(a) with leave of the Child Support Commissioner who gave the decision, or, where regulations made by the Lord Chancellor so provide, of a Child Support Commissioner selected in accordance with the regulations; or

(b) if the Child Support Commissioner refuses leave, with the leave of the appropriate court (ie either the Court of Appeal or the Court of Session).

The first application for leave must therefore always be to the Child Support Commissioner.

6.34   The parties who may apply for leave to appeal are specified in s 25(3), which provides that an application for leave to appeal against a decision of a Child Support Commissioner ('the appeal decision') may only be made by:

'(a)   a person who was a party to the proceedings in which the original decision, or appeal decision, was given;

(b)   the Secretary of State; or

(c)   any other person who is authorised to do so by regulations made by the Lord Chancellor.'

This is a modification of a somewhat convoluted provision in the original Bill, the effect of which would have been to enable an interested party to stand aside from any appeal until it reached the highest court, and then become involved. The intention of the present provision is that anyone who is dissatisfied by any decision has to go through all the stages of review, appeal to CSAT and so on and may not give notice of dissatisfaction and appeal when an appeal by one of the other parties reaches a certain level.

The regulations governing these matters are contained in reg 25 of the CSC(P) Regs 1992. An application to a commissioner under s 25 of the Act must be in writing and must be made within three months from the date on which the applicant was given written notice of the decision. Where the chief commissioner decides that it is impracticable or would cause undue delay for the same commissioner to determine the application, a different commissioner, or tribunal of commissioners, as the case may be, may determine the application.

6.35   The appeal to the Court of Appeal or Court of Session will follow the normal procedures for such appeals and lie outside this Act.

The Act does not need to provide that an appeal from the Court of Appeal lies, with leave, to the House of Lords; this is the case in any event.

8.   Provision for Other Appeals

6.36   As has been seen, the policy of the Act has been to exclude the jurisdiction of the courts both in the making of maintenance assessments and in dealing with appeals, in the latter case by providing for appeals to a system of tribunals and commissioners set up under the Act. However, s 45 contains provisions which run against that general policy.

Section 45(1) provides that the Lord Chancellor or, in relation to Scotland, the Lord Advocate, may by order make such provision as he considers necessary to secure that appeals, or such class of appeals as may be specified in the order

(a)   shall be made to a court instead of being made to a CSAT; or

(b)   shall be made in such circumstances as may be so specified.

'Court' is defined as:

'(a)   in relation to England and Wales and subject to any provision made under Schedule 11 to the Children Act 1989 (jurisdiction of courts with respect to certain proceedings relating to children) the High Court, a country court or a magistrates' court; and

(b)   in relation to Scotland, the Court of Session or the sheriff.'

Section 45(6) provides that where the effect of any order under subsection (1) is that there are no longer any appeals which fall to be dealt with by CSATs, the Lord Chancellor after consultation with the Lord Advocate may by order provide for the abolition of those tribunals.

6.37   The reasons why the government opted for appeals to tribunals rather than the courts were given by the Lord Chancellor during the legislative passage of the Bill (*House of Lords, Official Report*, 29 April 1991, col 553). He explained that social security tribunals had built up considerable expertise in assessing the needs of income-related benefit claimants to cover the living costs of children and that it was the government's intention to draw on and exploit that expertise for the benefit of children who are looking to an absent parent for support; SSATs provide a relatively speedy and informal forum in which the parties themselves, either alone or with the help of a friend or adviser, can present an appeal; many of the appeals will be of the detailed and technical kind in which tribunals like SSATs have become expert.

As to appeals to the courts which hear other family matters, the Lord Chancellor said that 'in England and Wales, at least, those courts, for the present, have their hands full in implementing the Children Act and, as I said the other evening, I do not think that it would be practical to expect the courts to take on that wholly new type of case, even were it desirable in practice'.

6.38   It might also have been said that, given that the powers of the appellate bodies are to be limited to ensuring that the rules as to the formulae for maintenance assessments have been correctly implemented, a tribunal is more appropriate than a court; the family jurisdiction of the courts involves the exercise of discretion, subject to statutory guidelines, and there is little room for discretion in the implementation of the maintenance formulae in the Act.

Nevertheless, the words of the Lord Chancellor quoted above were the preamble to his introduction of the clause which is now s 45 of the Act, and the Lord Chancellor continued as follows:

'However, the government realise that it may in the future become desirable to involve the courts. Circumstances change and the pros and cons of allocating appeals to the courts may weigh differently as a result and may weigh very differently when the system has settled down . . . The government has embarked upon a rolling programme to review the family justice system of which the Children Act 1989 was the first fruit. As part of that programme the government intends to review the organisation of family business. It is not possible for me to foresee at this stage what the result of that process will be; but new arrangements may well make it desirable in the future to concentrate appeals in specialist courts together with other family business. Further, experience of how the child support scheme under the Bill operates, especially in relation to connected court proceedings, may lead us to wish to reconsider the position.'

To cater for these possibilities, therefore, s 45(1) empowers the Lord Chancellor and, in Scotland, the Lord Advocate, to make orders to provide for appeals to go to courts rather than tribunals and, in fact, the Child Support Appeals (Jurisdiction of Courts) Order 1993 provides for appeals under s 20 to go to a court instead of a Child Support Appeal Tribunal, where the issue involved is whether a particular person is a parent of the child. 'Court' means a magistrates' court in the first instance; see para **6.8** above.

9. Judicial Review

6.39   Although, naturally enough, the Act does not mention it, the remedy of judicial review as a final method of challenging the operation of the Act and the system set up by it cannot be ignored. Since this is not a textbook on administrative law and since judicial review will only be appropriate in limited circumstances, the subject will not be considered at great length, but a preliminary outline of the place of judicial review in our system of law may assist.

6.40   Before 1977, a challenge to the actions of public authorities was made by way of one of the prerogative remedies of certiorari, prohibition or mandamus. In 1977 this was changed by means of a radical revision of procedure and the substitution of a new Order 53 of the Rules of the Supreme Court. This created a new procedure called an 'application for judicial review' in which it was unnecessary to select any one of the prerogative remedies. It enabled the High Court to exercise its powers to supervise the proceedings and decisions of, *inter alia*, tribunals and public bodies in a flexible and uniform manner.

Applications for judicial review must be made promptly, and in any event within three months of the act or omission in respect of which complaint is made. The first stage is to apply to a single judge for leave; this is normally dealt with without a hearing. If that application is refused, it may be renewed to a single judge in open court.

Where leave is granted the application proceeds by way of originating motion, the proceedings being assigned to the Crown Office list. The hearing will be before a single judge in open court.

6.41   In principle, therefore, the acts or omissions of a child support officer, a CSAT or a Child Support Commissioner might be the subject of an application for judicial review. However, it is necessary to bear in mind a number of important constraints.

First, judicial review is concerned with the decision-making process, not the merits of the decision itself (*Chief Constable of North Wales Police v Evans*

[1982] 1 WLR 1155, HL). In other words, provided the procedures have been properly employed, judicial review cannot be employed as a method of appeal against the substantive decision reached. Judicial review is therefore limited to ensuring that the person or body in question has acted within its powers and that the rules of natural justice have not been breached.

Secondly, judicial review will not normally be granted where there is another avenue of appeal. Save in the most exceptional circumstances the jurisdiction to grant judicial review will not be exercised where other remedies are available and have not been used (see *R v Epping and Harlow General Commissioners, ex parte Goldstraw* [1983] 3 All ER 257). Whether there are exceptional circumstances would, of course, depend on the facts of an individual case.

6.42 In applying these principles to the child support system, it must be remembered that until 1980 the only way to challenge the decision of a Social Security Commissioner was by way of judicial review. In 1980 this was changed, and the right of appeal from any decision of a Commissioner to the Court of Appeal, or, in Scotland, the Court of Session, was provided. This right of appeal is incorporated in the 1991 Act in respect of appeals against decisions of Child Support Commissioners. The 'supervisory jurisdiction' of the courts is therefore now exercised by the Court of Appeal by way of appeal, rather than by the Divisional Court by way of judicial review. Furthermore, an allegation that the rules of natural justice had not been observed would entitle an aggrieved party to claim that the decision was 'wrong in law' which will confer a right of appeal to the next stage of the system at all levels.

It will therefore be seen that judicial review is certainly not available as a routine method of challenging a decision made at any level of the new child support system. In order to persuade the courts to entertain such an application, it would be necessary to show that the act or omission complained of was so gross and unfair that it would not, or could not, be dealt with by way of the appeal procedures established by the Act.

6.43 However, it has already been seen (at para **3.7** above) that there are many occasions when the Secretary of State or the child support officer has a discretion as to whether to make some decision or do some act. In exercising that discretion, he is subject to s 2 of the Act which requires him to 'have regard to the welfare of any child likely to be affected by his decision'. Most of the matters set out at para **3.7** are not such as would be capable of review and appeal under ss 16 to 25, and, in those cases, it may well be that judicial review will be applicable.

10. The System at a Glance

6.44 The following chart may be a useful guide to understanding the system of reviews and appeals in outline. It should be noted that this list does not include appeals which raise the paternity of a child; these are referred to the court – see Paras **6.8** and **6.38** above.

Nature of Grievance	Remedy	Time-limit or other provision
1. Reduced benefit direction	1. Appeal to CSAT (s 46(7)) Or apply to CSO for review under reg 42, CS(MAP) Regs 1992	1. 28 days from notification. If late, leave of chairman required (s 20(2)) None
2. The making of, cancellation or refusal to cancel child maintenance assessment	2. Apply to Secretary of State for review (s 18(2)–(4))	2. Must be in writing (s 18(5)) 28 days
3. CSO's refusal to review in 2	3. Appeal to CSAT (s 20(1)(b))	3. As 1
4. Review in 2 carried out but not accepted	4. Appeal to CSAT (s 20(1)(a))	4. As 1
5. Change of circumstances of parent	5. Apply to CSO for review (s 17(1))	5. None
6. CSO refuses to review in 5	6. Apply to Secretary of State for review. Different CSO reviews (s 18(1))	6. As in 2
7. Review under 5 carried out but not accepted	7. As 6 (s 18(2))	7. As in 2
8. Decision of CSAT on question of law	8. Appeal to Child Support Commissioner (s 24(1))	8. Leave of CSAT or Commissioner required (s 24(6)). 3 months and/or 42 days
9. Decision of Child Support Commissioner on question of law	9. Appeal to Court of Appeal	3 months. Leave required

CHAPTER SEVEN

Collection and Enforcement

1. The Role of the Agency

7.1 The function of the Child Support Agency is to 'bring together in one organisation all matters to do with the assessment, collection and enforcement of child maintenance in the great majority of cases' (Mr Tony Newton, then Secretary of State for Social Services, *House of Commons, Official Report*, Vol 192, para 179). Assessment has already been considered in earlier chapters: the role of the agency in collection and enforcement must now be considered.

As is frequently the case with this Act, the role of the Agency will vary according to whether or not the person with care is in receipt of benefit. Under s 6(1), a person claiming or receiving certain benefits is obliged to authorise the Secretary of State to take action to recover child support maintenance from the absent parent; she has no option. By virtue of s 4(1), a person with care who is not in receipt of benefit may apply to the Secretary of State for a maintenance assessment, and, by s 4(2), may request that the Secretary of State arrange for the collection of the child support maintenance in accordance with the assessment, and the enforcement of the obligation to pay. In the case of the person not in receipt of benefit, therefore, there is a choice as to whether the Agency deals with the collection or a private arrangement is made. It seems that only the agency will be able to enforce an assessment.

7.2 The dual nature of the system is reflected in s 29(1) which provides that the Secretary of State may arrange for the collection of any child support maintenance payable in accordance with a maintenance assessment where:

(a)   the assessment is made by virtue of s 6 (benefit cases); or
(b)   an application has been made to the Secretary of State under s 4(3) or 7(3) (non-benefit cases) for him to arrange for its collection.

This has been described as an 'equal opportunity measure. It gives the facility of the Child Support Agency to those who are on the prescribed benefits, and are required to co-operate as well as to those who are not' (Ian Jack MP in committee on 11 June 1991, *House of Commons, Official Report*, para 26). The intention of the provisions was said to be 'to allow people not covered by clause 6 the voluntary use of the facilities provided in the Bill' (ibid).

7.3 There is, therefore, a power rather than a positive obligation on the Secretary of State, and accordingly on the Agency, to arrange for collection in the two classes described above. However, on page 3 of document CSA 1 (the child support maintenance application pack – see para **4.10** above) the following statement is made under the heading 'collection service':

'The Child Support Agency will provide an assessment service as described above. The collection service is also available and may involve direct payments between parents. Alternatively the Child Support Agency may collect payments from the absent parent and pass them on to you. If the absent parent falls into arrears, the Agency will consider taking enforcement action. The collection service will be provided if it is chosen by at least one parent.'

Section 29(2) provides that payments 'shall be made in accordance with regulations made by the Secretary of State' and some indication of the scope of the regulations is provided by s 29(3), which specifies certain particular matters for which the regulations may make provision. These are as follows:

'(a) for payments of child support maintenance to be made –
    (i) to the person caring for the child or children in question;
    (ii) to, or through, the Secretary of State; or
    (iii) to, or through, such other persons as the Secretary of State may, from time to time, specify;

(b) as to the method by which payments of child support maintenance are to be made;'

Prior to the Act the courts' powers to direct methods of payment were limited although the Maintenance Enforcement Act 1990 has improved the position (see para **2.11** above). Section 29(3) enables the regulations to provide for specific directions as to method of payment. The provision of s 29(3)(e) (see below) should also be noted:

'(c) as to the intervals at which such payments are to be made;

(d) as to the method and timing of the transmission of payments which are made, to or through the Secretary of State or any other person, in accordance with the regulations;

(e) empowering the Secretary of State to direct any person liable to make payments in accordance with the assessment –
    (i) to make them by standing orders or by any other method which requires one person to give his authority for payments to be made from an account of his to an account of another's on specific dates during the period for which the authority is in force and without the need for any further authority from him;
    (ii) to open an account from which payments under the assessment may be made in accordance with the method of payment which that person is obliged to adopt;'

The intention of these provisions is that the absent parent may be directed to pay by means of banker's order or direct debit; clearly a sensible idea.

However, the regulations will go further than mere exhortation. The absent parent may be 'required', or compelled, to give such authority; whether he will be so compelled from the outset, if he has a bank account, or merely as a means of enforcement, remains to be seen. Moreover, if he does not have a bank account he may be compelled to open one (and perhaps to keep it in funds) for the purpose of paying the assessment sums:

> '(f) providing for the making of representations with respect to matters with which the regulations are concerned.'

7.4 The regulations themselves are contained in Part II of the CS(CE)Regs 1992, the effect of which will be summarised below. It may be noted that reg 2(1) applies 'where a maintenance assessment has been made under the Act and the case is one to which s 29 of the Act applies'. This seems to be a tautology; s 29 applies wherever a maintenance assessment has been made and does not operate unless an assessment has been made; however, this may be of semantic interest only.

The effect of the regulations is as follows.

1. The Secretary of State may specify that payments of child support maintenance shall be made by the liable person:
    (a) to the person caring for the child or children (or in Scotland, in a s 7 application to the child);
    (b) to or through the Secretary of State; or
    (c) to or through such other persons as the Secretary of State may from time to time specify (reg 2(1)).
    This provision therefore allows for a different approach in benefit and non-benefit cases.
2. Payments shall be made by whichever of the following methods the Secretary of State specifies as being appropriate:
    (a) standing order;
    (b) direct debit;
    (c) an arrangement whereby one person gives authority for payments to be made from an account of his, or on his behalf, to another person;
    (d) cheque or postal order;
    (e) cash.
    The Secretary of State may direct a liable person to take all reasonable steps to open an account from which payments may be made (reg 3). The Secretary of State therefore has the choice as to which method of payment shall be adopted (subject to reg 6, below).
3. The Secretary of State shall specify the day and interval (ie weekly, monthly, etc) of payment and may from time to time vary such day or interval. In so doing he must have regard to the needs of the person entitled to receive payment, when the liable person's income is normally received, and any period necessary to enable clearance of cheques, etc (reg 4).
4. The Secretary of State may specify how payments are to be transmitted to the payee as follows:

    (a)   to an account;
    (b)   by cheque, girocheque, etc;
    (c)   in cash.

    The Secretary of State shall also specify the interval for payment (ie weekly, monthly, etc) which need not be the same interval as that referred to in reg 4. Again, the needs of the parties as to timing, etc must be considered (reg 5).

5.   The Secretary of State must, so far as is reasonably practicable, provide the liable person and the person entitled to receive payments with an opportunity to make representations about all the above matters, and he must have regard to those representations in exercising his powers (reg 6).

6.   The Secretary of State must send the liable person a notice stating the amount of child support maintenance, to whom it is to be paid, the method of payment and the day and interval of payment as soon as is reasonably practicable after the making of a maintenance assessment or any change in requirements (reg 7).

7.5   The Agency will therefore have wide powers to collect the maintenance assessment and to direct how payments shall be made. However, the Act envisages that the Agency may become involved in the collection of three further types of payment. First, s 30(1) provides that, where the Secretary of State is arranging for the collection of any payments under s 29 (ie under a maintenance assessment) or under s 30(2) (see below):

> 'he may also arrange for the collection of any periodical payments, or secured periodical payments, of a prescribed kind which are payable to or for the benefit of any person who falls within a prescribed category.'

The terms 'periodical payments' and 'secured periodical payments' are nowhere defined in the Act, so it must be taken that they have the same meaning as that contained in the Matrimonial Clauses Act 1973. Although s 30(1) envisages regulations which will prescribe the kind of periodical payments and payee to which it might apply, it must be the case that this refers to other 'maintenance' payable by the absent parent to a child or to the person with care herself. Clearly the 'topping-up' maintenance which the court may order under s 8(6) (see Chapter 8, para **8.10**) would be appropriate for this treatment.

Section 30(4) provides, in effect, for the Secretary of State to make regulations to enable any additional sums which may be collected by virtue of s 30 to be collected and enforced in exactly the same way as a child maintenance assessment.

7.6   Secondly, s 30(2) provides that the Secretary of State may arrange for the collection of periodical payments or secured periodical payments of a prescribed kind which are payable for the benefit of a child even though he is not arranging for the collection of child support maintenance with respect to that child.

What is envisaged here is that some orders of the court made before the coming into force of the Act may be collected through the Agency.

7.7   The Secretary of State's powers under s 5.30 have been exercised, and the regulations are contained in the CS(CEOFM)Regs 1992. By reg 2 the periodical payments and categories of person prescribed for the purposes of s 30 are as follows:

(a)   payments under a maintenance order made in relation to a child in accordance with the provisions of
section 8(6) (top-up orders)
section 8(7) (expenses for instruction or training)
section 8(8) (expenses due to disability);
(b)   any periodical payments under a maintenance order which are payable to or for the benefit of a spouse or former spouse who is the person with care of a qualifying child in respect of whom a maintenance assessment is in force and the Secretary of State has arranged for its collection under s 29.
(c)   any periodical payments under a maintenance order payable to, or for the benefit of, a former child of the family of the person against whom the order is made, that child having his home with the person with care.

7.8   The first two classes are clear enough: (a) relates to order made by courts as permitted by the Act in the case of qualifying children, (b) relates to spousal maintenance where there is an assessment in force.

As to (c), this relates to 'a child of the family', ie a non-qualifying child, residing with the person with care. No doubt this will only be collected by the agency where there is an assessment in force relating to other children.

7.9   Finally, when the powers of the courts are considered in Chapter 8, it will be seen that s 8(5) provides that some child maintenance orders may continue to be enforceable through the courts as consent orders.

7.10   What has been considered so far concerns the power of the Agency to stipulate what form of maintenance it will collect and how the absent parent is to pay. It is envisaged that the absent parent will co-operate in these arrangements and that payment will be made in accordance with the stipulations.

Not all absent parents will co-operate however, and the Agency therefore has to have powers of enforcement. These powers and remedies will now be considered in turn, but they may be summarised as follows:

(a)   deductions from earnings order;
(b)   liability order;
(c)   distress;
(d)   county court enforcement;
(e)   imprisonment.

2.   Enforcement by Deduction from Earnings Orders

7.11   Attachment of earnings is a well-known process for enforcing payments
of judgments and orders in England and Wales. Such orders are obtained from
county courts under the Attachment of Earnings Act 1971. The order stipulates a 'normal deduction rate', ie the sum to be deducted from the debtor's
earnings by the employer each week or month, and a 'protected earnings rate',
ie the sum below which the earnings must not be allowed to fall; the latter is
calculated according to income support rates.

It must be emphasised at the outset that deduction from earnings orders
under the Act are not the same as attachment of earnings orders. They are a
discrete form of enforcement arising only under this Act. The order is made by
the Secretary of State (the Agency) not by a court.

7.12   Section 31(1) describes any person liable to make payments of child
support maintenance as 'the liable person' and s 31(2) provides that the
Secretary of State may make a deduction from earnings order to secure the
payment of any amount due under the maintenance assessment in question.

It is clear that the Secretary of State has an unlimited discretion as to whether
or not to make a deduction from earnings order; this discretion will be
exercised by child support officers. A deduction from earnings order may not
only be made as a means of enforcement; there is no reason why the order
should not be made immediately the assessment is made. The DSS handbook
Notes to Advisers states that 'this method of collection will be used only in
limited circumstances where other methods have failed or are clearly likely to
fail'. This is a statement of intent but there is no similar restriction in the Act or
regulations.

This is made clear by s 31(3), which provides that a deduction of earnings
order may be made so as to secure the payment of:

'(a)   arrears of child support maintenance payable under the assessment;
 (b)   amounts of child support maintenance which will become due under
         the assessment; or
 (c)   both such arrears and such future amounts.'

It is not necessary to wait for arrears to accrue. It will also be remembered
that if the Secretary of State decides to collect periodical payments which are
not part of a maintenance assessment, he may use all the powers and remedies
available to him for collection and enforcement of a maintenance assessment
(see para **7.5** above). As will be seen below, although the making of any
deductions from earnings order may be challenged in a magistrates' court, the
general merits of the order may not be challenged.

7.13   Section 31(4) to (7) deal with the detail of any deduction from earnings
order. The order will be directed to the liable person's employer and will
instruct the employer to make deductions from the liable person's earnings and
pay the amounts deducted to the Secretary of State. The order must be served
on the employer and the liable person. It is the duty of the employer to comply

with the order, but he will not be liable for any non-compliance before the end of the period of seven days beginning with the date on which the copy of the order was served on him.

By s 31(8), 'earnings' has such meaning as may be prescribed. Regulations, therefore, specify the kind of regular payments which may be classed as 'earnings'.

7.14 Section 32(1) provides that the Secretary of State may 'by regulations make provision with respect to deduction from earnings orders' and the remainder of the section sets out the matters for which, in particular, the regulations may make provision. Some of these are so obvious as to require little or no comment. For example, regulations may require payments to be made in a prescribed manner; require the order to state the amounts to be deducted and the intervals for payment; require payment to the Secretary of State; allow the employer to make an administrative charge; require the employer to notify the Secretary of State if the liable person is not or ceases to be employed by him; and make provision for the variation, discharge or revival of orders. Under s 32(2)(a), the regulations may make provision as to the circumstances in which one person is to be treated as employed by another; this raises the same points as those made in relation to s 31(8) (see para **7.13** above).

The Crown is not to be exempt from deductions from earnings orders; regulations may make provision as to the operation of an order where the liable person is in the employment of the Crown (s 32(2)(i)). In fact, procedure already existed under the old law whereby a person entitled to a maintenance order against a person serving in HM Forces could send a copy of the order to his paymaster and have the order paid by way of attachment. It may be that the reason for specifying Crown employees as a separate class is that some similar arrangement is contemplated.

7.15 Section 32(3) deals specifically with the provision which regulations may make concerning changes of employment. It may be provided that while a deduction from earnings order is in force:

'(a) the liable person shall from time to time notify the Secretary of State, in the prescribed manner and within a prescribed period, of each occasion on which he leaves any employment or becomes employed, or re-employed . . .'

Thus far, this is unexceptional and is in line with the provisions as to attachment of earnings orders. However, the subsection continues:

'. . . and shall include in such a notification a statement of his earnings and expected earnings from the employment concerned and of such other matters as may be prescribed;'

Any indication of an increase in earnings might, of course, entitle the child support officer to make an increased assessment.

Similar obligations are imposed on 'any person who becomes the liable person's employer and knows that the order is in force' (s 32(3)(b)). Such a person must notify the Secretary of State 'in the prescribed manner and within a prescribed period, that he is the liable person's employer' and must give the same information as to earnings and expected earnings.

Employers will, therefore, have to familiarise themselves with the regulations, as sanctions may be imposed for failure to observe them (see para **7.22** below).

7.16 Section 32(4) envisages that some liable persons may have more than one deduction from earnings order made against them, and may also have attachment of earnings orders against them. It therefore provides that regulations may make provision with respect to the priority as between the various orders.

7.17 The detailed regulations as to all these matters are now contained in Part III of the CS(CE)Regs 1992. 'Earnings' are defined by reg 8(1), (3) and (4); the term includes wages, private pensions or compensation for loss of office, and statutory sick pay. It does not include pay from HM Forces, or pensions or benefits payable under any social security enactment. By reg 9 an order must specify, inter alia, a normal deduction rate and a protected earnings rate. By regs 19 and 11, respectively, these terms have the same meanings as those given by the Attachment of Earnings Act with the added requirement that the protected earnings rate must be the same as the liable person's exempt income as calculated at the date of the assessment.

By reg 12(6) an employer may deduct a sum not exceeding £1 in respect of his administrative costs; however, this sum is to be deducted from the earnings of the liable person (not from the child support maintenance) and may reduce the liable person's net earnings below the protected earning rate. Payments deducted under a deduction from earnings order must be paid to the Secretary of State by the 19th day of the month following the month in which the deduction is made (reg 14(1)).

The regulations contain provisions to ensure that information is supplied to the Secretary of State. By reg 15(1) the Secretary of State may require a liable person to provide details of his employer, his current and anticipated earnings, and his place of work and pay number; such details must be supplied within seven days of being given written notice to that effect. A liable person in respect of whom a deduction from earnings order is in force must notify the Secretary of State in writing within seven days of every occasion on which he leaves employment or becomes employed or re-employed (reg 15(2)). Employers are under similar duties (reg 16).

The regulations also contain detailed provisions as to power to vary (reg 18), discharge of orders (reg 20) and lapse of orders (reg 21).

7.18 Clearly, some provision had to be made to enable a liable person to challenge the making of a deduction from earnings order; otherwise the powers of child support officers would have been excessive. It is provided that regulations may include a provision that a liable person may appeal to a magistrates' court (or in Scotland to the sheriff) if he is aggrieved by the making of a deduction from earnings order against him, or by the terms of any such order, or if there is a dispute as to whether payments constitute earnings or as to any other prescribed matter relating to the order (s 32(5)).

The court hearing such an appeal may not question the maintenance assessment by reference to which the deduction from earnings order was made (s 32(6)).

Regulations may include provision as to the powers of the court in relation to an appeal 'which may include provision as to the quashing of a deduction from earnings order or a variation of the terms of such an order' (s 32(7)).

7.19 The regulations are contained in reg 22 of the CS(CE)Regs 1992, subpara (1) of which repeats that a liable person may appeal to the magistrates' court or, in Scotland, the sheriff, having jurisdiction in the area in which he resides. Such appeal will be by way of complaint and must be made within 28 days of the dates on which the matter appealed against arose.

By reg 22(3) an appeal may only be made on one or both of two very limited grounds, namely:

(a) that the deduction from earnings order is defective;
(b) that the payments in question do not constitute earnings.

'Defective' is not defined in the regulations. It is submitted, however, that its meaning must be confined to some formal defect and that as such para (a) does not provide a right of appeal against the deductions from earnings order, eg on the ground that it was unnecessary, unreasonable or inappropriate to make the order. It seems, therefore, that the general merits of the order cannot be challenged in an appeal to the magistrates.

7.20 As to para (b), the meaning of 'earnings' has been considered above. It may be that one frequent ground of appeal will be based on a contention that the liable person is not, in fact, employed. In this context, reg 8(2) provides that 'the relationship of employer and employee shall be treated as subsisting between two persons if one of them, as a principal and not as a servant or agent, pays to the other any sum defined as earnings (under these regulations)'.

By reg 22(4), where the court is satisfied that the appeal should be allowed, its powers are limited to either quashing the deduction from earnings order or specifying which, if any, of the payments in question, do not constitute earnings.

7.21 Regulation 24 contains provisions to govern priority as between different deduction from earnings orders or deduction from earnings orders and attachment of earnings orders. Deduction from earnings orders are dealt with in date order, so that the net earnings are compared with the protected earnings rate on the later order or orders after deduction of the previous order or orders. Deduction from earnings orders have priority over attachment of earnings orders where, again, the net earnings to be compared with the protected earnings rate are calculated after deduction of the sums done under the deduction from earnings order.

7.22 Persons who fail to comply with the requirements of a deduction from earnings order will, in the last resort, be liable to criminal sanctions. Section 32(8), which applies to liable persons and to their employers, provides that:

'If any person fails to comply with the requirements of a deduction from earnings order, or with any regulation under this section which is designated for the purposes of this subsection, he shall be guilty of an offence.'

By s 32(9), 'designated' means 'designated by the regulations'. Regulation 25 provides that the designated regulations are regs 15(1) and (2) (which relates to failure to provide details of employer, place of work or change of employment), 16(1), (2) and (3) (employer's duty to provide information) and 19(1) (employer's duty to comply with deductions from earnings orders).

The use of the term 'fails' imposes an absolute liability, which might have been regarded as oppressive had not s 32(10) provided that:

'It shall be a defence for a person charged with an offence under subsection (8) to prove that he took all reasonable steps to comply with the requirements in question.'

Once the failure itself has been established, the onus will be on the liable person or the employer to show why they should escape liability. Under s 32(11), any person guilty of an offence under subsection (8) will be liable on summary conviction to a fine not exceeding level two on the standard scale.

3. Liability Orders

7.23 It has been seen above that deduction from earnings orders will normally be available as a means of securing payment of sums due under a maintenance assessment. However, it is only possible to make a deduction from earnings order where there are earnings from employment to be attached. For this reason, the Act has to provide further means of enforcement; one of these, and probably the most important, is the liability order.

7.24 It is immediately clear that, unlike the deduction from earnings order, a liability order may only be made as a means of enforcement. The basis of the orders is set out in Section 33. Section 33(1) provides that the section applies where:

'(a)   a person who is liable to make payments of child support maintenance ("the liable person") fails to make one or more of those payments; and
 (b)   it appears to the Secretary of State that –
        (i)   it is inappropriate to make a deduction from earnings order against him (because, for example, he is not employed); or

    (ii)   although such an order has been made against him, it has proved ineffective as a means of securing that payments are made in accordance with the maintenance assessment in question.'

In order for the Secretary of State to make a valid decision to apply to the court for a liability order, therefore, two conditions have to be fulfilled. First, at least one payment of child support maintenance has to be in arrears. Secondly, the Secretary of State must consider whether a deduction from earnings order could and should be made. If it could not be made, eg because the liable person is not employed, that will be sufficient. If he is employed, two further possibilities arise. If no deductions from earnings order had ever been made, the Secretary of State would have to consider whether, nevertheless, it would be inappropriate to make such an order; s 33(1)(b) obviously contemplates the possibility that there might be some reason other than that the liable person was not employed which would make a deduction from earnings order inappropriate. A possible, if unlikely, example might be that it would be severely detrimental to the liable person if his employers discovered that he was in trouble with the Child Support Agency. The second possibility is that mentioned in s 33(1)(b)(ii), namely that a deduction from earnings order has been made but has proved ineffective.

The Secretary of State must, therefore, go through the process set out above before deciding to apply for a liability order. It is important to note, however, that as will be seen below at para **7.25** the court which is asked to make the liability order will be precluded from inquiring into the validity or reasonableness of the Secretary of State's decision to apply for a liability order, and the only vehicle for a liable person who questioned the validity of the decision would be judicial review.

7.25   By s 33(2), the Secretary of State may apply to a magistrates' court, or in Scotland to the sheriff, for an order known as a 'liability order' against the liable person. When such an application is made, s 33(3) provides that the court 'shall make the order if satisfied that the payments in question have become payable by the liable person and have not been paid'.

The making of a liability order is therefore mandatory; the discretion lies with the Secretary of State and, having made his decision, all that he has to prove is the making of a child maintenance assessment and that one or more payments is in arrears. The court will have no discretion to inquire into the question of whether it is an appropriate, or the most appropriate, means of enforcement; for example it could not consider the matters discussed in para **7.24** above. The only defence which might be raised relates to the provision for the need to be satisfied that 'the payments in question have become payable by the liable person'.

It must be remembered that the duty to consider the welfare of 'any child' likely to be affected by any decision falls on the child support officer and not on the court (which is precluded from considering any such matter). However, alleging failure to give proper weight to this duty might be another avenue of approach for an application for judicial review (see Chapter 6, para **6.39**).

7.26 Section 34 deals with the regulations about liability orders which the Secretary of State may make; these will include provision as to the procedure to be followed and the forms to be used. In particular, the regulations may provide that where a liability order has been made, and for so long as the amount in respect of which the order was made remains wholly or partly unpaid, the liable person shall be under a duty to supply relevant information to the Secretary of State. Section 34(2) provides that:

> '"relevant information" means any information of a prescribed description which is in the possession of the liable person and which the Secretary of State has asked him to supply.'

There does not appear to be a specific sanction for breach of such a requirement. The regulations are contained in Part IV of the CS(CE)Regs 1992, the most relevant of which in this context is that by reg 28(1) the Secretary of State must give the liable person at least seven days' notice of his intention to apply for a liability order, which notice must contain the amount of child support maintenance which it is alleged is unpaid.

7.27 Once a liability order specifying a sum of money which is unpaid has been made, it may be enforced in a variety of ways. These will now be considered in subsequent sections.

4. Enforcement of Liability Orders by Distress

7.28 Section 35 provides for the enforcement of liability orders by means of distress, ie the seizure and sale of the liable person's goods. Where a liability order has been made against the liable person the Secretary of State may 'levy the appropriate amount by distress and sale of the liable person's goods' (s 35(1)). Section 35(2) defines 'appropriate amount' as:

> 'the aggregate of –
> (a) the amount in respect of which the order was made, to the extent that it remains unpaid; and
> (b) an amount, determined in such manner as may be prescribed, in respect of the charges connected with the distress.'

7.29 The amount to be recovered by distress is therefore the unpaid balance of the liability order and the costs of distress. Section 35(3) sets out what the Secretary of State may seize when levying distress, namely:

> '(a)   any of the liable person's goods except –
> (i)   such tools, books, vehicles and other items of equipment as are necessary to him for use personally by him in his employment, business or vocation;

    (ii)   such clothing, bedding, furniture, household equipment and provisions as are necessary for satisfying his basic domestic needs; and

  (b) any money, banknotes, bills of exchange, promissory notes, bonds, specialties or securities for money belonging to the liable person.'

The liable person's domestic needs are to be taken to include those of any member of his family with whom he resides (s 35(4)).

7.30 The remainder of s 35 deals with procedural matters which are commonplace and with the inevitable conferring on the Secretary of State of the power to make regulations supplementing the section's provisions. Regulation 30 of the CS(CE)Regs 1992 in fact only provides for the documents which the person levying distress must carry with him and hand to the liable person. However, it should be noted that by s 35(8)(c) regulations may 'provide for an appeal to a magistrates' court by any person aggrieved by the levying of, or an attempt to levy, a distress under this section'. The question of what kind of appeal it will be possible to make therefore arises.

It must be said that appeal against the liability order itself will not be possible; under s 33(3), the magistrates' court, or sheriff, will already have had to consider, in limited terms, whether or not a liability order should be made and that decision cannot be challenged under these provisions. Regulation 31 of the CS(CE)Regs 1992, which deals with appeals in connection with distress, does not amplify the position as set out in the Act. Subpara (1) merely provides that 'a person aggrieved by the levy of, or an attempt to levy, a distress, may appeal to the magistrates court having jurisdiction in the area in which he resides'; the appeal is by way of complaint for an order.

Regulation 31(3) provides that if the court is satisfied that the levy was irregular it may order the goods to be discharged, award compensation equal to the value of the goods (if sold) or require the Secretary of State to desist from levying (in the case of attempted levy).

The only ground on which the court may act under these regulations (and therefore the only ground for appeal under the regulations) is therefore that 'the levy was irregular'. This can only apply to some procedural defect in the levy and cannot go to the root of the decision to levy. The general merits of the case cannot, therefore, be addressed by these means.

Since 'any person aggrieved' has the right of appeal, it follows that the liable person's new wife or cohabitee and, presumably, children will have the same right to be heard as the liable person. It may be that the magistrates will have to deal with what will amount to interpleader proceedings, where a third party claims that goods over which distress has been levied are that party's property and not the property of the debtor.

7.31 Section 37 contains provisions as to the enforcement of liability orders in Scotland which are outside the scope of this part of the book. It should be noted, however, that s 39 empowers the Secretary of State to make regulations for a liability order made in one part of the United Kingdom to be enforced in any other part. An order made in Scotland or Northern Ireland will accordingly be enforceable in England and Wales in the same way as if the order had been made in England and Wales, and reg 29 of the CS(CE)Regs 1992 makes provision for these matters.

5. Enforcement of Liability Orders in County Courts

7.32 Another form of enforcement of a liability order open to the Secretary of State is to seek to recover the amount due through a county court as if it were a judgment or order of the county court. A similar procedure is already available, for example, to enforce an award of an industrial tribunal.

Section 36(1) provides that, where a liability order has been made against a person, the amount in respect of which the order was made, to the extent that it remains unpaid, shall, if a county court so orders, be recoverable by means of garnishee proceedings or a charging order, as if it were payable under a county court order. Unusually, no power to make regulations is conferred on the Secretary of State, so the procedure will be dealt with by means of amendment to the County Court Rules. A number of matters worthy of comment arise.

First, the similarity with orders of an industrial tribunal is not exact, since in those cases the county court has to make an order for payment which may then be enforced; under s 36, the liability order will be recoverable immediately as if it were payable under a county court order. The order for payment for an industrial tribunal award normally requires the debtor to pay within a stated period, determined by the county court. The liability order will be enforceable immediately.

Secondly, the powers of the county court will be limited to making a garnishee order, eg against a liable person's bank or debtors, or a charging order, eg over the liable person's real property, shares or investments. In either case the first stage in the process is to obtain an order nisi, which is obtained without notice to the liable person. The liable person will first become aware of the county court proceedings when he is served with the order nisi, which will contain the date and place of the hearing of the application for an order absolute.

Thirdly, although the liability order may be enforced by these means 'if the county court so orders', there will be no question of the county court inquiring into the merits of the liability order; no doubt the order will be proved by an affidavit filed on behalf of the Secretary of State. The court's discretion will therefore be limited to such discretion as it has when making any garnishee order or charging order. Clearly it will have to be satisfied that the proposed garnishee does indeed owe money to the liable person or that the liable person in fact has an interest in the real and personal property in respect of which a charge is sought. Once those matters are proved, it will be for the liable person, on the hearing of the application for the order absolute, to show cause why the order should not be made; the principal reason why a court would consider such an order inappropriate would be the competing interests of other creditors. Although the Act does not so specify, a charging order absolute may be enforced by an application for an order for the sale of property charged.

6.   Enforcement by Commitment to Prison

7.33   When all other means of enforcement have failed, the Secretary of State may adopt the final and drastic method of applying for the liable person to be committed to prison. Section 40(1) provides that, where the Secretary of State has sought to levy an amount by distress under the Act, or to recover an amount by virtue of s 36 (enforcement through the county court) and that amount or any portion of it remains unpaid, he may apply to a magistrates' court for the issue of a warrant committing the liable person to prison.

To arrive at this stage, therefore, two conditions have to have been fulfilled, namely:

(a)   A liability order must have been made by a magistrates' court or the sheriff; this in itself must have involved a decision by the Secretary of State that a deduction from earnings order was either inappropriate or had been made and had proved ineffective.

(b)   Either distress must have been levied and must have proved wholly or partly ineffective, or an attempt to recover the sum due by means of an application in the county court for a garnishee order or charging order must have failed to recover the whole sum due.

7.34   If these conditions are fulfilled the application to the magistrates' court may be made. The court cannot proceed to its inquiry unless the liable person is present; the inquiry must be 'in the presence of the liable person' (s 40(2)). If, therefore, the liable person does not attend the hearing of the application, it will have to be adjourned. Section 40(11) provides that the Secretary of State may make regulations including provision:

'(d)   that, for the purpose of enabling an inquiry to be made as to the liable person's conduct and means, a justice of the peace may issue a summons to him to appear before a magistrates' court and (if he does not obey) may issue a warrant for his arrest;

(e)   that for the purpose of enabling such an inquiry, a justice of the peace may issue a warrant for the liable person's arrest without issuing a summons.'

The relevant regulations are regs 33 and 34 of the CS(CE)Regs 1992. A justice of the peace may either issue a summons for the liable person to appear before a magistrates' court for the purpose of the inquiry or issue a warrant for his arrest without issuing a summons (reg 33(1)).

7.35   Once the liable person is before the court, the court must inquire as to:

'(a)   the liable person's means; and

(b)   whether there has been wilful refusal or culpable neglect on his part'
(s 40(2)).

No doubt the two will be closely linked. If a liable person has not paid simply because he has no money, he can hardly be accused of wilful refusal or culpable neglect. Presumably it will be at this stage that the court may inquire into whether a liable person is genuinely able to pay the assessment. This is probably the only time in the whole operation of the Act that anyone may go behind the rigidity of the formula and take account of the overall financial position of a liable person. This is plain from the wording of s 40(3) which provides as follows:

'If, but only if, the court is of the opinion that there has been wilful refusal or culpable neglect on the part of the liable person it may –
(a)   issue a warrant of commitment against him; or
(b)   fix a term of imprisonment and postpone the issue of the warrant until such time and on such conditions (if any) as it thinks just.'

The court may order imprisonment, whether suspended or not, only if it is satisfied that there has been wilful refusal or capable neglect; even then it has a discretion as to whether to make such an order. It is submitted that, in order to be so satisfied, the court would have to find that the liable person had the means to pay and that he had either deliberately decided not to pay or had unreasonably refused to apply his mind to the question of payment.

As to evidence, among the matters for which the Secretary of State may make provision by regulations under s 40(11) is the following:

'(c)   that a statement in writing to the effect that wages of any amount have been paid to the liable person during any period, purporting to be signed by or on behalf of his employer, shall be evidence of the facts stated.' This provision in the Act is repeated, more or less verbatim, in reg 33(2).

Such a statement would therefore be admissible as evidence; it would not be conclusive if the liable person challenged it, in which case it might be necessary to call the employer to give oral evidence.

7.36   The proper approach of justices in very similar cases was considered in *R v Luton Magistrates' Court* [1992] 2 FLR 201, which was concerned with the powers of justices to commit under s 76 of the Magistrates' Court Act 1980 for arrears of maintenance; the terminology used in the Act ('wilful refusal or culpable neglect') is identical with that contained in s 40(2). Waite J commented that 'the power under s 76 to issue a writ committing a spouse to prison in such cases was "a power of extreme severity".' He continued as follows:

'Indeed, it might be argued that the existence of such a power in a society which long ago closed the Marshalsea Prison and abandoned imprisonment as a remedy for enforcement of debts, is anomalous. Certainly Parliament has made it plain that the power is to be exercised sparingly and only as a last resort.'

His Lordship emphasised that any order of commitment must be preceded by an inquiry in the presence of the defendant as to whether his default did indeed amount to wilful refusal or culpable neglect and that the court was expressly prohibited for exercising the power, unless satisfied that all other methods of enforcing payment have been tried or considered, and either have proved unsuccessful or are likely to do so. He also commented adversely on the fact that the justices had not allowed the defendant to obtain legal advice.

7.37 For further guidance as to whether or not a warrant of commitment should be made it may also be that magistrates will be referred to the case law in respect of community charge defaulters. The Community Charges (Administration and Enforcement) Regulations 1989, which govern enforcement of the so-called 'poll tax' are, in fact, remarkably similar to the regulations governing enforcement of child support maintenance. There is the same provision for a magistrates' court to make a liability order and the same provision for applications for warrants of commitment, with precisely the same terms of reference for the inquiry by the court. While it is not suggested that the poll tax cases will be followed in every detail it may well be that magistrates will at least regard them as useful pointers. Some of the cases, in fact, predate the community charge and are survivors from enforcement of the rating legislation but, again, they are based on the same formulae.

For example, in both *R v Liverpool JJ, ex parte Lanckiret* [1977] Rating Appeals 85 and *R v Richmond JJ, ex parte Atkins* [1983] RVR 148, it was held that a committal is unlawful if a proper means inquiry is not carried out or insufficient questions are put to the debtor to elicit his true financial position.

In *R v Birmingham JJ, ex parte Mansell* (1988) *The Independent*, April 21, it was held that justices had erred because they had failed to consider whether other enforcement methods could be used. In *R v Manchester City Magistrates' Court, ex parte Davies* [1988] 1 All ER 930, it was emphasised that no one, especially someone who had never been in prison, should ever be sent to prison lightly, and where there were no means to pay the court should bear in mind that the local authority could always renew its application if the debtor's financial position improved.

In *R v Poole JJ, ex parte Benham* [1992] JP 156, it was held that when examining whether or not there had been culpable refusal or wilful neglect the court is confined to examining the conduct of the debtor only between the bill and the liability order. As to means, the court may only consider the debtor's means on the day of the hearing.

Finally, on a different point, in *Re Smith (a Bankrupt), ex parte Braintree District Council* [1990] 2 AC 215, it was held that committal proceedings are a 'legal process' with the meaning of the Insolvency Act 1986, s 286 and may be stayed by a county court in bankruptcy.

7.38   Where the court has power to issue a warrant of commitment, it has the choice of making an outright order or a suspended order. Under s 40(4), the amount in respect of which the warrant is made, which must be stated on the warrant, is:

' (i)   the amount mentioned in s 35(1) or so much of it as remains outstanding; and
 (ii)   an amount (determined in accordance with regulations made by the Secretary of State) in respect of the costs of commitment.'

The amount mentioned in s 35(1) is the 'appropriate amount' to be levied on distress, as defined by s 35(2) (see para **7.28** above). This amount will be significant for two reasons. First, if a postponed order is made, no doubt the order will state the amount to be paid and the rate of payment. Secondly, by s 40(6), a warrant issued under Section 40 shall order the liable person:

'(a)   to be imprisoned for a specified period; but
 (b)   to be released (unless he is in custody for some other reason) on payment of the amount stated in the warrant.'

7.39   The maximum term of imprisonment which may be imposed is to be calculated in accordance with Sch 4 to the Magistrates' Courts Act 1980 but must not exceed six weeks (s 40(7)). Regulations are to make provision for the reduction of the term of imprisonment specified in any warrant where there is part payment of the amount in respect of which the warrant was issued (s 40(8)).

Regulation 34(5) of the CS(CE)Regs 1992 provides that where, after the issue of a warrant, part payment of the amount stated in it is made, the period of imprisonment shall be reduced proportionately, so that for the period of imprisonment stated in the warrant, there shall be substituted a period of such number of days as bears the same proportion to the number of days specified in the warrant as the amount remaining unpaid under the warrant bears to the amount specified in the warrant. For example, if the warrant had specified 28 days' imprisonment and a sum of £1000 outstanding, and the debtor then paid £750, the term of 7 days' imprisonment (25% of the original term) would be substituted for the original term. Regulation 34(6) provides that where the part payment would reduce the period to the number of days already served, the period of imprisonment shall be reduced to the period already served plus one day.

7.40   Section 40(1) to (11) do not apply to Scotland (s 40(12). Commitment to prison in Scotland is dealt with by s 38 and is beyond the scope of this chapter.

7.   Arrears Generally

7.41   Section 41 deals with the manner in which the Secretary of State may treat arrears of child support maintenance recovered from an absent parent. It applies in any case where the Secretary of State is authorised to collect child support maintenance and where the absent parent has failed to make one or more payments due from him. The two matters specifically dealt with are the approach in benefit cases and the question of interest.

7.42   As to benefit cases, the section authorises the Secretary of State to retain arrears collected and not to pay them to the person with care, when that person has been in receipt of benefit. Regulations allow the Secretary of State to retain arrears:

'. . . if he is satisfied that the amount of any benefit paid to the person with care . . . would have been less had the absent parent not been in arrears with his payments of child support maintenance.'

7.43   Section 41(3) provides that in such circumstances as may be prescribed:

'the absent parent shall be liable to make such payments of interest with respect to the arrears of child support maintenance as may be prescribed.'

Regulations as to the rate of interest and other matters have been made under s 41(4). It is clearly intended that interest will be payable in arrears, either to the Secretary of State or to the person with care, if he is not on receipt of benefit. Interest will be recoverable and enforceable in exactly the same way as child support maintenance (s 41(5)).

The regulations are contained in the CS(AIAMA)Regs 1992 and need not be repeated in detail here. However, the following points may be noted:

(a)   when the Secretary of State is considering taking action where there are arrears he must serve an arrears notice on the absent parent, setting out the arrears and the provisions as to arrears and interest contained in the regulations and requesting payment of all outstanding arrears (reg 2(2) and (3));

(b)   interest is payable on any child support maintenance due and not paid on the due date (reg 3(1)) – the rate of interest is 1% per annum above the median base rate prevailing, calculated on a daily basis (reg 6(1)). Interest is only payable on the arrears of child support maintenance, not on accrued interest (reg 6(2));

(c)   where there are arrears due, the Secretary of State may attribute any payment of child support maintenance made by an absent parent to child support maintenance due as he thinks fit (reg 9);

(d)   where a new or fresh maintenance assessment has retrospective effect the child support officer may adjust the amount payable under that assessment for the purpose of taking account of the retrospective effect; however, he may not increase the amount payable under the assessment for this purpose by more than 1.5 times the assessment (in the case of a new assessment) or 1.5 times the difference between the original assessment and the fresh assessment (in the case of a fresh assessment) (reg 10(1) and (4)).

CHAPTER EIGHT

The Role of the Courts, and Maintenance Agreements

1. Introduction

8.1 One of the fundamental objectives of the Act is the removal from the courts of the task of assessing child maintenance and the transfer of this responsibility, together with the collection and enforcement of child mainte-nance, to the Child Support Agency. Two principal reasons for this were given. First, it was said that the courts were unpredictable in that there was a wide disparity in the level of awards of maintenance in similar cases, and that maintenance orders were generally too low. Secondly, the enforcement of maintenance orders was ineffective and unsatisfactory, and an unacceptably high proportion of orders were allowed to be in arrears. This had regrettable consequences for the parent with care of the child or children, and for the 'taxpayer' who had to subsidise feckless parents when they failed to pay and the parent with care was in receipt of benefit.

So it is that that courts have been relieved of their role in child maintenance cases. However, as will be seen, it would be incorrect to assume that the courts are left with no role at all in this field. After the general principle has been considered the various exceptions will be set out, and it will then be necessary to consider the effect which the Act will have on other related proceedings in respect of which the courts retain jurisdiction.

8.2 The general principle is set out in s 8. It provides:

'In any case where subsection (1) applies, no court shall exercise any power which it would otherwise have to make, vary or revive any maintenance order in relation to the child and absent parent concerned.' (s 8(3))

This does not prevent a court from revoking a maintenance order (s 8(4)).

It is therefore necessary to refer to s 8(1) to see to what classes of case it applies. This provides that it (subsection (1)) applies:

'in any case where a child support officer would have jurisdiction to make a maintenance assessment with respect to a qualifying child and an absent parent of his on an application duly made by a person entitled to apply for such an assessment with respect to that child.'

In other words, where a child support officer could make a maintenance assessment, the jurisdiction of the court is excluded. The child must be a 'qualifying child' as defined by s 3(1) and there must be an 'absent parent' (see Chapter 3, para **3.3**).

Subsection (1) applies even though the circumstances of the case are such that a child support officer would not make an assessment if it were applied for (s 8(2)); the courts cannot be used as a 'fall back' position where the Agency would decline to make an assessment.

8.3 It will be seen therefore that, quite apart from the specific exceptions contained in the section, the courts will continue to have jurisdiction in respect of children who are not qualifying children or where for some other reason the child support officer would not have jurisdiction. The section goes on to provide that the courts shall not be precluded from exercising their powers in certain specified cases; these will be considered in turn in the remainder of this chapter, but, for the sake of convenience, they may be summarised as follows:

(a) where the child support officer has no jurisdiction;

(b) in respect of children who are not the adopted or natural children of both parties to a marriage;

(c) in respect of children who are between 17 and 19 years of age and are not in full-time education;

(d) in respect of children who are aged 19 or older;

(e) where 'topping-up' orders under s 8(6) may be made;

(f) where orders in respect of additional educational expenses may be made under s 8(7);

(g) where orders for expenses of disabled or blind children may be made under s 8(8);

(h) in making lump sum or property adjustment orders for children;

(i) in the case of orders made against the person with care of the child;

(j) subject to order of the Lord Chancellor, in certain kinds of consent orders.

In addition, it will be seen that the courts will have jurisdiction in the case of enforcement of sums due under maintenance agreements and have a potentially important role in respect of certain types of appeal.

The courts will continue to exercise their jurisdiction in the remainder of matrimonial cases, many of which involve children who are qualifying children, and it will be necessary for the courts in those cases to have regard to the liability which the absent parent is likely to incur and the sum which the parent with care is likely to receive. This will be considered below (see paras **8.21** to **8.30**).

The removal of jurisdiction from the courts means that any order which purports to be made by a court after the coming into force of s 8 would be without jurisdiction and void. Existing orders will continue until a maintenance assessment is made.

2.   Where Child Support Officer Lacks Jurisdiction

8.4   Jurisdiction is covered by s 44 and is dealt with at Chapter 4, para **4.3**. Briefly, the child support officer has jurisdiction only if the person with care, the absent parent and the qualifying child are all habitually resident in the United Kingdom. If any one of the three is not so resident, there will be no jurisdiction and any application for child maintenance will have to be dealt with through the courts.

3.   Stepchildren and 'Children of the Family'

8.5   In order to be a qualifying child, a child must either be the natural (ie biological) child of both the parents or must have been adopted by those parents. This is an area where the Act departs from the general law, since a party to a marriage has an obligation in principle to maintain a child who is a child of the family, defined by s 52 of the Matrimonial Causes Act 1973 as:

'(a)   a child of both those parties; and
 (b)   any other child, not being a child who has been boarded-out with those parties by a local authority or voluntary organisation, who has been treated by both those parties as a child of their family.'

The meaning of 'treated' is considered at Chapter 1, para **1.9**, but it will be clear in most cases; the most common example is where the child is the child of one of the parties to the marriage by a previous union and becomes a stepchild of the other party.

8.6   It will not be possible to claim maintenance for such children through the Agency, although it should be noted that the Agency will have powers to collect maintenance for such children which is payable under a court order where it is collecting child maintenance assessments in respect of qualifying children in the same family (see Chapter 7, para **7.4**). In such cases it will normally be necessary to apply to the courts for an order.

The procedure for the application will depend on whether the applicant chooses to apply under the Matrimonial Causes Act 1973 or the Children Act 1989. This matter is considered at Chapter 1, para **1.24**.

4.   Children aged 17 or 18

8.7   In order to be a qualifying child, it is necessary to be a child as defined by the Act. Section 55(1) was considered fully at Chapter 4, para **4.4** and need not be set out in full here.

8.8   This means that a 17 or 18-year-old will be excluded from the ambit of the Agency if:

(a)   he is not in full-time education of whatever kind, or

(b)   he is receiving 'advanced education' as defined by the regulations.

The regulations, and the general position, are considered in more detail at para **4.4** et seq.

In such cases, if maintenance is sought, it will be necessary to make application to the courts. Where the parents are unmarried, application is made under the Children Act 1989. Where they are or were married, application may be made either under the 1989 Act, under the Matrimonial Causes Act 1973 or under the Domestic Proceedings and Magistrates' Courts Act 1978 (see Chapter 1, para **1.3**).

5.   Children aged 19 and over

8.9   For the purposes of the Act, a person is a child, as defined by s 55(1), only if he is under 16 or, in certain circumstances, under 19. It follows that a person who is 19 or over cannot in any circumstances be a child and cannot be the subject of a child maintenance assessment. However, persons aged 19 and over are not uncommonly dependent on their parents, for example when they are pursuing full-time education; local education authorities take into account the means of parents when assessing eligibility for grants with the result that many students have to look to their parents for support.

The Child Support Agency will be unable to deal with such cases which means that application will have to be made to the courts either under the Children Act 1989 or, if the parents are or were married, under the Matrimonial Causes Act 1973 or Domestic Proceedings and Magistrates' Courts Act 1978.

6.   'Topping up' under s 8(6)

8.10   It was seen in Chapter 5 that the maintenance assessment formula consisted of two elements, namely a basic element and an additional element. The latter is designed to provide additional maintenance where the means of the parents exceed a certain level. However, even this additional element stops when it reaches a certain level, so that there is, in effect, a maintenance ceiling when assessments are made by the Agency, no matter how wealthy the parents are. This ceiling on the formula award is reached when the additional element is calculated according to the 'alternative formula'.

The Act recognises, however, that there will be cases where it may be inappropriate to limit the maintenance in this way and in those cases the courts are allowed to retain jurisdiction as regards the additional amounts (but not the formula sums). Section 8(6) therefore provides that nothing in that section shall prevent a court from exercising any power which it has to make a maintenance order in relation to a child if:

'(a)   a maintenance assessment is in force with respect to the child;

(b)   the amount of the child support maintenance payable in accordance with the assessment was determined by reference to the alternative formula mentioned in paragraph 4(3) of Schedule 1; and

(c)   the court is satisfied that the circumstances of the case make it appropriate for the absent parent to make or secure the making of periodical payments under a maintenance order in addition to the child support maintenance payable by him in accordance with the maintenance assessment.'

8.11   In order to satisfy the court that it has jurisdiction therefore, the initial requirement is that the applicant prove that a maintenance assessment has been made and that it includes an additional element, the whole assessment being calculated according to the alternative formula (see Chapter 5, para **5.12**). Presumably this can only be done by the production of the assessment itself, showing how the calculation was made.

Section 8(6) does not say, in terms, that the limit on the maintenance assessment must have been reached. It merely says that the assessment must have been made using the alternative formula. However, the whole point of the alternative formula is that it produces a lower figure than that produced by the normal additional element calculation and it therefore follows that if the alternative formula has been applied the ceiling has been reached.

8.12   The task confronting the court therefore will be to assess the needs of the child and the ability of the absent parent to pay, after making allowance for the means of the parent with care. If the resulting sum exceeds the child mainte- nance assessment an order could be made in respect of the balance.

Section 8(6) only applies to periodical payments. Lump sum orders and property adjustment orders are considered below (see para **8.18**).

As to backdating, see para **8.39**.

For procedure, see para **8.45**.

7.   Additional Educational Expenses

8.13   Section 8(7) is what might be called the 'school fees exception', al- though, as will be seen, it is not limited to school fees. It provides that the court shall not be prevented from exercising any power which it has to make a maintenance order in relation to a child if:

'(a)   the child is, will be or (if the order were to be made) would be receiving instruction at an educational establishment or undergoing training for a trade, profession or vocation (whether or not while in gainful employment); and

(b)   the order is made solely for the purposes of requiring the person making or securing the making of periodical payments fixed by the order to meet some or all of the expenses incurred in connection with the provision of the instruction or training.'

The first point to be noted about this is that there is no question of additional maintenance or topping up involved; this subsection does not assume that there will be a child maintenance assessment made by the Agency to provide for everyday requirements, although there may be (there is no reason why an application should not be made jointly under s 8(6) and (7) if that were appropriate). Secondly, the term 'educational establishment' is not defined by the Act, unlike 'recognised educational establishment' which is defined by s 55(3). Accordingly the normal plain meaning afforded by the English language applies and the term must mean school, college or university.

It is, however, important not to lose sight of the fact that the child must be a child as defined by s 55(1). This may have a circular effect for children aged between 16 and 18, because it may be that the person concerned will only be a 'child' if attending a 'recognised educational establishment'. If the institution in question is not a recognised educational establishment, and the person does not come within the meaning of any other part of the definition in s 55(1), then the person concerned will not be a child within s 55(1) and so will be unable to take advantage of s 8(7). However, if he were outside the jurisdiction of the child support officer, a court would have jurisdiction in any event.

8.14   Provided the person in question is a child within the meaning of s 55(1), various classes of expenses would appear to be claimable under s 8(7). School fees and extra expenses incurred at school are the obvious examples. Fees charged by any other educational establishment, such as a college, would be another example. However, 'expenses incurred in connection with the provision of the instruction or training' has a wider meaning than merely fees. It could include accommodation charges, travel expenses or the provision of special clothing or books and equipment. Whatever the nature of the expenses, it will be necessary to show that these are directly attributable to the provision of the instruction or training.

8.15   When the expenses arise out of training for a trade, profession or vocation, the fact that the child is in gainful employment is not a bar. Bearing in mind that a child in gainful employment would probably be over the age of 16, however, it would be necessary to ensure that the child was a 'child' within the meaning of s 55(1).

Having said that, if the child is not a child under s 55(1), the whole of the provisions of the Act, including s 8, cease to apply; the parties and the child would be released from the constraints of the Act and the position under the Matrimonial Causes Act 1973, the Domestic Proceedings and Magistrates' Courts Act 1978 or the Children Act 1989 would have to be considered.

For procedure, see para **8.45**.

8. Disabled or Blind Children

8.16 Disabled and blind children frequently have additional special needs and expenses which cannot be accommodated within an all-embracing formula. Accordingly, the cost of those expenses may be recovered through the courts.

Section 8(8) provides that a court shall not be prevented from exercising any power which it has to make a maintenance order in relation to a child if:

'(a) a disability living allowance is paid to or in respect of him; or
(b) no such allowance is paid but he is disabled,
and the order is made solely for the purpose of requiring the person making or securing the making of periodical payments fixed by the order to meet some or all of any expenses attributable to the child's disability.'

A child is disabled if he is blind, deaf or dumb or is substantially and permanently handicapped by illness, injury, mental disorder or congenital deformity or such other disability as may be prescribed (s 8(9)).

8.17 Speaking to the amendments leading to the subsection as it now appears, the Lord Chancellor said that this provision:

'. . . will mean that a person with care of a disabled child will be able to make such an application [ie a maintenance application] to the courts as well as being able to ask the Child Support Agency to make a maintenance assessment for everyday living expenses. So a disabled child will not be excluded from the benefits of the new system but there will be the additional ability to apply to the courts for a top up award . . . there is widespread agreement that provision for these costs involves a large element of discretion because individual circumstances can vary so much.' (*House of Lords, Official Report*, 22 July 1991, col 517).

As with s 8(7), it is not a prerequisite of an application that a maintenance assessment be in force, although it is probable that this will be so. The purpose of this provision is limited to the recovery of expenses attributable to the child's disability.

For procedure, see para **8.45**.

9. Lump Sums or Property Adjustment Orders

8.18 The effect of s 8(1) and (3) is that the courts are prevented from making 'a maintenance order in relation to a child' in the specified circumstances. Section 8(11) defines 'maintenance order' as 'an order which requires the making or securing of periodical payments to or for a child'.

It follows from this that the various other forms of financial relief for a child are not brought under the umbrella of the Act and the powers of the courts in relation to such orders remain. Accordingly, the courts still have the power to

order a lump sum in favour of a child under s 24(1) of the Matrimonial Causes
Act 1973. Such orders are uncommon (see Chapter 1, para **1.7**) and it is
unlikely that the practice of the courts will change. However, it should be noted
that that part of the jurisdiction of the court has not been removed.

10.   Appeals

8.19   For the sake of completeness, it should be noted that, notwithstanding
the intention contained in the Act that appeals shall lie to special tribunals,
there is a reserve power under which the Lord Chancellor may direct that
appeals be heard by a specified court. This is discussed further at Chapter 6,
para **6.39**.

11.   The Effect of the Act on Related Court Proceedings

8.20   One of the principal concerns expressed during the legislative passage of
the Act by those inside and outside Parliament with an interest in these matters
has been the relationship between the Act and the remainder of matrimonial
financial litigation with which the Act does not deal. The doubts expressed
relate almost entirely to matrimonial cases and not to cases where the parents
had not been married. Until the coming into force of the Act, all issues relating
to financial disputes between the parties to a marriage, including maintenance
for children, will be dealt with by the same court on the same occasion. Since
the children were part of the family of the parent with care of them, it is
regarded as appropriate to look at the needs of the family as a whole and to make
a 'package deal' order.

The effect of the Act is that one aspect of the financial life of the family,
namely the maintenance of the children, has been removed from the ambit of
the court and is to be determined according to a formula which leaves no room
for discretion. Fears were therefore expressed about the likely effect of this.
First, it was said, it was unrealistic in principle to hive off one limited aspect of
family finance in this way. Children do not exist in a vacuum.

Secondly, it was feared that the rigid imposition of the formula amounts,
which would apply in benefit cases whether the parent with care of the children
wanted it to or not, would lead to more disputed litigation. It was said that
absent parents who previously might have been willing to surrender their
interest in a matrimonial home to the parent with care of the children in return
for a reduction in the maintenance payable would now be unwilling to make
such an arrangement and fewer cases would be settled.

Thirdly, it was argued that injustice would be caused to a husband who left
his wife and children in the former matrimonial home and went to live
elsewhere, if the formula award did not permit him to establish a new home for
himself. It was said that courts were able to recognise the realities of life and to

make corresponding allowances in their orders. This would be impossible under the formula.

Finally, it was thought that the whole concept of the 'clean break' was under attack. Since 1984, if not earlier, the tendency of lawyers and their clients involved in matrimonial proceedings had been to resolve the capital disputes between the parties, and to leave as few continuing obligations and links as possible. (It has to be said that this tendency has extended to cases which the original advocates of the clean break never envisaged, such as cases where mothers with care of young children were receiving state benefits and were incapable of self-sufficiency; nevertheless many such orders were made, with the apparent approval of the parties.) It was feared that the high level of the formula awards, including as they do an element of maintenance for the parent with care, would discourage the development of the clean break and put back the clock.

8.21 The attitude of the proponents of the Act has been that where there are young children there cannot be a completely clean break. There must be an element of continuing obligation. Moreover, it was said, the notion of a clean break in most cases is false, because the obligations of the absent parent are merely being passed on to the state. It was wrong in principle that 'the taxpayer' should be asked to relieve absent parents of obligations which they wished to shed and, in effect, to finance a new deal between the parents. It was further argued that the formula does in fact allow for the cost of rehousing of an absent parent and that there is sufficient flexibility in the system to refute the charges of rigidity and unfairness.

8.22 It will have been seen that many of the arguments centre round the former matrimonial home. More people in the United Kingdom own their own homes (subject to mortgage) than ever before and this is reflected in the divorcing population. In most cases, the main concern of the parties is what is to happen to the former matrimonial home. It is in this area that many of the arguments over the merits of the Act have centred.

Clearly it is no part of the purpose of this book to become involved in the arguments on either side; the Act is now law and will be coming into operation shortly. What must now be considered is what effect it is likely to have on the way the courts deal with applications relating to matrimonial property.

8.23 For an idea of the way the formula is intended to work in practice in cases involving a matrimonial home, the Solicitor General (in Standing Committee A on 18 June 1991) referred to example no 7 in the White Paper *Children Come First*. The facts given in that example were as follows:

Angela and Robert have been divorced. They have two children aged 10 and 12 who live with Angela. Robert lives alone, and his net income is £200 per week. Angela's net income is £140 per week.

The maintenance bill is £65 per week. Robert's interest in the former matrimonial home has been transferred to Angela who now pays the mortgage payments of £70 per week. Robert has no capital and pays rent of £35 per week.

Robert's exempt income is £71.70 per week (personal allowance plus rent); his assessable income is therefore £128 per week. 50% of this is £64 and this is what he pays under the child maintenance assessment. He therefore retains net income of £136 per week.

Robert then decides to buy himself a house. He will need a large mortgage because he has no capital. His mortgage payments are therefore £90 per week, net of tax relief.

His exempt income is now:

Personal allowance	£36.70 per week
Mortgage	£90.00 per week
Total	£126.70 per week

This reduces his assessable income to £73 per week, 50% of which is £37. This is what he pays as maintenance assessment. He therefore retains £163 (82% of his net income) for himself. (The figures used in the example are now, of course, out of date.)

8.24   The Solicitor General's comments in Standing Committee were as follows:

'If the caring person has acquired equity in the family home, the committee will appreciate that her housing costs are likely to be lower than would otherwise be the case. Her exempt income will be lower, her assessable income higher, and her contribution to maintenance higher. The absent parent's contribution to maintenance can, therefore, be lower. If, however, the caring parent has acquired a liability in the form of mortgage commitments – that is, a house not free from encumbrance but with, for example, a £40,000 mortgage on it and hundreds of pounds a month to be paid on that mortgage – her housing costs will be higher, her exempt income higher, her assessable income lower and her contribution to maintenance lower. The absent parent's contribution to maintenance can, therefore, be higher.

. . . all those ingredients are contained in the formula. If the absent parent has foregone his share in the family home and consequently has little or no capital with which to start again in the housing market, his housing costs will be higher, his exempt income higher, his assessable income lower and his maintenance obligation lower.'

8.25   The only way in which the formula is said to take account of property adjustment orders is, therefore, by taking account of the increased housing costs incurred by the absent parent. However, this self-adjusting mechanism might not operate in the following cases:

(a)   Where the additional housing costs assumed by the absent parent were, in the view of the child support officer, excessive. The regulations which govern the amounts that may be claimed are considered below.

(b)   Where the absent parent shared housing costs with a new partner who had means of her own; those means, or the partner's ability to share housing costs, will be taken into account when calculating the absent parent's exempt income.

(c)   Where, for some fortuitous reason, the absent parent had no housing costs; for example, where he lives rent free with relatives or in tied rent free accommodation.

To a limited extent, that part of the CS(MASC)Regs 1992 which deals with housing costs in relation to the calculation of exempt income and protected income, makes some concession to the absent parent who is not residing in the former family home. Regulation 18 specifies what are excessive housing costs, and provides essentially that housing costs may not exceed the greater of £80 per week or one-half of net income (for the detail see para **5.24**). However, by reg 18(2) it is provided that this restriction shall not apply where 'the absent parent is responsible for making payments in respect of housing costs which are higher than they would be otherwise by virtue of the unavailability of his share of the equity of the property formerly occupied with his partner and which remains occupied by that former partner'. Where an absent parent is in this position, therefore, the restriction on housing costs (and therefore on exempt or protected income) does not apply.

Generally speaking, therefore, the only way in which an absent parent's transfer of his share in a former matrimonial home to his spouse can be recognised by the formula is if he deliberately increases his housing costs. It may be very difficult for a court deciding whether or not to make a property adjustment order to predict what the absent parent's housing costs will be in the future.

8.26   What is certain, however, is that the courts dealing with ancillary relief applications, and advocates appearing before them, will have to calculate what the financial position of both parents is likely to be once the child maintenance assessment has been made. This will involve calculating all the figures in the same way as the child support officer would do, and working out the assessment on the basis of the present means of the parties. If an assessment had already been made, this would be a known factor which would have to be taken into account. It will also be necessary to predict how the parties will stand financially as a result of any order which is suggested and to see what the maintenance assessment would be then.

The courts, and practitioners, must therefore get used to doing this in the same way as they once became used to calculating the tax consequences of orders and in the way they have adjusted to the requirement to have regard to the net effect of any orders which may be made.

8.27   It is difficult to predict what effect this is going to have on the way the courts deal with ancillary relief applications involving a former matrimonial home. Clearly the basic principles will still be the same; the first consideration of the court will be the welfare of the minor children of the family, and the natural inclination of the court will be towards making such order as will permit the parent with care and the children to go on living in the home, at least until the children have ceased their full-time education.

What may change is the disposition of the equity in the home. While it may be, for the sake of convenience, that the legal title in the property will continue to be transferred to the parent with care, it may also be that the arguments of absent parents in favour of granting them a charge over the property to be realised at some date in the foreseeable future will receive a sympathetic hearing. Among the factors in s 25 of the Matrimonial Causes Act 1973 to which the court must have regard are:

'(b) the financial needs, obligations and responsibilities which each of the parties to the marriage has or is likely to have in the foreseeable future'

and:

'(f) the contributions which each of the parties has made or is likely in the foreseeable future to make to the welfare of the family, including any contribution by looking after the home or caring for the family.'

If, on the figures available, it seems that the absent parent will be obliged to pay child maintenance assessments calculated according to the formula, this will be an obligation and a contribution which cannot be ignored. Child maintenance assessments will generally be considerably higher than maintenance orders have been in the past and, of course, they include an element for the parent with care. It may therefore be that the courts will be more ready to grant to the absent parent some capital sum, payable at a future date and secured by a charge over the property, to reflect these matters.

8.28 In this respect, as in many others previously mentioned, the position where the parent with care is in receipt of benefit is very different from that where she is not. A person who is, or is likely to be, in receipt of benefit cannot contract out of the child support scheme nor give any undertaking to apply for an assessment; by virtue of s 6 she has to apply and has no say in the amount of the assessment. The making of an assessment in such cases must, therefore, be regarded as a fact of life.

Where the parent with care is not in receipt of benefit she has a choice as to whether or not to apply for an assessment. If, however, she does apply for an assessment, the amount payable will be the formula amount and there is no discretion to award any lower or higher amount. In such cases, parents, and their legal advisers, may wish to consider how they can negotiate payment of a sum different from the formula assessment, and indeed the courts may wish to try to provide for such payments. One way in which this could be done is by a maintenance agreement which may be converted into a court order; this aspect is dealt with below (see paras **8.31** to **8.34**) and need not be considered further here save to say that it does not provide, during the transitional period at any rate, a way for 'non-benefit' parents to contract out of the Act.

By virtue of s 8(3), the court is precluded from making an order in respect of the children. There are, however, two ways in which an arrangement made between the parents could be incorporated into a court order. First, the absent parent could give an undertaking to pay certain regular amounts for the benefit of the children. This would have the disadvantage of all undertakings given in relation to ancillary relief, namely the difficulty of enforcing them; however, the undertakings could be worded in such a way that they constituted an agreement and arrears could be recovered as a civil debt.

Secondly, the absent parent could agree to make periodical payments to the parent with care for herself; these payments could run during the minority of the children and be for a fixed term, after which neither party would be entitled to make any further application. This option would not be open if the parent with care remarried.

Neither of these options would be available if the person with care were in receipt of state benefits, so caution would have to be exercised if she might in future become in receipt of such benefits. By virtue of s 9(3) and (4) (see para **8.33** below), any agreement or undertaking not to apply for a child maintenance assessment would be void. In any event, it seems that these possibilities could only exist with the agreement of the parties. It is difficult to see how a court could impose either alternative on an unwilling party.

8.29   As regards maintenance orders in respect of those children where the court has retained jurisdiction, it may well be that the amounts ordered will increase. In Australia, where the power of the courts to make orders for some children co-exists with the child support scheme, it has been noted that the levels of court orders have risen, reflecting the 'benchmarks' laid down by the Agency. It is highly likely that this will happen here; in that way the Act will have changed the way in which the courts regard maintenance of children.

12.   Maintenance Agreements and 'Consent Orders'

8.30   It has always been possible for parents to make agreements to regulate the maintenance payable in respect of their children. Such agreements could be incorporated into consent orders of the court but, if not, they established contractual obligations which could be sued upon like any other contract.

It will remain possible for parents to make agreements but the Act changes the position in several respects. In particular, where a parent with care is in receipt of benefit, there is little point in making a maintenance agreement since s 6 compels such a person to apply for a child maintenance assessment.

8.31   Maintenance agreements are dealt with under s 9. It defines 'maintenance agreement' as 'any agreement for the making, or for securing the making, of periodical payments by way of maintenance, or in Scotland aliment, to or for the benefit of any child' (s 9(1)). The general principle is then set out, namely 'nothing in this Act shall be taken to prevent any person from entering into a maintenance agreement' (s 9(2)). Freedom of contract therefore still exists in this respect.

8.32 However, the following two subsections are designed to attempt to ensure that the jurisdiction of the Child Support Agency shall not be ousted. There is nothing surprising in this; it was always the case that the jurisdiction of the court in relation to child maintenance could not be ousted or restricted.
Section 9(3) provides that:

'The existence of a maintenance agreement shall not prevent any party to the agreement, or any other person, from applying for a maintenance assessment with respect to any child to or for whose benefit periodical payments are to be made or secured under the agreement.'

This is followed by s 9(4) which provides that:

'Where any agreement contains a provision which purports to restrict the right of any person to apply for a maintenance assessment, that provision shall be void.'

Any person who enters into a maintenance agreement is therefore entitled to resile from it at any stage and to apply to the Agency for a child maintenance assessment. A person who is in receipt of benefit may be compelled to do so.

8.33 The provisions of s 8, which prevent the courts from making maintenance orders in relation to children in cases where the child support officer would have jurisdiction to make an assessment, extend to the powers of the court to vary a maintenance agreement pursuant to ss 34 to 36 of the Matrimonial Causes Act 1973. Section 9(5) provides that, where s 8 would prevent any court from making a maintenance order in relation to a child and an absent parent of his, no court shall exercise any power that it has to vary any agreement so as:

'(a)   to insert a provision requiring that absent parent to make or secure the making of periodical payments by way of maintenance, or in Scotland aliment, to or for the benefit of the child; or
 (b)   to increase the amount payable under such a provision.'

A party who was dissatisfied with the terms of an agreement and could not negotiate a satisfactory new agreement would therefore have no choice except to apply for a maintenance assessment.
Arrears due under a maintenance agreement can be enforced like any other civil debt (by suing and obtaining judgment), but the option of obtaining a maintenance order instead of an agreement has been closed in cases to which s 8(1) applies.

8.34 However, what is set out above must be read in the light of s 8(5) which states that the Lord Chancellor, or in Scotland the Lord Advocate, may by order provide that in such circumstances as may be specified by the order the court shall not be prevented from exercising its powers if:

(a)   a written agreement (whether or not enforceable) provides for the making or securing by an absent parent of the child of periodical payments to or for the benefit of the child; and

(b)   the maintenance order which the court makes is, in all material respects, in the same terms as that agreement.

This order has now been made, in the shape of the Child Maintenance (Consent Order) Order 1993, which provides that s 8 shall not prevent a court from exercising its powers in any circumstances in which paras (a) and (b) of s 8(5) apply.

Close examination of the wording of the order shows that the words 'consent orders' in its title are a misnomer. It may be that most of the applications made to the court under s 8(5) are consent applications but they do not have to be; s 8(5) and the order itself merely refer to a 'maintenance order'. Accordingly, it will be possible for the court to make an order against the wishes of one party provided it is identical in substance with the terms of a written agreement.

The significance of this, during the transitional period at least, will be that in non-benefit cases the jurisdiction of the child support officer will be ousted where, whether by consent or otherwise, the court makes an order pursuant to s 8(5). This aspect of the transitional provisions is considered further at para **9.4**.

In any event, the Lord Chancellor's department has emphasised that this is likely to be a temporary expedient, since it is hoped that in due course the child support agency will be able to register, collect and enforce maintenance agreements itself. The department has also stressed that in benefit cases assessments will be mandatory. This does not mean that the court will not be able to make a consent order where the parent with care is receiving benefit, but that few if any absent parents will wish to agree to a consent order in addition to an assessment.

13.   The Relationship between Assessments and Court Orders

8.35   Section 10 contains various provisions which, in the words of the Lord Chancellor:

> '. . . will allow us the alternatives of either continuing to make child maintenance agreements effective through the courts as consent orders or through the new agency's collection and enforcement powers. They will allow the agency, when resources are available, to collect and enforce any other form of child maintenance or spousal maintenance where the agency is collecting related child maintenance.' (*House of Lords, Official Report*, 22 July 1991, col 515).

The amendments to which the Lord Chancellor was speaking included what is now s 30 (collection and enforcement of other forms of maintenance); this is dealt with in more detail in Chapter 7 at para **7.5**.

The upshot of all these provisions is that the Secretary of State may:

'. . . collect and where necessary enforce the payment of two different classes of periodical payment. First he can arrange to collect any periodical payments which are payable for the benefit of children regardless of whether they arise from court orders or binding agreements. Such orders may have been made because the child fell outside the scope of child support maintenance; for example because the order was made against his stepfather. Secondly, the Secretary of State can arrange to collect any periodical payments which are payable to or for the benefit of people other than children but only when he is also arranging the collection of child maintenance. The second class is designed so that maintenance which is linked can be collected together . . . I should add that the main task of the agency will be to collect maintenance for children who fall within the child support scheme and it may not be possible for its services to be extended in this way at the outset' (ibid).

8.36 Section 10 envisages that regulations will be made to prescribe its operation and the kind of orders and agreements to which it will apply. A mere recital of the terms of the section would not be particularly informative, but it is hoped that the words of the Lord Chancellor set out above may help to put it into context. Provision for consent orders has already been dealt with at para **8.34** above.

Section 10(1) provides that where an order of a kind prescribed for the purposes of the subsection is in force with respect to any qualifying child with respect to whom a maintenance assessment is made, the order:

'(a) shall, so far as it relates to the making or securing of periodical payments, cease to have effect to such extent as may be determined in accordance with regulations made by the Secretary of State;

 (b) where the regulations so provide, shall, so far as it so relates, have effect subject to such modifications as may so be determined.'

In other words, regulations will dictate which orders remain in force, which cease to have effect and which shall be modified.

8.37 Similar provisions exist in relation to maintenance agreements. Where an agreement of a prescribed kind is in force with respect to any qualifying child with respect to whom a maintenance assessment is made, the agreement:

'shall, so far as it relates to the making or securing of periodical payments, be unenforceable to such extent as may be determined in accordance with regulations made by the Secretary of State (s 10(2)(a))'.

Section 10(2)(b) is in exactly the same terms as s 10(1)(b) above.

Again, therefore, the regulations will dictate whether, and to what extent, a maintenance agreement remains enforceable once an assessment is made.

8.38 The regulations are contained in the CS(MAJ)Regs 1992. The enactments, orders under which are prescribed for the purposes of s 10(1) (ie the enactments and orders to which that section applies), are as follows:

(a)   Affiliation Proceedings Act 1957;
(b)   Part II of Matrimonial Causes Act 1973;
(c)   The Domestic Proceedings and Magistrates' Courts Act 1978;
(d)   Part III of the Matrimonial and Family Proceedings Act 1984;
(e)   Family Law (Scotland) Act 1985;
(f)   Schedule 1 to the Children Act 1989 (reg 3(1)).

Any order made under any of the above provisions is 'caught' by the provisions of the regulations when a maintenance assessment is made. Regulation 3(2) applies when a maintenance assessment is made with respect to:

(a)   all of the children with respect to whom an order under any of the above enactments is in force; or
(b)   one or more but not all of the children with respect to whom an order is made under any of these enactments is in force and where the amount payable under the order to or for the benefit of each child is separately specified.

In such circumstances, by virtue of reg 3(2), the order shall, so far as it relates to the making or securing of periodical payments to or for the benefit of the children with respect to whom the maintenance assessment has been made, cease to have effect.

8.39   There are two exceptions to this. The first is where the order was made under s 8(7) or (8) of the Act (ie for educational expenses or where the child is disabled). The second relates to Scotland and is considered in Chapter 10. Subject to this, in circumstances to which reg 3(1) and (2) apply, the maintenance assessment will take effect two days after the assessment is made and the maintenance order will cease to have effect from that date (the effective date of the assessment) (reg 3(5) and (6)).

8.40   The CS(MAJ)Regs 1992 contain similar provisions relating to maintenance agreements. By reg 4(1) maintenance agreements within the meaning of s 9(1) of the Act are prescribed for the purposes of s 10(2); such agreements are referred to as 'any agreement for the making, or for securing the making, of periodical payments by way of maintenance, or in Scotland aliment, to or for the benefit of any child'.
By reg 4(2) where a maintenance assessment is made with respect to:

(a)   all of the children with respect to whom an agreement is in force; or
(b)   one or more, but not all, of the children with respect to whom an agreement is in force and where the amount payable under the agreement to or for the benefit of each child is separately specified,

that agreement shall, so far as it relates to the making or securing of periodical payments to or for the benefit of the children with respect to whom the maintenance assessment has been made, become unenforceable from the effective date of the assessment.

It will remain unenforceable until such date as a child support office no longer has jurisdiction to make a maintenance assessment with respect to that child (reg 4(3)).

8.41   Regulations 5 and 6 contain provisions to ensure co-operation between the agency and the courts. In effect, when a child support officer is aware of the existence of a relevant court order and considers that it may be affected by an assessment, he must notify all parties and the court of the assessment and its effective date. Similarly, where the court is aware of an assessment and makes an order which it considers has affected or is likely to affect the assessment, the court must notify the Secretary of State to that effect.

8.42   Section 10(3) is also concerned with the power of the Secretary of State to make regulations. Regulations enable the Secretary of State to prescribe agreements, orders and periods of time and how they are to be treated. Arrears may be recovered, and applications in the court may be treated as applications for orders to be revoked.

8.43   Provision had to be made for the overlapping jurisdiction of the agency and the courts, and the first measure to deal with this is the Maintenance Orders (Backdating) Order 1993. As its name suggests, this deals with the power of courts to backdate orders and its effect may be summarised as follows:

(a)   Amendments are made to Matrimonial Causes Act 1973, s 29(5), Domestic Proceedings and Magistrates' Courts Act 1978, s 5(5) and Children Act 1989, Sch 1, para 3(5) to enable a court to backdate any order made under s 8(6) (the 'top-up' provisions) to the date of the assessment made by the child support officer. However, as a protection for the absent parent, it is also provided that the backdating provision shall only apply where the application for the top up order is made within six months of the assessment. This effectively places a limit on backdating of six months before the application. It is submitted that this does not mean that an application to top up may not be made after six months from the date of the assessment; it merely means that if such an application is made 'out of time' the order can only be backdated to the date of the application.

(b)   Amendments are made to Matrimonial Causes Act 1973, s 31(12) and Domestic Proceedings and Magistrates' Courts Act 1978, s 20(9B) to deal with the position where an order has been made for children and spouse, and an agency assessment supersedes the children's order; in such circumstances, the spouse might wish to apply to vary the order which related to her. It is provided that any variation order made in such circumstances may be backdated to the date of the assessment, with the same safeguard as to a six months' limit.

(c)   Amendments are made to Matrimonial Causes Act 1973, s 29(7), Domestic Proceedings and Magistrates' Courts Act 1978, s 5(7) and

Children Act 1989, Sch 1, para 3(7) to provide for the position where cases move out of the jurisdiction of the agency and are either terminated automatically or cancelled by the child support officer. In such cases there will inevitably be delay pending any application to the court and, once again, any order of the court may be backdated by up to six months to the date of the termination or cancellation.

(d) Amendments are made to Matrimonial Causes Act 1973, s 31(11), Domestic Proceedings and Magistrates' Courts Act 1978, s 20(9A) and Children Act 1989, Sch 1, para 6(9) to govern the position where an absent father applies to vary an order covering more than one child following an agency assessment in respect of one or more but not all the children. In such a case the onus will be on the absent father to apply to vary, and if a variation order is made it may be backdated to the time when the assessment took effect.

8.44 Procedures have had to be devised to deal with the position where there is a dispute as to whether the court or the agency has jurisdiction and these are contained in new FPR, rr 10.24 to 10.26. This can best be understood by assuming that the parent with care has applied to a county court for a periodical payments order for a child. Court staff will be alerted to sift and check such applications, and where either the proper officer or the district judge considers that the court does not have jurisdiction, the applicant will be informed to that effect. (It should be added here that forms of application for ancillary relief have been amended to require the applicant to state whether or not an assessment has been made or applied for and to identify cases where the court might have jurisdiction.)

If the applicant persists with the application the proper officer, if it was he who made the original decision, will refer the matter to the district judge who will either inform the applicant that there appears to be no jurisdiction or give directions for a hearing, which may be ex parte. (Where the district judge made the original decision this stage may be omitted.)

If the applicant still persists and there has been no hearing, the district judge will give directions for a hearing, which may be ex parte.

After the hearing, if the district judge declines jurisdiction, the parties will be given reasons in writing. That decision will be subject to the applicant's right to appeal to a circuit judge.

8.45 For the sake of completeness, some mention should be made of the procedure for applying to the courts for orders in respect of a qualifying child or children where this is still permitted (ie in those cases set out in paras **8.10** to **8.16** above). When the application is made to a county court in a matrimonial cause one of the forms contained in Appendix 2 of the FPR will be used in the normal way, probably Form M11. This and other forms have been amended to require the applicant to tick a box to indicate whether the application is for a stepchild, 'in addition to child support maintenance already paid under a Child Support Agency assessment' and so on, over all the possibilities. In the same way, Form CHA 13 which may be used in a county court or magistrates' court has been amended to enable these points to be clarified at the outset.

Pro forma statements and affidavits of means have been amended to include details of receipts from, and payments to, the Child Support Agency.

With these minor exceptions, procedure will be unchanged.

CHAPTER NINE

Transitional Provisions

1. Introduction

9.1 The Child Support Act 1991 comes into effect on 5 April 1993. However, this does not mean that the full effect of the formula assessments will be visited on absent parents immediately. The introduction of such a complex and all-embracing system has proved difficult and accordingly it has now been decided to phase in the operation of the new system. This has been effected by the Child Support Act 1991 (Commencement No 3 and Transitional Provisions) Order 1992; in this chapter this order will be referred to as 'the order'.

9.2 Before the provisions of the order are considered it should be noted that the general effect of assessments on court orders has been dealt with in Chapter 8, paras **8.20** to **8.29** and readers are referred to those paragraphs for a detailed account of how the agency and the courts will deal with the interlocking of their separate jurisdictions.

9.3 Finally, by way of introduction, it will be remembered that the general effect of s 8 of the Act is that the jurisdiction of the courts is excluded in all cases where the Child Support Office would have jurisdiction to make an assessment, ie with certain defined exceptions, most cases where maintenance for a child is sought. This exclusion applies to new orders from 5 April 1993; as from that date the courts will be precluded from making orders where no order has been made before. However, as will be seen below, the power to vary an existing order will subsist.

2. Phasing in between 1993 and 1997

9.4 Paragraph 1 of the order defines a transitional period of the period between 5 April 1993 and 6 April 1997. Subject to what is said in para **9.7** below about phasing in during 1996/7, during the transitional period no application for child support maintenance under s 4 may be made where:

  (a) there is in force a maintenance order or maintenance agreement in respect of the qualifying child or children, or there is pending before any court an application for such a maintenance order; or
  (b) benefit is being paid to a parent of the child or children.

Several points of interest arise out of (a) above. First, 'maintenance order' does not include an order made under s 8(6), (7) or (8) i.e. a 'top up' order, an order for educational experience or an order for a disabled child.

Secondly, the order does not state that the maintenance order must have been made before 5 April 1993. In most cases this will be so, of course, because in most cases the court loses its jurisdiction on that date. However, the court may still make an order (which does not have to be a consent order) in the same terms as those contained in a written agreement (see para **8.34** above) and this may be done at any time. Such an order would fall within the definition of 'maintenance order' which would therefore have the effect of ousting the jurisdiction of the child support officer in a non benefit case during the transitional period.

Thirdly, as matters stand, the 'maintenance agreement' does not have to be in writing. This would have had the unfortunate effect that the jurisdiction of the child support officer under s 4 would have been excluded and the oral agreement could not have been varied by the court (there being no jurisdiction to vary an oral agreement order MCA 1973). This would clearly have been unjust and it is understood that this part of the order is to be amended so that it applies to written agreements only.

9.5   It will be noted that para 1 is limited to applications under s 4. There will be nothing to prevent the Secretary of State requiring a person with care in receipt of benefit to authorise an application under s 6, and it is understood that much of the work of the agency during the transitional period is to be devoted to make assessments in benefit cases. (The only effect of the restriction under para 6, set out above, is to prevent someone receiving benefit from making application in their own right under s 4.)

The effect of the provisions is, therefore, that applications under s 4 will be confined to those cases where there is no court order.

9.6   Persons with care who have the benefit of a court order and wish it to be increased may well wonder whether the exclusion of the court's jurisdiction (including applications to vary) under s 8 will mean that the order is frozen until 1997. Clearly this could not have been allowed, and the effect of para 5 of Sch 1 to the order is that, for so long as the prohibition on applications under s 4 continues, the courts will retain their power to vary existing orders.

9.7   As indicated in para **9.4** above, there is an exception to the prohibition on s 4 applications during the transitional period which, in effect, provides for phasing in all cases 'caught' by these provisions between 8 April 1966 and 6 January 1997. Paragraph 4 of Sch 1 to the order provides that the restriction on s 4 applications shall not apply to persons with care whose surnames begin with a certain letter from certain specified dates. The letters, and dates, are as follows:

Initial letter of surname	*Date*
A to D	8 April 1996
E to K	1 July 1996
L to R	7 October 1996
S to Z	6 January 1997

The effect of this is that, for example, a person with care called Smith would be entitled to make a s 4 application from 6 January 1997, notwithstanding that there was an existing court order or that she was receiving benefit.

9.8   Paragraph 4(2) of Sch 1 to the order provides for the position where, as at 5 April 1993, an application for a child maintenance order has been made (ie filed with the court), but no order has yet been made. In such a case, an application for a maintenance assessment under s 4 may be made and if it is made the jurisdiction of the court will be excluded. Until an application for an assessment is made the court will be able to make an order. Once an order is made, of course, the prohibition on s 4 assessments during the transitional period will apply.

3.   Modification of Assessment

9.9   Part II of the schedule to the order contains provisions designed to soften the blow of an assessment in certain limited circumstances. These provisions apply to cases where:

(a) on 4 April 1993 there is in force, in respect of all the qualifying children for whom an application for a maintenance assessment is made, and the absent parent concerned, one or more
  (i) maintenance orders, or
  (ii) orders under s 151 of the Army Act 1955 (or similar legislation for the other Forces), or
  (iii) maintenance agreements (being agreements which are made or evidenced in writing); and
(b) the absent parent is responsible for maintaining a child or children residing with him, other than the children in respect of which the application is made; and
(c) the formula amount (ie the amount of child support maintenance which would be payable under an assessment) is not more than £60; and
(d) the formula amount exceeds the aggregate weekly amount which was payable under the order, agreements or arrangements by more than £20 per week.

Where, but only where, all these conditions apply, the amount payable under the assessment shall be 'the modified amount', ie an amount which is £20 greater than the aggregate amount which was payable under the orders, agreements or arrangements.

9.10 This modified amount will be payable for one year from the date on which the original assessment takes effect or, if shorter, until any of the conditions set out in para **9.9** is no longer satisfied. Thereafter the full assessment amount will be payable.

CHAPTER TEN

Child Maintenance: A Scottish Perspective

10.1 The Child Support Act 1991 is a UK measure. The system analysed in the previous chapters applies equally to Scotland, and England and Wales (and Northern Ireland). However, there are some provisions which apply only to Scotland. These are largely concerned with enforcement of liability orders where the corresponding provisions relating to England are not applicable north of the border. Moreover, there is one major difference between the system of child maintenance in Scotland and England, namely that a qualifying child aged 12 or over can apply for a maintenance assessment in Scotland (s 7 of the 1991 Act). These Scottish provisions will be discussed in this chapter. However, the primary purpose of this chapter is to place the Child Support Act 1991 in a Scottish context and, in particular, to discuss its implications for the law of aliment for children and financial provision on divorce which are radically different from the corresponding law in England. To avoid duplication, I have taken the order of the preceding chapters as the structure of this chapter.

1. The Law before the Child Support Act 1991

10.2 By s 1(1)(c) of the Family Law (Scotland) Act 1985, a father or mother owes an obligation to aliment his or her child. Both parents, therefore, have an obligation to aliment their children. The obligation arises under s 1(1)(c) when there is a blood tie between the parents and the child, or when the child has been adopted. The fact that the parents have never married is irrelevant. By s 1(1)(d), a person who has accepted a child as a child of the family owes an obligation to aliment the child. The absence of a blood tie is irrelevant. Thus, for example, a grandparent who brings up a grandchild, or an uncle or aunt who brings up a niece or nephew, owes an obligation to aliment the child: *Inglis v Inglis and Mathew* 1987 SCLR 608. Section 1(1)(d) is most important in practice, where a parent marries a spouse who is not the father or mother of the child: if the spouse accepts the child as a child of the family, then the stepparent owes an obligation to aliment the stepchild. For the purpose of s 1(1)(d), a family includes a one-parent family. Whether or not a person has accepted a child as a child of his or her family is a question of fact: it is not clear in Scots law whether a person can accept a child as a child of the family if he did not know that the child was not his natural child.

For the purposes of an award of aliment, a child is a person under the age of 18. However, where a child is reasonably and appropriately undergoing instruction at an educational establishment, or training for employment or for a trade, profession or vocation, the obligation to aliment the child can continue until the child reaches the age of 25 (s 1(5)(a) and (b)). Thus, for example, a child between the ages of 18 and 25 who is attending university can sue his or her parents for aliment.

10.3 The obligation of aliment is to provide such support as is reasonable in the circumstances, having regard to the factors which the courts use to determine the amount of aliment (s 1(2)). These factors are the needs and resources of the parties, their earning capacities and generally all the circumstances of the case (s 4(1)). Hitherto the courts have given weight to the needs of the child; accordingly, when the child is an infant, awards of aliment have been small; see, for example, *McGeachie v McGeachie* 1989 SCLR 99. The court may take account of the fact that the defender is maintaining dependants in his household even if he does not owe an obligation of aliment to the dependant (s 4(3)(a)). So, for example, the fact that a father is maintaining his cohabitee can be taken into account to reduce the award of aliment for his child. The conduct of a party is *not* taken into account unless it would be manifestly inequitable to leave it out of account (s 4(3)(b)). The fact that a woman conceived a child as a result of a failure to take contraceptive measures or refused to terminate her pregnancy, will not constitute conduct which it would be manifestly inequitable to leave out of account (*Bell v McCurdie* 1981 SLT 159).

In the majority of cases, at least two persons will owe an obligation to aliment a child. In these circumstances, there is no order of liability. Instead, the court, in deciding how much, if any, aliment to award against any of those persons, must have regard to the obligation of aliment owed to the child by the other person(s) (s 4(2) and see, for example, *Inglis v Inglis and Mathew* 1987 SCLR 608). Thus, in a claim for aliment against a father, the court must take into account the fact that the child's mother also has an obligation to aliment the child.

10.4 An action for aliment can be brought by the child when the child reaches the age of 16 (Age of Legal Capacity (Scotland) Act 1991, s 1(1)). When a child is below the age of 18, the action may be brought on the child's behalf by the child's parent or guardian, or any person entitled to or seeking or having custody or care of the child (s 2(4)(a) and (c) of the Family Law (Scotland) Act 1985). If the child is below the age of 16, the action must be brought on the child's behalf by one of those persons. A woman, whether married or not, may bring an action for aliment on behalf of her unborn child, but no action can be heard or disposed of before the child is born (s 2(5)).

An action of aliment for a child can be raised even if the child is living with the defender (s 2(6)). The defender has, in these circumstances, a defence if he or she can show that he or she is fulfilling the obligation of aliment and is continuing to do so: s 2(7). If the child is not living with the defender, it is a defence for the defender to make an offer to receive the child into his or her household and to fulfil the obligation of aliment, provided it is reasonable to expect the child to accept the offer (s 2(8), (9) and see, for example, *McKay v McKay* 1980 SLT (Sh Ct) 111). However, this defence is not available if the child is under the age of 16.

An action for aliment *simpliciter* is competent in the Court of Session and Sheriff Court (s 2(1)). In practice, however, the claim is most likely to arise in the course of other proceedings. These would include actions for declarator of parentage, actions for parental rights, custody and separation (s 2(2)). The most common case is, of course, an action of divorce and a claim for financial provision. Here a spouse will often seek aliment from the other spouse in respect of the children of the marriage under s 1(1)(c) (the couple's natural children) or s 1(1)(d) (any stepchild accepted by either spouse as a child of the family). It should be stressed that in matrimonial proceedings it is the child's independent right to aliment which is sought to be enforced: the claim for aliment for the child is therefore separate from any claim by the spouses for financial provision on divorce. It is submitted that a child's claim for aliment should be satisfied *before* the court considers a spouse's claim for financial provision on divorce. If, at any stage of the proceedings, an action for divorce or separation is dismissed, the court can nevertheless make, inter alia, an order for aliment for any children of the family (s 9(1) of the Matrimonial Proceedings (Children) Act 1958; s 21 of the Family Law (Scotland) Act 1985).

10.5   An award of aliment takes the form of periodical payments which can be ordered for a definite or indefinite period or until the happening of a specified event (s 3(1)(a)). The court cannot substitute a lump sum for a periodical payment (s 3(2)). The court can, however, award alimentary payments of an occasional or special nature which it would be unreasonable to expect the claimant to meet out of the periodical payments of aliment (s 3(1)(b)). These could include inlying, funeral or educational expenses. While such claims can take the form of lump-sum payments, it has been held that a claim for educational expenses can take the form of an annual periodical allowance (*MacDonald v MacDonald* 1992 OH, unreported). An award of aliment can be backdated to the date of the bringing of the action or a later date and, on special cause shown, a date prior to the bringing of the action (s 3(1)(c)).

On a material change of circumstances, an award of aliment can be varied or recalled (s 5(1)). The variation can be backdated as above (s 5(2), incorporating s 3(1)(c) by inference and see, for example, *Abrahams v Abrahams* 1989 SLT (Sh Ct) 11). These provisions are retrospective (s 5(1); *Nixon v Nixon* 1987 SLT 602).

Where the children are from families on low incomes, any award of aliment will be small. In practice, resort will be made to income support. Where a parent has failed to aliment a child under the age of 16, the DSS can take proceedings against the parent for a contribution to any income support paid in relation to the child (Social Security Administration Act 1992, s 106). (See *Secretary of State for Social Services v McMillan* 1987 SLT 52.)

When a child is received into care, the parent or guardian's obligation to aliment a child under the age of 16 continues, even if parental rights have been assumed (Social Work (Scotland) Act 1968, s 17(6)). The local authority has the right to seek a contribution towards the maintenance of a child while in care (Part VI of the Social Work (Scotland) Act 1968). These provisions do not extend to recovery of arrears of maintenance (*Tayside Regional Council v Thaw* 1987 SLT 69).

2.   The Background to the Child Support Act 1991

10.6   As the 1991 Act applies throughout the United Kingdom, the background to the Act discussed in Chapter 2 is of importance to Scots lawyers.

3.   The General Principles and Characteristics of the Act

10.7   The general principles of the Act are the same in Scotland as in England. In particular, the terms 'qualifying child', 'absent parent' and 'person with care' are new to Scots law and the statutory definitions should be carefully noted. In relation to the definition of parent, the provisions in ss 27 and 28 of the Human Fertilisation and Embryology Act 1990 are applicable in Scotland. It should be noted that the common law presumptions as to parentage have been abolished in Scots law and replaced by the presumptions in s 5 of the Law Reform (Parent and Child) (Scotland) Act 1986. By s 5(1)(a) of that Act, a man is presumed to be the father of a child if he was married to the mother of the child at any time during the period beginning with the conception and ending with the birth of the child. The presumption does not apply where a child was conceived and born before the couple were married. The presumption applies in the case of a void, voidable and irregular marriage in the same way as it applies in the case of a valid and regular marriage (s 5(2)). By s 5(1)(b), a man is presumed to be the father of a child, if *both* he and the mother of the child have acknowledged that he is the father, and the child has been registered as such.

The Act is concerned with the obligations of a parent to maintain his and her natural or adopted children, when the parent(s) does not live in the same household as the child and the child lives with a person with care who provides for the child. The Act does not therefore apply where a person owes an obligation to aliment a child by virtue of s 1(1)(d) of the Family Law (Scotland) Act 1985, namely when the child has been accepted by the person as a child of his or her family. So, for example, an action for aliment is still competent by a stepchild against a stepparent who has accepted the child as a child of the family.

The terms 'maintenance assessment' and 'child support maintenance' are equally applicable in Scotland as in England.

10.8 Because a child has an independent right to aliment and his or her interests are not the primary concern of the court in relation to a claim for financial provision on divorce *by a spouse*, it is less difficult in Scots law to apply the new system of child maintenance in the context of marriage breakdown: such difficulties as are likely to be experienced are discussed below. The obligation of the Secretary of State in s 2 of the 1991 Act to 'have regard to the welfare of any child likely to be affected by his decision' should be contrasted with the obligation of the court in s 3(2) of the Law Reform (Parent and Child) (Scotland) Act 1986 to regard the welfare of the child as the paramount consideration in any proceedings relating to parental rights.

4. Procedure for Obtaining Assessment

10.9 As a general rule, the procedure for obtaining a maintenance assessment is the same in Scotland as in England. The child support officer must have jurisdiction and the child must be a 'qualifying child'. There must be 'an absent parent'. A parent or person having the right to the custody of the child cannot be excluded from being 'a person with care' if the child has his home and receives day-to-day care from the parent or person with custody (s 3(3), (4)(a) and (d) of the 1991 Act). When more than one person has care of the child, and one or more, but not all, have parental rights in respect of the child, an application cannot be brought by the person who does not have parental rights. Thus, for example, if a parent and stepparent care for the child, an application cannot be brought by the stepparent unless the stepparent has obtained parental rights under s 3(1) of the Law Reform (Parent and Child) (Scotland) Act 1986.

The fundamental principle that a person with care who is in receipt of benefit will be directed to apply for a maintenance assessment from the absent parent applies in Scotland. Where the person with care is not in receipt of benefit, he or she is not obliged to make an application but, as we shall see, in most cases an application cannot be made to the courts for aliment for the child.

10.10 There is one important difference between the new system of child maintenance in Scots and English law. By s 7(1) of the 1991 Act, a qualifying child who has attained the age of 12 and is habitually resident in Scotland may apply to a child support officer for a maintenance assessment to be made in respect of him or herself. The child cannot apply if: (i) there has been an application for maintenance assessment by a person with care of the child or who is an absent parent of the child; or (ii) if the Secretary of State has been authorised under s 6 to recover child support maintenance from the absent parent by the person with care of the child, ie when the person with care is in receipt of benefit (s 7(1)(a) and (b)). If an application is made under s 7(1), the Secretary of State may make an assessment for any other qualifying children in the care of the same person as the child making the application (s 7(2)). If such assessment is made, the child – or the person with care or the absent parent – may apply to the Secretary of State to arrange for the collection of the child support maintenance and the enforcement of the obligation to pay the maintenance in accordance with the assessment (s 7(3)). The child, the person with care and the absent parent must comply – so far as they reasonably can – with any regulations in respect of supplying information to enable the absent parent to be traced, the amount of child support maintenance to be assessed and the amount to be recovered from the absent parent (s 7(5)). The child who made the application may, at any time, request the Secretary of State to cease acting under s 7 (s 7(6)).

This right of a child aged 12 to apply on his or her own behalf for a maintenance assessment reflects the right of a child to seek aliment under the 1985 Act. However, as we have seen, the child has no active legal capacity to institute proceedings for aliment until he or she reaches the age of 16. Giving a child the statutory right to apply for maintenance assessment at the age of 12 is therefore an important exception to the general principle that a person only reaches the age of legal capacity in Scots law at the age of 16 (s 1 of the Age of Legal Capacity (Scotland) Act 1991).

The procedures in respect of the assessment, interim assessments, reviews and termination are the same in Scotland as in England, but are also applicable in respect of applications by a child under s 7 of the 1991 Act.

5. How Child Maintenance is Assessed

10.11   Child maintenance will be assessed in Scotland in exactly the same way as it will be assessed in England.

6. Disputes as to Parentage, Reviews and Appeals

10.12   The treatment of disputes as to parentage discussed in Chapter 6 is applicable to Scotland. However, s 27 of the 1991 Act does not apply to Scotland, but s 28 gives the Secretary of State for Social Services title to sue for a declarator of parentage under s 7 of the Law Reform (Parent and Child) (Scotland) Act 1986 and to defend an action for declarator of non-parentage or illegitimacy brought by a person named as the alleged parent in an application for maintenance assessment.

10.13   While it may prove to be pedantic, it should be noted that Case F in s 26 refers to 'affiliation proceedings': these are defined in s 26(3) in relation to Scotland as any action of 'affiliation and aliment'. There are, however, *dicta* that actions of affiliation and aliment may no longer be competent (*Conlon v O'Dowd* 1987 SCLR 771). It is thought that actions of affiliation and aliment are technically no longer competent, having been replaced by actions of declarator of parentage and aliment under the Law Reform (Parent and Child) (Scotland) Act 1986. However, the general point is clear and, no doubt, any procedural difficulties can be resolved by purposive interpretation of s 26(3).

10.14   The system of reviews applies to both Scotland and England, and the treatment of appeals in Chapter 6 already covers the Scottish position. It should be noted, however, that under s 25(4) of the 1991 Act the Court of Session has jurisdiction to hear an appeal from a decision of a Child Support Commissioner only if the Child Support Commissioner, to whom the application for leave is made, directs that the Court of Session is the appropriate court having regard 'to the circumstances of the case, and in particular the convenience of the persons who may be parties to the appeal'. It is thought that where the parties to the appeal are resident in Scotland, the Court of Session will be regarded as the appropriate court, but it may also be the appropriate court where, for example, the parties live in Carlisle.

Where a judicial review is sought in Scotland, the application for the judicial review will, of course, be made to the Court of Session in the usual way.

7.   Collection and Enforcement

10.15   The wide powers of the Child Support Agency to arrange for the collection of the maintenance assessment should be noted. This is an important innovation in Scottish family law. Similarly, deduction from earnings orders which can be made by the Agency is a new – and important – remedy in Scots law. The treatment of liability orders already covers the Scottish position, ie the liability order will be made, where appropriate, by the sheriff. The defender is under a duty to provide information to the Secretary of State while any sums due under the order remain unpaid (ss 37(2) and 34(2)).

10.16   In any proceedings before the sheriff in relation to the Act, a party will be able to be represented by a person who is neither a solicitor nor an advocate (s 49). However, the 1991 Act does not introduce any new method of enforcing liability orders in Scots law. Instead, s 38(1) provides that a liability order is to be a warrant:

(a)   for the Secretary of State to charge the defender to pay the appropriate amount (ie the amount unpaid) and to recover that amount by a poinding and sale under Part II of the Debtors (Scotland) Act 1987 and, in connection therewith, for the opening of shut and lockfast places;

(b)   for an arrestment (other than an arrestment of the person's earnings in the hands of his employers) and action of furthcoming or sale.

Moreover, a liability order can be used to found a Bill of Inhibition or action of adjudication at the instance of the Secretary of State (s 38(1)). A sum payable under a liability order is expressly stipulated to be a sum decerned for aliment for the purposes of the Debtors (Scotland) Act 1880 and the Civil Imprisonment (Scotland) Act 1882 (s 40(13)). But only the Secretary of State is to be regarded as the creditor for the purposes of s 4 of the Civil Imprisonment (Scotland) Act 1882 and only he can exercise the powers leading to the imprisonment of the debtor for failure to pay the liability order (s 40(14)).

There are provisions for the mutual enforcement of liability orders throughout the UK (s 39).

8.   The Role of the Courts and Maintenance Agreements

10.17   It is a major objective of the 1991 Act that the courts have no function in assessing child maintenance: instead, this, and the task of collection and enforcement of child maintenance, are transferred to the Child Support Agency. Accordingly, where an application for a child maintenance assessment is competent, the jurisdiction of the courts to award aliment has been removed. However, as we shall see, the courts will continue to have jurisdiction to award aliment in certain circumstances.

The general principle is set out in s 8. Section 8(1) provides:

'This subsection applies in any case where a child support officer would have jurisdiction to make a maintenance assessment with respect to a qualifying child and an absent parent of his on an application duly made by a person entitled to apply for such an assessment with respect to that child.'

By s 8(3), where s 8(1) applies, 'no court shall exercise any power which it would otherwise have to make, vary or revive any maintenance order in relation to the child and the absent parent concerned'. In Scotland, a maintenance order is an order for aliment for a child under the Family Law (Scotland) Act 1985. Thus, if an application for maintenance assessment could be made – even if the child support officer would not make an assessment in the circumstances (s 8(3)) – the court is precluded from making, varying or reviving an order for aliment in respect of the child. This will include the situation where a child could apply for maintenance assessment under s 7. However, existing orders for aliment will continue until a maintenance assessment is actually made, although they cannot be varied or revived. Moreover, the court will continue to have the power to revoke an order for aliment (s 8(4)).

It is important to appreciate the scope of s 8(1) and (3). The child support officer must have jurisdiction, ie the person with care, the qualifying child and the absent parent must be habitually resident in the UK. If this is not the case, s 8(3) does not apply, and the court retains jurisdiction to award aliment.

10.18 Section 8(1) and (3) only removes the court's jurisdiction in relation to awards of aliment in respect of the qualifying child and *the absent parent*. Section 8(10) expressly stipulates that the court retains jurisdiction to make an award of aliment against the person with care; in Scotland, that will arise if the person with care owes the child an obligation of aliment, ie if the person with care is the child's parent (s 1(1)(c) of the 1985 Act) or a person who has accepted the child as a child of his or her family (s 1(1)(d) of the 1985 Act). Thus, a child can bring an action of aliment under s 2(6) where the defender is living with the child, but the defender will, of course, have a defence under s 2(7) in appropriate circumstances (see discussion above). A fortiori, a claim for aliment under s 2(6) remains competent if there is no absent parent, ie the child's parent is living with the child and the person with care, who may also be liable in aliment under s 1(1)(c) (if he or she is also the child's parent) or under s 1(1)(d) (if he or she has accepted the child as a child of the family).

10.19 Before s 8(1) and (3) applies, the child must be a qualifying child. To be a qualifying child, the child must be the natural child of both parents or have been adopted by those parents. Where the child is a stepchild of a party to the marriage, then the child is not a qualifying child *vis-à-vis* the stepparent. If the stepparent has accepted the child as a child of the family, an action for aliment against the stepparent remains competent, for example on divorce, because the child is not a qualifying child.

A qualifying child is defined as a child under the age of 16 (s 55(1)(a)). Therefore, an action of aliment prima facie remains competent when the child is over the age of 16. However, where the child is between the ages of 16 and 19, the child remains a qualifying child if he or she is receiving full-time education – not being 'advanced education'; thus, if the child is at school, as opposed to university, he or she remains a qualifying child and an action for aliment is incompetent (s 55(1)(b)). Under s 55(1)(c) a child between the ages of 16 and 18 may continue to be a qualifying child even if the child is not receiving full-time education, if he or she satisfies conditions prescribed by the Secretary of State: if these conditions are satisfied, an action of aliment will be excluded. When a child reaches the age of 19, the child can no longer be a qualifying child under any circumstances. Therefore, if the child is reasonably and appropriately undergoing instruction at an educational establishment, or training for employment or for a trade, profession or vocation, an action of aliment remains competent until he or she reaches the age of 25.

10.20 By s 8(6), the court can continue to make or vary an award of aliment where a maintenance assessment order has been made which includes 'an additional element', if satisfied that in the circumstances an award of aliment by the absent parent in addition to the maintenance assessment order is justified. This 'topping-up' award of aliment is unlikely to be used except in the case of very wealthy parents. Even where the child is a qualifying child, the court retains jurisdiction to make an order for aliment in relation to the child's school fees, and educational and training expenses (s 8(7)). The court can only award a periodical allowance in these circumstances. The jurisdiction of the court under s 3(1)(b) of the 1985 Act to make occasional payment for these purposes therefore continues to be excluded unless the child is *not* a qualifying child, for example because a child is over 16 and receiving advanced education. The court's jurisdiction also continues in respect of additional needs for disabled or blind children (s 8(8) and (9)).

It is an important feature of the new system of child maintenance that the assessment contains an element of support for the person with care of the child. Because aliment was concerned with support for the child, no account could be taken of the financial needs of the carer of the child. However, para 5 of Sch 5 to the 1991 Act adds a new s 4(4) to the Family Law (Scotland) Act 1985. This provides that:

> 'Where a court makes an award of aliment in an action brought by or on behalf of a child under the age of 16 years, it may include in that award such provision as it considers to be in all the circumstances reasonable in respect of the expenses incurred wholly or partly by the person having the care of the child for the purpose of caring for the child.'

Thus, in those circumstances where an action of aliment is competent, the court can make provision for the carer of the child, thus bringing the law of aliment into line with the formula in relation to maintenance assessment.

10.21 It remains competent for persons to enter into agreements in relation to aliment for children (s 9(1) and (2)). However, the existence of such an agreement does not prevent any party to the agreement or any other person, for example the child, from applying for a maintenance assessment (s 9(1) and (3)). Any provision in the agreement restricting the right to apply for a maintenance assessment is void (s 9(4)). If s 8 would prevent the court from making an award of aliment in relation to a child and an absent parent, the court cannot use any power to vary the agreement so as to insert a provision requiring the absent parent to aliment the child or to increase the amount of aliment due under the agreement. The court retains its power to interpone its authority in terms of any such agreement (s 8(5)). Where a person with care is not in receipt of benefit, an agreement in respect of aliment for the children may be an attractive proposition, but where the carer is in receipt of benefit, there is little point in entering an agreement for aliment as s 6 compels such a person to apply for maintenance assessment. But, as noted above, if an increase in the agreed aliment is sought, if s 8 would be applicable, the court has no jurisdiction to vary the periodical allowance in the agreement and therefore the parties must negotiate a new agreement or make an application for maintenance assessment.

9. The Effect of Maintenance Assessment on Financial Provision on Divorce

10.22 It is thought that in many cases the amount of child maintenance to be paid by the absent parent will be considerably greater than the amount currently awarded as aliment for a child. Solicitors will have to familiarise themselves with the statutory formula for assessment of child maintenance in order to negotiate settlements for those clients who are not compelled to apply for maintenance assessment, ie who are not in receipt of benefit. But even if a settlement is reached, the person with care can still apply for maintenance assessment so that a financial 'clean break' is even less likely than at present. In the case of clients who are in receipt of benefit or on low incomes, it is thought that the new system has many advantages, particularly in relation to collection and enforcement of maintenance assessment.

10.23 Because the levels of maintenance assessment will be higher than current levels of aliment, this will have a 'knock-on' effect in relation to claims for financial provision on divorce as it will reduce the resources of the absent parent. A party's resources are, of course, relevant in claims for financial provision under s 9(1)(c), (d) and (e) of the Family Law (Scotland) Act 1985 (s 11(3)(g), (4)(d) and (5)(e)). More importantly, any order for financial provision must not only be justified by a s 9 principle, but also be 'reasonable having regard to the resources of the parties' (s 8(2)(b)). Once the new system of child assessment is operative, we can expect that orders for financial provision may become less generous because the levels currently awarded will no longer be reasonable in the light of the potential payer's resources, which will be considerably reduced if child assessment is being paid. In particular, it is thought that courts may become even more reluctant to make a property transfer order of the absent parent's interest in the matrimonial home in favour of the custodial parent. On the other hand, it must always be remembered that the maintenance assessment contains an element of financial support for the parent with care of the children. This will also result in a reduction of claims for financial provision on divorce based on s 9(1)(c), namely that the economic burden of caring, after divorce, for a child of the marriage under the age of 16, should be shared fairly between the parties.

10. Conclusion

10.24 This chapter has explored those aspects of the new system of child maintenance which are peculiar to Scots law. It has also attempted to place the system of child maintenance in a Scottish context. However, as explained at the outset, the Child Support Act 1991 is a UK measure and the system of maintenance assessment – and its administrative structure – applies in both Scotland and England. Scots lawyers will therefore have to become familiar with the new law which has been fully discussed in the preceding chapters.

APPENDIX 1
CHILD SUPPORT ACT 1991
(1991 c 48)

ARRANGEMENT OF SECTIONS

The basic principles

An Act to make provision for the assessment, collection and enforcement of periodical maintenance payable by certain parents with respect to children of theirs who are not in their care; for the collection and enforcement of certain other kinds of maintenance; and for connected purposes.

[25th July 1991]

The basic principles

1 The duty to maintain

(1) For the purposes of this Act, each parent of a qualifying child is responsible for maintaining him.

(2) For the purposes of this Act, an absent parent shall be taken to have met his responsibility to maintain any qualifying child of his by making periodical payments of maintenance with respect to the child of such amount, and at such intervals, as may be determined in accordance with the provisions of this Act.

(3) Where a maintenance assessment made under this Act requires the making of periodical payments, it shall be the duty of the absent parent with respect to whom the assessment was made to make those payments.

2 Welfare of children: the general principle

Where, in any case which falls to be dealt with under this Act, the Secretary of State or any child support officer is considering the exercise of any discretionary power conferred by this Act, he shall have regard to the welfare of any child likely to be affected by his decision.

3 Meaning of certain terms used in this Act

(1) A child is a 'qualifying child' if –
- (a)   one of his parents is, in relation to him, an absent parent; or
- (b)   both of his parents are, in relation to him, absent parents.

(2) The parent of any child is an 'absent parent', in relation to him, if –
- (a)   that parent is not living in the same household with the child; and
- (b)   the child has his home with a person who is, in relation to him, a person with care.

(3) A person is a 'person with care', in relation to any child, if he is a person –
- (a)   with whom the child has his home;
- (b)   who usually provides day to day care for the child (whether exclusively or in conjunction with any other person); and
- (c)   who does not fall within a prescribed category of person.

(4) The Secretary of State shall not, under subsection (3)(c), prescribe as a category –
- (a)   parents;
- (b)   guardians;
- (c)   persons in whose favour residence orders under section 8 of the Children Act 1989 are in force;
- (d)   in Scotland, persons having the right to custody of a child.

(5) For the purposes of this Act there may be more than one person with care in relation to the same qualifying child.

(6) Periodical payments which are required to be paid in accordance with a maintenance assessment are referred to in this Act as 'child support maintenance'.

(7) Expressions are defined in this section only for the purposes of this Act.

4 Child support maintenance

(1) A person who is, in relation to any qualifying child or any qualifying children, either the person with care or the absent parent may apply to the Secretary of State for a maintenance assessment to be made under this Act with respect to that child, or any of those children.

(2) Where a maintenance assessment has been made in response to an application under this section the Secretary of State may, if the person with care or absent parent with respect to whom the assessment was made applies to him under this subsection, arrange for –

    (a)   the collection of the child support maintenance payable in accordance with the assessment;

    (b)   the enforcement of the obligation to pay child support maintenance in accordance with the assessment.

(3) Where an application under subsection (2) for the enforcement of the obligation mentioned in subsection (2)(b) authorises the Secretary of State to take steps to enforce that obligation whenever he considers it necessary to do so, the Secretary of State may act accordingly.

(4) A person who applies to the Secretary of State under this section shall, so far as that person reasonably can, comply with such regulations as may be made by the Secretary of State with a view to the Secretary of State or the child support officer being provided with the information which is required to enable –

    (a)   the absent parent to be traced (where that is necessary);

    (b)   the amount of child support maintenance payable by the absent parent to be assessed; and

    (c)   that amount to be recovered from the absent parent.

(5) Any person who has applied to the Secretary of State under this section may at any time request him to cease acting under this section.

(6) It shall be the duty of the Secretary of State to comply with any request made under subsection (5) (but subject to any regulations made under subsection (8)).

(7) The obligation to provide information which is imposed by subsection (4) –

    (a)   shall not apply in such circumstances as may be prescribed; and

    (b)   may, in such circumstances as may be prescribed, be waived by the Secretary of State.

(8) The Secretary of State may by regulations make such incidental, supplemental or transitional provision as he thinks appropriate with respect to cases in which he is requested to cease to act under this section.

(9) No application may be made under this section if there is in force with respect to the person with care and absent parent in question a maintenance assessment made in response to an application under section 6.

5 Child support maintenance: supplemental provisions

(1) Where –

    (a)   there is more than one person with care of a qualifying child; and

    (b)   one or more, but not all, of them have parental responsibility for (or, in Scotland, parental rights over) the child;

no application may be made for a maintenance assessment with respect to the child by any of those persons who do not have parental responsibility for (or, in Scotland, parental rights over) the child.

(2) Where more than one application for a maintenance assessment is made with respect to the child concerned, only one of them may be proceeded with.

(3) The Secretary of State may by regulations make provision as to which of two or more applications for a maintenance assessment with respect to the same child is to be proceeded with.

6 Applications by those receiving benefit

(1) Where income support, family credit or any other benefit of a prescribed kind is claimed by or in respect of, or paid to or in respect of, the parent of a qualifying child she shall, if –

(*a*)   she is a person with care of the child; and

(*b*)   she is required to do so by the Secretary of State,

authorise the Secretary of State to take action under this Act to recover child support maintenance from the absent parent.

(2) The Secretary of State shall not require a person ('the parent') to give him the authorisation mentioned in subsection (1) if he considers that there are reasonable grounds for believing that –

(*a*)   if the parent were to be required to give that authorisation; or

(*b*)   if she were to give it,

there would be a risk of her, or of any child living with her, suffering harm or undue distress as a result.

(3) Subsection (2) shall not apply if the parent requests the Secretary of State to disregard it.

(4) The authorisation mentioned in subsection (1) shall extend to all children of the absent parent in relation to whom the parent first mentioned in subsection (1) is a person with care.

(5) That authorisation shall be given, without unreasonable delay, by completing and returning to the Secretary of State an application –

(*a*)   for the making of a maintenance assessment with respect to the qualifying child or qualifying children; and

(*b*)   for the Secretary of State to take action under this Act to recover, on her behalf, the amount of child support maintenance so assessed.

(6) Such an application shall be made on a form ("a maintenance application form") provided by the Secretary of State.

(7) A maintenance application form shall indicate in general terms the effect of completing and returning it.

(8) Subsection (1) has effect regardless of whether any of the benefits mentioned there is payable with respect to any qualifying child.

(9) A person who is under the duty imposed by subsection (1) shall, so far as she reasonably can, comply with such regulations as may be made by the Secretary of State with a view to the Secretary of State or the child support officer being provided with the information which is required to enable –

(*a*)   the absent parent to be traced;

(*b*)   the amount of child support maintenance payable by the absent parent to be assessed; and

(*c*)   that amount to be recovered from the absent parent.

(10) The obligation to provide information which is imposed by subsection (9) –

(*a*)   shall not apply in such circumstances as may be prescribed; and

(*b*)   may, in such circumstances as may be prescribed, be waived by the Secretary of State.

(11) A person with care who has authorised the Secretary of State under subsection (1) but who subsequently ceases to fall within that subsection may request the Secretary of State to cease acting under this section.

(12) It shall be the duty of the Secretary of State to comply with any request made under subsection (11) (but subject to any regulations made under subsection (13)).

(13) The Secretary of State may by regulations make such incidental or transitional provision as he thinks appropriate with respect to cases in which he is requested under subsection (11) to cease to act under this section.

(14) The fact that a maintenance assessment is in force with respect to a person with care shall not prevent the making of a new maintenance assessment with respect to her in response to an application under this section.

7 Right of child in Scotland to apply for assessment

(1) A qualifying child who has attained the age of 12 years and who is habitually resident in Scotland may apply to the Secretary of State for a maintenance assessment to be made with respect to him if –

    (*a*) no such application has been made by a person who is, with respect to that child, a person with care or an absent parent; or

    (*b*) the Secretary of State has not been authorised under section 6 to take action under this Act to recover child support maintenance from the absent parent (other than in a case where he has waived any requirement that he should be so authorised).

(2) An application made under subsection (1) shall authorise the Secretary of State to make a maintenance assessment with respect to any other children of the absent parent who are qualifying children in the care of the same person as the child making the application.

(3) Where a maintenance assessment has been made in response to an application under this section the Secretary of State may, if the person with care, the absent parent with respect to whom the assessment was made or the child concerned applies to him under this subsection, arrange for –

    (*a*) the collection of the child support maintenance payable in accordance with the assessment;

    (*b*) the enforcement of the obligation to pay child support maintenance in accordance with the assessment.

(4) Where an application under subsection (3) for the enforcement of the obligation mentioned in subsection (3)(*b*) authorises the Secretary of State to take steps to enforce that obligation whenever he considers it necessary to do so, the Secretary of State may act accordingly.

(5) Where a child has asked the Secretary of State to proceed under this section, the person with care of the child, the absent parent and the child concerned shall, so far as they reasonably can, comply with such regulations as may be made by the Secretary of State with a view to the Secretary of State or the child support officer being provided with the information which is required to enable –

    (*a*) the absent parent to be traced (where that is necessary);

    (*b*) the amount of child support maintenance payable by the absent parent to be assessed; and

    (*c*) that amount to be recovered from the absent parent.

(6) The child who has made the application (but not the person having care of him) may at any time request the Secretary of State to cease acting under this section.

(7) It shall be the duty of the Secretary of State to comply with any request made under subsection (6) (but subject to any regulations made under subsection (9)).

(8) The obligation to provide information which is imposed by subsection (5) –

    (*a*) shall not apply in such circumstances as may be prescribed by the Secretary of State; and

    (*b*) may, in such circumstances as may be so prescribed, be waived by the Secretary of State.

(9) The Secretary of State may by regulations make such incidental, supplemental or transitional provision as he thinks appropriate with respect to cases in which he is requested to cease to act under this section.

8 Role of the courts with respect to maintenance for children

(1) This subsection applies in any case where a child support officer would have jurisdiction to make a maintenance assessment with respect to a qualifying child and an absent parent of his on an application duly made by a person entitled to apply for such an assessment with respect to that child.

(2) Subsection (1) applies even though the circumstances of the case are such that a child support officer would not make an assessment if it were applied for.

(3) In any case where subsection (1) applies, no court shall exercise any power which it would otherwise have to make, vary or revive any maintenance order in relation to the child and absent parent concerned.

(4) Subsection (3) does not prevent a court from revoking a maintenance order.

(5) The Lord Chancellor or in relation to Scotland the Lord Advocate may by order provide that, in such circumstances as may be specified by the order, this section shall not prevent a court from exercising any power which it has to make a maintenance order in relation to a child if –
- (*a*) a written agreement (whether or not enforceable) provides for the making, or securing, by an absent parent of the child of periodical payments to or for the benefit of the child; and
- (*b*) the maintenance order which the court makes is, in all material respects, in the same terms as that agreement.

(6) This section shall not prevent a court from exercising any power which it has to make a maintenance order in relation to a child if –
- (*a*) a maintenance assessment is in force with respect to the child;
- (*b*) the amount of the child support maintenance payable in accordance with the assessment was determined by reference to the alternative formula mentioned in paragraph 4(3) of Schedule 1; and
- (*c*) the court is satisfied that the circumstances of the case make it appropriate for the absent parent to make or secure the making of periodical payments under a maintenance order in addition to the child support maintenance payable by him in accordance with the maintenance assessment.

(7) This section shall not prevent a court from exercising any power which it has to make a maintenance order in relation to a child if –
- (*a*) the child is, will be or (if the order were to be made) would be receiving instruction at an educational establishment or undergoing training for a trade, profession or vocation (whether or not while in gainful employment); and
- (*b*) the order is made solely for the purposes of requiring the person making or securing the making of periodical payments fixed by the order to meet some or all of the expenses incurred in connection with the provision of the instruction or training.

(8) This section shall not prevent a court from exercising any power which it has to make a maintenance order in relation to a child if –
- (*a*) a disability living allowance is paid to or in respect of him; or
- (*b*) no such allowance is paid but he is disabled,

and the order is made solely for the purpose of requiring the person making or securing the making of periodical payments fixed by the order to meet some or all of any expenses attributable to the child's disability.

(9) For the purposes of subsection (8), a child is disabled if he is blind, deaf or dumb or is substantially and permanently handicapped by illness, injury, mental disorder or congenital deformity or such other disability as may be prescribed.

(10) This section shall not prevent a court from exercising any power which it has to make a maintenance order in relation to a child if the order is made against a person with care of the child.

(11) In this Act "maintenance order", in relation to any child, means an order which requires the making or securing of periodical payments to or for the benefit of the child and which is made under –
- (*a*) Part II of the Matrimonial Causes Act 1973;
- (*b*) the Domestic Proceedings and Magistrates' Courts Act 1978;
- (*c*) Part III of the Matrimonial and Family Proceedings Act 1984;
- (*d*) the Family Law (Scotland) Act 1985;
- (*e*) Schedule 1 to the Children Act 1989; or
- (*f*) any other prescribed enactment,

and includes any order varying or reviving such an order.

9 Agreements about maintenance

(1) In this section 'maintenance agreement' means any agreement for the making, or for securing the making, of periodical payments by way of maintenance, or in Scotland aliment, to or for the benefit of any child.

(2) Nothing in this Act shall be taken to prevent any person from entering into a maintenance agreement.

(3) The existence of a maintenance agreement shall not prevent any party to the agreement, or any other person, from applying for a maintenance assessment with respect to any child to or for whose benefit periodical payments are to be made or secured under the agreement.

(4) Where any agreement contains a provision which purports to restrict the right of any person to apply for a maintenance assessment, that provision shall be void.

(5) Where section 8 would prevent any court from making a maintenance order in relation to a child and an absent parent of his, no court shall exercise any power that it has to vary any agreement so as –

    (*a*) to insert a provision requiring that absent parent to make or secure the making of periodical payments by way of maintenance, or in Scotland aliment, to or for the benefit of that child; or

    (*b*) to increase the amount payable under such a provision.

10 Relationship between maintenance assessments and certain court orders and related matters

(1) Where an order of a kind prescribed for the purposes of this subsection is in force with respect to any qualifying child with respect to whom a maintenance assessment is made, the order –

    (*a*) shall, so far as it relates to the making or securing of periodical payments, cease to have effect to such extent as may be determined in accordance with regulations made by the Secretary of State; or

    (*b*) where the regulations so provide, shall, so far as it so relates, have effect subject to such modifications as may be so determined.

(2) Where an agreement of a kind prescribed for the purposes of this subsection is in force with respect to any qualifying child with respect to whom a maintenance assessment is made, the agreement –

    (*a*) shall, so far as it relates to the making or securing of periodical payments, be unenforceable to such extent as may be determined in accordance with regulations made by the Secretary of State; or

    (*b*) where the regulations so provide, shall, so far as it so relates, have effect subject to such modifications as may be so determined.

(3) Any regulations under this section may, in particular, make such provision with respect to –

    (*a*) any case where any person with respect to whom an order or agreement of a kind prescribed for the purposes of subsection (1) or (2) has effect applies to the prescribed court, before the end of the prescribed period, for the order or agreement to be varied in the light of the maintenance assessment and of the provisions of this Act;

    (*b*) the recovery of any arrears under the order or agreement which fell due before the coming into force of the maintenance assessment,

as the Secretary of State considers appropriate and may provide that, in prescribed circumstances, an application to any court which is made with respect to an order of a prescribed kind relating to the making or securing of periodical payments to or for the benefit of a child shall be treated by the court as an application for the order to be revoked.

(4) The Secretary of State may by regulations make provision for –

    (*a*) notification to be given by the child support officer concerned to the prescribed person in any case where that officer considers that the making of a maintenance assessment has affected, or is likely to affect, any order of a kind prescribed for the purposes of this subsection;

    (*b*) notification to be given by the prescribed person to the Secretary of State in any case where a court makes an order which it considers has affected, or is likely to affect, a maintenance assessment.

(5) Rules may be made under section 144 of the Magistrates' Courts Act 1980 (rules of procedure) requiring any person who, in prescribed circumstances, makes an application to a magistrates' court for a maintenance order to furnish the court with a statement in a prescribed form, and signed by a child support officer, as to whether or not, at the time when the statement is made, there is a maintenance assessment in force with respect to that person or the child concerned.

    In this subsection –

        'maintenance order' means an order of a prescribed kind for the making or securing of periodical payments to or for the benefit of a child; and

        'prescribed' means prescribed by the rules.

Maintenance assessments

11 Maintenance assessments

(1) Any application for a maintenance assessment made to the Secretary of State shall be referred by him to a child support officer whose duty it shall be to deal with the application in accordance with the provision made by or under this Act.

(2) The amount of child support maintenance to be fixed by any maintenance assessment shall be determined in accordance with the provisions of Part I of Schedule 1.

(3) Part II of Schedule 1 makes further provision with respect to maintenance assessments.

12 Interim maintenance assessments

(1) Where it appears to a child support officer who is required to make a maintenance assessment that he does not have sufficient information to enable him to make an assessment in accordance with the provision made by or under this Act, he may make an interim maintenance assessment.

(2) The Secretary of State may by regulations make provision as to interim maintenance assessments.

(3) The regulations may, in particular, make provision as to –

    (*a*) the procedure to be followed in making an interim maintenance assessment; and

    (*b*) the basis on which the amount of child support maintenance fixed by an interim assessment is to be calculated.

(4) Before making any interim assessment a child support officer shall, if it is reasonably practicable to do so, give written notice of his intention to make such an assessment to –

    (*a*) the absent parent concerned;

    (*b*) the person with care concerned; and

    (*c*) where the application for a maintenance assessment was made under section 7, the child concerned.

(5) Where a child support officer serves notice under subsection (4), he shall not make the proposed interim assessment before the end of such period as may be prescribed.

13   Child support officers

(1) The Secretary of State shall appoint persons (to be known as child support officers) for the purpose of exercising functions –
  (a)   conferred on them by this Act, or by any other enactment; or
  (b)   assigned to them by the Secretary of State.

(2) A child support officer may be appointed to perform only such functions as may be specified in his instrument of appointment.

(3) The Secretary of State shall appoint a Chief Child Support Officer.

(4) It shall be the duty of the Chief Child Support Officer to –
  (a)   advise child support officers on the discharge of their functions in relation to making, reviewing or cancelling maintenance assessments;
  (b)   keep under review the operation of the provision made by or under this Act with respect to making, reviewing or cancelling maintenance assessments; and
  (c)   report to the Secretary of State annually, in writing, on the matters with which the Chief Child Support Officer is concerned.

(5) The Secretary of State shall publish, in such manner as he considers appropriate, any report which he receives under subsection (4)(c).

(6) Any proceedings (other than for an offence) in respect of any act or omission of a child support officer which, apart from this subsection, would fall to be brought against a child support officer resident in Northern Ireland may instead be brought against the Chief Child Support Officer.

(7) For the purposes of any proceedings brought by virtue of subsection (6), the acts or omissions of the child support officer shall be treated as the acts or omissions of the Chief Child Support Officer.

Information

14   Information required by Secretary of State

(1) The Secretary of State may make regulations requiring any information or evidence needed for the determination of any application under this Act, or any question arising in connection with such an application, or needed in connection with the collection or enforcement of child support or other maintenance under this Act, to be furnished –
  (a)   by such persons as may be determined in accordance with regulations made by the Secretary of State; and
  (b)   in accordance with the regulations.

(2) Where the Secretary of State has in his possession any information acquired by him in connection with his functions under any of the benefit Acts, he may –
  (a)   make use of that information for purposes of this Act; or
  (b)   disclose it to the Department of Health and Social Services for Northern Ireland for purposes of any enactment corresponding to this Act and having effect with respect to Northern Ireland.

(3) The Secretary of State may by regulations make provision authorising the disclosure by him or by child support officers, in such circumstances as may be prescribed, of such information held by them for purposes of this Act as may be prescribed.

(4) The provisions of Schedule 2 (which relate to information which is held for purposes other than those of this Act but which is required by the Secretary of State) shall have effect.

15 Powers of inspectors

(1) Where, in a particular case, the Secretary of State considers it appropriate to do so for the purpose of acquiring information which he or any child support officer requires for purposes of this Act, he may appoint a person to act as an inspector under this section.

(2) Every inspector shall be furnished with a certificate of his appointment.

(3) Without prejudice to his being appointed to act in relation to any other case, or being appointed to act for a further period in relation to the case in question, an inspector's appointment shall cease at the end of such period as may be specified.

(4) An inspector shall have power –
    (*a*)   to enter at all reasonable times –
        (i)   any specified premises, other than premises used solely as a dwelling-house; and
        (ii)   any premises which are not specified but which are used by any specified person for the purpose of carrying on any trade, profession, vocation or business; and
    (*b*)   to make such examination and enquiry there as he considers appropriate.

(5) An inspector exercising his powers may question any person aged 18 or over whom he finds on the premises.

(6) If required to do so by an inspector exercising his powers, any person who is or has been –
    (*a*)   an occupier of the premises in question;
    (*b*)   an employer or an employee working at or from those premises;
    (*c*)   carrying on at or from those premises any trade, profession, vocation or business;
    (*d*)   an employee or agent of any person mentioned in paragraphs (*a*) to (*c*),
shall furnish to the inspector all such information and documents as the inspector may reasonably require.

(7) No person shall be required under this section to answer any question or to give any evidence tending to incriminate himself or, in the case of a person who is married, his or her spouse.

(8) On applying for admission to any premises in the exercise of his powers, an inspector shall, if so required, produce his certificate.

(9) If any person –
    (*a*)   intentionally delays or obstructs any inspector exercising his powers; or
    (*b*)   without reasonable excuse, refuses or neglects to answer any question or furnish any information or to produce any document when required to do so under this section,
he shall be guilty of an offence and liable on summary conviction to a fine not exceeding level 3 on the standard scale.

(10) In this section –
    "certificate" means a certificate of appointment issued under this section;
    "inspector" means an inspector appointed under this section;
    "powers" means powers conferred by this section; and
    "specified" means specified in the certificate in question.

Reviews and appeals

16 Periodical reviews

(1) The Secretary of State shall make such arrangements as he considers necessary to secure that, where any maintenance assessment has been in force for a prescribed period, the amount of child support maintenance fixed by that assessment ("the original assessment") is reviewed by a child support officer under this section as soon as is reasonably practicable after the end of that prescribed period.

(2) Before conducting any review under this section, the child support officer concerned shall give, to such persons as may be prescribed, such notice of the proposed review as may be prescribed.

(3) A review shall be conducted under this section as if a fresh application for a maintenance assessment had been made by the person in whose favour the original assessment was made.

(4) On completing any review under this section, the child support officer concerned shall make a fresh maintenance assessment, unless he is satisfied that the original assessment has ceased to have effect or should be brought to an end.

(5) Where a fresh maintenance assessment is made under subsection (4), it shall take effect –

  (*a*) on the day immediately after the end of the prescribed period mentioned in subsection (1); or

  (*b*) in such circumstances as may be prescribed, on such later date as may be determined in accordance with regulations made by the Secretary of State.

(6) The Secretary of State may by regulations prescribe circumstances (for example, where the maintenance assessment is about to terminate) in which a child support officer may decide not to conduct a review under this section.

17   Reviews on change of circumstances

(1) Where a maintenance assessment is in force –

  (*a*) the absent parent or person with care with respect to whom it was made; or

  (*b*) where the application for the assessment was made under section 7, either of them or the child concerned,

may apply to the Secretary of State for the amount of child support maintenance fixed by that assessment ('the original assessment') to be reviewed under this section.

(2) An application under this section may be made only on the ground that, by reason of a change of circumstance since the original assessment was made, the amount of child support maintenance payable by the absent parent would be significantly different if it were to be fixed by a maintenance assessment made by reference to the circumstances of the case as at the date of the application.

(3) The child support officer to whom an application under this section has been referred shall not proceed unless, on the information before him, he considers that it is likely that he will be required by subsection (6) to make a fresh maintenance assessment if he conducts the review applied for.

(4) Before conducting any review under this section, the child support officer concerned shall give to such persons as may be prescribed, such notice of the proposed review as may be prescribed.

(5) A review shall be conducted under this section as if a fresh application for a maintenance assessment had been made by the person in whose favour the original assessment was made.

(6) On completing any review under this section, the child support officer concerned shall make a fresh maintenance assessment, unless –

  (*a*) he is satisfied that the original assessment has ceased to have effect or should be brought to an end; or

  (*b*) the difference between the amount of child support maintenance fixed by the original assessment and the amount that would be fixed if a fresh assessment were to be made as a result of the review is less than such amount as may be prescribed.

18   Reviews of decisions of child support officers

(1) Where –

  (*a*) an application for a maintenance assessment is refused; or

  (*b*) an application, under section 17, for the review of a maintenance assessment which is in force is refused,

the person who made that application may apply to the Secretary of State for the refusal to be reviewed.

(2) Where a maintenance assessment is in force –

  (*a*) the absent parent or person with care with respect to whom it was made; or

  (*b*) where the application for the assessment was made under section 7, either of them or the child concerned,

may apply to the Secretary of State for the assessment to be reviewed.

(3) Where a maintenance assessment is cancelled the appropriate person may apply to the Secretary of State for the cancellation to be reviewed.

(4) Where an application for the cancellation of a maintenance assessment is refused, the appropriate person may apply to the Secretary of State for the refusal to be reviewed.

(5) An application under this section shall give the applicant's reasons (in writing) for making it.

(6) The Secretary of State shall refer to a child support officer any application under this section which is duly made; and the child support officer shall conduct the review applied for unless in his opinion there are no reasonable grounds for supposing that the refusal, assessment or cancellation in question –
  (*a*) was made in ignorance of a material fact;
  (*b*) was based on a mistake as to a material fact;
  (*c*) was wrong in law.

(7) The Secretary of State shall arrange for a review under this section to be conducted by a child support officer who played no part in taking the decision which is to be reviewed.

(8) Before conducting any review under this section, the child support officer concerned shall give to such persons as may be prescribed, such notice of the proposed review as may be prescribed.

(9) If a child support officer conducting a review under this section is satisfied that a maintenance assessment or (as the case may be) a fresh maintenance assessment should be made, he shall proceed accordingly.

(10) In making a maintenance assessment by virtue of subsection (9), a child support officer shall, if he is aware of any material change of circumstance since the decision being reviewed was taken, take account of that change of circumstance in making the assessment.

(11) The Secretary of State may make regulations –
  (*a*) as to the manner in which applications under this section are to be made;
  (*b*) as to the procedure to be followed with respect to such applications; and
  (*c*) with respect to reviews conducted under this section.

(12) In this section "appropriate person" means –
  (*a*) the absent parent or person with care with respect to whom the maintenance assessment in question was, or remains, in force; or
  (*b*) where the application for that assessment was made under section 7, either of those persons or the child concerned.

19 Reviews at instigation of child support officers

(1) Where a child support officer is not conducting a review under section 16, 17 or 18 but is nevertheless satisfied that a maintenance assessment which is in force is defective by reason of –
  (*a*) having been made in ignorance of a material fact;
  (*b*) having been based on a mistake as to a material fact; or
  (*c*) being wrong in law,
he may make a fresh maintenance assessment on the assumption that the person in whose favour the original assessment was made has made a fresh application for a maintenance assessment.

(2) Where a child support officer is not conducting such a review but is nevertheless satisfied that if an application were to be made under section 17 or 18 it would be appropriate to make a fresh maintenance assessment, he may do so.

(3) Before making a fresh maintenance assessment under this section, a child support officer shall give to such persons as may be prescribed such notice of his proposal to make a fresh assessment as may be prescribed.

20 Appeals

(1) Any person who is aggrieved by the decision of a child support officer –
  (*a*) on a review under section 18;

(*b*)   to refuse an application for such a review,

may appeal to a child support appeal tribunal against that decision.

(2) Except with leave of the chairman of a child support appeal tribunal, no appeal under this section shall be brought after the end of the period of 28 days beginning with the date on which notification was given of the decision in question.

(3) Where an appeal under this section is allowed, the tribunal shall remit the case to the Secretary of State, who shall arrange for it to be dealt with by a child support officer.

(4) The tribunal may, in remitting any case under this section, give such directions as it considers appropriate.

21   Child support appeal tribunals

(1) There shall be tribunals to be known as child support appeal tribunals which shall, subject to any order made under section 45, hear and determine appeals under section 20.

(2) The Secretary of State may make such regulations with respect to proceedings before child support appeal tribunals as he considers appropriate.

(3) The regulations may in particular make provision –
   (*a*)   as to procedure;
   (*b*)   for the striking out of appeals for want of prosecution;
   (*c*)   as to the persons entitled to appear and be heard on behalf of any of the parties;
   (*d*)   requiring persons to attend and give evidence or to produce documents;
   (*e*)   about evidence;
   (*f*)   for authorising the administration of oaths;
   (*g*)   as to confidentiality;
   (*h*)   for notification of the result of an appeal to be given to such persons as may be prescribed.

(4) Schedule 3 shall have effect with respect to child support appeal tribunals.

22   Child Support Commissioners

(1) Her Majesty may from time to time appoint a Chief Child Support Commissioner and such number of other Child Support Commissioners as she may think fit.

(2) The Chief Child Support Commissioner and the other Child Support Commissioners shall be appointed from among persons who –
   (*a*)   have a 10 year general qualification; or
   (*b*)   are advocates or solicitors in Scotland of 10 years' standing.

(3) The Lord Chancellor, after consulting the Lord Advocate, may make such regulations with respect to proceedings before Child Support Commissioners as he considers appropriate.

(4) The regulations –
   (*a*)   may, in particular, make any provision of a kind mentioned in section 21(3); and
   (*b*)   shall provide that any hearing before a Child Support Commissioner shall be in public except in so far as the Commissioner for special reasons directs otherwise.

(5) Schedule 4 shall have effect with respect to Child Support Commissioners.

23   Child Support Commissioners for Northern Ireland

(1) Her Majesty may from time to time appoint a Chief Child Support Commissioner for Northern Ireland and such number of other Child Support Commissioners for Northern Ireland as she may think fit.

(2) The Chief Child Support Commissioner for Northern Ireland and the other Child Support Commissioners for Northern Ireland shall be appointed from among persons who are barristers or solicitors of not less than 10 years' standing.

(3) Schedule 4 shall have effect with respect to Child Support Commissioners for Northern Ireland, subject to the modifications set out in paragraph 8.

(4) Subject to any Order made after the passing of this Act by virtue of subsection (1)(*a*) of section 3 of the Northern Ireland Constitution Act 1973, the matters to which this subsection applies shall not be transferred matters for the purposes of that Act but shall for the purposes of subsection (2) of that section be treated as specified in Schedule 3 to that Act.

(5) Subsection (4) applies to all matters relating to Child Support Commissioners, including procedure and appeals, other than those specified in paragraph 9 of Schedule 2 to the Northern Ireland Constitution Act 1973.

24 Appeal to Child Support Commissioner

(1) Any person who is aggrieved by a decision of a child support appeal tribunal, and any child support officer, may appeal to a Child Support Commissioner on a question of law.

(2) Where, on an appeal under this section, a Child Support Commissioner holds that the decision appealed against was wrong in law he shall set it aside.

(3) Where a decision is set aside under subsection (2), the Child Support Commissioner may –
- (*a*) if he can do so without making fresh or further findings of fact, give the decision which he considers should have been given by the child support appeal tribunal;
- (*b*) if he considers it expedient, make such findings and give such decision as he considers appropriate in the light of those findings; or
- (*c*) refer the case, with directions for its determination, to a child support officer or, if he considers it appropriate, to a child support appeal tribunal.

(4) Any reference under subsection (3) to a child support officer shall, subject to any direction of the Child Support Commissioner, be to a child support officer who has taken no part in the decision originally appealed against.

(5) On a reference under subsection (3) to a child support appeal tribunal, the tribunal shall, subject to any direction of the Child Support Commissioner, consist of persons who were not members of the tribunal which gave the decision which has been appealed against.

(6) No appeal lies under this section without the leave –
- (*a*) of the person who was the chairman of the child support appeal tribunal when the decision appealed against was given or of such other chairman of a child support appeal tribunal as may be determined in accordance with regulations made by the Lord Chancellor; or
- (*b*) subject to and in accordance with regulations so made, of a Child Support Commissioner.

(7) The Lord Chancellor may by regulations make provision as to the manner in which, and the time within which, appeals under this section are to be brought and applications for leave under this section are to be made.

(8) Where a question which would otherwise fall to be determined by a child support officer first arises in the course of an appeal to a Child Support Commissioner, he may, if he thinks fit, determine it even though it has not been considered by a child support officer.

(9) Before making any regulations under subsection (6) or (7), the Lord Chancellor shall consult the Lord Advocate.

25 Appeal from Child Support Commissioner on question of law

(1) An appeal on a question of law shall lie to the appropriate court from any decision of a Child Support Commissioner.

(2) No such appeal may be brought except –
  (a)   with leave of the Child Support Commissioner who gave the decision or, where regulations made by the Lord Chancellor so provide, of a Child Support Commissioner selected in accordance with the regulations; or
  (b)   if the Child Support Commissioner refuses leave, with the leave of the appropriate court.

(3) An application for leave to appeal under this section against a decision of a Child Support Commissioner ('the appeal decision') may only be made by –
  (a)   a person who was a party to the proceedings in which the original decision, or appeal decision, was given;
  (b)   the Secretary of State; or
  (c)   any other person who is authorised to do so by regulations made by the Lord Chancellor.

(4) In this section –
"appropriate court" means the Court of Appeal unless in a particular case the Child Support Commissioner to whom the application for leave is made directs that, having regard to the circumstances of the case, and in particular the convenience of the persons who may be parties to the appeal, the appropriate court is the Court of Session; and
"original decision" means the decision to which the appeal decision in question relates.

(5) The Lord Chancellor may by regulations make provision with respect to –
  (a)   the manner in which and the time within which applications must be made to a Child Support Commissioner for leave under this section; and
  (b)   the procedure for dealing with such applications.

(6) Before making any regulations under subsection (2), (3) or (5), the Lord Chancellor shall consult the Lord Advocate.

26   Disputes about parentage

(1) Where a person who is alleged to be a parent of the child with respect to whom an application for a maintenance assessment has been made ('the alleged parent') denies that he is one of the child's parents, the child support officer concerned shall not make a maintenance assessment on the assumption that the alleged parent is one of the child's parents unless the case falls within one of those set out in subsection (2).

(2) The Cases are –

CASE A

Where the alleged parent is a parent of the child in question by virtue of having adopted him.

CASE B

Where the alleged parent is a parent of the child in question by virtue of an order under section 30 of the Human Fertilisation and Embryology Act 1990 (parental orders in favour of gamete donors).

CASE C

Where –
  (a)   either –
        (i)   a declaration that the alleged parent is a parent of the child in question (or a declaration which has that effect) is in force under section 56 of the Family Law Act 1986 (declarations of parentage); or
        (ii)   a declarator by a court in Scotland that the alleged parent is a parent of the child in question (or a declarator which has that effect) is in force; and
  (b)   the child has not subsequently been adopted.

CASE D

Where –
   (*a*)   a declaration to the effect that the alleged parent is one of the parents of the child in question has been made under section 27; and
   (*b*)   the child has not subsequently been adopted.

CASE E

Where –
   (*a*)   the child is habitually resident in Scotland;
   (*b*)   the child support officer is satisfied that one or other of the presumptions set out in section 5(1) of the Law Reform (Parent and Child) (Scotland) Act 1986 applies; and
   (*c*)   the child has not subsequently been adopted.

CASE F

Where –
   (*a*)   the alleged parent has been found, or adjudged, to be the father of the child in question –
      (i)   in proceedings before any court in England and Wales which are relevant proceedings for the purposes of section 12 of the Civil Evidence Act 1968; or
      (ii)   in affiliation proceedings before any court in the United Kingdom,
      (whether or not he offered any defence to the allegation of paternity) and that finding or adjudication still subsists; and
   (*b*)   the child has not subsequently been adopted.

(3) In this section –
   "adopted" means adopted within the meaning of Part IV of the Adoption Act 1976 or, in relation to Scotland, Part IV of the Adoption (Scotland) Act 1978; and
   "affiliation proceedings", in relation to Scotland, means any action of affiliation and aliment.

27   Reference to court for declaration of parentage

(1) Where –
   (*a*)   a child support officer is considering whether to make a maintenance assessment with respect to a person who is alleged to be a parent of the child, or one of the children, in question ("the alleged parent");
   (*b*)   the alleged parent denies that he is one of the child's parents; and
   (*c*)   the child support officer is not satisfied that the case falls within one of those set out in section 26(2),
the Secretary of State or the person with care may apply to the court for a declaration as to whether or not the alleged parent is one of the child's parents.

(2) If, on hearing any application under subsection (1), the court is satisfied that the alleged parent is, or is not, a parent of the child in question it shall make a declaration to that effect.

(3) A declaration under this section shall have effect only for the purposes of this Act.

(4) In this section "court" means, subject to any provision made under Schedule 11 to the Children Act 1989 (jurisdiction of courts with respect to certain proceedings relating to children) the High Court, a county court or a magistrates' court.

(5) In the definition of "relevant proceedings" in section 12(5) of the Civil Evidence Act 1968 (findings of paternity etc. as evidence in civil proceedings) the following paragraph shall be added at the end –
   "(*d*)   section 27 of the Child Support Act 1991."

(6) This section does not apply to Scotland.

28   Power of Secretary of State to initiate or defend actions of declarator: Scotland

(1) Where –
  (a) a child support officer is considering whether to make a maintenance assessment with respect to a person who is alleged to be a parent of the child, or one of the children, in question ("the alleged parent");
  (b) the alleged parent denies that he is a parent of the child in question; and
  (c) the child support officer is not satisfied that the case falls within one of those set out in section 26(2),
the Secretary of State may bring an action for declarator of parentage under section 7 of the Law Reform (Parent and Child) (Scotland) Act 1986.

(2) The Secretary of State may defend an action for declarator of non-parentage or illegitimacy brought by a person named as the alleged parent in an application for a maintenance assessment.

(3) This section applies to Scotland only.

Collection and enforcement

29   Collection of child support maintenance

(1) The Secretary of State may arrange for the collection of any child support maintenance payable in accordance with a maintenance assessment where –
  (a) the assessment is made by virtue of section 6; or
  (b) an application has been made to the Secretary of State under section 4(2) or 7(3) for him to arrange for its collection.

(2) Where a maintenance assessment is made under this Act, payments of child support maintenance under the assessment shall be made in accordance with regulations made by the Secretary of State.

(3) The regulations may, in particular, make provision –
  (a) for payments of child support maintenance to be made –
    (i)   to the person caring for the child or children in question;
    (ii) to, or through, the Secretary of State; or
    (iii) to, or through, such other person as the Secretary of State may, from time to time, specify;
  (b) as to the method by which payments of child support maintenance are to be made;
  (c) as to the intervals at which such payments are to be made;
  (d) as to the method and timing of the transmission of payments which are made, to or through the Secretary of State or any other person, in accordance with the regulations;
  (e) empowering the Secretary of State to direct any person liable to make payments in accordance with the assessment –
    (i) to make them by standing order or by any other method which requires one person to give his authority for payments to be made from an account of his to an account of another's on specific dates during the period for which the authority is in force and without the need for any further authority from him;
    (ii) to open an account from which payments under the assessment may be made in accordance with the method of payment which that person is obliged to adopt;
  (f) providing for the making of representations with respect to matters with which the regulations are concerned.

30   Collection and enforcement of other forms of maintenance

(1) Where the Secretary of State is arranging for the collection of any payments under section 29 or subsection (2), he may also arrange for the collection of any periodical payments, or secured periodical payments, of a prescribed kind which are payable to or for the benefit of any person who falls within a prescribed category.

(2) The Secretary of State may arrange for the collection of any periodical payments or secured periodical payments of a prescribed kind which are payable for the benefit of a child even though he is not arranging for the collection of child support maintenance with respect to that child.

(3) Where –
   (a) the Secretary of State is arranging, under this Act, for the collection of different payments ("the payments") from the same absent parent;
   (b) an amount is collected by the Secretary of State from the absent parent which is less than the total amount due in respect of the payments; and
   (c) the absent parent has not stipulated how that amount is to be allocated by the Secretary of State as between the payments,
the Secretary of State may allocate that amount as he sees fit.

(4) In relation to England and Wales, the Secretary of State may by regulations make provision for sections 29 and 31 to 40 to apply, with such modifications (if any) as he considers necesssary or expedient, for the purpose of enabling him to enforce any obligation to pay any amount which he is authorised to collect under this section.

(5) In relation to Scotland, the Secretary of State may by regulations make provision for the purpose of enabling him to enforce any obligation to pay any amount which he is authorised to collect under this section –
   (a) empowering him to bring any proceedings or take any other steps (other than diligence against earnings) which could have been brought or taken by or on behalf of the person to whom the periodical payments are payable;
   (b) applying sections 29, 31 and 32 with such modifications (if any) as he considers necessary or expedient.

31 Deduction from earnings orders

(1) This section applies where any person ("the liable person") is liable to make payments of child support maintenance.

(2) The Secretary of State may make an order ("a deduction from earnings order") against a liable person to secure the payment of any amount due under the maintenance assessment in question.

(3) A deduction from earnings order may be made so as to secure the payment of –
   (a) arrears of child support maintenance payable under the assessment;
   (b) amounts of child support maintenance which will become due under the assessment; or
   (c) both such arrears and such future amounts.

(4) A deduction from earnings order –
   (a) shall be expressed to be directed at a person ("the employer") who has the liable person in his employment; and
   (b) shall have effect from such date as may be specified in the order.

(5) A deduction from earnings order shall operate as an instruction to the employer to –
   (a) make deductions from the liable person's earnings; and
   (b) pay the amounts deducted to the Secretary of State.

(6) The Secretary of State shall serve a copy of any deduction from earnings order which he makes under this section on –
   (a) the person who appears to the Secretary of State to have the liable person in question in his employment; and
   (b) the liable person.

(7) Where –
   (a) a deduction from earnings order has been made; and
   (b) a copy of the order has been served on the liable person's employer,

it shall be the duty of that employer to comply with the order; but he shall not be under any liability for non-compliance before the end of the period of 7 days beginning with the date on which the copy was served on him.

(8) In this section and in section 32 "earnings" has such meaning as may be prescribed.

32 Regulations about deduction from earnings orders

(1) The Secretary of State may by regulations make provision with respect to deduction from earnings orders.

(2) The regulations may, in particular, make provision –
- (a) as to the circumstances in which one person is to be treated as employed by another;
- (b) requiring any deduction from earnings under an order to be made in the prescribed manner;
- (c) requiring an order to specify the amount or amounts to which the order relates and the amount or amounts which are to be deducted from the liable person's earnings in order to meet his liabilities under the maintenance assessment in question;
- (d) requiring the intervals between deductions to be made under an order to be specified in the order;
- (e) as to the payment of sums deducted under an order to the Secretary of State;
- (f) allowing the person who deducts and pays any amount under an order to deduct from the liable person's earnings a prescribed sum towards his administrative costs;
- (g) with respect to the notification to be given to the liable person of amounts deducted, and amounts paid, under the order;
- (h) requiring any person on whom a copy of an order is served to notify the Secretary of State in the prescribed manner and within a prescribed period if he does not have the liable person in his employment or if the liable person ceases to be in his employment;
- (i) as to the operation of an order where the liable person is in the employment of the Crown;
- (j) for the variation of orders;
- (k) similar to that made by section 31(7), in relation to any variation of an order;
- (l) for an order to lapse when the employer concerned ceases to have the liable person in his employment;
- (m) as to the revival of an order in such circumstances as may be prescribed;
- (n) allowing or requiring an order to be discharged;
- (o) as to the giving of notice by the Secretary of State to the employer concerned that an order has lapsed or has ceased to have effect.

(3) The regulations may include provision that while a deduction from earnings order is in force –
- (a) the liable person shall from time to time notify the Secretary of State, in the prescribed manner and within a prescribed period, of each occasion on which he leaves any employment or becomes employed, or re-employed, and shall include in such a notification a statement of his earnings and expected earnings from the employment concerned and of such other matters as may be prescribed;
- (b) any person who becomes the liable person's employer and knows that the order is in force shall notify the Secretary of State, in the prescribed manner and within a prescribed period, that he is the liable person's employer, and shall include in such a notification a statement of the liable person's earnings and expected earnings from the employment concerned and of such other matters as may be prescribed.

(4) The regulations may include provision with respect to the priority as between a deduction from earnings order and –
- (a) any other deduction from earnings order;
- (b) any order under any other enactment relating to England and Wales which provides for deductions from the liable person's earnings;
- (c) any diligence against earnings.

(5) The regulations may include a provision that a liable person may appeal to a magistrates' court (or in Scotland to the sheriff) if he is aggrieved by the making of a deduction from earnings order against him, or by the terms of any such order, or there is a dispute as to whether payments constitute earnings or as to any other prescribed matter relating to the order.

(6) On an appeal under subsection (5) the court or (as the case may be) the sheriff shall not question the maintenance assessment by reference to which the deduction from earnings order was made.

(7) Regulations made by virtue of subsection (5) may include provision as to the powers of a magistrates' court, or in Scotland of the sheriff, in relation to an appeal (which may include provision as to the quashing of a deduction from earnings order or the variation of the terms of such an order).

(8) If any person fails to comply with the requirements of a deduction from earnings order, or with any regulation under this section which is designated for the purposes of this subsection, he shall be guilty of an offence.

(9) In subsection (8) "designated" means designated by the regulations.

(10) It shall be a defence for a person charged with an offence under subsection (8) to prove that he took all reasonable steps to comply with the requirements in question.

(11) Any person guilty of an offence under subsection (8) shall be liable on summary conviction to a fine not exceeding level two on the standard scale.

33   Liability orders

(1) This section applies where –
   (a)   a person who is liable to make payments of child support maintenance ("the liable person") fails to make one or more of those payments; and
   (b)   it appears to the Secretary of State that –
      (i)   it is inappropriate to make a deduction from earnings order against him (because, for example, he is not employed); or
      (ii)   although such an order has been made against him, it has proved ineffective as a means of securing that payments are made in accordance with the maintenance assessment in question.

(2) The Secretary of State may apply to a magistrates' court or, in Scotland, to the sheriff for an order ("a liability order") against the liable person.

(3) Where the Secretary of State applies for a liability order, the magistrates' court or (as the case may be) sheriff shall make the order if satisfied that the payments in question have become payable by the liable person and have not been paid.

(4) On an application under subsection (2), the court or (as the case may be) the sheriff shall not question the maintenance assessment under which the payments of child support maintenance fell to be made.

34   Regulations about liability orders

(1) The Secretary of State may make regulations in relation to England and Wales –
   (a)   prescribing the procedure to be followed in dealing with an application by the Secretary of State for a liability order;
   (b)   prescribing the form and contents of a liability order; and
   (c)   providing that where a magistrates' court has made a liability order, the person against whom it is made shall, during such time as the amount in respect of which the order was made remains wholly or partly unpaid, be under a duty to supply relevant information to the Secretary of State.

(2) In subsection (1) "relevant information" means any information of a prescribed description which is in the possession of the liable person and which the Secretary of State has asked him to supply.

35   Enforcement of liability orders by distress

(1) Where a liability order has been made against a person ("the liable person"), the Secretary of State may levy the appropriate amount by distress and sale of the liable person's goods.

(2) In subsection (1), "the appropriate amount" means the aggregate of –
   (a)   the amount in respect of which the order was made, to the extent that it remains unpaid; and
   (b)   an amount, determined in such manner as may be prescribed, in respect of the charges connected with the distress.

(3) The Secretary of State may, in exercising his powers under subsection (1) against the liable person's goods, seize –
   (a)   any of the liable person's goods except –
      (i)   such tools, books, vehicles and other items of equipment as are necessary to him for use personally by him in his employment, business or vocation;
      (ii)   such clothing, bedding, furniture, household equipment and provisions as are necessary for satisfying his basic domestic needs; and
   (b)   any money, banknotes, bills of exchange, promissory notes, bonds, specialties or securities for money belonging to the liable person.

(4) For the purposes of subsection (3), the liable person's domestic needs shall be taken to include those of any member of his family with whom he resides.

(5) No person levying a distress under this section shall be taken to be a trespasser –
   (a)   on that account; or
   (b)   from the beginning, on account of any subsequent irregularity in levying the distress.

(6) A person sustaining special damage by reason of any irregularity in levying a distress under this section may recover full satisfaction for the damage (and no more) by proceedings in trespass or otherwise.

(7) The Secretary of State may make regulations supplementing the provisions of this section.

(8) The regulations may, in particular –
   (a)   provide that a distress under this section may be levied anywhere in England and Wales;
   (b)   provide that such a distress shall not be deemed unlawful on account of any defect or want of form in the liability order;
   (c)   provide for an appeal to a magistrates' court by any person aggrieved by the levying of, or an attempt to levy, a distress under this section;
   (d)   make provision as to the powers of the court on an appeal (which may include provision as to the discharge of goods distrained or the payment of compensation in respect of goods distrained and sold).

36   Enforcement in county courts

(1) Where a liability order has been made against a person, the amount in respect of which the order was made, to the extent that it remains unpaid, shall, if a county court so orders, be recoverable by means of garnishee proceedings or a charging order, as if it were payable under a county court order.

(2) In subsection (1) "charging order" has the same meaning as in section 1 of the Charging Orders Act 1979.

37   Regulations about liability orders; Scotland

(1) Section 34(1) does not apply to Scotland.

(2) In Scotland, the Secretary of State may make regulations providing that where the sheriff has made a liability order, the person against whom it is made shall, during such time as the amount in respect of which the order was made remains wholly or partly unpaid, be under a duty to supply relevant information to the Secretary of State.

(3) In this section "relevant information" has the same meaning as in section 34(2).

38   Enforcement of liability orders by diligence: Scotland

(1) In Scotland, where a liability order has been made against a person, the order shall be warrant anywhere in Scotland –
  (a)   for the Secretary of State to charge the person to pay the appropriate amount and to recover that amount by a poinding and sale under Part II of the Debtors (Scotland) Act 1987 and, in connection therewith, for the opening of shut and lockfast places;
  (b)   for an arrestment (other than an arrestment of the person's earnings in the hands of his employers) and action of furthcoming or sale,
and shall be apt to found a Bill of Inhibition or an action of adjudication at the instance of the Secretary of State.

(2) In subsection (1) the "appropriate amount" means the amount in respect of which the order was made, to the extent that it remains unpaid.

39   Liability orders: enforcement throughout United Kingdom

(1) The Secretary of State may by regulations provide for –
  (a)   any liability order made by a court in England and Wales; or
  (b)   any corresponding order made by a court in Northern Ireland,
to be enforced in Scotland as if it had been made by the sheriff.

(2) The power conferred on the Court of Session by section 32 of the Sheriff Courts (Scotland) Act 1971 (power of Court of Session to regulate civil procedure in the sheriff court) shall extend to making provision for the registration in the sheriff court for enforcement of any such order as is referred to in subsection (1).

(3) The Secretary of State may by regulations make provision for, or in connection with, the enforcement in England and Wales of –
  (a)   any liability order made by the sheriff in Scotland; or
  (b)   any corresponding order made by a court in Northern Ireland,
as if it had been made by a magistrates' court in England and Wales.

(4) Regulations under subsection (3) may, in particular, make provision for the registration of any such order as is referred to in that subsection in connection with its enforcement in England and Wales.

40   Commitment to prison

(1) Where the Secretary of State has sought –
  (a)   to levy an amount by distress under this Act; or
  (b)   to recover an amount by virtue of section 36,
and that amount, or any portion of it, remains unpaid he may apply to a magistrates' court for the issue of a warrant committing the liable person to prison.

(2) On any such application the court shall (in the presence of the liable person) inquire as to –
  (a)   the liable person's means; and
  (b)   whether there has been wilful refusal or culpable neglect on his part.

(3) If, but only if, the court is of the opinion that there has been wilful refusal or culpable neglect on the part of the liable person it may –
  (a)   issue a warrant of commitment against him; or

(b)   fix a term of imprisonment and postpone the issue of the warrant until such time and on such conditions (if any) as it thinks just.

(4) Any such warrant –
(a)   shall be made in respect of an amount equal to the aggregate of –
  (i)   the amount mentioned in section 35(1) or so much of it as remains outstanding; and
  (ii) an amount (determined in accordance with regulations made by the Secretary of State) in respect of the costs of commitment; and
(b)   shall state that amount.

(5) No warrant may be issued under this section against a person who is under the age of 18.

(6) A warrant issued under this section shall order the liable person –
(a)   to be imprisoned for a specified period; but
(b)   to be released (unless he is in custody for some other reason) on payment of the amount stated in the warrant.

(7) The maximum period of imprisonment which may be imposed by virtue of subsection (6) shall be calculated in accordance with Schedule 4 to the Magistrates' Courts Act 1980 (maximum periods of imprisonment in default of payment) but shall not exceed six weeks.

(8) The Secretary of State may by regulations make provision for the period of imprisonment specified in any warrant issued under this section to be reduced where there is part payment of the amount in respect of which the warrant was issued.

(9) A warrant issued under this section may be directed to such person or persons as the court issuing it thinks fit.

(10) Section 80 of the Magistrates' Courts Act 1980 (application of money found on defaulter) shall apply in relation to a warrant issued under this section against a liable person as it applies in relation to the enforcement of a sum mentioned in subsection (1) of that section.

(11) The Secretary of State may by regulations make provision –
(a)   as to the form of any warrant issued under this section;
(b)   allowing an application under this section to be renewed where no warrant is issued or term of imprisonment is fixed;
(c)   that a statement in writing to the effect that wages of any amount have been paid to the liable person during any period, purporting to be signed by or on behalf of his employer, shall be evidence of the facts stated;
(d)   that, for the purposes of enabling an inquiry to be made as to the liable person's conduct and means, a justice of the peace may issue a summons to him to appear before a magistrates' court and (if he does not obey) may issue a warrant for his arrest;
(e)   that for the purpose of enabling such an inquiry, a justice of the peace may issue a warrant for the liable person's arrest without issuing a summons;
(f)   as to the execution of a warrant for arrest.

(12) Subsections (1) to (11) do not apply to Scotland.

(13) For the avoidance of doubt, it is declared that a sum payable under a liability order is a sum decerned for aliment for the purposes of the Debtors (Scotland) Act 1880 and the Civil Imprisonment (Scotland) Act 1882.

(14) Where a liability order has been made, the Secretary of State (and he alone) shall be regarded as, and may exercise all the powers of, the creditor for the purposes of section 4 (imprisonment for failure to obey decree for alimentary debt) of the Civil Imprisonment (Scotland) Act 1882.

41   Arrears of child support maintenance

(1) This section applies where –
(a)   the Secretary of State is authorised under section 4, 6 or 7 to recover child support

maintenance payable by an absent parent in accordance with a maintenance assessment; and

(b)   the absent parent has failed to make one or more payments of child support maintenance due from him in accordance with that assessment.

(2) Where the Secretary of State recovers any such arrears he may, in such circumstances as may be prescribed and to such extent as may be prescribed, retain them if he is satisfied that the amount of any benefit paid to the person with care of the child or children in question would have been less had the absent parent not been in arrears with his payments of child support maintenance.

(3) In such circumstances as may be prescribed, the absent parent shall be liable to make such payments of interest with respect to the arrears of child support maintenance as may be prescribed.

(4) The Secretary of State may by regulations make provision –
  (a)   as to the state of interest payable by virtue of subsection (3);
  (b)   as to the time at which, and person to whom, any such interest shall be payable;
  (c)   as to the circumstances in which, in a case where the Secretary of State has been acting under section 6, any such interest may be retained by him;
  (d)   for the Secretary of State, in a case where he has been acting under section 6 and in such circumstances as may be prescribed, to waive any such interest (or part of any such interest).

(5) The provisions of this Act with respect to –
  (a)   the collection of child support maintenance;
  (b)   the enforcement of any obligation to pay child support maintenance,
shall apply equally to interest payable by virtue of this section.

(6) Any sums retained by the Secretary of State by virtue of this section shall be paid by him into the Consolidated Fund.

Special cases

42   Special cases

(1) The Secretary of State may by regulations provide that in prescribed circumstances a case is to be treated as a special case for the purposes of this Act.

(2) Those regulations may, for example, provide for the following to be special cases –
  (a)   each parent of a child is an absent parent in relation to the child;
  (b)   there is more than one person who is a person with care in relation to the same child;
  (c)   there is more than one qualifying child in relation to the same absent parent but the person who is the person with care in relation to one of those children is not the person who is the person with care in relation to all of them;
  (d)   a person is an absent parent in relation to more than one child and the other parent of each of those children is not the same person;
  (e)   the person with care has care of more than one qualifying child and there is more than one absent parent in relation to those children;
  (f)   a qualifying child has his home in two or more separate households.

(3) The Secretary of State may by regulations make provision with respect to special cases.

(4) Regulations made under subsection (3) may, in particular –
  (a)   modify any provision made by or under this Act, in its application to any special case or any special case falling within a prescribed category;
  (b)   make new provision for any such case; or
  (c)   provide for any prescribed provision made by or under this Act not to apply to any such case.

43   Contribution to maintenance by deduction from benefit

(1) This section applies where –
- (a)   by virtue of paragraph 5(4) of Schedule 1, an absent parent is taken for the purposes of that Schedule to have no assessable income; and
- (b)   such conditions as may be prescribed for the purposes of this section are satisfied.

(2) The power of the Secretary of State to make regulations under section 51 of the Social Security Act 1986 by virtue of subsection (*1*)(*r*), (deductions from benefits) may be exercised in relation to cases to which this section applies with a view to securing that –
- (a)   payments of prescribed amounts are made with respect to qualifying children in place of payments of child support maintenance; and
- (b)   arrears of child support maintenance are recovered.

Jurisdiction

44   Jurisdiction

(1) A child support officer shall have jurisdiction to make a maintenance assessment with respect to a person who is –
- (a)   a person with care;
- (b)   an absent parent; or
- (c)   a qualifying child,

only if that person is habitually resident in the United Kingdom.

(2) Where the person with care is not an individual, subsection (1) shall have effect as if paragraph (a) were omitted.

(3) The Secretary of State may by regulations make provision for the cancellation of any maintenance assessment where –
- (a)   the person with care, absent parent or qualifying child with respect to whom it was made ceases to be habitually resident in the United Kingdom;
- (b)   in a case falling within subsection (2), the absent parent or qualifying child with respect to whom it was made ceases to be habitually resident in the United Kingdom; or
- (c)   in such circumstances as may be prescribed, a maintenance order of a prescribed kind is made with respect to any qualifying child with respect to whom the maintenance assessment was made.

45   Jurisdiction of courts in certain proceedings under this Act

(1) The Lord Chancellor or, in relation to Scotland, the Lord Advocate may by order make such provision as he considers necessary to secure that appeals, or such class of appeals as may be specified in the order –
- (a)   shall be made to a court instead of being made to a child support appeal tribunal; or
- (b)   shall be so made in such circumstances as may be so specified.

(2) In subsection (1), "court" means –
- (a)   in relation to England and Wales and subject to any provision made under Schedule 11 to the Children Act 1989 (jurisdiction of courts with respect to certain proceedings relating to children) the High Court, a county court or a magistrates' court; and
- (b)   in relation to Scotland, the Court of Session or the sheriff.

(3) Schedule 11 to the Act of 1989 shall be amended in accordance with subsections (4) and (5).

(4) The following sub-paragraph shall be inserted in paragraph 1, after sub-paragraph (2) –
"(2A) Sub-paragraphs (1) and (2) shall also apply in relation to proceedings –
- (a)   under section 27 of the Child Support Act 1991 (reference to court for declaration of parentage); or
- (b)   which are to be dealt with in accordance with an order made under section 45 of that Act (jurisdiction of courts in certain proceedings under that Act)".

(5) In paragraphs 1(3) and 2(3), the following shall be inserted after "Act 1976" –
"(*bb*) section 20 (appeals) or 27 (reference to court for declaration of parentage) of the Child Support Act 1991;"

(6) Where the effect of any order under subsection (1) is that there are no longer any appeals which fall to be dealt with by child support appeal tribunals, the Lord Chancellor after consultation with the Lord Advocate may by order provide for the abolition of those tribunals.

(7) Any order under subsection (1) or (6) may make –
    (*a*)   such modifications of any provision of this Act or of any other enactment; and
    (*b*)   such transitional provision,
as the Minister making the order considers appropriate in consequence of any provision made by the order.

Miscellaneous and supplemental

46   Failure to comply with obligations imposed by section 6

(1) This section applies where any person ("the parent") –
    (*a*)   fails to comply with a requirement imposed on her by the Secretary of State under section 6(1); or
    (*b*)   fails to comply with any regulation made under section 6(9).

(2) A child support officer may serve written notice on the parent requiring her, before the end of the specified period, either to comply or to give him her reasons for failing to do so.

(3) When the specified period has expired, the child support officer shall consider whether, having regard to any reasons given by the parent, there are reasonable grounds for believing that, if she were to be required to comply, there would be a risk of her or of any children living with her suffering harm or undue distress as a result of complying.

(4) If the child support officer considers that there are such reasonable grounds, he shall –
    (*a*)   take no further action under this section in relation to the failure in question; and
    (*b*)   notify the parent, in writing, accordingly.

(5) If the child support officer considers that there are no such reasonable grounds, he may give a reduced benefit direction with respect to the parent.

(6) Where the child support officer gives a reduced benefit direction he shall send a copy of it to the parent.

(7) Any person who is aggrieved by a decision of a child support officer to give a reduced benefit direction may appeal to a child support appeal tribunal against that decision.

(8) Sections 20(2) to (4) and 21 shall apply in relation to appeals under subsection (7) as they apply in relation to appeals under section 20.

(9) A reduced benefit direction shall take effect on such date as may be specified in the direction.

(10) Reasons given in response to a notice under subsection (2) may be given either in writing or orally.

(11) In this section –
"comply" means to comply with the requirement or with the regulation in question; and "complied" and "complying" shall be construed accordingly;
"reduced benefit direction" means a direction, binding on the adjudication officer, that the amount payable by way of any relevant benefit to, or in respect of, the parent concerned be reduced by such amount, and for such period, as may be prescribed;
"relevant benefit" means income support, family credit or any other benefit of a kind prescribed for the purposes of section 6; and
"specified", in relation to any notice served under this section, means specified in the notice; and

the period to be specified shall be determined in accordance with regulations made by the Secretary of State.

47 Fees

(1) The Secretary of State may by regulations provide for the payment, by the absent parent or the person with care (or by both), of such fees as may be prescribed in cases where the Secretary of State takes any action under section 4 or 6.

(2) The Secretary of State may by regulations provide for the payment, by the absent parent, the person with care or the child concerned (or by any or all of them), of such fees as may be prescribed in cases where the Secretary of State takes any action under section 7.

(3) Regulations made under this section –
  (a) may require any information which is needed for the purpose of determining the amount of any such fee to be furnished, in accordance with the regulations, by such person as may be prescribed;
  (b) shall provide that no such fees shall be payable by any person to or in respect of whom income support, family credit or any other benefit of a prescribed kind is paid; and
  (c) may, in particular, make provision with respect to the recovery by the Secretary of State of any fees payable under the regulations.

48 Right of audience

(1) Any person authorised by the Secretary of State for the purposes of this section shall have, in relation to any proceedings under this Act before a magistrates' court, a right of audience and the right to conduct litigation.

(2) In this section "right of audience" and "right to conduct litigation" have the same meaning as in section 119 of the Courts and Legal Services Act 1990.

49 Right of audience: Scotland

In relation to any proceedings before the sheriff under any provision of this Act, the power conferred on the Court of Session by section 32 of the Sheriff Courts (Scotland) Act 1971 (power of Court of Session to regulate civil procedure in sheriff court) shall extend to the making of rules permitting a party to such proceedings, in such circumstances as may be specified in the rules, to be represented by a person who is neither an advocate nor a solicitor.

50 Unauthorised disclosure of information

(1) Any person who is, or has been, employed in employment to which this section applies is guilty of an offence if, without lawful authority, he discloses any information which –
  (a) was acquired by him in the course of that employment; and
  (b) relates to a particular person.

(2) It is not an offence under this section –
  (a) to disclose information in the form of a summary or collection of information so framed as not to enable information relating to any particular person to be ascertained from it; or
  (b) to disclose information which has previously been disclosed to the public with lawful authority.

(3) It is a defence for a person charged with an offence under this section to prove that at the time of the alleged offence –
  (a) he believed that he was making the disclosure in question with lawful authority and had no reasonable cause to believe otherwise; or
  (b) he believed that the information in question had previously been disclosed to the public with lawful authority and had no reasonable cause to believe otherwise.

(4) A person guilty of an offence under this section shall be liable –

(*a*) on conviction on indictment, to imprisonment for a term not exceeding two years or a fine or both; or

(*b*) on summary conviction, to imprisonment for a term not exceeding six months or a fine not exceeding the statutory maximum or both.

(5) This section applies to employment as –

(*a*) the Chief Child Support Officer;

(*b*) any other child support officer;

(*c*) any clerk to, or other officer of, a child support appeal tribunal;

(*d*) any member of the staff of such a tribunal;

(*e*) a civil servant in connection with the carrying out of any functions under this Act.

and to employment of any other kind which is prescribed for the purposes of this section.

(6) For the purposes of this section a disclosure is to be regarded as made with lawful authority if, and only if, it is made –

(*a*) by a civil servant in accordance with his official duty; or

(*b*) by any other person either –

(i) for the purposes of the function in the exercise of which he holds the information and without contravening any restriction duly imposed by the responsible person; or

(ii) to, or in accordance with an authorisation duly given by the responsible person;

(*c*) in accordance with any enactment or order of a court;

(*d*) for the purpose of instituting, or otherwise for the purposes of, any proceedings before a court or before any tribunal or other body or person mentioned in this Act; or

(*e*) with the consent of the appropriate person.

(7) "The responsible person" means –

(*a*) the Lord Chancellor;

(*b*) the Secretary of State;

(*c*) any person authorised by the Lord Chancellor, or Secretary of State, for the purposes of this subsection; or

(*d*) any other prescribed person, or person falling within a prescribed category.

(8) "The appropriate person" means the person to whom the information in question relates, except that if the affairs of that person are being dealt with –

(*a*) under a power of attorney;

(*b*) by a receiver appointed under section 99 of the Mental Health Act 1983;

(*c*) by a Scottish mental health custodian, that is to say –

(i) a curator bonis, tutor or judicial factor; or

(ii) the managers of a hospital acting on behalf of that person under section 94 of the Mental Health (Scotland) Act 1984; or

(*d*) by a mental health appointee, that is to say –

(i) a person directed or authorised as mentioned in sub-paragraph (*a*) of rule 41(1) of the Court of Protection Rules 1984; or

(ii) a receiver ad interim appointed under sub-paragraph (*b*) of that rule;

the appropriate person is the attorney, receiver, custodian or appointee (as the case may be) or, in a case falling within paragraph (*a*), the person to whom the information relates.

51 Supplementary powers to make regulations

(1) The Secretary of State may by regulations make such incidental, supplemental and transitional provision as he considers appropriate in connection with any provision made by or under this Act.

(2) The regulations may, in particular, make provision –

(*a*) as to the procedure to be followed with respect to –

(i) the making of applications for maintenance assessments;

(ii) the making, cancellation or refusal to make maintenance assessments;

(iii) reviews under sections 16 to 19;

(*b*) extending the categories of case to which section 18 or 19 applies;

(c)   as to the date on which an application for a maintenance assessment is to be treated as having been made;

(d)   for attributing payments made under maintenance assessments to the payment of arrears;

(e)   for the adjustment, for the purpose of taking account of the retrospective effect of a maintenance assessment, of amounts payable under the assessment;

(f)   for the adjustment, for the purpose of taking account of over-payments or under-payments of child support maintenance, of amounts payable under a maintenance assessment;

(g)   as to the evidence which is to be required in connection with such matters as may be prescribed;

(h)   as to the circumstances in which any official record or certificate is to be conclusive (or in Scotland, sufficient) evidence;

(i)   with respect to the giving of notices or other documents;

(j)   for the rounding up or down of any amounts calculated, estimated or otherwise arrived at in applying any provision made by or under this Act.

(3) No power to make regulations conferred by any other provision of this Act shall be taken to limit the powers given to the Secretary of State by this section.

52   Regulations and orders

(1) Any power conferred on the Lord Chancellor, the Lord Advocate or the Secretary of State by this Act to make regulations or orders (other than a deduction from earnings order) shall be exercisable by statutory instrument.

(2) No statutory instrument containing (whether alone or with other provisions) regulations made under section 4(7), 5(3), 6(1), (9) or (10), 7(8), 12(2), 41(2), (3) or (4), 42, 43(1), 46 or 47 or under Part I of Schedule 1, or an order made under section 45(1) or (6), shall be made unless a draft of this instrument has been laid before Parliament and approved by a resolution of each House of Parliament.

(3) Any other statutory instrument made under this Act (except an order made under section 58(2)) shall be subject to annulment in pursuance of a resolution of either House of Parliament.

(4) Any power of a kind mentioned in subsection (1) may be exercised –
    (a)   in relation to all cases to which it extends, in relation to those cases but subject to specified exceptions or in relation to any specified cases or classes of case;
    (b)   so as to make, as respects the cases in relation to which it is exercised –
        (i)   the full provision to which it extends or any lesser provision (whether by way of exception or otherwise);
        (ii)   the same provision for all cases, different provision for different cases or classes of case or different provision as respects the same case or class of case but for different purposes of this Act;
        (iii)   provision which is either unconditional or is subject to any specified condition;
    (c)   so to provide for a person to exercise a discretion in dealing with any matter.

53   Financial provisions

Any expenses of the Lord Chancellor or the Secretary of State under this Act shall be payable out of money provided by Parliament.

54   Interpretation

In this Act –
    "absent parent", has the meaning given in section 3(2);
    "adjudication officer" has the same meaning as in the benefit Acts;
    "assessable income" has the meaning given in paragraph 5 of Schedule 1;
    "benefit Acts" means the Social Security Acts 1975 to 1991;
    "Chief Adjudication Officer" has the same meaning as in the benefit Acts;

"Chief Child Support Officer" has the meaning given in section 13;

"child benefit" has the same meaning as in the Child Benefit Act 1975;

"child support appeal tribunal" means a tribunal appointed under section 21;

"child support maintenance" has the meaning given in section 3(6);

"child support officer" has the meaning given in section 13;

"deduction from earnings order" has the meaning given in section 31(2);

"disability living allowance" has the same meaning as in the Social Security Act 1975;

"family credit" has the same meaning as in the benefit Acts;

"general qualification" shall be construed in accordance with section 71 of the Courts and Legal Services Act 1990 (qualification for judicial appointments);

"income support" has the same meaning as in the benefit Acts;

"interim maintenance assessment" has the meaning given in section 12;

"liability order" has the meaning given in section 33(2);

"maintenance agreement" has the meaning given in section 9(1);

"maintenance assessment" means an assessment of maintenance made under this Act and, except in prescribed circumstances, includes an interim maintenance assessment;

"maintenance order" has the meaning given in section 8(11);

"maintenance requirement" means the amount calculated in accordance with paragraph 1 of Schedule 1;

"parent", in relation to any child, means any person who is in law the mother or father of the child;

"parental responsibility" has the same meaning as in the Children Act 1989;

"parental rights" has the same meaning as in the Law Reform (Parent and Child) (Scotland) Act 1986;

"person with care" has the meaning given in section 3(3);

"prescribed" means prescribed by regulations made by the Secretary of State;

"qualifying child" has the meaning given in section 3(1);

55 Meaning of "child"

(1) For the purposes of this Act a person is a child if –
 (a) he is under the age of 16;
 (b) he is under the age of 19 and receiving full-time education (which is not advanced education) –
  (i) by attendance at a recognised educational establishment; or
  (ii) elsewhere, if the education is recognised by the Secretary of State; or
 (c) he does not fall within paragraph (a) or (b) but –
  (i) he is under the age of 18, and
  (ii) prescribed conditions are satisfied with respect to him.

(2) A person is not a child for the purposes of this Act if he –
 (a) is or has been married;
 (b) has celebrated a marriage which is void; or
 (c) has celebrated a marriage in respect of which a decree of nullity has been granted.

(3) In this section –
 "advanced education" means education of a prescribed description; and
 "recognised educational establishment" means an establishment recognised by the Secretary of State for the purposes of this section as being, or as comparable to, a university, college or school.

(4) Where a person has reached the age of 16, the Secretary of State may recognise education provided for him otherwise than at a recognised educational establishment only if the Secretary of State is satisfied that education was being so provided for him immediately before he reached the age of 16.

(5) The Secretary of State may provide that in prescribed circumstances education is or is not to be treated for the purposes of this section as being full-time.

(6) In determining whether a person falls within subsection (1)(*b*), no account shall be taken of such interruptions in his education as may be prescribed.

(7) The Secretary of State may by regulations provide that a person who ceases to fall within subsection (1) shall be treated as continuing to fall within that subsection for a prescribed period.

(8) No person shall be treated as continuing to fall within subsection (1) by virtue of regulations made under subsection (7) after the end of the week in which he reaches the age of 19.

56   Corresponding provision for and co-ordination with Northern Ireland

(1) An Order in Council made under paragraph 1(1)(b) of Schedule 1 to the Northern Ireland Act 1974 which contains a statement that it is made only for purposes corresponding to those of the provisions of this Act, other than provisions which relate to the appointment of Child Support Commissioners for Northern Ireland –
- (*a*)   shall not be subject to sub-paragraphs (4) and (5) of paragraph 1 of that Schedule (affirmative resolution of both Houses of Parliament); but
- (*b*)   shall be subject to annulment in pursuance of a resolution of either House of Parliament.

(2) The Secretary of State may make arrangements with the Department of Health and Social Services for Northern Ireland with a view to securing, to the extent allowed for in the arrangements, that –
- (*a*)   the provision made by or under this Act ("the provision made for Great Britain"); and
- (*b*)   the provision made by or under any corresponding enactment having effect with respect to Northern Ireland ("the provision made for Northern Ireland"),
provide for a single system within the United Kingdom.

(3) The Secretary of State may make regulations for giving effect to any such arrangements.

(4) The regulations may, in particular –
- (*a*)   adapt legislation (including subordinate legislation) for the time being in force in Great Britain so as to secure its reciprocal operation with the provision made for Northern Ireland; and
- (*b*)   make provision to secure that acts, omissions and events which have any effect for the purposes of the provision made for Northern Ireland have a corresponding effect for the purposes of the provision made for Great Britain.

57   Application to Crown

(1) The power of the Secretary of State to make regulations under section 14 requiring prescribed persons to furnish information may be excercised so as to require information to be furnished by persons employed in the service of the crown or otherwise in the discharge of Crown functions.

(2) In such circumstances, and subject to such conditions, as may be prescribed, an inspector appointed under section 15 may enter any Crown premises for the purpose of exercising any powers conferred on him by that section.

(3) Where such an inspector duly enters any Crown premises for those purposes, section 15 shall apply in relation to persons employed in the service of the Crown or otherwise in the discharge of Crown functions as it applies in relation to other persons.

(4) Where a liable person is in the employment of the Crown, a deduction from earnings order may be made under section 31 in relation to that person; but in such a case subsection (8) of section 32 shall apply only in relation to the failure of that person to comply with any requirement imposed on him by regulations made under section 32.

58   Short title, commencement and extent, etc.

(1) This Act may be cited as the Child Support Act 1991.

(2) Section 56(1) and subsections (1) to (11) and (14) of this section shall come into force on the passing of this Act but otherwise this Act shall come into force on such date as may be appointed by order made by the Lord Chancellor, the Secretary of State or Lord Advocate, or by any of them acting jointly.

(3) Different dates may be appointed for different provisions of this Act and for different purposes (including, in particular, for different cases or categories of case).

(4) An order under subsection (2) may make such supplemental, incidental or transitional provision as appears to the person making the order to be necessary or expedient in connection with the provisions brought into force by the order, including such adaptations or modifications of –
- (a) the provisions so brought into force;
- (b) any provisions of this Act then in force; or
- (c) any provision of any other enactment,

as appear to him to be necessary or expedient.

(5) Different provision may be made by virtue of subsection (4) with respect to different periods.

(6) Any provision made by virtue of subsection (4) may, in particular, include provision for –
- (a) the enforcement of a maintenance assessment (including the collection of sums payable under the assessment) as if the assessment were a court order of a prescribed kind;
- (b) the registration of maintenance assessments with the appropriate court in connection with any provision of a kind mentioned in paragraph (a);
- (c) the variation, on application made to a court, of the provisions of a maintenance assessment relating to the method of making payments fixed by the assessment or the intervals at which such payments are to be made;
- (d) a maintenance assessment, or an order of a prescribed kind relating to one or more children, to be deemed, in prescribed circumstances, to have been validly made for all purposes or for such purposes as may be prescribed.

In paragraph (c) "court" includes a single justice.

(7) The Lord Chancellor, the Secretary of State or the Lord Advocate may by order make such amendments or repeals in, or such modifications of, such enactments as may be specified in the order, as appear to him to be necessary or expedient in consequence of any provision made by or under this Act (including any provision made by virtue of subsection (4)).

(8) This Act shall, in its application to the Isles of Scilly, have effect subject to such exceptions, adaptations and modifications as the Secretary of State may by order prescribe.

(9) Sections 27, 35 and 48 and paragraph 7 of Schedule 5 do not extend to Scotland.

(10) Sections 7, 28 and 49 extend only to Scotland.

(11) With the exception of sections 23 and 56(1), subsections (1) to (3) of this section and Schedules 2 and 4, and (in so far as it amends any enactment extending to Northern Ireland) Schedule 5, this Act does not extend to Northern Ireland.

(12) Until Schedule 1 to the Disability Living Allowance and Disability Working Allowance Act 1991 comes into force, paragraph 1(1) of Schedule 3 shall have effect with the omission of the words "and disability appeal tribunals" and the insertion, after "social security appeal tribunals", of the word "and".

(13) The consequential amendments set out in Schedule 5 shall have effect.

(14) In Schedule 1 to the Children Act 1989 (financial provision for children), paragraph 2(6)(b) (which is spent) is hereby repealed.

Schedules

MAINTENANCE ASSESSMENTS

PART I

CALCULATION OF CHILD SUPPORT MAINTENANCE

The maintenance requirement

1.—(1) In this Schedule "the maintenance requirement" means the amount, calculated in accordance with the formula set out in sub-paragraph (2), which is to be taken as the minimum amount necessary for the maintenance of the qualifying child or, where there is more than one qualifying child, all of them.

(2) The formula is –

$$MR = AG - CB$$

where –

MR is the amount of the maintenance requirement;

AG is the aggregate of the amounts to be taken into account under sub-paragraph (3); and

CB is the amount payable by way of child benefit (or which would be so payable if the person with care of the qualifying child were an individual) or, where there is more than one qualifying child, the aggregate of the amounts so payable with respect to each of them.

(3) The amounts to be taken into account for the purpose of calculating AG are –

 (*a*) such amount or amounts (if any), with respect to each qualifying child, as may be prescribed;

 (*b*) such amount or amounts (if any), with respect to the person with care of the qualifying child or qualifying children, as may be prescribed; and

 (*c*) such further amount or amounts (if any) as may be prescribed.

(4) For the purposes of calculating CB it shall be assumed that child benefit is payable with respect to any qualifying child at the basic rate.

(5) In sub-paragraph (4) "basic rate" has the meaning for the time being prescribed.

The general rule

2.—(1) In order to determine the amount of any maintenance assessment, first rcalculate –

$$(A + C) \times P$$

where –

A is the absent parent's assessable income;

C is the assessable income of the other parent, where that parent is the person with care, and otherwise has such value (if any) as may be prescribed; and

P is such number greater than zero but less than 1 as may be prescribed.

(2) Where the result of the calculation made under sub-paragraph (1) is an amount which is equal to, or less than, the amount of the maintenance requirement for the qualifying child or qualifying children, the amount of maintenance payable by the absent parent for that child or those children shall be an amount equal to –

$$A \times P$$

where A and P have the same values as in the calculation made under sub-paragraph (1).

(3) Where the result of the calculation made under sub-paragraph (1) is an amount which exceeds the amount of the maintenance requirement for the qualifying child or qualifying children, the amount of maintenance payable by the absent parent for that child or those children shall consist of –

(*a*)   a basic element calculated in accordance with the provisions of paragraph 3; and

(*b*)   an additional element calculated in accordance with the provisions of paragraph 4.

The basic element

3.—(1) The basic element shall be calculated by applying the formula –

$$BE = A \times G \times P$$

where –

BE is the amount of the basic element;

A and P have the same values as in the calculation made under paragraph 2(1); and

G has the value determined under sub-paragraph (2).

(2) The value of G shall be determined by applying the formula –

$$G = \frac{MR}{(A + C) \times P}$$

where –

MR is the amount of the maintenance requirement for the qualifying child or qualifying children; and

A, C and P have the same values as in the calculation made under paragraph 2(1).

The additional element

4.—(1) Subject to sub-paragraph (2), the additional element shall be calculated by applying the formula –

$$AE = (1 - G) \times A \times R$$

where –

AE is the amount of the additional element;

A has the same value as in the calculation made under paragraph 2(1);

G has the value determined under paragraph 3(2); and

R is such number greater than zero but less than 1 as may be prescribed.

(2) Where applying the alternative formula set out in sub-paragraph (3) would result in a lower amount for the additional element, that formula shall be applied in place of the formula set out in sub-paragraph (1).

(3) The alternative formula is –

$$AE = Z \times Q \times \frac{A}{A + C}$$

where –

A and C have the same values as in the calculation made under paragraph 2(1);

Z is such number as may be prescribed; and

Q is the aggregate of –

(*a*)   any amount taken into account by virtue of paragraph 1(3)(*a*) in calculating the maintenance requirement; and

(*b*)   any amount which is both taken into account by virtue of paragraph 1(3)(*c*) in making that calculation and is an amount prescribed for the purposes of this paragraph.

Assessable income

5.—(1) The assessable income of an absent parent shall be calculated by applying the formula –

$$A = N - E$$

where –
  A is the amount of that parent's assessable income;
  N is the amount of that parent's net income, calculated or estimated in accordance with
     regulations made by the Secretary of State for the purposes of this sub-paragraph; and
  E is the amount of that parent's exempt income, calculated or estimated in accordance with
     regulations made by the Secretary of State for those purposes.

(2) The assessable income of a parent who is a person with care of the qualifying child or children
shall be calculated by applying the formula –

$$C = M - F$$

where –
  C is the amount of that parent's assessable income;
  M is the amount of that parent's net income, calculated or estimated in accordance with
     regulations made by the Secretary of State for the purposes of this sub-paragraph; and
  F is the amount of that parent's exempt income, calculated or estimated in accordance with
     regulations made by the Secretary of State for those purposes.

(3) Where the preceding provisions of this paragraph would otherwise result in a person's
assessable income being taken to be a negative amount his assessable income shall be taken to be
nil.

(4) Where income support or any other benefit of a prescribed kind is paid to or in respect of a
parent who is an absent parent or a person with care that parent shall, for the purposes of this
Schedule, be taken to have no assessable income.

Protected income

6.—(1) This paragraph applies where –
  (*a*) one or more maintenance assessments have been made with respect to an absent parent;
        and
  (*b*) payment by him of the amount, or the aggregate of the amounts, so assessed would
        otherwise reduce his disposable income below his protected income level.

(2) The amount of the assessment, or (as the case may be) of each assessment, shall be adjusted in
accordance with such provisions as may be prescribed with a view to securing so far as is reasonably
practicable that payment by the absent parent of the amount, or (as the case may be) aggregate of
the amounts, so assessed will not reduce his disposable income below his protected income level.

(3) Regulations made under sub-paragraph (2) shall secure that, where the prescribed minimum
amount fixed by regulations made under paragraph 7 applies, no maintenance assessment is
adjusted so as to provide for the amount payable by an absent parent in accordance with that
assessment to be less than that amount.

(4) The amount which is to be taken for the purposes of this paragaph as an absent parent's
disposable income shall be calculated, or estimated, in accordance with regulations made by the
Secretary of State.

(5) Regulations made under sub-paragraph (4) may, in particular, provide that, in such circumstances and to such extent as may be prescribed –
  (*a*) income of any child who is living in the same household with the absent parent; and
  (*b*) where the absent parent is living together in the same household with another adult of the
        opposite sex (regardless of whether or not they are married), income of that other adult,
is to be treated as the absent parent's income for the purposes of calculating his disposable income.

(6) In this paragraph the "protected income level" of a particular absent parent means an amount
of income calculated, by reference to the circumstances of that parent, in accordance with
regulations made by the Secretary of State.

The minimum amount of child support maintenance

7.—(1) The Secretary of State may prescribe a minimum amount for the purposes of this paragraph.

(2) Where the amount of child support maintenance which would be fixed by a maintenance assessment but for this paragraph is nil, or less than the prescribed minimum amount, the amount to be fixed by the assessment shall be the prescribed minimum amount.

(3) In any case to which section 43 applies, and in such other cases (if any) as may be prescribed, sub-paragraph (2) shall not apply.

Housing costs

8.— Where regulations under this Schedule require a child support officer to take account of the housing costs of any person in calculating, or estimating, his assessable income or disposable income, those regulations may make pro vision –
  (*a*)   as to the costs which are to be treated as housing costs for the purpose of the regulations;
  (*b*)   for the apportionment of housing costs; and
  (*c*)   for the amount of housing costs to be taken into account for prescribed purposes not to exceed such amount (if any) as may be prescribed by, or determined in accordance with, the regulations.

Regulations about income and capital

9.— The Secretary of State may by regulations provide that, in such circumstances and to such extent as may be prescribed –
  (*a*)   income of a child shall be treated as income of a parent of his;
  (*b*)   where the child support officer concerned is satisfied that a person has intentionally deprived himself of a source of income with a view to reducing the amount of his assessable income, his net income shall be taken to include income from that source of an amount estimated by the child support officer;
  (*c*)   a person is to be treated as possessing capital or income which he does not possess;
  (*d*)   capital or income which a person does possess is to be disregarded;
  (*e*)   income is to be treated as capital;
  (*f*)   capital is to be treated as income.

References to qualifying children

10.— References in this Part of this Schedule to "qualifying children" are to those qualifying children with respect to whom the maintenance assessment falls to be made.

PART II
GENERAL PROVISIONS ABOUT MAINTENANCE ASSESSMENTS

Effective date of assessment

11.—(1) A maintenance assessment shall take effect on such date as may be determined in accordance with regulations made by the Secretary of State.

(2) That date may be earlier than the date on which the assessment is made.

Form of assessment

12.— Every maintenance assessment shall be made in such form and contain such information as the Secretary of State may direct.

Assessments where amount of child support is nil

13.— A child support officer shall not decline to make a maintenance assessment only on the ground that the amount of the assessment is nil.

Consolidated applications and assessments

14.— The Secretary of State may by regulations provide –
- (*a*) for two or more applications for maintenance assessments to be treated, in prescribed circumstances, as a single application; and
- (*b*) for the replacement, in prescribed circumstances, of a maintenance assessment made on the application of one person by a later maintenance assessment made on the application of that or any other person.

Separate assessments for different periods

15.— Where a child support officer is satisfied that the circumstances of a case require different amounts of child support maintenance to be assessed in respect of different periods, he may make separate maintenance assessments each expressed to have effect in relation to a different specified period.

Termination of assessments

16.—(1) A maintenance assessment shall cease to have effect –
- (*a*) on the death of the absent parent, or of the person with care, with respect to whom it was made;
- (*b*) on there no longer being any qualifying child with respect to whom it would have effect;
- (*c*) on the absent parent with respect to whom it was made ceasing to be a parent of –
    - (i) the qualifying child with respect to whom it was made; or
    - (ii) where it was made with respect to more than one qualifying child, all of the qualifying children with respect to whom it was made;
- (*d*) where the absent parent and the person with care with respect to whom it was made have been living together for a continuous period of six months;
- (*e*) where a new maintenance assessment is made with respect to any qualifying child with respect to whom the assessment in question was in force immediately before the making of the new assessment.

(2) A maintenance assessment made in response to an application under section 4 or 7 shall be cancelled by a child support officer if the person on whose application the assessment was made asks him to do so.

(3) A maintenance assessment made in response to an application under section 6 shall be cancelled by a child support officer if –
- (*a*) the person on whose application the assessment was made ("the applicant") asks him to do so; and
- (*b*) he is satisfied that the applicant has ceased to fall within subsection (1) of that section.

(4) Where a child support officer is satisfied that the person with care with respect to whom a maintenance assessment was made has ceased to be a person with care in relation to the qualifying child, or any of the qualifying children, with respect to whom the assessment was made, he may cancel the assessment with effect from the date on which, in his opinion, the change of circumstances took place.

(5) Where –
- (*a*) at any time a maintenance assessment is in force but a child support officer would no longer have jurisdiction to make it if it were to be applied for at that time; and
- (*b*) the assessment has not been cancelled, or has not ceased to have effect, under or by virtue of any other provision made by or under this Act,

it shall be taken to have continuing effect unless cancelled by a child support officer in accordance with such prescribed provision (including provision as to the effective date of cancellation) as the Secretary of State considers it appropriate to make.

(6) Where both the absent parent and the person with care with respect to whom a maintenance assessment was made request a child support officer to cancel the assessment, he may do so if he is satisfied that they are living together.

(7) Any cancellation of a maintenance assessment under sub-paragraph (5) or (6) shall have effect from such date as may be determined by the child support officer.

(8) Where a child support officer cancels a maintenance assessment, he shall immediately notify the absent parent and person with care, so far as that is reasonably practicable.

(9) Any notice under sub-paragraph (8) shall specify the date with effect from which the cancellation took effect.

(10) A person with care with respect to whom a maintenance assessment is in force shall provide the Secretary of State with such information, in such circumstances, as may be prescribed, with a view to assisting the Secretary of State or a child support officer in determining whether the assessment has ceased to have effect, or should be cancelled.

(11) The Secretary of State may by regulations make such supplemental, incidental or transitional provision as he thinks necessary or expedient in consequence of the provisions of this paragraph.

SCHEDULE 2

Provision of Information to Secretary of State

Inland Revenue records

1.—(1) This paragraph applies where the Secretary of State or the Department of Health and Social Services for Northern Ireland requires information for the purpose of tracing –
    (*a*)   the current address of an absent parent; or
    (*b*)   the current employer of an absent parent.

(2) In such a case, no obligation as to secrecy imposed by statute or otherwise on a person employed in relation to the Inland Revenue shall prevent any information obtained or held in connection with the assessment or collection of income tax from being disclosed to –
    (*a*)   the Secretary of State;
    (*b*)   the Department of Health and Social Services for Northern Ireland; or
    (*c*)   an officer of either of them authorised to receive such information in connection with the operation of this Act or of any corresponding Northern Ireland legislation.

(3) This paragraph extends only to disclosure by or under the authority of the Commissioners of Inland Revenue.

(4) Information which is the subject of disclosure to any person by virtue of this paragraph shall not be further disclosed to any person except where the further disclosure is made –
    (*a*)   to a person to whom disclosure could be made by virtue of sub-paragraph (2); or
    (*b*)   for the purposes of any proceedings (civil or criminal) in connection with the operation of this Act or of any corresponding Northern Ireland legislation.

Local authority records

2.—(1) This paragraph applies where –
    (*a*)   the Secretary of State requires relevant information in connection with the discharge by him, or by any child support officer, of functions under this Act, or
    (*b*)   the Department of Health and Social Services for Northern Ireland requires relevant information in connection with the discharge of any functions under any corresponding Northern Ireland legislation.

(2) The Secretary of State may give a direction to the appropriate authority requiring them to give him such relevant information in connection with any housing benefit or community charge benefit to which an absent parent or person with care is entitled as the Secretary of State considers necessary in connection with his determination of –

(a) that person's income of any kind;

(b) the amount of housing costs to be taken into account in determining that person's income of any kind; or

(c) the amount of that person's protected income.

(3) The Secretary of State may give a similar direction for the purposes of enabling the Department of Health and Social Services for Northern Ireland to obtain such information for the purposes of any corresponding Northern Ireland legislation.

(4) In this paragraph –

"appropriate authority" means –

(a) in relation to housing benefit, the housing or local authority concerned; and

(b) in relation to community charge benefit, the charging authority or, in Scotland, the levying authority; and

"relevant information" means information of such a description as may be prescribed.

SCHEDULE 3

Child Support Appeal Tribunals

The President

1.—(1) The person appointed under Schedule 10 to the Social Security Act 1975 as President of the social security appeal tribunals, medical appeal tribunals and disability appeal tribunals shall, by virtue of that appointment, also be President of the child support appeal tribunals.

(2) It shall be the duty of the President to arrange such meetings of the chairmen and members of child support appeal tribunals, and such training for them, as he considers appropriate.

(3) The President may, with the consent of the Secretary of State as to numbers, remuneration and other terms and conditions of service, appoint such officers and staff as he thinks fit for the child support appeal tribunals and their full-time chairmen.

Membership of child support appeal tribunals

2.—(1) A child support appeal tribunal shall consist of a chairman and two other persons.

(2) The chairman and the other members of the tribunal must not all be of the same sex.

(3) Sub-paragraph (2) shall not apply to any proceedings before a child support appeal tribunal if the chairman of the tribunal rules that it is not reasonably practicable to comply with that sub-paragraph in those proceedings.

The chairmen

3.—(1) The chairman of a child support appeal tribunal shall be nominated by the president.

(2) The President may nominate himself or a person drawn –

(a) from the appropriate panel appointed by the Lord Chancellor, or (as the case may be) the Lord President of the Court of Session, under section 7 of the Tribunals and Inquiries Act 1971;

(b) from among those appointed under paragraph 4; or

(c) from among those appointed under paragraph 1A of Schedule 10 to the Social Security Act 1975 to act as full-time chairmen of social security appeal tribunals.

(3) Subject to any regulations made by the Lord Chancellor, no person shall be nominated as a chairman of a child support appeal tribunal by virtue of sub-paragraph (2)(*a*) unless he has a 5 year general qualification or is an advocate or solicitor in Scotland of 5 years' standing.

4.—(1) The Lord Chancellor may appoint regional and other full-time chairmen for child support appeal tribunals.

(2) A person is qualified to be appointed as a full-time chairman if he has a 7 year general qualification or is an advocate or solicitor in Scotland of 7 years' standing.

(3) A person appointed to act as a full-time chairman shall hold and vacate office in accordance with the terms of his appointment, except that he must vacate his office at the end of the completed year of service in which he reaches the age of 72 unless his appointment is continued under subparagraph (4).

(4) Where the Lord Chancellor considers it desirable in the public interest to retain a full-time chairman in office after the end of the completed year of service in which he reaches the age of 72, he may from time to time authorise the continuance of that person in office until any date not later than that on which that person reaches the age of 75.

(5) A person appointed as a full-time chairman may be removed from office by the Lord Chancellor, on the ground of misbehaviour or incapacity.

(6) Section 75 of the Courts and Legal Services Act 1990 (judges etc. barred from legal practice) shall apply to any person appointed as a full-time chairman under this Schedule as it applies to any person holding as a full-time appointment any of the offices listed in Schedule 11 to the Act.

(7) The Secretary of State may pay, or make such payments towards the provision of, such remuneration, pensions, allowances or gratuities to or in respect of persons appointed as full-time chairmen under this paragraph as, with the consent of the Treasury, he may determine.

Other members of child support appeal tribunals

5.—(1) The members of a child support appeal tribunal other than the chairman shall be drawn from the appropriate panel constituted under this paragraph.

(2) The panels shall be constituted by the President for the whole of Great Britain, and shall –
  (*a*) act for such areas; and
  (*b*) be composed of such persons,
as the President thinks fit.

(3) The panel for an area shall be composed of persons appearing to the President to have knowledge or experience of conditions in the area and to be representative of persons living or working in the area.

(4) Before appointing members of a panel, the President shall take into consideration any recommendations from such organisations or persons as he considers appropriate.

(5) The members of the panels shall hold office for such period as the President may direct.

(6) The President may at any time terminate the appointment of any member of a panel.

Clerks of tribunals

6.—(1) Each child support appeal tribunal shall be serviced by a clerk appointed by the President.

(2) The duty of summoning members of a panel to serve on a child support appeal tribunal shall be performed by the clerk to the tribunal.

Expenses of tribunal members and others

7.—(1) The Secretary of State may pay –
  (*a*) to any member of a child support appeal tribunal, such remuneration and travelling and other allowances as the Secretary of State may determine with the consent of the Treasury;

(b) to any person required to attend at any proceedings before a child support appeal tribunal, such travelling and other allowances as may be so determined; and

(c) such other expenses in connection with the work of any child support appeal tribunal as may be so determined.

(2) In sub-paragraph (1), references to travelling and other allowances include references to compensation for loss of remunerative time.

(3) No compensation for loss of remunerative time shall be paid to any person under this paragraph in respect of any time during which he is in receipt of other remuneration so paid.

Consultation with Lord Advocate

8.— Before exercising any of his powers under paragraph 3(3) or 4(1), (4) or (5), the Lord Chancellor shall consult the Lord Advocate.

SCHEDULE 4

CHILD SUPPORT COMMISSIONERS

Tenure of office

1.—(1) Every Child Support Commissioner shall vacate his office at the end of the completed year of service in which he reaches the age of 72.

(2) Where the Lord Chancellor considers it desirable in the public interest to retain a Child Support Commissioner in office after the end of the completed year of service in which he reaches the age of 72, he may from time to time authorise the continuance of that Commissioner in office until any date not later than that on which he reaches the age of 75.

(3) A Child Support Commissioner may be removed from office by the Lord Chancellor on the ground of misbehaviour or incapacity.

Commissioners' remuneration and their pensions

2.—(1) The Lord Chancellor may pay, or make such payments towards the provision of such remuneration, pensions, allowances or gratuities to or in respect of persons appointed as Child Support Commissioners as, with the consent of the Treasury, he may determine.

(2) The Lord Chancellor shall pay to a Child Support Commissioner such expenses incurred in connection with his work as such a Commissioner as may be determined by the Treasury.

Commissioners barred from legal practice

3.— Section 75 of the Courts and Legal Services Act 1990 (judges etc. barred from legal practice) shall apply to any person appointed as a Child Support Commissioner as it applies to any person holding as a full-time appointment any of the offices listed in Schedule 11 to that Act.

Deputy Child Support Commissioners

4.—(1) The Lord Chancellor may appoint persons to act as Child Support Commissioners (but to be known as deputy Child Support Commissioners) in order to facilitate the disposal of the business of Child Support Commissioners,

(2) A deputy Child Support Commissioner shall be appointed –

(a) from among persons who have a 10 year general qualification or are advocates or solicitors in Scotland of 10 years' standing; and

(b) for such period or on such occasions as the Lord Chancellor thinks fit.

(3) Paragraph 2 applies to deputy Child Support Commissioners as if the reference to pensions were omitted and paragraph 3 does not apply to them.

Tribunals of Commissioners

5.—(1) If it appears to the Chief Child Support Commissioner (or, in the case of his inability to act, to such other of the Child Support Commissioners as he may have nominated to act for the purpose) that an appeal falling to be heard by one of the Child Support Commissioners involves a question of law of special difficulty, he may direct that the appeal be dealt with by a tribunal consisting of any three of the Child Support Commissioners.

(2) If the decision of such a tribunal is not unanimous, the decision of the majority shall be the decision of the tribunal.

Finality of decisions

6.—(1) Subject to section 25, the decision of any Child Support Commissioner shall be final.

(2) Sub-paragraph (1) shall not be taken to make any finding of fact or other determination embodied in, or necessary to, a decision, or on which it is based, conclusive for the purposes of any further decision.

Consultation with Lord Advocate

7.— Before exercising any of his powers under paragraph 1(2) or (3), or 4(1) or (2)(*b*), the Lord Chancellor shall consult the Lord Advocate.

Northern Ireland

8.— In its application to Northern Ireland this Schedule shall have effect as if –
  (*a*) for any reference to a Child Support Commissioner (however expressed) there were substituted a corresponding reference to a Child Support Commissioner for Northern Ireland;
  (*b*) in paragraph 2(1), the word "pensions" were omitted;
  (*c*) for paragraph 3, there were substituted –
  "3. A Child Support Commissioner for Northern Ireland, so long as he holds office as such, shall not practise as a barrister or act for any remuneration to himself as arbitrator or referee or be directly or indirectly concerned in any matter as a conveyancer, notary public or solicitor.";
  (*d*) in paragraph 4 –
    (i) for paragraph (*a*) of sub-paragraph (2) there were substituted –
      "(*a*) from among persons who are barristers or solicitors of not less than 10 years' standing; and";
    (ii) for sub-paragraph (3) there were substituted –
      "(3) Paragraph 2 applies to deputy Child Support Commissioners for Northern Ireland, but paragraph 3 does not apply to them."; and
  (*e*) paragraphs 5 to 7 were omitted.

SCHEDULE 5

CONSEQUENTIAL AMENDMENTS

The Tribunals and Inquiries Act 1971 (c.62)

1.—(1) In section 7(3) of the Tribunals and Inquiries Act 1971 (chairmen of certain tribunals to be drawn from panels) after "paragraph" there shall be inserted "4A".

(2) In Schedule 1 to that Act (tribunals under the general supervision of the Council on Tribunals) the following entry shall be inserted at the appropriate place –

"Child support maintenance

4A(*a*)   The child support appeal tribunals established under section 21 of the Child Support Act 1991.

(*b*)   A Child Support Commissioner appointed under section 22 of the Child Support Act 1991 and any tribunal presided over by such a Commissioner."

The Northern Ireland Constitution Act 1973 (c. 36)

2.—   In paragraph 9 of Schedule 2 to the Northern Ireland Constitution Act 1973 (certain judicial appointments to be an excepted matter), after the words "for Northern Ireland", where they first occur, there shall be inserted "the Chief and other Child Support Commissioners for Northern Ireland".

The House of Commons Disqualification Act 1975 (c.24)

3.—(1)   The House of Commons Disqualification Act 1975 shall be amended as follows.

(2)   In Part I (disqualifying judicial offices), the following entries shall be inserted at the appropriate places –
"Chief or other Child Support Commissioner (excluding a person appointed under paragraph 4 of Schedule 4 to the Child Support Act 1991)."
"Chief or other Child Support Commissioner for Northern Ireland (excluding a person appointed under paragraph 4 of Schedule 4 to the Child Support Act 1991)."

(3)   In Part III (other disqualifying offices), the following entry shall be inserted at the appropriate place –
"Regional or other full-time chairman of a child support appeal tribunal established under section 21 of the Child Support Act 1991".

The Northern Ireland Assembly Disqualification Act 1975 (c.25)

4.—(1)   In Part I of the Northern Ireland Assembly Disqualification Act 1975 (disqualifying judicial offices), the following entries shall be inserted at the appropriate places –
"Chief or other Child Support Commissioner (excluding a person appointed under paragraph 4 of Schedule 4 to the Child Support Act 1991)."
"Chief or other Child Support Commissioner for Northern Ireland (excluding a person appointed under paragraph 4 of Schedule 4 to the Child Support Act 1991)."

The Family Law (Scotland) Act 1985 (c.37)

5.—   In section 4 (amount of aliment) of the Family Law (Scotland) Act 1985, at the end there shall be added –
"(4)   Where a court makes an award of aliment in an action brought by or on behalf of a child under the age of 16 years, it may include in that award such provision as it considers to be in all the circumstances reasonable in respect of the expenses incurred wholly or partly by the person having care of the child for the purpose of caring for the child."

Bankruptcy (Scotland) Act 1985 (c.66)

6.—(1)   The Bankruptcy (Scotland) Act 1985 shall be amended as follows.

(2)   In section 32 (vesting of estate and dealings of debtor after sequestration) –
   (*a*)   in subsection (3) –
      (i)   after paragraph (*b*) there shall be inserted –
         "(*c*)   any obligation of his to pay child support maintenance under the Child Support Act 1991,";

    (ii) after "relevant obligations" where second occurring there shall be inserted "referred to in paragraphs (*a*) and (*b*) above";
  (*b*) in subsection (5) after "Diligence" there shall be inserted "(which, for the purposes of this section, includes the making of a deduction from earnings order under the Child Support Act 1991)".

(3) In section 37 (effect of sequestration on diligence), in subsection (5A) for "or a conjoined arrestment order" there is substituted ", a conjoined arrestment order or a deduction from earnings order under the Child Support Act 1991".

(4) In section 55 (effect of discharge under section 54), in subsection (2)(*d*) –
  (*a*) after "being" there shall be inserted "(i)";
  (*b*) at the end there shall be inserted –
    "or
    (i) child support maintenance within the meaning of the Child Support Act 1991 which was unpaid in respect of any period before the date of sequestration of –
      (*aa*) any person by whom it was due to be paid; or
      (*bb*) any employer by whom it was, or was due to be, deducted under section 31(5) of that Act.".

The Insolvency Act 1986 (c.45)

7.— In section 281(5)(*b*) of the Insolvency Act 1986 (effect of discharge of bankrupt), after "family proceedings" there shall be inserted "or under a maintenance assessment made under the Child Support Act 1991".

The Debtors (Scotland) Act 1987 (c.18)

8.—(1) The Debtors (Scotland) Act 1987 shall be amended as follows.

(2) In section 1(5) (time to pay directions not competent in certain cases) after paragraph (c) there shall be inserted –
    "(*cc*) in connection with a liability order within the meaning of the Child Support Act 1991;".

(3) In section 15(3) (interpretation of Part I), in the definition of "decree or other document", after "maintenance order" there shall be inserted ", a liability order within the meaning of the Child Support Act 1991".

(4) In section 54(1) (maintenance arrestment to be preceded by default) in paragraph (c) for "the aggregate of 3 instalments" there shall be substituted "one instalment".

(5) In section 72 (effect of sequestration on diligence against earnings) –
  (*a*) in subsection (2) after "order" there shall be inserted "or deduction from earnings order under the Child Support Act 1991";
  (*b*) after subsection (3) there shall be inserted –
    "(3A) Any sum deducted by the employer under such a deduction from earnings order made before the date of sequestration shall be paid to the Secretary of State, notwithstanding that the date of payment will be after the date of sequestration.";
  (*c*) after subsection (4) there shall be inserted –
    "(4A) A deduction from earnings order under the said Act shall not be competent after the date of sequestration to secure the payment of any amount due by the debtor under a maintenance assessment within the meaning of that Act in respect of which a claim could be made in the sequestration.".

(6) In section 73(1) (interpretation of Part III), in the definition of "net earnings",
  (*a*) in paragraph (c) for "within the meaning of the Wages Councils Act 1979" there shall be substituted ", namely any enactment, rules, deed or other instrument providing for the payment of annuities or lump sums –

    (i)   to the persons with respect to whom the instrument has effect on their retirement at a specified age or on becoming incapacitated at some earlier age, or

    (ii) to the personal representatives or the widows, relatives or dependants of such persons on their death or otherwise,

whether with or without any further or other benefit;"; and

   (*b*)   at the end there shall be added –

      "(*d*)   any amount deductible by virtue of a deduction from earnings order which, in terms of regulations made under section 32(4)(*c*) of the Child Support Act 1991, is to have priority over diligences against earnings."

(7) In section 106 (interpretation) in the definition of "maintenance order" –

   (*a*)   the word "or" where it appears after paragraph (*g*), shall be omitted; and

   (*b*)   at the end there shall be inserted "or

      (*j*)   a maintenance assessment within the meaning of the Child Support Act 1991.".

APPENDIX 2

CHILD SUPPORT ACT 1991 (COMMENCEMENT NO 1) ORDER 1992
(SI 1992/1431)

1. Citation

This Order may be cited as the Child Support Act 1991 (Commencement No 1) Order 1992.

2. Date appointed for the coming into force of certain provisions of the Child Support Act 1991

The date appointed for the coming into force of the provisions of the Child Support Act 1991 specified in the Schedule to this Order is 17th June 1992.

SCHEDULE

Provision of the Child Support Act 1991	Subject Matter
Section 3(3)(c)	Meaning of certain terms used in the Act.
Section 4(4), (7) and (8)	Child support maintenance.
Section 5(3)	Child support maintenance: supplemental provisions.
Section 6(1) (in so far as it confers power to prescribe kinds of benefit for the purposes of that subsection), (9), (10) and (13)	Applications by those receiving benefit.
Section 7(5), (8) and (9)	Right of child in Scotland to apply for assessment.
Section 8(5), (9) and (11)(f)	Role of the courts with respect to maintenance for children.
Section 10	Relationship between maintenance assessments and certain court orders and related matters.
Section 12(2), (3) and (5)	Interim maintenance assessments.
Section 14(1) and (3)	Information required by Secretary of State.
Section 16(1), (2), (5) and (6)	Periodical reviews.

Provision of the Child Support Act 1991	*Subject Matter*
Section 17(4) and (6)(b)	Reviews on change of circumstances.
Section 18(8) and (11)	Reviews of decisions of child support officers.
Section 21(2) and (3)	Child support appeal tribunals.
Section 22(3) and (4)	Child Support Commissioners.
Section 24(6) and (7)	Appeal to Child Support Commissioner.
Section 25(2)(a), (3)(c), (5) and (6)	Appeal from Child Support Commissioner on question of law.
Section 29(2) and (3)	Collection of child support maintenance.
Section 30(1), (4) and (5)	Collection and enforcement of other forms of maintenance.
Section 31(8)	Deduction from earnings orders.
Section 32(1) to (5) and (7) to (9)	Regulations about deduction from earnings orders.
Section 34(1)	Regulations about liability orders.
Section 35(2)(b), (7) and (8)	Enforcement of liability orders by distress.
Section 39	Liability orders: enforcement throughout United Kingdom.
Section 40(4)(a)(ii), (8) and (11)	Commitment to prison.
Section 41(2), (3) and (4)	Arrears of child support maintenance.
Section 42	Special cases.
Section 43(1)(b) and (2)(a)	Contribution to maintenance by deduction from benefit.
Section 44(3)	Jurisdiction.
Section 45	Jurisdiction of courts in certain proceedings under the Act.
Section 46(11)	Failure to comply with obligations imposed by section 6.
Section 47	Fees.
Section 49	Right of audience: Scotland.
Section 50(5) and (7)(b)	Unauthorised disclosure of information.
Section 51	Supplementary powers to make regulations.
Section 52	Regulations and orders.
Section 54	Interpretation.
Section 55	Meaning of "child".

Provision of the Child Support Act 1991	*Subject Matter*
Section 56(2), (3) and (4)	Corresponding provision for and co-ordination with Northern Ireland.
Section 57	Application to Crown.
Schedule 1 in the respects specified below and section 11, so far as it relates to them—paragraphs 1(3) and (5), 2(1), 4(1) and (3), 5(1), (2) and (4), 6(2) to (6), 7 to 9, 11, 14 and 16(5), (10) and (11)	Maintenance assessments.
Paragraph 2(4) of Schedule 2 and section 14(4) so far as it relates to that sub-paragraph	Provision of information to Secretary of State.
Paragraph 3(3) of Schedule 3 and section 21(4) so far as it relates to that sub-paragraph	Child Support Appeal Tribunals.

CHILD SUPPORT ACT 1991 (COMMENCEMENT NO 2) ORDER 1992
(SI 1992/1938)

1. Citation

This Order may be cited as the Child Support Act 1991 (Commencement No 2) Order 1992.

2. Date appointed for the coming into force of certain provisions of the Child Support Act 1991

The date appointed for the coming into force of the following provisions of the Child Support Act 1991 is 1st September 1992—

Section 13 (Child Support Officers);

Section 21(1) and (4) and Schedule 3 (Child Support Appeal Tribunals) in so far as they are not already in force;

Section 22(1), (2) and (5) and Schedule 4 (Child Support Commissioners);

Section 23 (Child Support Commissioners for Northern Ireland);

Section 24(9) (Appeal to Child Support Commissioner);

Paragraphs 1 to 4 of Schedule 5 and section 58(13) so far as it relates to those paragraphs (Consequential Amendments).

CHILD SUPPORT ACT 1991 (COMMENCEMENT NO 3 AND TRANSITIONAL PROVISIONS) ORDER 1992
(SI 1992/2644)

1. Citation

This Order may be cited as the Child Support Act 1991 (Commencement No 3 and Transitional Provisions) Order 1992.

2. Date appointed for the coming into force of certain provisions of the Child Support Act 1991

Subject to the following provisions of this Order, the date appointed for the coming into force of all the provisions of the Child Support Act 1991, in so far as they are not already in force, except sections 19(3), 30(2), 34(2), 37(2) and (3) and 58(12), is 5th April 1993.

3. Transitional Provisions

The transitional provisions set out in the Schedule to this Order shall have effect.

SCHEDULE
PART I

Phased take-on of cases

1. In this Part of this Schedule—

"the Act" means the Child Support Act 1991;
"benefit" means income support, family credit, or disability working allowance under Part VII of the Social Security Contributions and Benefits Act 1992, or any other benefit prescribed under section 6(1) of the Act (applications by persons receiving benefit); and
"transitional period" means the period beginning with 5th April 1993 and ending with 6th April 1997.

2. Subject to paragraph 4 below, during the transitional period no application under section 4 of the Act (applications for child support maintenance) in relation to a qualifying child or any qualifying children may be made at any time when—

(a) there is in force a maintenance order or maintenance agreement in respect of that qualifying child or those qualifying children and the absent parent, or there is pending before any court an application for such a maintenance order; or
(b) benefit is being paid to a parent of that child or those children.

3. Subject to paragraph 4 below, during the transitional period no application under section 7 of the Act (right of child in Scotland to apply for assessment) may be made by a qualifying child at any time when there is in force a maintenance order or maintenance agreement in respect of that child and the absent parent, or there is pending before any court an application for such a maintenance order.

4. (1) Paragraphs 2 and 3 above do not apply to an application made—

    (a) in that part of the transitional period beginning with 8th April 1996, if the surname of the person with care begins with any of the letters A to D inclusive;

    (b) in that part of the transitional period beginning with 1st July 1996, if the surname of the person with care begins with any of the letters E to K inclusive;

    (c) in that part of the transitional period beginning with 7th October 1996, if the surname of the person with care begins with any of the letters L to R inclusive; and

    (d) in that part of the transitional period beginning with 6th January 1997, if the surname of the person with care begins with any of the letters S to Z inclusive.

(2) Where paragraph 2 or 3 applies to a case because there is pending before a court an application for a maintenance order, and that application was made before 5th April 1993, those paragraphs shall not prevent the making of an application for a maintenance assessment under section 4 or, as the case may be, section 7 of the Act; but in such a case section 8(3) of the Act shall not have effect until such an application is actually made.

5. For so long as paragraph 2 or 3 above operates in a case so as to prevent an application being made under section 4 of the Act or, as the case may be, section 7 of the Act, and no application has been made under section 6 of the Act, then in relation to that case section 8(3) of the Act (role of the courts with respect to maintenance orders) shall be modified so as to have effect as if the word "vary" was omitted.

PART II

6. Modification of maintenance assessment in certain cases

In this Part of this Schedule—

    "the Act" means the Child Support Act 1991;

    "formula amount" means the amount of child support maintenance that would, but for the provisions of this Part of this Schedule, be payable under an original assessment, or any fresh assessment made during the period specified in paragraph 8 consequent on a review under section 17, 18 or 19 of the Act;

    "the Maintenance Assessment Procedure Regulations" means the Child Support (Maintenance Assessment Procedure) Regulations 1992;

    "modified amount" means an amount which is £20 greater than the aggregate weekly amount which was payable under the orders, agreements or arrangements mentioned in paragraph 7(1)(a) below; and

    "original assessment" means a maintenance assessment made in respect of a qualifying child where no previous such assessment has been made or, where the assessment is made in respect of more than one child, where no previous such assessment has been made in respect of any of those children.

7. (1) Subject to sub-paragraph (2), the provisions of this Part of this Schedule apply to cases where—

    (a) on 4th April 1993 there is in force, in respect of all the qualifying children in respect of whom an application for a maintenance assessment is made under the Act and the absent parent concerned, one or more—

        (i) maintenance orders;

        (ii) orders under section 151 of the Army Act 1955 (deductions from pay for maintenance of wife or child) or section 151 of the Air Force Act 1955 (deductions from pay for maintenance of wife or child) or arrangements corresponding to such an order and made under Article 1(b) or 3 of the Naval and Marine Pay and Pensions (Deductions for Maintenance) Order 1959; or

(iii) maintenance agreements (being agreements which are made or evidenced in writing); and

(b) the absent parent is responsible for maintaining a child or children residing with him other than the child or children in respect of whom the application is made; and

(c) the formula amount is not more than £60; and

(d) the formula amount exceeds the aggregate weekly amount which was payable under the orders, agreements or arrangements mentioned in sub-paragraph (a) above by more than £20 a week.

(2) Nothing in this Part of this Schedule applies to an interim maintenance assessment made under section 12 of the Act.

8. In a case to which this Part of this Schedule applies, the amount payable under an original assessment, or any fresh assessment made consequent on a review under section 17, 18 or 19 of the Act, during the period of one year beginning with the date on which the original assessment takes effect or, if shorter, until any of the conditions specified in paragraph (7)(1) is no longer satisfied, shall, instead of being the formula amount, be the modified amount.

9. For the purpose of determining the aggregate weekly amount payable under the orders, agreements or arrangements mentioned in paragraph 7(1)(a) above any payments in kind and any payments made to a third party on behalf of or for the benefit of the qualifying child or qualifying children or the person with care shall be disregarded.

10. If, in making a maintenance assessment, a child support officer has applied the provisions of this Part of this Schedule, regulation 10(2) of the Maintenance Assessment Procedure Regulations shall have effect as if there was added at the end—

"(g) the aggregate weekly amount which was payable under the orders, agreements or arrangements specified in paragraph 7(1)(a) of the Schedule to the Child Support Act 1991 (Commencement No.3 and Transitional Provisions) Order 1992 (modification of maintenance assessment in certain cases).".

11. The first review of an original assessment under section 16 of the Act (periodical reviews) shall be conducted on the basis that the amount payable under the assessment immediately before the review takes place was the formula amount.

12. (1) The provisions of the following sub-paragraphs shall apply where there is a review of a previous assessment under section 17 of the Act (reviews on change of circumstances) at any time when the amount payable under that assessment is the modified amount.

(2) Where the child support officer determines that, were a fresh assessment to be made as a result of the review, the amount payable under it (disregarding the provisions of this Part of this Schedule) (in this paragraph called "the reviewed formula amount") would be—

(a) more than the formula amount, the amount of child support maintenance payable shall be the modified amount plus the difference between the formula amount and the reviewed formula amount;

(b) less than the formula amount but more than the modified amount, the amount of child support maintenance payable shall be the modified amount;

(c) less than the modified amount, the amount of child support maintenance payable shall be the reviewed formula amount.

(3) The child support officer shall, in determining the reviewed formula amount, apply the provisions of regulations 20 to 22 of the Maintenance Assessment Procedure Regulations.

CHILD SUPPORT (INFORMATION, EVIDENCE AND DISCLOSURE) REGULATIONS 1992
(SI 1992/1812)

ARRANGEMENT OF REGULATIONS

PART I
General

1. Citation, commencement and interpretation

(1) These Regulations may be cited as the Child Support (Information, Evidence and Disclosure) Regulations 1992 and shall come into force on 5th April 1993.

(2) In these Regulations, unless the context otherwise requires—

"the Act" means the Child Support Act 1991;
"appropriate authority" means—

(a) in relation to housing benefit, the housing or local authority concerned; and
(b) in relation to council tax benefit, the billing authority or, in Scotland, the levying authority;

"local authority" means, in relation to England and Wales, the council of a county, a metropolitan district, a London Borough or the Common Council of the City of London and, in relation to Scotland, a regional council or an islands council;
"Maintenance Assessments and Special Cases Regulations" means the Child Support (Maintenance Assessments and Special Cases) Regulations 1992;
"Maintenance Assessment Procedure Regulations" means the Child Support (Maintenance Assessment Procedure) Regulations 1992;
"parent with care" means a person who, in respect of the same child or children, is both a parent and a person with care;
"related proceedings" means proceedings in which a relevant court order was or is being sought;
"relevant court order" means—

(a) an order as to periodical or capital provision or as to variation of property rights made under an enactment specified in paragraphs (a) to (e) of section 8(11) of the Act or prescribed under section 8(11)(f) of the Act in relation to a qualifying child or a relevant person; or
(b) an order under Part II of the Children Act 1989 (Orders With Respect To Children In Family Proceedings) in relation to a qualifying child or, in Scotland, an order under section 3 of the Law Reform (Parent and Child) (Scotland) Act 1986 or a decree of declarator under section 7 of that Act in relation to a qualifying child;

"relevant person" means—

(a) a person with care;
(b) an absent parent;
(c) a parent who is treated as an absent parent under regulation 20 of the Maintenance Assessments and Special Cases Regulations;
(d) where the application for an assessment is made by a child under section 7 of the Act, that child,

in respect of whom a maintenance assessment has been applied for or is or has been in force.

(3) In these Regulations, unless the context otherwise queries, a reference—

(a) to a numbered regulation is to the regulation in these Regulations bearing that number;
(b) in a regulation to a numbered paragraph is to the paragraph in that regulation bearing that number;
(c) in a paragraph to a lettered or numbered sub-paragraph is to the sub-paragraph in that paragraph bearing that letter or number.

PART II
Furnishing of information or evidence

2. Persons under a duty to furnish information or evidence

(1) Where an application for a maintenance assessment has been made under the Act, a person falling within a category listed in paragraph (2) shall, subject to the restrictions specified in that paragraph, furnish such information or evidence as is required by the Secretary of State and which is needed to enable a determination to be made in relation to one or more of the matters listed in regulation 3(1), and the person concerned has that information or evidence in his possession or can reasonably be expected to acquire that information or evidence.

(2) The persons who may be required to furnish information or evidence, and the matter or matters with respect to which such information or evidence may be required, are as follows—

(a) the relevant persons, with respect to the matters listed in regulation 3(1);
(b) a person who is alleged to be a parent of a child with respect to whom an application for a maintenance assessment has been made who denies that he is one of that child's parents, with respect to the matters listed in sub-paragraphs (b) and (d) of regulation 3(1);
(c) the current or recent employer of the absent parent or the parent with care in relation to whom an application for a maintenance assessment has been made, with respect to the matters listed in sub-paragraphs (d), (e), (f), (h) and (j) of regulation 3(1);
(d) the local authority in whose area a person falling within a category listed in sub-paragraphs (a) and (b) above resides or has resided, with respect to the matter listed in sub-paragraph (a) of regulation 3(1);
(e) a person specified in paragraph (3) below, in any case where, in relation to the qualifying child or qualifying children or the absent parent—

(i) there is or has been a relevant court order; or
(ii) there have been, or are pending, related proceedings before a court,

with respect to the matters listed in sub-paragraph (g), (h) and (k) of regulation 3(1).

(3) The persons who may be required to furnish information or evidence in relation to a relevant court order or related proceedings under the provisions of paragraph (2)(e) are—

(a) in England and Wales—

(i) in relation to the High Court, the senior district judge of the principal registry of the Family Division or, where proceedings were instituted in a district registry, the district judge;
(ii) in relation to a county court, the proper officer of that court within the meaning of Order 1, Rule 3 of the County Court Rules 1981;
(iii) in relation to a magistrates' court, the clerk to the justices of that court;

(b) in Scotland—

(i) in relation to the Court of Session, the Deputy Principal Clerk of Session;
(ii) in relation to a sheriff court, the sheriff clerk.

3. Purposes for which information or evidence may be required

(1) The Secretary of State may require information or evidence under the provisions of regulation 2 only if that information or evidence is needed to enable—

(a) a decision to be made as to whether, in relation to an application for a maintenance assessment, there exists a qualifying child, an absent parent and a person with care;
(b) a decision to be made as to whether a child support officer has jurisdiction to make a maintenance assessment under section 44 of the Act;
(c) a decision to be made, where more than one application has been made, as to which application is to be proceeded with;
(d) an absent parent to be identified;
(e) an absent parent to be traced;
(f) the amount of child support maintenance payable by an absent parent to be assessed;
(g) the amount payable under a relevant court order to be ascertained;

(h) the amounts specified in sub-paragraphs (f) and (g) to be recovered from an absent parent;

(i) the amount of interest payable with respect to arrears of child support maintenance to be determined;

(j) the amount specified in sub-paragraph (i) to be recovered from an absent parent;

(k) any related proceedings to be identified.

(2) The information or evidence to be furnished in accordance with regulation 2 may in particular include information and evidence as to—

(a) the habitual residence of the person with care, the absent parent and any child in respect of whom an application for a maintenance assessment has been made;

(b) the name and address of the person with care and of the absent parent, their marital status, and the relationship of the person with care to any child in respect of whom the application for a maintenance assessment has been made;

(c) the name, address and date of birth of any such child, that child's marital status, and any education that child is undergoing;

(d) the persons who have parental responsibility for (or, in Scotland, parental rights over) any qualifying child where there is more than one person with care;

(e) the time spent by a qualifying child in respect of whom an application for a maintenance assessment has been made with each person with care, where there is more than one such person;

(f) the matters relevant for determining, in a case falling within section 26 of the Act (disputes about parentage), whether that case falls within one of the Cases set out in subsection (2) of that section, and if it does not, the matters relevant for determining the parentage of a child whose parentage is in dispute;

(g) the name and address of any current or recent employer of an absent parent or a parent with care, and the gross earnings and the deductions from those earnings deriving from each employment;

(h) the address from which an absent parent or parent with care who is self-employed carries on his trade or business, the trading name, and the gross receipts and expenses and other outgoings of the trade or business;

(i) any other income of an absent parent and a parent with care;

(j) any income, other than earnings, of a qualifying child;

(k) amounts payable and paid under a relevant court order or a maintenance agreement;

(l) the persons living in the same household as the absent parent or living in the same household as the parent with care, their relationship to the absent parent or the parent with care, as the case may be, and to each other, and, in the case of the children of any such party, the dates of birth of those children;

(m) the matters set out in sub-paragraphs (g) and (h) in relation to the persons specified in sub-paragraph (1) other than any children living in the same household as the absent parent or the parent with care, as the case may be;

(n) income other than earnings of the persons living in the same household as the absent parent or the parent with care;

(o) benefits related to disability that the absent parent, parent with care and other persons living in the same household as the absent parent or the parent with care are entitled to or would be entitled to if certain conditions were satisfied;

(p) the housing costs to be taken into account for the purposes of determining assessable or disposable income;

(q) the identifying details of any bank, building society or similar account held in the name of the absent parent or the person with care, and statements relating to any such account;

(r) the matters relevant for determining whether—

  (i) a maintenance assessment has ceased to have effect or should be cancelled under the provisions of paragraph 16 or Schedule 1 to the Act;
  (ii) a person is a child within the meaning of section 55 of the Act.

4. Information from an appropriate authority in connection with housing benefit or council tax benefit

For the purposes of paragraph 2 of Schedule 2 to the Act, "relevant information" means—

  (a) information as to the amount of housing costs of an absent parent or person with care which are treated as eligible rent for housing benefit purposes, and the entitlement to housing benefit at the date the Secretary of State gives a direction under paragraph 2(2) of that Schedule;
  (b) information as to the amount of council tax payable by an absent parent or person with care, and as to the entitlement to council tax benefit at the date the Secretary of State gives a direction under paragraph 2(2) of that Schedule.

5. Time within which information or evidence is to be furnished

Subject to the provisions of regulations 2(5), 6(1), 17(5) and 19(2) of the Maintenance Assessment Procedure Regulations, any information or evidence furnished in accordance with regulations 2 and 3 shall be furnished as soon as is reasonably practicable in the particular circumstances of the case.

6. Continuing duty of persons with care

Where a person with care with respect to whom a maintenance assessment has been made believes that, by virtue of section 44 or 55 of, or paragraph 16 of Schedule 1 to, the Act the assessment has ceased to have effect or should be cancelled, she shall, as soon as is reasonably practicable, inform the Secretary of State of that belief, and of the reasons for it, and shall provide such other information as the Secretary of State may reasonably require, with a view to assisting the Secretary of State or a child support officer in determining whether the assessment has ceased to have effect, or should be cancelled.

7. Powers of inspectors in relation to Crown residences

Subject to Her Majesty not being in residence, an inspector appointed under section 15 of the Act may enter any Crown premises for the purpose of exercising any powers conferred on him by that section.

PART III
Disclosure of information

8. Disclosure of information to a court or tribunal

The Secretary of State or a child support officer may disclose any information held by them for the purposes of the Act to—

  (a) a court;
  (b) any tribunal or other body or person mentioned in the Act;
  (c) any tribunal established under the benefit Acts,

where such disclosure is made for the purposes of any proceedings before any of those bodies relating to this Act or to the benefit Acts.

9. Disclosure of information to an appropriate authority for use in the exercise of housing benefit or council tax benefit functions

The Secretary of State or a child support officer may disclose information held by him for the purposes of the Act to, and as required by, an appropriate authority for use in the exercise of its functions relating to housing benefit or council tax benefit.

10. Disclosure of information to the Secretary of State

A child support officer may disclose any information held by him for the purposes of the Act to, and as required by, the Secretary of State for use in connection with the functions of the Secretary of State under any of the benefit Acts.

11. Employment to which section 50 of the Act applies

For the purposes of section 50 of the Act (unauthorised disclosure of information) the following kinds of employment are prescribed in addition to those specified in paragraphs (a) to (e) of section 50(5)—

    (a) the Comptroller and Auditor General;
    (b) the Parliamentary Commissioner for Administration;
    (c) the Health Service Commissioner for England;
    (d) the Health Service Commissioner for Wales;
    (e) the Health Service Commissioner for Scotland;
    (f) any member of the staff of the National Audit Office;
    (g) any other person who carries out the administrative work of that Office, or who provides, or is employed in the provision of, services to it;
    (h) any officer of any of the Commissioners referred to in paragraph (b) to (e) above; and
    (i) any person who provides, or is employed in the provision of, services to the Department of Social Security.

CHILD SUPPORT (MAINTENANCE ASSESSMENT PROCEDURE) REGULATIONS 1992
(SI 1992/1813)

ARRANGEMENT OF REGULATIONS

PART X

Miscellaneous provisions

SCHEDULES

PART I

General

1. Citation, commencement and interpretation

(1) These Regulations may be cited as the Child Support (Maintenance Assessment Procedure) Regulations 1992 and shall come into force on 5th April 1993.

(2) In these Regulations, unless the context otherwise requires—

"the Act" means the Child Support Act 1991;
"applicable amount" is to be construed in accordance with Part IV of the Income Support Regulations;
"applicable amounts Schedule" means Schedule 2 to the Income Support Regulations;
"award period" means a period in respect of which an award of family credit or disability working allowance is made;
"balance of the reduction period" means, in relation to a direction that is or has been in force, the portion of the period specified in a direction in respect of which no reduction of relevant benefit has been made;
"benefit week", in relation to income support, has the same meaning as in the Income Support Regulations, and, in relation to family credit and disability working allowance, is to be construed in accordance with the Social Security (Claims and Payments) Regulations 1987;
"direction" means reduced benefit direction;
"disability working allowance" has the same meaning as in the Social Security Contributions and Benefits Act 1992;
"day to day care" has the same meaning as in the Maintenance Assessments and Special Cases Regulations;
"effective application" means any application that complies with the provisions of regulation 2;
"effective date" means the date on which a maintenance assessment takes effect for the purposes of the Act;

"Income Support Regulations" means the Income Support (General) Regulations 1987;

"Information, Evidence and Disclosure Regulations" means the Child Support (Information, Evidence and Disclosure) Regulations 1992;

"Maintenance Assessments and Special Cases Regulations" means the Child Support (Maintenance Assessments and Special Cases) Regulations 1992;

"maintenance period" has the meaning prescribed in regulation 33;

"obligation imposed by section 6 of the Act" is to be construed in accordance with section 46(1) of the Act;

"parent with care" means a person who, in respect of the same child or children, is both a parent and a person with care;

"the parent concerned" means the parent with respect to whom a direction is given;

"protected income level" has the same meaning as in paragraph 6(6) of Schedule 1 to the Act;

"relevant benefit" means income support, family credit or disability working allowance;

"relevant person" means—

(a) a person with care;
(b) an absent parent;
(c) a parent who is treated as an absent parent under regulation 20 of the Maintenance Assessments and Special Cases Regulations;
(d) where the application for an assessment is made by a child under section 7 of the Act, that child,

in respect of whom a maintenance assessment has been applied for or is or has been in force.

(3) In these Regulations, references to a direction as being "in operation" "suspended", or "in force" shall be construed as follows—

a direction is "in operation" if, by virtue of that direction, relevant benefit is currently being reduced;
a direction is "suspended" if either—

(a) after that direction has been given, relevant benefit ceases to be payable, or becomes payable at one of the rates indicated in regulation 40(3); or
(b) at the time that the direction is given, relevant benefit is payable at one of the rates indicated in regulation 40(3),

and these Regulations provide for relevant benefit payable from a later date to be reduced by virtue of the same direction;
a direction is "in force" if it is either in operation or is suspended.

and cognate terms shall be construed accordingly.

(4) The provisions of Schedule 1 shall have effect to supplement the meaning of "child" in section 55 of the Act.

(5) The provisions of these Regulations shall have general application to cases prescribed in regulations 19 to 26 of the Maintenance Assessments and Special Cases Regulations as cases to be treated as special cases for the purposes of the Act, and the terms "absent parent" and "person with care" shall be construed accordingly.

(6) Except where express provision is made to the contrary, where, by any provision of the Act or of these Regulations—

(a) any document is given or sent to the Secretary of State, that document shall, subject to paragraph (7), be treated as having been so given or sent on the day it is received by the Secretary of State, and

(b) any document is given or sent to any person, that document shall, if sent by post to that person's last known or notified address, and subject to paragraph (8), be treated as having been given or sent on the second day after the day of posting, excluding any Sunday or any day which is a bank holiday in England, Wales, Scotland or Northern Ireland under the Banking and Financial Dealings Act 1971.

(7) Except where the provisions of regulation 8(6), 24(2), 29(3) or 31(6)(a) apply, the Secretary of State may treat a document given or sent to him as given or sent on such day, earlier than the day it was received by him, as he may determine, if he is satisfied that there was unavoidable delay in his receiving the document in question.

(8) Where, by any provision of the Act or of these Regulations, and in relation to a particular application, notice or notification—

(a) more than one document is required to be given or sent to a person, and more than one such document is sent by post to that person but not all the documents are posted on the same day; or

(b) documents are required to be given or sent to more than one person, and not all such documents are posted on the same day,

all those documents shall be treated as having been posted on the later or, as the case may be, the latest day of posting.

(9) In these Regulations, unless the context otherwise requires, a reference—

(a) to a numbered Part is to the Part of these Regulations bearing that number;

(b) to a numbered Schedule is to the Schedule to these Regulations bearing that number;

(c) to a numbered regulation is to the regulation in these Regulations bearing that number;

(d) in a regulation or Schedule to a numbered paragraph is to the paragraph in that regulation or Schedule bearing that number;

(e) in a paragraph to a lettered or numbered sub-paragraph is to the sub-paragraph in that paragraph bearing that letter or number.

PART II

Applications for a maintenance assessment

2. Applications under section 4, 6 or 7 or the Act

(1) Any person who applies for a maintenance assessment under section 4 or 7 of the Act shall do so on a form (a "maintenance application form") provided by the Secretary of State.

(2) Maintenance application forms provided by the Secretary of State under section 6 of the Act or under paragraph (1) shall be supplied without charge by such persons as the Secretary of State appoints or authorises for that purpose.

(3) A completed maintenance application form shall be given or sent to the Secretary of State.

(4) Subject to paragraph (5), an application for a maintenance assessment under the Act shall be an effective application if it is made on a maintenance application form and that

form has been completed in accordance with the Secretary of State's instructions.

(5) Where an application is not effective under the provisions of paragraph (4), the Secretary of State may—

(a) give or send the maintenance application form to the person who made the application, together, if he thinks appropriate, with a fresh maintenance application form, and request that the application be re-submitted so as to comply with the provisions of that paragraph; or

(b) request the person who made the application to provide such additional information or evidence as the Secretary of State specifies,

and if a completed application form or, as the case may be, the additional information or evidence requested is received by the Secretary of State within 14 days of the date of his request, he shall treat the application as made on the date on which the earlier or earliest application would have been treated as made had it been effective under the provisions of paragraph (4).

(6) Subject to paragraph (7), a person who has made an effective application may amend his application by notice in writing to the Secretary of State at any time before a maintenance assessment is made.

(7) No amendment under paragraph (6) shall relate to any change of circumstances arising after the effective date of a maintenance assessment resulting from an effective application.

3. Applications on the termination of a maintenance assessment

(1) Where a maintenance assessment has been in force with respect to a person with care and a qualifying child and that person is replaced by another person with care, an application for a maintenance assessment with respect to that person with care and that qualifying child may for the purposes of regulation 30(2)(b)(ii) and subject to paragraph (3) be treated as having been received on a date earlier than that on which it was received.

(2) Where a maintenance assessment has been made in response to an application by a child under section 7 of the Act and either—

(a) a child support officer cancels that assessment following a request from that child; or

(b) that child ceases to be a child for the purposes of the Act,

any application for a maintenance assessment with respect to any other children who were qualifying children with respect to the earlier maintenance assessment may for the purposes of regulation 30(2)(b)(ii) and subject to paragraph (3) be treated as having been received on a date earlier than that on which it was received.

(3) No application for a maintenance assessment shall be treated as having been received under paragraph (1) or (2) on a date—

(a) more than 8 weeks earlier than the date on which the application was received; or

(b) on or before the first day of the maintenance period in which the earlier maintenance assessment ceased to have effect.

4. Multiple applications

(1) The provisions of Schedule 2 shall apply in cases where there is more than one application for a maintenance assessment.

(2) The provisions of paragraphs 1, 2 and 3 of Schedule 2 relating to the treatment of two or more applications as a single application shall apply where no request is received for the Secretary of State to cease acting in relation to all but one of the applications.

(3) Where, under the provisions of paragraph 1, 2 or 3 of Schedule 2, two or more applications are to be treated as a single application, that application shall be treated as an application for a maintenance assessment to be made with respect to all of the qualifying children mentioned in the applications, and the effective date of that assessment shall be determined by reference to the earlier or earliest application.

5. Notice to other persons of an application for a maintenance assessment

(1) Where an effective application for a maintenance assessment has been made the Secretary of State shall as soon as is reasonably practicable give notice in writing of that application to the relevant persons other than the applicant.

(2) The Secretary of State shall give or send to any person to whom notice has been given under paragraph (2) a form (a "maintenance enquiry form") and a written request that the form be completed and returned to him for the purpose of enabling the application for the maintenance assessment to be proceeded with.

(3) Where the person to whom notice is being given under paragraph (1) is an absent parent, that notice shall specify the effective date of the maintenance assessment if one is to be made, and set out in general terms the provisions relating to interim maintenance assessments.

6. Response to notification of an application for a maintenance assessment

(1) Any person who has received a maintenance enquiry form given or sent under regulation 5(2) shall complete that form in accordance with the Secretary of State's instructions and return it to the Secretary of State within 14 days of its having been given or sent.

(2) Subject to paragraph (3), a person who has returned a completed maintenance enquiry form may amend the information he has provided on that form at any time before a maintenance assessment is made by notifying the Secretary of State in writing of the amendments.

(3) No amendment under paragraph (2) shall relate to any change of circumstances arising after the effective date of any maintenance assessment made in response to the application in relation to which the maintenance enquiry form was given or sent.

7. Death of a qualifying child

(1) Where the child support officer concerned is informed of the death of a qualifying child with respect to whom an application for a maintenance assessment has been made, he shall—

(a) proceed with the application as if it had not been made with respect to that child if he has not yet made an assessment;
(b) treat any assessment already made by him as not having been made if the relevant persons have not been notified of it and proceed with the application as if it had not been made with respect to that child.

(2) Where all of the qualifying children with respect to whom an application for a maintenance assessment has been made have died, and either the assessment has not been made or the relevant persons have not been notified of it, the child support officer shall treat the application as not having being made.

PART III

Interim maintenance assessments

8. Amount and duration of an interim maintenance assessment

(1) Where a child support officer serves notice under section 12(4) of the Act of his intention to make an interim maintenance assessment, he shall not make the interim assessment before the end of a period of 14 days commencing with the date that notice was given or sent.

(2) The amount of child support maintenance fixed by an interim maintenance assessment shall be 1.5 multiplied by the amount of the maintenance requirement in respect of the qualifying child or qualifying children concerned calculated in accordance with the provisions of paragraph 1 of Schedule 1 to the Act, and paragraphs 2 to 9 of that Schedule shall not apply to interim maintenance assessments.

(3) Where the provisions of regulation 30(2)(a) and (4) apply, the effective date of an interim maintenance assessment shall be such date, being not earlier than the first and not later than the seventh day following the expiry of the period of 14 days specified in paragraph (1), as falls on the same day of the week as the date specified in regulation 30(2)(a).

(4) Where a maintenance assessment is made after an interim maintenance assessment has been in force, child support maintenance calculated in accordance with Part I of Schedule 1 to the Act shall be payable in respect of the period preceding that during which the interim maintenance assessment was in force.

(5) The child support maintenance payable under the provisions of paragraph (4) shall be payable in respect of the period between the effective date of the assessment (or, where separate assessments are made for different periods under paragraph 15 of Schedule 1 to the Act, the effective date of the assessment in respect of the earliest such period) and the effective date of the interim maintenance assessment.

(6) Where a child support officer is satisfied that there was unavoidable delay by the absent parent in completing and returning a maintenance enquiry form under the provisions of regulation 6(1), or in providing information or evidence that is required by the Secretary of State for the determination of an application for a maintenance assessment, he may cancel an interim maintenance assessment which is in force.

(7) An interim maintenance assessment shall not be cancelled under paragraph (6) with effect from a date earlier than that on which the provisions of regulation 6(1) could have been complied with.

(8) Subject to paragraphs (6), (7) and (10), the child support maintenance payable in respect of any period in respect of which an interim maintenance assessment is in force shall not be adjusted following the making of a maintenance assessment.

(9) An interim maintenance assessment shall cease to have effect on the first day of the maintenance period during which the Secretary of State receives the information which

enables a child support officer to make the maintenance assessment or assessments in relation to the same absent parent, person with care, and qualifying child or qualifying children, calculated in accordance with Part I of Schedule 1 to the Act.

(10) Where a maintenance assessment calculated in accordance with Part I of Schedule 1 to the Act is made following an interim maintenance assessment and the amount of child support maintenance payable under that assessment in respect of the period during which the interim maintenance assessment was in force is higher than the amount fixed by the interim maintenance assessment determined in accordance with paragraph (2), the amount of child support maintenance payable in respect of that period shall be that fixed by the maintenance assessment calculated in accordance with Part I of Schedule 1 to the Act.

(11) Subject to regulation 9(6), for the purposes of sections 17 and 18 of the Act a maintenance assessment shall not include an interim maintenance assessment.

(12) The provisions of regulations 29, 31, 32, 33(5) and 55 shall not apply to interim maintenance assessments.

9. Cancellation of an interim maintenance assessment

(1) An absent parent with respect to whom an interim maintenance assessment is in force may apply to a child support officer for that interim assessment to be cancelled.

(2) Any application made under paragraph (1) shall be in writing, and shall include a statement of the grounds for the application.

(3) A child support officer who receives an application under the provisions of paragraph (1), shall—

  (a) decide whether the interim maintenance assessment is to be cancelled and, if so, the date with effect from which it is to be cancelled;
  (b) in any case where he does cancel an interim maintenance assessment, decide whether it is appropriate for a maintenance assessment to be made in accordance with the provisions of Part I of Schedule 1 to the Act;
  (c) in any case where he has decided that it is appropriate for a maintenance assessment to be made in accordance with the provisions of Part I of Schedule 1 to the Act, make that assessment.

(4) Where a child support officer has made a decision under paragraph (3), he shall immediately notify the applicant, so far as that is reasonably practicable, and shall give the reasons for his decision in writing.

(5) A notification under paragraph (4) shall include information as to the provisions of sections 18 and 20 of the Act and regulation 24(1), and, where an assessment is made in accordance with the provisions of Part I of Schedule 1 to the Act, the provisions of sections 16 and 17 of the Act.

(6) Where a child support officer has made a decision following an application under paragraph (1), the absent parent may apply to the Secretary of State for a review of that decision and, subject to the modification set out in paragraph (7), the provisions of section 18(5) to (8) of the Act shall apply to such a review.

(7) The modification referred to in paragraph (6) is that section 18(6) of the Act shall have effect as if for "the refusal, assessment or cancellation in question" there is

substituted "the decision following an application under regulation 9(1) of the Child Support (Maintenance Assessment Procedure) Regulations 1992".

(8) Regulations 10, 11 and 25 shall apply to reviews under paragraph (6).

PART IV

Notifications following certain decisions by child support officers

10. Notification of a new or a fresh maintenance assessment

(1) Where a child support officer makes a new or a fresh maintenance assessment following—

    (a) an application under section 4, 6 or 7 of the Act; or
    (b) a review under section 16, 17, 18 or 19 of the Act,

he shall immediately notify the relevant persons, so far as that is reasonably practicable, of the amount of the child support maintenance under that assessment.

(2) A notification under paragraph (1) shall set out, in relation to the maintenance assessment in question—

    (a) the maintenance requirement;
    (b) the effective date of the assessment;
    (c) the absent parent's assessable income and, where relevant, his protected income level;
    (d) the assessable income of a parent with care;
    (e) details as to the minimum amount of child support maintenance payable by virtue of regulations made under paragraph 7 of Schedule 1 to the Act; and
    (f) details as to apportionment where a case is to be treated as a special case for the purposes of the Act under section 42 of the Act.

(3) Except where a person gives written permission to the Secretary of State that the information, in relation to him, mentioned in sub-paragraphs (a) and (b) below may be conveyed to other persons, any document given or sent under the provisions of paragraph (1) or (2) shall not contain—

    (a) the address of any person other than the recipient of the document in question (other than the address of the office of the child support officer concerned) or any other information the use of which could reasonably be expected to lead to any such person being located;
    (b) any other information the use of which could reasonably be expected to lead to any person, other than a qualifying child or a relevant person, being identified.

(4) A notification under paragraph (1) shall include information as to the following provisions—

    (a) where a new maintenance assessment is made following an application under the Act or a fresh maintenance assessment is made following a review under section 16 of the Act, sections 16, 17 and 18 of the Act;
    (b) where a fresh maintenance assessment is made following a review under section 17 of the Act, or following a review under section 19 of the Act where the child support officer conducting such a review is satisfied that if an application were to be made under section 17 of the Act it would be appropriate to make a fresh maintenance assessment, sections 16 and 18 of the Act;
    (c) where a fresh maintenance assessment is made following a review under section 18 of the Act, or following a review under section 19 of the Act where the child support officer conducting such a review is satisfied that if an application were to

be made under section 18 of the Act, it would be appropriate to make a fresh maintenance assessment, sections 16, 17 and 20 of the Act.

11. Notification of a refusal to conduct a review

(1) Where a child support officer refuses an application for a review under section 17 of the Act on the grounds set out in section 17(3) of the Act, or an application for a review under section 18 of the Act on the grounds set out in section 18(6) of the Act, he shall immediately notify the applicant, so far as that is reasonably practicable, and shall give the reasons for his refusal in writing.

(2) A notification under paragraph (1) shall include information as to the following provisions—

    (a) where the refusal is on the grounds set out in section 17(3) of the Act, sections 16 and 18 of the Act and regulations 24(1) and 31(7);
    (b) where the refusal is on the grounds set out in section 18(6) of the Act, sections 16, 17 and 20 of the Act.

12. Notification of a refusal to make a new or a fresh maintenance assessment

(1) Where a child support officer refuses an application for a maintenance assessment under the Act, or refuses to make a fresh assessment following a review under section 17 or 18 of the Act, he shall immediately notify the following persons, so far as that is reasonably practicable—

    (a) where an application for a maintenance assessment under section 4 or 6 of the Act is refused, the applicant;
    (b) where an application for a maintenance assessment under section 7 of the Act is refused, the applicant child and the other relevant persons who have been notified of the application;
    (c) where there is a refusal to make a fresh assessment following a review under section 17 or 18 of the Act, the relevant persons,

and shall give the reasons for his refusal in writing.

(2) A notification under paragraph (1) shall include information as to the following provisions—

    (a) where an application for a maintenance assessment under the Act is refused, section 18 of the Act and regulation 24(1);
    (b) where there is a refusal to make a fresh assessment following a review under section 17 of the Act, sections 16 and 18 of the Act and regulation 24(1);
    (c) where there is a refusal to make a fresh assessment following a review under section 18 of the Act, sections 16, 17 and 20 of the Act.

13. Notification of a refusal to cancel a maintenance assessment

(1) Where a child support officer refuses a request under paragraph 16 of Schedule 1 to the Act for a maintenance assessment to be cancelled, or refuses to cancel a maintenance assessment following a review under section 18 of the Act, he shall immediately notify the following persons, so far as that is reasonably practicable—

    (a) where a request for a cancellation under paragraph 16 of Schedule 1 to the Act is refused, the applicant, or, as the case may be, the applicants;
    (b) where the cancellation of a maintenance assessment following a review under section 18 of the Act is refused, the relevant persons,

and shall give the reasons for his refusal in writing.

(2) A notification under paragraph (1) shall include information as to the following provisions—

   (a) where a request for a cancellation under paragraph 16 of Schedule 1 to the Act is refused, sections 16 and 18 of the Act and regulation 24(1);
   (b) where the cancellation of a maintenance assessment following a review under section 18 of the Act is refused, sections 16, 17 and 20 of the Act.

14. Notification of a cancellation of a maintenance assessment

(1) Where a child support officer cancels a maintenance assessment, he shall immediately notify the relevant persons, so far as that is reasonably practicable, and shall give the reasons for the cancellation in writing.

(2) A notification under paragraph (1) shall include information as to the provisions of section 18 of the Act and regulations 24(1) and 31(8).

15. Notification of a refusal to reinstate a cancelled maintenance assessment

(1) Where a child support officer, following a review under section 18(3) of the Act, refuses to reinstate a maintenance assessment that has been cancelled, he shall immediately notify the relevant persons, so far as that is reasonably practicable, and shall give the reasons for his refusal in writing.

(2) A notification under paragraph (1) shall include information as to the provisions of section 20 of the Act.

16. Notification when an applicant under section 7 of the Act ceases to be a child

Where a maintenance assessment has been made in response to an application by a child under section 7 of the Act and that child ceases to be a child for the purposes of the Act, a child support officer shall immediately notify, so far as that is reasonably practicable—

   (a) the other qualifying children over the age of 12 and the absent parent with respect to whom that maintenance assessment was made; and
   (b) the person with care.

PART V
Periodical reviews

17. Intervals between periodical reviews and notice of a periodical review

(1) Subject to regulation 18(1), a maintenance assessment that has been in force for a period of 52 weeks shall be reviewed by a child support officer under section 16 of the Act.

(2) Where a review under section 17 of the Act results in a fresh maintenance assessment, the next review under the provisions of paragraph (1) shall be conducted when that fresh assessment has been in force for a period of 52 weeks.

(3) A child support officer may decide not to conduct a review under paragraph (1) if a fresh maintenance assessment following such a review would cease to have effect within 28 days of the effective date of that fresh assessment.

(4) Before a child support officer conducts a review under section 16 of the Act, he shall give 14 days' notice of the proposed review to the relevant persons.

(5) Subject to paragraphs (6) and (7), a child support officer shall request every person to whom he is giving notice under paragraph (4) to provide, within 14 days, and in accordance with the provisions of regulations 2 and 3 of the Information, Evidence and Disclosure Regulations such information or evidence as to his current circumstances as may be specified.

(6) The provisions of paragraph (5) shall not apply in relation to any person to whom or in respect of whom income support is payable or to a person with care where income support is payable to or in respect of the absent parent.

(7) The provisions of paragraph (5) shall not apply in relation to a relevant person where—

    (a) a case is prescribed in regulation 22 or 23 of the Maintenance Assessments and Special Cases Regulations as a case to be treated as a special case for the purposes of the Act;
    (b) there has been a review under section 16 or 17 of the Act in relation to another maintenance assessment in force relating to that person;
    (c) the child support officer concerned has notified that person of the assessments following that review not earlier than 13 weeks prior to the date a review under section 16 of the Act is due under paragraph (1); and
    (d) the child support officer has no reason to believe that there has been a change in that person's circumstances.

18. Review under section 17 of the Act treated as a review under section 16 of the Act

(1) Where, under the provisions of regulation 19(1), a child support officer gives notice of a review under section 17 of the Act, that notice is given or sent not earlier than 8 weeks prior to the next review, under the provisions of regulation 17(1), of the maintenance assessment in force, and the review under section 17 of the Act does not result in a fresh maintenance assessment by virtue of the provisions of regulation 20, 21 or 22, that review shall be treated as a review under section 16 of the Act, and the fresh assessment that would have been made but for the provisions of regulation 20, 21 or 22, as the case may be, shall be the assessment following that review.

(2) Where there is a fresh assessment under the provisions of paragraph (1), the next review under the provisions of regulation 17(1) shall be of that fresh assessment.

PART VI
Reviews on a change of circumstances

19. Conduct of a review on a change of circumstances

(1) Where a child support officer proposes to conduct a review under section 17 of the Act, he shall give 14 days' notice of the proposed review to the relevant persons.

(2) Subject to paragraphs (3) and (4), and except where the circumstances set out in regulation 17(7) apply, a child support officer proposing to conduct a review under section 17 of the Act shall request every person to whom he is giving notice under paragraph (1) to provide within 14 days, and in accordance with the provisions of

regulations 2 and 3 of the Information, Evidence and Disclosure Regulations, such information or evidence as to his current circumstances as may be specified.

(3) The provisions of paragraph (2) shall not apply in relation to any person to whom or in respect of whom income support is payable.

(4) Where an application for a review under section 17 of the Act is made at the time that a review under section 16 of the Act is being conducted, the child support officer concerned may proceed with the review under section 17 of the Act notwithstanding that he has not complied with the provisions of paragraph (2) if in his opinion such compliance is not required in the particular circumstances of the case.

(5) Where a maintenance assessment is in force with respect to a parent with care and an absent parent in response to an application by the parent with care under section 6 of the Act, and the parent with care authorises the Secretary of State to take action under the Act to recover child support maintenance from that absent parent in relation to an additional child of whom she is a parent with care and he is an absent parent, that authorisation shall be treated by the Secretary of State as an application for a review under section 17 of the Act.

20. Fresh assessments following a review on a change of circumstances

(1) Subject to paragraphs (2) and (3) and regulations 21 and 22, a child support officer who has completed a review under section 17 of the Act shall not make a fresh assessment if the difference between the amount of child support maintenance fixed by the assessment currently in force and the amount that would be fixed if a fresh assessment were to be made as a result of the review is less than £10.00 per week.

(2) Where a child support officer who has completed a review under section 17 of the Act determines that, were a fresh assessment to be made as a result of the review, the circumstances of the absent parent are such that the provisions of paragraph 6 of Schedule 1 to the Act would apply to that assessment, he shall not make a fresh assessment if the difference between the amount of child support maintenance fixed by the original assessment and the amount that would be fixed if a fresh assessment were to be made as a result of the review is less than £1.00 per week.

(3) Where a child support officer who has completed a review under section 17 of the Act determines that, were a fresh assessment to be made as a result of the review, the children in respect of whom that assessment would be made are not identical with the children in respect of whom the original assessment was made, he shall not make a fresh assessment if the difference between the amount of child support maintenance fixed by the original assessment and the amount that would be fixed if a fresh assessment were to be made as a result of the review is less than £1.00 per week.

21. Fresh assessments following a review on a change of circumstances: special case prescribed by regulation 22 of the Maintenance Assessments and Special Cases Regulations

(1) The provisions of paragraphs (2) and (3) shall apply on a review under section 17 of the Act where a case is to be treated as a special case for the purposes of the Act by virtue of regulation 22 of the Maintenance Assessments and Special Cases Regulations.

(2) Where there is a change in the circumstances of the absent parent (whether or not there is also a change in the circumstances of one or more of the persons with care), a child support officer shall not make fresh assessments if the difference between the

aggregate amount of child support maintenance fixed by the assessments currently in force and the aggregate amount that would be fixed if fresh assessments were to be made as a result of the review is less than £10.00 per week or, where the circumstances of the absent parent are such that the provisions of paragraph 6 of Schedule 1 to the Act would apply to those fresh assessments, that difference is less than £1.00 per week.

(3) Where there is a change in the circumstances of one or more of the persons with care but not in that of the absent parent, the provisions of regulation 20 shall apply in relation to each fresh assessment.

22. Fresh assessments following a review on a change of circumstances: special case prescribed by regulation 23 of the Maintenance Assessments and Special Cases Regulations

(1) The provisions of paragraph (2) shall apply on a review under section 17 of the Act where a case is to be treated as a special case for the purposes of the Act by virtue of regulation 23 of the Maintenance Assessment and Special Cases Regulations.

(2) Where there is a change in the circumstances of the person with care or in the circumstances of one or more of the absent parents, the provisions of regulation 20 shall apply to each fresh assessment.

23. Reviews conducted under section 19 of the Act as if a review under section 17 of the Act had been applied for

The provisions of regulations 20, 21 and 22 shall apply to a review under section 19 of the Act which has been conducted as if an application for a review under section 17 of the Act had been made.

PART VII

Reviews of a decision by a child support officer

24. Time limits for an application for a review of a decision by a child support officer

(1) Subject to paragraph (2), the Secretary of State shall not refer any application for a review under section 18(1), (3) or (4) of the Act or under section 18 of the Act as extended by regulation 9(6) to a child support officer unless that application is received by the Secretary of State within 28 days of the date of notification to the applicant of the decision whose review he seeks.

(2) Where the Secretary of State receives an application for a review under section 18(1), (3) or (4) of the Act or under section 18 of the Act as extended by regulation 9(6) more than 28 days after the date of notification to the applicant of the decision whose review he seeks, the Secretary of State may refer that application to a child support officer if he is satisfied that there was unavoidable delay in making the application.

25. Notice of a review of a decision by a child support officer

(1) Where on an application for a review under section 18 of the Act a child support officer proposes to conduct such a review, he shall give 14 days' notice of the proposed review to the relevant persons.

(2) A child support officer proposing to conduct a review under section 18 of the Act shall—

    (a) send to the relevant persons the applicant's reasons for making the application for the review;

    (b) where a maintenance assessment is in force, send to the relevant persons the information that was included, under the provisions of regulation 10(2), in the notification of that assessment made under the provisions of regulation 10(1);

    (c) invite representations, either in person or in writing, from the relevant persons on any matter relating to the review and set out the provisions of paragraphs (3) to (6) in relation to such representations.

(3) Subject to paragraph (4), where the child support officer conducting the review does not within 14 days of the date on which notice of the review was given receive a request from a relevant person to make representations in person, or receives such a request and arranges for an appointment for such representations to be made but that appointment is not kept, he may complete the review in the absence of such representations from that person.

(4) Where the child support officer conducting the review is satisfied that there was good reason for failure to keep an appointment, he shall provide for a further opportunity for the making of representations by the relevant person concerned before he completes the review.

(5) Where the child support officer conducting the review does not receive written representations from a relevant person within 14 days of the date on which notice of the review was given, he may complete the review in the absence of written representations from that person.

(6) Except where a person gives written permission to the Secretary of State that the information, in relation to him, mentioned in sub-paragraphs (a) and (b) below may be conveyed to other persons, any document given or sent under the provisions of paragraph (1) or (2) shall not contain—

    (a) the address of any person other than the recipient of the document in question (other than the address of the office of the child support officer concerned) or any other information the use of which could reasonably be expected to lead to any such person being located;

    (b) any other information the use of which could reasonably be expected to lead to any person other than a qualifying child or relevant person being identified.

26. Procedure on a review of a decision by a child support officer

(1) Where the Secretary of State has referred more than one application for a review to a child support officer under section 18 of the Act in relation to the same decision and that child support officer proposes to conduct a review but has not given notice under regulation 25(1), he shall give notice to the relevant persons under regulation 25(1) and shall conduct one review taking account of all the representations made and all the evidence before him.

(2) Where the child support officer conducting a review under section 18 of the Act has given notice under regulation 25(1) and has a further application referred to him by the Secretary of State in relation to the same decision before he has completed his review, he shall notify the person who has made that further application that he is already conducting a review of that decision and that he will take into account the information contained in that application.

27. Review following an application under section 18(1)(b) of the Act

Where a child support officer has completed a review following an application for a review under section 18(1)(b) of the Act, regulations 20 to 22 shall apply in relation to any fresh assessment following that review.

28. Reviews conducted under section 19 of the Act as if a review under section 18(1)(b) of the Act had been applied for

The provisions of regulation 27 shall apply to a review under section 19 of the Act which has been conducted as if an application for a review under section 18(1)(b) of the Act had been made.

29. Extension of provisions of section 18(2) of the Act

(1) The provisions of section 18(2) of the Act shall apply where a maintenance assessment has been in force but is no longer in force if the condition specified in paragraph (2) is satisfied.

(2) The condition mentioned in paragraph (1) is that, subject to paragraph (3), the application for a review under section 18(2) of the Act as extended by this regulation is received by the Secretary of State within 28 days of the date of notification to the applicant of the maintenance assessment whose review he seeks.

(3) Where the Secretary of State receives such an application more than 28 days after the date of notification to the applicant of the maintenance assessment whose review he seeks, the Secretary of State may refer that application to a child support officer if he is satisfied that there was unavoidable delay.

PART VIII

Commencement and termination of maintenance assessments and maintenance periods

30. Effective dates of new maintenance assessments

(1) Subject to regulation 8(3), the effective date of a new maintenance assessment following an application under section 4, 6 or 7 of the Act shall be the date determined in accordance with paragraphs (2) to (4).

(2) Where no maintenance assessment is in force with respect to the person with care and absent parent, the effective date of a new assessment shall be—

    (a) the date a maintenance enquiry form is given or sent to an absent parent in a case where the application for a maintenance assessment is made by a person with care or by a child under section 7 of the Act; or

    (b) the date an effective maintenance application form is received by the Secretary of State in a case where the application for a maintenance assessment—

        (i) is made by an absent parent, or

        (ii) is an application in relation to which the provisions of regulation 3 have been applied.

(3) The provisions of regulation 1(6)(b) shall not apply to paragraph (2)(a).

(4) Where a child support officer is satisfied that an absent parent has deliberately avoided receipt of a maintenance enquiry form, he may determine the date on which the

form would have been given or sent but for such avoidance, and that date shall be the relevant date for the purposes of paragraph (2)(a).

31. Effective dates of maintenance assessments following a review under sections 16 to 19 of the Act

(1) Where a fresh maintenance assessment is made following a review under section 16 of the Act, the effective date of that assessment shall be 52 weeks after the effective date of the previous assessment.

(2) Subject to paragraph (4), where an application is made under section 17 of the Act for a review of a maintenance assessment in force, and a fresh maintenance assessment is made in accordance with the provisions of regulation 20, 21 or 22, the effective date of that assessment shall be the first day of the maintenance period in which the application is received.

(3) Where a case falls within regulation 18(1), the effective date of the fresh assessment shall be the first day of the maintenance period in which the assessment is made.

(4) Where an application is made under section 17 of the Act for a review of a maintenance assessment in force following the death of a qualifying child and a fresh maintenance assessment is made in accordance with the provisions of regulation 20, 21 or 22, the effective date of that assessment shall be the first day of the maintenance period during the course of which that child died.

(5) Where, following a review under section 18(1)(a) of the Act, a maintenance assessment is made following a refusal to make a maintenance assessment, the effective date of that assessment shall be the effective date of the assessment that would have been made if the application for a maintenance assessment had not been refused.

(6) Subject to paragraphs (7), (10) and (11), where an application is made under section 18(2) of the Act for a review of a maintenance assessment in force, the effective date of a fresh assessment (if one is made) following such a review shall be—

    (a) where the application is received by the Secretary of State within 28 days of the date of notification of that assessment, or on a later date but the Secretary of State is satisfied that there was unavoidable delay, the effective date as determined on the review;

    (b) subject to sub-paragraph (a), where the application is received by the Secretary of State later than 28 days after the date of notification of that assessment, the first day of the maintenance period in which the application is received.

(7) Where an application is made under section 18(1)(b) of the Act for a review of a refusal of an application under section 17 of the Act for the review of a maintenance assessment which is in force, the effective date of a fresh maintenance assessment (if one is made) shall be the date determined under paragraph (2).

(8) Where, following a review under section 18(3) of the Act, a cancelled maintenance assessment is reinstated, the effective date of the reinstated assessment shall be the date on which the cancelled assessment ceased to have effect.

(9) Where there has been a misrepresentation or failure to disclose a material fact on the part of the person with care or absent parent in connection with an application for a maintenance assessment under the Act, or a review under section 16 or 17 of the Act, and that misrepresentation or failure has resulted in an incorrect assessment or a series

of incorrect assessments, the effective date of a fresh assessment (or of a fresh assessment in relation to the earliest relevant period) following discovery of the misrepresentation or failure shall be the effective date of the incorrect assessment or the first incorrect assessment, as the case may be.

(10) Where a fresh maintenance assessment is made on a review under section 18 or 19 of the Act by reason of an assessment having been made in ignorance of a material fact or having been based on a mistake as to a material fact and that ignorance or mistake, as the case may be, is attributable to an operational or administrative error on the part of the Secretary of State or of a child support officer, the effective date of that fresh assessment shall be the effective date of the assessment that has been reviewed.

(11) Subject to paragraphs (9), (10), (12), (13) and (14), where a fresh maintenance assessment is made under section 19 of the Act, the effective date of the assessment shall be the first day of the maintenance period in which the assessment is made.

(12) Where a fresh maintenance assessment is made under section 19 of the Act following the death of a qualifying child, the effective date of that assessment shall be the first day of the maintenance period during which that child died.

(13) Where a child support officer on a review under section 18 or 19 of the Act is satisfied that a maintenance assessment which is or has been in force is defective by reason of a mistake as to the effective date of that assessment, the effective date of a fresh assessment shall be that determined in accordance with regulation 30 or in accordance with paragraphs (1) to (12), as the case may be.

(14) Where a child support officer on a review under section 19 of the Act is satisfied that if an application were to be made under section 18 of the Act it would be appropriate to make a fresh maintenance assessment, and does so, the effective date of that fresh assessment shall be determined in accordance with paragraphs (5) to (8).

32. Cancellation of a maintenance assessment

Where a child support officer cancels a maintenance assessment under paragraph 16(2) or (3) of Schedule 1 to the Act, the assessment shall cease to have effect from the date of receipt of the request for the cancellation of the assessment or from such later date as the child support officer may determine.

33. Maintenance periods

(1) The child support maintenance payable under a maintenance assessment shall be calculated at a weekly rate and be in respect of successive maintenance periods, each such period being a period of 7 days.

(2) Subject to paragraph (6), the first maintenance period shall commence on the effective date of the first maintenance assessment, and each succeeding maintenance period shall commence on the day immediately following the last date of the preceding maintenance period.

(3) The maintenance periods in relation to a fresh maintenance assessment following a review under section 16, 17, 18 or 19 of the Act shall coincide with the maintenance periods in relation to the earlier assessment, had it continued in force, and the first maintenance period in relation to a fresh assessment shall commence on the day following the last day of the last maintenance period in relation to the earlier assessment.

(4) The amount of child support maintenance payable in respect of a maintenance period which includes the effective date of a fresh maintenance assessment shall be the amount of maintenance payable under that fresh assessment.

(5) The amount of child support maintenance payable in respect of a maintenance period during the course of which a cancelled maintenance assessment ceases to have effect shall be the amount of maintenance payable under that assessment.

(6) Where a case is to be treated as a special case for the purposes of the Act by virtue of regulation 22 of the Maintenance Assessments and Special Cases Regulations (multiple applications relating to an absent parent) and an application is made by a person with care in relation to an absent parent where there is already a maintenance assessment in force in relation to that absent parent and a different person with care, the maintenance periods in relation to an assessment made in response to that application shall coincide with the maintenance periods in relation to the earlier maintenance assessment, and the first such period shall commence not later than 7 days after the date of notification to the relevant persons of the later maintenance assessment.

PART IX

Reduced benefit directions

34. Prescription of disability working allowance for the purposes of section 6 of the Act

Disability working allowance shall be a benefit of a prescribed kind for the purposes of section 6 of the Act.

35. Periods for compliance with obligations imposed by section 6 of the Act

(1) Where the Secretary of State considers that a parent has failed to comply with an obligation imposed by section 6 of the Act we shall serve written notice on that parent that, unless she complies with that obligation, he intends to refer the case to a child support officer for the child support officer to take action under section 46 of the Act if the child support officer considers such action to be appropriate.

(2) The Secretary of State shall not refer a case to a child support officer prior to the expiry of a period of 6 weeks from the date he serves notice under paragraph (1) on the parent in question, and the notice shall contain a statement to that effect.

(3) Where the Secretary of State refers a case to a child support officer and the child support officer serves written notice on a parent under section 46(2) of the Act, the period to be specified in that notice shall be 14 days.

36. Amount of and period of reduction of relevant benefit under a reduced benefit direction

(1) The reduction in the amount payable by way of a relevant benefit to, or in respect of, the parent concerned and the period of such reduction by virtue of a direction shall be determined in accordance with paragraphs (2) to (9).

(2) Subject to paragraph (6) and regulations 37, 38(7) and 40, there shall be a reduction for a period of 26 weeks from the day specified in the direction under the provisions of section 46(9) of the Act in respect of each such week equal to

$$0.2 \times B$$

where B is an amount equal to the weekly amount, in relation to the week in question, specified in column (2) of paragraph 1(1)(e) of the applicable amounts Schedule.

(3) Subject to paragraph (6) and regulations 37, 38(7) and 40, at the end of the period specified in paragraph (2) there shall be a reduction from the day immediately succeeding the last day of that period for a period of 52 weeks of an amount in respect of each such week equal to

$$0.1 \times B$$

where B has the same meaning as in paragraph (2).

(4) Subject to paragraph (5), a direction shall come into operation on the first day of the second benefit week following the review, carried out by the adjudication officer in consequence of the direction, of the relevant benefit that is payable.

(5) Where the relevant benefit is income support and the provisions of regulation 26(2) of the Social Security (Claims and Payments) Regulations 1987 (deferment of payment of different amount of income support) apply, a direction shall come into operation on such later date as may be determined by the Secretary of State in accordance with those provisions.

(6) Where the benefit payable is income support and there is a change in the benefit week whilst a direction is in operation, the periods of the reductions specified in paragraphs (2) and (3) shall be—

(a) where the reduction is that specified in paragraph (2), a period greater than 25 weeks but less than 26 weeks;
(b) where the reduction is that specified in paragraph (3), a period greater than 51 weeks but less than 52 weeks;

and ending on the last day of the last benefit week falling entirely within the period of 26 weeks specified in paragraph (2), or the period of 52 weeks specified in paragraph (3), as the case may be.

(7) Where the weekly amount specified in column (2) of paragraph 1(1)(e) of the applicable amounts Schedule changes on a day when a direction is in operation, the amount of the reduction of the relevant benefit shall be changed—

(a) where the benefit is income support, from the first day of the first benefit week to commence for the parent concerned on or after the day that weekly amount changes;
(b) where the benefit is family credit or disability working allowance, from the first day of the next award period of that benefit for the parent concerned commencing on or after the day that weekly amount changes;

(8) Only one direction in relation to a parent shall be in force at any one time.

(9) Where a direction has been in operation for the aggregate of the periods specified in paragraphs (2) and (3) ("the full period"), no further direction shall be given with respect to the same parent on account of that parent's failure to comply with the obligations imposed by section 6 of the Act in relation to any child in relation to whom the direction that has been in operation for the full period was given.

37. Modification of reduction under a reduced benefit direction to preserve minimum entitlement to relevant benefit

Where in respect of any benefit week the amount of the relevant benefit that would be payable after it has been reduced following a direction would, but for this regulation, be nil or less than the minimum amount of that benefit that is payable as determined—

(a) in the case of income support, by regulation 26(4) of the Social Security (Claims and Payments) Regulations 1987;

(b) in the case of family credit and disability working allowance, by regulation 27(2) of those Regulations.

the amount of that reduction shall be decreased to such extent as to raise the amount of that benefit to the minimum amount that is payable.

38. Suspension of a reduced benefit direction when relevant benefit ceases to be payable

(1) Where relevant benefit ceases to be payable to, or in respect of, the parent concerned at a time when a direction is in operation, that direction shall, subject to paragraph (2), be suspended for a period of 52 weeks from the date the relevant benefit has ceased to be payable.

(2) Where a direction has been suspended for a period of 52 weeks and no relevant benefit is payable at the end of that period, it shall cease to be in force.

(3) Where a direction is suspended and relevant benefit again becomes payable to or in respect of the parent concerned, the amount payable by way of that benefit shall, subject to regulations 40, 41 and 42, be reduced in accordance with that direction for the balance of the reduction period.

(4) The amount or, as the case may be, amounts of the reduction to be made during the balance of the reduction period shall be determined in accordance with regulation 36(2) and (3).

(5) No reduction in the amount of benefit under paragraph (3) shall be made before the expiry of a period of 14 days from service of the notice specified in paragraph (6), and the provisions of regulation 36(4) shall apply as to the date when the direction again comes into operation.

(6) Where relevant benefit again becomes payable to or in respect of a parent with respect to whom a direction is suspended she shall be notified in writing by a child support officer that the amount of relevant benefit paid to or in respect of her will again be reduced, in accordance with the provisions of paragraph (3), if she continues to fail to comply with the obligations imposed by section 6 of the Act.

(7) Where a direction has ceased to be in force by virtue of the provisions of paragraph (2), a further direction in respect of the same parent given on account of that parent's failure to comply with the obligations imposed by section 6 of the Act in relation to one or more of the same qualifying children shall, unless it also ceases to be in force by virtue of the provisions of paragraph (2), be in operation for the balance of the reduction period relating to the direction that has ceased to be in force, and the provisions of paragraph (4) shall apply to it.

39. Reduced benefit direction where family credit or disability working allowance is payable and income support becomes payable

(1) Where a direction is in operation in respect of a parent to whom or in respect of whom family credit or disability working allowance is payable, and income support becomes payable to or in respect of that parent, income support shall become a relevant benefit for the purposes of that direction, and the amount payable by way of income support shall be reduced in accordance with that direction for the balance of the reduction period.

(2) The amount or, as the case may be, the amounts of the reduction to be made during the balance of the reduction period shall be determined in accordance with regulation 36(2) and (3).

40. Suspension of a reduced benefit direction when a modified applicable amount is payable

(1) Where a direction is given or is in operation at a time when income support is payable to or in respect of the parent concerned but her applicable amount falls to be calculated under the provisions mentioned in paragraph (3), that direction shall be suspended for so long as the applicable amount falls to be calculated under the provisions mentioned in that paragraph, or 52 weeks, whichever period is the shorter.

(2) Where a case falls within paragraph (1) and a direction has been suspended for a period of 52 weeks, it shall cease to be in force.

(3) The provisions of paragraph (1) shall apply where the applicable amount in relation to the parent concerned falls to be calculated under—

    (a) regulation 19 of the Schedule 4 to the Income Support Regulations (applicable amounts for persons in residential care and nursing homes);
    (b) regulation 21 of the paragraphs 1 to 3 of Schedule 7 to the Income Support Regulations (patients);
    (c) regulation 21 of the paragraphs 10B, 10C, 10D and 13 of Schedule 7 to the Income Support Regulations (persons in residential accommodation).

41. Termination of a reduced benefit direction following compliance with obligations imposed by section 6 of the Act

(1) Where a parent with care with respect to whom a direction is in force complies with the obligations imposed by section 6 of the Act, that direction shall cease to be in force on the date determined in accordance with paragraph (2) or (3), as the case may be.

(2) Where the direction is in operation, it shall cease to be in force on the last day of the benefit week during the course of which the parent concerned complied with the obligations imposed by section 6 of the Act.

(3) Where the direction is suspended, it shall cease to be in force on the date on which the parent concerned complied with the obligations imposed by section 6 of the Act.

42. Review of a reduced benefit direction

(1) Where a parent with care with respect to whom a direction is in force gives the Secretary of State reasons—

    (a) additional to any reasons given by her in response to the notice served on her under section 46(2) of the Act for having failed to comply with the obligations imposed by section 6 of the Act; or

(b) as to why she should no longer be required to comply with the obligations imposed by section 6 of the Act,

the Secretary of State shall refer the matter to a child support officer who shall conduct a review of the direction ("a review") to determine whether the direction is to continue or is to cease to be in force.

(2) Where a parent with care with respect to whom a direction is in force gives a child support officer reasons of the kind mentioned in paragraph (1), a child support officer shall conduct a review to determine whether the direction is to continue or is to cease to be in force.

(3) A review shall not be carried out by the child support officer who gave the direction with respect to the parent concerned.

(4) Where the child support officer who is conducting a review considers that the parent concerned is no longer to be required to comply with the obligations imposed by section 6 of the Act, the direction shall cease to be in force on the date determined in accordance with paragraph (5) or (6), as the case may be.

(5) Where the direction is in operation, it shall cease to be in force on the last day of the benefit week during the course of which the parent concerned gave the reasons specified in paragraph (1).

(6) Where the direction is suspended, it shall cease to be in force on the date on which the parent concerned gave the reasons specified in paragraph (1).

(7) The provisions of section 20 of the Act shall apply in relation to a decision of a child support officer following a review.

(8) A child support officer shall on completing a review immediately notify the parent concerned of his decision, so far as that is reasonably practicable, and shall give the reasons for his decision in writing.

(9) A notification under paragraph (8) shall include information as to the provisions of section 20 of the Act.

43. Termination of a reduced benefit direction where a maintenance assessment is made following an application by a child under section 7 of the Act

Where a qualifying child of a parent with respect to whom a direction is in force applies for a maintenance assessment to be made with respect to him under section 7 of the Act, and an assessment is made in response to that application in respect of all of the qualifying children in relation to whom the parent concerned failed to comply with the obligations imposed by section 6 of the Act, that direction shall cease to be in force from the date determined in accordance with regulation 45.

44. Termination of a reduced benefit direction where a maintenance assessment is made following an application by an absent parent under section 4 of the Act

Where—

(a) an absent parent applies for a maintenance assessment to be made under section 4 of the Act with respect to all of his qualifying children in relation to whom the other parent of those children is a person with care;

(b) a direction is in force with respect to that other parent following her failure to comply with the obligations imposed by section 6 of the Act in relation to those qualifying children; and

(c) an assessment is made in response to that application by the absent parent for a maintenance assessment,

that direction shall cease to be in force on the date determined in accordance with regulation 45.

45. Date from which a reduced benefit direction ceases to be in force following a termination under regulation 43 or 44

(1) The date a direction ceases to be in force under the provisions of regulation 43 or 44 shall be determined in accordance with paragraphs (2) and (3).

(2) Where the direction is in operation, it shall cease to be in force on the last day of the benefit week during the course of which the Secretary of State is supplied with the information that enables a child support officer to make the assessment.

(3) Where the direction is suspended, it shall cease to be in force on the date on which the Secretary of State is supplied with the information that enables a child support officer to make the assessment.

46. Cancellation of a reduced benefit direction in cases of error

Where a child support officer is satisfied that a direction was given as a result of an error on the part of the Secretary of State or a child support officer, or though not given as a result of such an error has not subsequently ceased to be in force as a result of such an error, the child support officer shall cancel the direction and it shall be treated as not having been given, or as having ceased to be in force on the date it would have ceased to be in force if that error had not been made, as the case may be.

47. Reduced benefit directions where there is an additional qualifying child

(1) Where a direction is in operation or would be in operation but for the provisions of regulation 40 and a child support officer gives a further direction with respect to the same parent on account of that parent failing to comply with the obligations imposed by section 6 of the Act in relation to an additional qualifying child of whom she is a person with care, the earlier direction shall cease to be in force on the last day of the benefit week preceding the benefit week on the first day of which, in accordance with the provisions of regulation 36(4), the further direction comes into operation, or would come into operation but for the provisions of regulation 40.

(2) Where a further direction comes into operation in a case falling within paragraph (1), the provisions of regulation 36 shall apply to it.

(3) Where a direction has ceased to be in force by virtue of regulation 38(2) and a child support officer gives a direction with respect to the same parent on account of that parent's failure to comply with the obligations imposed by section 6 of the Act in relation to an additional qualifying child, no further direction shall be given with respect to that parent on account of her failure to comply with the obligations imposed by section 6 of the Act in relation to one or more children in relation to whom the direction that has ceased to be in force by virtue of regulation 38(2) was given.

(4) Where a case falls within paragraph (1) or (3) and the further direction, but for the provisions of this paragraph would cease to be in force by virtue of the provisions of regulation 41 or 42, but the earlier direction would not have ceased to be in force by virtue of the provisions of those regulations, the later direction shall continue in force for a period ("the extended period") calculated in accordance with the provisions of paragraph (5) and the reduction of relevant benefit shall be determined in accordance with paragraphs (6) and (7).

(5) The extended period for the purposes of paragraph (4) shall be

$$(78 - F - S) \text{ weeks}$$

where—

> F is the number of weeks for which the earlier direction was in operation; and
> S is the number of weeks for which the later direction has been in operation.

(6) Where the extended period calculated in accordance with paragraph (5) is greater than 52 weeks, there shall be a reduction of relevant benefit in respect of the number of weeks in excess of 52 determined in accordance with regulation 36(2), and a reduction of relevant benefit in respect of the remaining 52 weeks determined in accordance with regulation 36(3).

(7) Where the extended period calculated in accordance with paragraph (5) is equal to or less than 52 weeks, there shall be a reduction of relevant benefit in respect of that period determined in accordance with regulation 36(3).

(8) In this regulation "an additional qualifying child" means a qualifying child of whom the parent concerned is a person with care and who was either not such a qualifying child at the time the earlier direction was given or had not been born at the time the earlier direction was given.

48. Suspension and termination of a reduced benefit direction where the sole qualifying child ceases to be a child or where the parent concerned ceases to be a person with care

(1) Where, whilst a direction is in operation—

> (a) there is, in relation to that direction, only one qualifying child, and that child ceases to be a child within the meaning of the Act; or
> (b) the parent concerned ceases to be a person with care,

the direction shall be suspended from the last day of the benefit week during the course of which the child ceases to be a child within the meaning of the Act, or the parent concerned to be a person with care, as the case may be.

(2) Where, under the provisions of paragraph (1), a direction has been suspended for a period of 52 weeks and no relevant benefit is payable at that time, it shall cease to be in force.

(3) If during the period specified in paragraph (1) the former child again becomes a child within the meaning of the Act or the parent concerned again becomes a person with care and relevant benefit is payable to or in respect of that parent, a reduction in the amount of that benefit shall be made in accordance with the provisions of paragraphs (3) to (7) of regulation 38.

49. Notice of termination of a reduced benefit direction

(1) Where a direction ceases to be in force under the provisions of regulations 41 to 44 or 46 to 48, or is suspended under the provisions of regulation 48, a child support officer shall serve notice of such termination or suspension, as the case may be, on the adjudication officer and shall specify the date on which the direction ceases to be in force or is suspended, as the case may be.

(2) Any notice served under paragraph (1) shall set out the reasons why the direction has ceased to be in force or has been suspended.

(3) The parent concerned shall be served with a copy of any notice served under paragraph (1).

50. Rounding provisions

Where any calculation made under this Part of these Regulations results in a fraction of a penny, that fraction shall be treated as a penny if it exceeds one half, and shall otherwise be disregarded.

PART X

Miscellaneous provisions

51. Persons who are not persons with care

(1) For the purposes of the Act the following categories of person shall not be persons with care—

    (a) a local authority;
    (b) a person with whom a child who is looked after by a local authority is placed by that authority under the provisions of the Children Act 1989,
    (c) in Scotland, a person with whom a child is boarded out by a local authority under the provisions of section 21 of the Social Work (Scotland) Act 1968.

(2) In paragraph (1) above—

"local authority" means, in relation to England and Wales, the council of a county, a metropolitan district, a London Borough or the Common Council of the City of London and, in relation to Scotland, a regional council or an islands council;

"a child who is looked after by a local authority" has the same meaning as in section 22 of the Children Act 1989.

52. Terminations of maintenance assessments

(1) Where the Secretary of State is satisfied that a question arises as to whether a maintenance assessment has ceased to have effect under the provisions of paragraph 16(1)(a) to (d) of Schedule 1 to the Act, he shall refer that question (a "termination question") to a child support officer.

(2) Where a child support officer has made a decision on a termination question (a "termination decision") he shall immediately notify the following persons of his decision, so far as that is reasonably practicable—

    (a) in a case falling within paragraph 16(1)(a) of Schedule 1 to the Act, the surviving relevant persons;
    (b) in a case falling within paragraph 16(1)(b), (c) or (d) of Schedule 1 to the Act, the relevant persons.

(3) Any notification under paragraph (2) shall give the reasons for the termination decision made, include information as to the provisions of section 18 of the Act, and explain the provisions of paragraph (4).

(4) The persons specified in paragraph (2) may apply to the Secretary of State for a review of a termination decision as if it were a case falling within section 18 of the Act and, subject to the modifications set out in paragraph (5), section 18(5) to (9) and (11) of the Act shall apply to such a review.

(5) The modifications referred to in paragraph (4) are—

(a) section 18(6) of the Act shall have effect as if for "the refusal, assessment or cancellation" there is substituted "the termination decision";

(b) section 18(9) of the Act shall have effect as if for "a maintenance assessment or (as the case may be) a fresh maintenance assessment" there is substituted "a different termination decision".

(6) The provisions of regulation 24 as to time limits for an application for a review of a decision by a child support officer shall apply to reviews under paragraph (4).

(7) Where a child support officer has completed a review of a termination decision he shall immediately notify the persons specified in paragraph (2), so far as that is reasonably practicable, of the review decision, give the reasons for that decision in writing, and notify them of the provisions of section 20 of the Act.

(8) Where a case falls within regulation 19 of the Maintenance Assessments and Special Cases Regulations and both absent parents have made an application for a maintenance assessment under section 4 of the Act, the Secretary of State shall be under the duty imposed by section 4(6) of the Act only if both absent parents have, under section 4(5) of the Act, requested the Secretary of State to cease acting under section 4 of the Act.

53. Authorisation of representative

(1) A person may authorise a representative, whether or not legally qualified, to receive notices and other documents on his behalf and to act on his behalf in relation to the making of applications and the supply of information under any provision of the Act or these Regulations.

(2) Where a person has authorised a representative for the purposes of paragraph (1) who is not legally qualified, he shall confirm that authorisation in writing to the Secretary of State.

54. Correction of accidental errors in decisions

(1) Subject to regulation 56, accidental errors in any decision or record of a decision may at any time be corrected by a child support officer and a correction made to, or to the record of, a decision shall be deemed to be part of the decision or of that record.

(2) A child support officer who has made a correction under the provisions of paragraph (1) shall immediately notify the persons who were notified of the decision that has been corrected, so far as that is reasonably practicable.

55. Setting aside of decisions on certain grounds

(1) Subject to paragraph (7) and regulation 56, on an application made by a relevant person, a decision may be set aside by a child support officer on the grounds that the

interests of justice so require, and in particular that a relevant document in relation to that decision was not sent to, or was not received at an appropriate time by the person making the application or his representative or was sent but not received at an appropriate time by the child support officer who gave the decision.

(2) Any application made under paragraph (1) shall be in writing, shall include a statement of the grounds for the application, and shall be made by giving or sending it to the Secretary of State within 28 days of the date of notification of the decision in question.

(3) Where an application to set aside a decision is being considered by a child support officer under paragraph (1), he shall notify the relevant persons other than the applicant of the application and they shall be given 14 days to make representations as to that application.

(4) The provisions of regulation 25(6) shall apply to notifications under paragraph (5).

(5) A child support officer who has made a determination on an application to set aside a decision shall immediately notify the relevant persons, so far as that is reasonably practicable, and shall give the reasons for his determination in writing.

(6) For the purposes of determining an application to set aside a decision under this regulation, there shall be disregarded regulation 1(6)(b) and any provision in any enactment or instrument to the effect that any notice or other document required or authorised to be given or sent to any person shall be deemed to have been given or sent if it was sent by post to that person's last known or notified address.

(7) The provisions of paragraphs (1) to (6) shall not apply to any document given or sent under any provision of Part IX.

56. Provisions common to regulations 54 and 55

(1) In determining whether the time limits specified in regulation 17, 19, 24 or 25 have been complied with, there shall be disregarded any day falling before the day on which notification is given of a correction made to, or to the record of, a decision made under regulation 54 or on which notification is given that a decision shall not be set aside following an application made under regulation 55, as the case may be.

(2) The power to correct errors under regulation 54 or set aside decisions under regulation 55 shall not be taken to limit any other powers to correct errors or set aside decisions that are exercisable apart from these Regulations.

SCHEDULE 1

Meaning of "child" for the purposes of the Act

1. Persons of 16 or 17 years of age who are not in full-time non-advanced education

(1) Subject to sub-paragraph (3), the conditions which must be satisfied for a person to be a child within section 55(1)(c) of the Act are—

   (a) the person is registered for work or for training under youth training with—

      (i) the Department of Employment;
      (ii) the Ministry of Defence;

  (iii) in England and Wales, a local education authority within the meaning of the Education Acts 1944 to 1992;
  (iv) in Scotland, an education authority within the meaning of section 135(1) of the Education (Scotland) Act 1980 (interpretation); or
  (v) for the purposes of applying Council Regulation (EEC) No. 1408/71, any corresponding body in another member State;

(b) the person is not engaged in remunerative work, other than work of a temporary nature that is due to cease before the end of the extension period which applies in the case of that person;
(c) the extension period which applies in the case of that person has not expired; and
(d) immediately before the extension period begins, the person is a child for the purposes of the Act without regard to this paragraph.

(2) For the purposes of paragraphs (b), (c) and (d) of sub-paragraph (1), the extension period—

(a) begins on the first day of the week in which the person would no longer be a child for the purposes of the Act but for this paragraph; and
(b) where a person ceases to fall within section 55(1)(a) of the Act or within paragraph 5—

  (i) on or after the first Monday of September, but before the first Monday in January of the following year, ends on the last day of the week which falls immediately before the week which includes the first Monday in January in that year;
  (ii) on or after the first Monday in January but before the Monday following Easter Monday in that year, ends on the last day of the week which falls 12 weeks after the week which includes the first Monday in January in that year;
  (iii) at any other time of the year, ends on the last day of the week which falls 12 weeks after the week which includes the Monday following Easter Monday in that year.

(3) A person shall not be a child for the purposes of the Act under this paragraph if—

(a) he is engaged in training under youth training; or
(b) he is entitled to income support.

2. Meaning of "advanced education" for the purposes of section 55 of the Act

For the purposes of section 55 of the Act "advanced education" means education of the following description—

(a) a course in preparation for a degree, a Diploma of Higher Education, a higher national diploma, a higher national diploma or higher national certificate of the Business and Technician Education Council or the Scottish Vocational Education Council or a teaching qualification; or
(b) any other course which is of a standard above that of an ordinary national diploma, a national diploma or national certificate of the Business and Technician Education Council or the Scottish Vocational Education Council, and advanced level of the General Certificate of Education, a Scottish certificate of education (higher level) or a Scottish certificate of sixth year studies.

3. Circumstances in which education is to be treated as full-time education

For the purposes of section 55 of the Act education shall be treated as being full-time if it is received by a person attending a course of education at a recognised educational establishment and the time spent receiving instruction or tuition, undertaking supervised study, examination or practical work or taking part in any exercise, experiment or project for which provision is made in the curriculum of the course, exceeds 12 hours per week, so however that in calculating the time spent in pursuit of the course, no account shall be taken of time occupied by meal breaks or spent on unsupervised study, whether undertaken on or off the premises of the educational establishment.

4. Interruption of full-time education

(1) Subject to sub-paragraph (2), in determining whether a person falls within section 55(1)(b) of the Act no account shall be taken of a period (whether beginning before or after the person concerned attains age 16) of up to 6 months of any interruption to the extent to which it is accepted that the interruption is attributable to a cause which is reasonable in the particular circumstances of the case; and where the interruption or its continuance is attributable to the illness or disability of mind or body of the person concerned, the period of 6 months may be extended for such further period as a child support officer considers reasonable in the particular circumstances of the case.

(2) The provisions of sub-paragraph (1) shall not apply to any period of interruption of a person's full-time education which is likely to be followed immediately or which is followed immediately by a period during which—

(a) provision is made for the training of that person, and for an allowance to be payable to that person, under youth training; or
(b) he is receiving education by virtue of his employment or of any office held by him.

5. Circumstances in which a person who has ceased to receive full-time education is to be treated as continuing to fall within section 55(1) of the Act

(1) Subject to sub-paragraphs (2) and (5), a person who has ceased to receive full-time education (which is not advanced education) shall, if—

(a) he is under the age of 16 when he so ceases, from the date on which he attains that age; or
(b) he is 16 or over when he so ceases, from the date on which he so ceases.

be treated as continuing to fall within section 55(1) of the Act up to and including the week including the terminal date or if he attains the age of 19 on or before that date up to and including the week including the last Monday before he attains that age.

(2) In the case of a person specified in sub-paragraph (1)(a) or (b) who had not attained the upper limit of compulsory school age when he ceased to receive full-time education, the terminal date in his case shall be that specified in paragraph (a), (b) or (c) of sub-paragraph (3), whichever next follows the date on which he would have attained that age.

(3) In this paragraph the "terminal date" means—

(a) the first Monday in January; or
(b) the Monday following Easter Monday; or
(c) the first Monday in September,

whichever first occurs after the date on which the person's said education ceased.

(4) In this paragraph "compulsory school age" means—

  (a) in England and Wales, compulsory school age as determined in accordance with section 9 of the Education Act 1962;
  (b) in Scotland, school age as determined in accordance with sections 31 and 33 of the Education (Scotland) Act 1980.

(5) A person shall not be treated as continuing to fall within section 55(1) of the Act under this paragraph if he is engaged in remunerative work, other than work of a temporary nature that is due to cease before the terminal date.

(6) Subject to sub-paragraphs (5) and (8), a person whose name was entered as a candidate for any external examination in connection with full-time education (which is not advanced education), which he was receiving at that time, shall so long as his name continued to be so entered before ceasing to receive such education be treated as continuing to fall within section 55(1) of the Act for any week in the period specified in sub-paragraph (7).

(7) Subject to sub-paragraph (8), the period specified for the purposes of sub-paragraph (6) is the period beginning with the date when that person ceased to receive such education ending with—

  (a) whichever of the dates in sub-paragraph (3) first occurs after the conclusion of the examination (or the last of them, if there are more than one); or
  (b) the expiry of the week which includes the last Monday before his 19th birthday, whichever is the earlier.

(8) The period specified in sub-paragraph (7) shall, in the case of a person who has not attained the age of 16 when he so ceased, begin with the date on which he attained that age.

6. Interpretation

In this Schedule—

  "Education Acts 1944 to 1992" has the meaning prescribed in section 94(2) of the Further and Higher Education Act 1992;
  "remunerative work" means work of not less than 24 hours a week—

  (a) in respect of which payment is made; or
  (b) which is done in expectation of payment;

  "week" means a period of 7 days beginning with a Monday;
  "youth training" means—

  (a) arrangements made under section 2 of the Employment and Training Act 1973 (functions of the Secretary of State) or section 2 of the Enterprise and New Towns (Scotland) Act 1990;
  (b) arrangements made by the Secretary of State for persons enlisted in Her Majesty's forces for any special term of service specified in regulations made under section 2 of the Armed Forces Act 1966 (power of Defence Council to make regulations as to engagement of persons in regular forces); or
  (c) for the purposes of the application of Council Regulation (EEC) No. 1408/71, any corresponding provisions operated in another member State,

for purposes which include the training of persons who, at the beginning of their training, are under the age of 18.

SCHEDULE 2

Multiple applications

1. No maintenance assessment in force: more than one application for a maintenance assessment by the same person under section 4 or 6 or under sections 4 and 6 of the Act

(1) Where a person makes an effective application for a maintenance assessment under section 4 or 6 of the Act and, before that assessment is made, makes a subsequent effective application under that section with respect to the same absent parent or person with care, as the case may be, those applications shall be treated as a single application.

(2) Where a parent with care makes an effective application for a maintenance assessment—

   (a) under section 4 of the Act; or
   (b) under section 6 of the Act,

and, before that assessment is made, makes a subsequent effective application—

   (c) in a case falling within paragraph (a), under section 6 of the Act; or
   (d) in a case falling within paragraph (b), under section 4 of the Act,

with respect to the same absent parent, those applications shall, if the parent with care does not cease to fall within section 6(1) of the Act, be treated as a single application under section 6 of the Act, and shall otherwise be treated as a single application under section 4 of the Act.

2. No maintenance assessment in force: more than one application by a child under section 7 of the Act

Where a child makes an effective application for a maintenance assessment under section 7 of the Act and, before that assessment is made, makes a subsequent effective application under that section with respect to the same person with care and absent parent, both applications shall be treated as a single application for a maintenance assessment.

3. No maintenance assessment in force: applications by different persons for a maintenance assessment

(1) Where the Secretary of State receives more than one effective application for a maintenance assessment with respect to the same person with care and absent parent, he shall refer each such application to a child support officer and, if no maintenance assessment has been made in relation to any of the applications, the child support officer shall determine which application he shall proceed with in accordance with sub-paragraphs (2) to (11).

(2) Where there is an application by a person with care under section 4 or 6 of the Act and an application by an absent parent under section 4 of the Act, the child support officer shall proceed with the application of the person with care.

(3) Where there is an application for a maintenance assessment by a qualifying child under section 7 of the Act and a subsequent application is made with respect to that child by a person who is, with respect to that child, a person with care or an absent parent, the child support officer shall proceed with the application of that person with care or absent parent, as the case may be.

(4) Where, in a case falling within sub-paragraph (3), there is more than one subsequent application, the child support officer shall apply the provisions of sub-paragraph (2), (8), (9) or (11), as is appropriate in the circumstances of the case, to determine which application he shall proceed with.

(5) Where there is an application for a maintenance assessment by more than one qualifying child under section 7 of the Act in relation to the same person with care and absent parent, the child support officer shall proceed with the application of the elder or, as the case may be, eldest of the qualifying children.

(6) Where a case is to be treated as a special case for the purposes of the Act under regulation 19 of the Maintenance Assessments and Special Cases Regulations (both parents are absent) and an effective application is received from each absent parent, the child support officer shall proceed with both applications, treating them as a single application for a maintenance assessment.

(7) Where, under the provisions of regulation 20 of the Maintenance Assessments and Special Cases Regulations (persons treated as absent parents), two persons are to be treated as absent parents and an effective application is received from each such person, the child support officer shall proceed with both applications, treating them as a single application for a maintenance assessment.

(8) Where there is an application under section 6 of the Act by a parent with care and an application under section 4 of the Act by another person with care who has parental responsibility for (or, in Scotland, parental rights over) the qualifying child or qualifying children with respect to whom the application under section 6 of the Act was made, the child support officer shall proceed with the application under section 6 of the Act by the parent with care.

(9) Where—

    (a) more than one person with care makes an application for a maintenance assessment under section 4 of the Act in respect of the same qualifying child or qualifying children (whether or not any of those applications is also in respect of other qualifying children);

    (b) each such person has parental responsibility for (or, in Scotland, parental rights over) that child or children, and

    (c) under the provisions of regulation 20 of the Maintenance Assessments and Special Cases Regulations one of those persons is to be treated as an absent parent,

the child support officer shall proceed with the application of the person who does not fall to be treated as an absent parent under the provisions of regulation 20 of those Regulations.

(10) Where, in a case falling within sub-paragraph (9), there is more than one person who does not fall to be treated as an absent parent under the provisions of regulation 20 of those Regulations, the child support officer shall apply the provisions of paragraph (11) to determine which application he shall proceed with.

(11) Where—

    (a) more than one person with care makes an application for a maintenance assessment under section 4 of the Act in respect of the same qualifying child or qualifying children (whether or not any of those applications is also in respect of other qualifying children); and

(b) either—
  (i) none of those persons has parental responsibility for (or, in Scotland, parental rights over) that child or children; or
  (ii) the case falls within sub-paragraph (9)(b) but the child support officer has not been able to determine which application he is to proceed with under the provisions of sub-paragraph (9).

the child support officer shall proceed with the application of the principal provider of day to day care, as determined in accordance with sub-paragraph (12).

(12) Where—
  (a) the applications are in respect of one qualifying child, the application of that person with care with whom the child spends the greater or, as the case may be, the greatest proportion of his time;
  (b) the applications are in respect of more than one qualifying child, the application of that person with care with whom the children spend the greater or, as the case may be, the greatest proportion of their time, taking account of the time each qualifying child spends with each of the persons with care in question;
  (c) the child support officer cannot determine which application he is to proceed with under paragraph (a) or (b), and child benefit is paid in respect of the qualifying child or qualifying children to one but not any other of the applicants, the application of the applicant to whom child benefit is paid;
  (d) the child support officer cannot determine which application he is to proceed with under paragraph (a), (b) or (c), the application of that applicant who in the opinion of the child support officer is the principal provider of day to day care for the child or children in question.

(13) Subject to sub-paragraph (14), where, in any case falling within sub-paragraphs (2) to (11), the applications are not in respect of identical qualifying children, the application that the child support officer is to proceed with as determined by those paragraphs shall be treated as an application with respect to all of the qualifying children with respect to whom the applications were made.

(14) Where the child support officer is satisfied that the same person with care does not provide the principal day to day care for all of the qualifying children with respect to whom an assessment would but for the provisions of this paragraph be made under sub-paragraph (13), he shall make separate assessments in relation to each person with care providing such principal day to day care.

4. Maintenance assessment in force: subsequent application for a maintenance assessment with respect to the same persons

Where a maintenance assessment is in force and a subsequent application is made under the same section of the Act for an assessment with respect to the same person with care, absent parent, and qualifying child or qualifying children as those with respect to whom the assessment in force has been made, that application shall not be proceeded with unless the Secretary of State treats that application as an application for a review under section 17 of the Act.

5. Maintenance assessment in force: subsequent application for a maintenance assessment under section 6 of the Act

Where a maintenance assessment is in force following an application under section 4 or 7 of the Act and the person with care makes an application under section 6 of the Act, any maintenance assessment made in response to that application shall replace the assessment currently in force.

6. Maintenance assessment in force: subsequent application for a maintenance assessment in respect of additional children

(1) Where a maintenance assessment made in response to an application by an absent parent under section 4 of the Act is in force and that assessment is not in respect of all of his children who are in the care of the person with care with respect to whom that assessment has been made, an assessment made in response to an application by that person with care under section 4 of the Act with respect to—

  (a) the children in respect of whom the assessment currently in force was made; and
  (b) the additional child or, as the case may be, one or more of the additional children in that person's care who are children of that absent parent,

shall replace the assessment currently in force.

(2) Where—

  (a) a maintenance assessment made in response to an application by an absent parent or a person with care under section 4 of the Act is in force;
  (b) that assessment is not in respect of all of the children of the absent parent who are in the care of the person with respect to whom that assessment has been made; and
  (c) the absent parent makes a subsequent application in respect of an additional qualifying child or additional qualifying children of his in the care of the same person,

that application shall be treated as an application for a maintenance assessment in respect of all of the qualifying children concerned, and the assessment made shall replace the assessment currently in force.

(3) Where a maintenance assessment made in response to an application by a child under section 7 of the Act is in force and the person with care of that child makes an application for a maintenance assessment under section 4 of the Act in respect of that child and all other children of the absent parent who are in her care, that assessment shall replace the assessment currently in force.

CHILD SUPPORT (MAINTENANCE ASSESSMENTS AND SPECIAL CASES) REGULATIONS 1992
(SI 1992/1815)

ARRANGEMENT OF REGULATIONS

PART I
General

PART II
Calculation or estimation of child support maintenance

PART III
Special cases

SCHEDULES

PART I

General

1. Citation, commencement and interpretation

(1) These Regulations may be cited as the Child Support (Maintenance Assessment and Special Cases) Regulations 1992 and shall come into force on 5th April 1993.

(2) In these Regulations, unless the context otherwise requires—

"the Act" means the Child Support Act 1991;

"claimant" means a claimant for income support;

"Contributions and Benefits Act" means the Social Security Contributions and Benefits Act (1992);

"council tax benefit" has the same meaning as in the Local Government Finance Act 1992;

"course of advanced education" means

(a) a full-time course leading to a postgraduate degree or comparable qualification, a first degree or comparable qualification, a Diploma of Higher Education, a higher national diploma, a higher national diploma or higher national certificate of the Business and Technician Education Council or the Scottish Vocational Education Council or a teaching qualification; or

(b) any other full-time course which is a course of a standard above that of an ordinary national diploma, a national diploma or national certificate of the Business and Technician Education Council or the Scottish Vocational Education Council, the advanced level of the General Certificate of Education, a Scottish certificate of education (higher level) or a Scottish certificate of sixth year studies;

"covenant income" means the gross income payable to a student under a Deed of Covenant by a parent;

"day" includes any part of a day;

"day to day care" means care of not less than 2 nights per week on average during—

(a) the 12 month period ending with the relevant week; or

(b) such other period, ending with the relevant week, as in the opinion of the child support officer is more representative of the current arrangements for the care of the child in question;

and for the purposes of this definition, where a child is a boarder at a boarding school or is an in-patient in a hospital, the person who, but for those cirumstances, would otherwise provide day to day care of the child, shall be treated as providing day to day care during the periods in question.

"disability working allowance" has the same meaning as in section 129 of the Contributions and Benefits Act;

"earnings" has the meaning assigned to it by paragraph 1 or 3, as the case may be, of Schedule 1;

"effective date" means the date on which a maintenance assessment takes effect for the purposes of the Act;

"eligible housing costs" shall be construed in accordance with Schedule 3;

"employed earner" has the same meaning as in section 2(1)(a) of the Contributions and Benefits Act;

"family" means—

(a) a married or unmarried couple (including the members of a polygamous marriage) and any child or children living with them for whom at least one member of that couple has day to day care,

(b) where a person who is not a member of a married or unmarried couple has day to day care of a child, that person and any such child or children;

and for the purposes of this definition a person shall not be treated as having day to day care of a child who is a member of that person's household where the child in question is being looked after by a local authority within the meaning of section 22 of the Children Act 1989 or, in Scotland, where the child is boarded out with that person by a local authority under the provisions of section 21 of the Social Work (Scotland) Act 1968;

"grant" means any kind of educational grant or award and includes any scholarship, exhibition, allowance or bursary but does not include a payment made under section 100 of the Education Act 1944 or section 73 of the Education (Scotland) Act 1980;

"grant contribution" means any amount which a Minister of the Crown or an education authority treats as properly payable by another person when assessing the amount of a student's grant and by which that amount is, as a consequence, reduced;

"home" means—

(a) the dwelling in which a person and any family of his normally live; or

(b) if he or they normally live in more than one home, the principal home of that person and any family of his,

and for the purpose of determining the principal home in which a person normally lives no regard shall be had to residence in a residential care home or a nursing home during the period which does not exceed 52 weeks or, where it appears to the child support officer that the person will return to his principal home after that period has expired, such longer period as that officer considers reasonable to allow for the return of that person to that home;

"housing benefit" has the same meaning as in section 130 of the Contributions and Benefits Act;

"Housing Benefit Regulations" means the Income Support (General) Regulations 1987;

"Income Support Regulations" means the Income Support (General) Regulations 1987;

"Maintenance Assessment Procedure Regulations" means the Child Support (Maintenance Assessment Procedure) Regulations 1992;

"married couple" means a man and a woman who are married to each other and are members of the same household;

"non-dependant" means a person who is a non-dependant for the purposes of either—

(a) regulation 3 of the Income Support Regulations; or

(b) regulation 3 of the Housing Benefit Regulations,

or who would be a non-dependant for those purposes if another member of the household in which he is living were entitled to income support or housing benefit as the case may be;

"nursing home" has the same meaning as in regulation 19(3) of the Income Support Regulations;

"occupational pension scheme" has the same meaning as in section 66(1) of the Social Security Pensions Act 1975;

"ordinary clothing or footwear" means clothing or footwear for normal daily use, but does not include school uniforms, or clothing or footwear used solely for sporting activities;

"parent with care" means a person who, in respect of the same child or children, is both a parent and a person with care;

"partner" means—

(a) in relation to a member of a married or unmarried couple who are living together, the other member of that couple;

(b) in relation to a member of a polygamous marriage, any other member of that marriage with whom he lives;

"patient" means a person (other than a person who is serving a sentence of imprisonment or detention in a young offender institution within the meaning of the Criminal Justice Act 1982 as amended by the Criminal Justice Act 1988 who is regarded as receiving free in-patient treatment within the meaning of the Social Security (Hospital In-Patients) Regulations 1975;

"person" does not include a local authority;

"personal pension scheme" has the same meaning as in section 84(1) of the Social Security Act 1986 and, in the case of a self-employed earner, includes a scheme approved by the Inland Revenue under Chapter IV of Part XIV of the Income and Corporation Taxes Act 1988;

"polygamous marriage" means any marriage during the subsistence of which a party to it is married to more than one person and in respect of which any ceremony of marriage took place under the law of a country which at the time of that ceremony permitted polygamy;

"prisoner" means a person who is detained in custody pending trial or sentence upon conviction or under a sentence imposed by a court other than a person whose detention is under the Mental Health Act 1983 or the Mental Health (Scotland) Act 1984;

"relevant child" means a child of an absent parent or a parent with care who is a member of the same family as that parent;

"relevant Schedule" means Schedule 2 to the Income Support Regulations (income support applicable amounts);

"relevant week" means—

(a) in relation to an application for child support maintenance—

(i) in the case of the person making the application, the period of 7 days immediately preceding the date on which the appropriate maintenance assessment application form is submitted to the Secretary of State;

(ii) in the case of a person to whom a maintenance assessment enquiry form is given or sent as a result of such application, the period of 7 days immediately preceding the date on which that form is to be treated as given or sent under regulation 1(6)(b) of the Maintenance Assessment Procedure Regulations;

(b) in relation to a review of a maintenance assessment under section 16 or 17 of the Act, the period of 7 days immediately preceding the date on which a maintenance assessment review enquiry form given or sent to the person in question is to be treated as having been given or sent under regulation 1(6)(b) of the Maintenance Assessment Procedure Regulations;

"residential care home" has the same meaning as in regulation 19(3) of the Income Support Regulations;

"retirement annuity contract" means an annuity contract for the time being approved by the Board of Inland Revenue as having for its main object the provision of a life annuity in old age or the provision of an annuity for a partner or dependant and in respect of which relief from income tax may be given on any premium;

"self-employment earner" has the same meaning as in section 2(1)(b) of the Contributions and Benefits Act;

"student" means a person, other than a person in receipt of a training allowance, who is aged less than 19 and attending a full-time course of advanced education or who is aged 19 or over and attending a full-time course of study at an educational establishment; and for the purposes of this definition—

(a) a person who has started on such a course shall be treated as attending it throughout any period of term or vacation within it, until the last day of the course or such earlier date as he abandons it or is dismissed from it;
(b) a person on a sandwich course (within the meaning of paragraph 1(1) of Schedule 5 to the Education (Mandatory Awards) Regulations 1988) shall be treated as attending a full-time course of advanced education or, as the case may be, of study;

"student loan" means a loan which is made to a student pursuant to arrangements made under section 1 of the Education (Student Loans) Act 1990);

"the Independent Living Fund" means the charitable trust of that name established out of funds provided by the Secretary of State for the purpose of providing financial assistance to those persons incapacitated by or otherwise suffering from very severe disability who are in need of such assistance to enable them to live independently;

"training allowance" has the same meaning as in regulation 2 of the Income Support Regulations;

"unmarried couple" means a man and a woman who are not married to each other but are living together as husband and wife;

"weekly council tax" means the annual amount of the council tax in question payable in respect of the year in which the effective date falls, divided by 52;

"year" means a period of 52 weeks;

"youth training" means—

(a) arrangements made under section 2 of the Employment and Training Act 1973 or section 2 of the Enterprise and New Towns (Scotland) Act 1990; or
(b) arrangements made by the Secretary of State for persons enlisted in Her Majesty's forces for any special term of service specified in regulations made under section 2 of the Armed Forces Act 1966 (power of Defence Council to make regulations as to engagement of persons in regular forces);

for purposes which include the training of persons who, at the beginning of their training, are under the age of 18.

(3) In these Regulations, unless the context otherwise requires, a reference—

(a) to a numbered Part is to the Part of these Regulations bearing that number;
(b) to a numbered Schedule is to the Schedule to these Regulations bearing that number;
(c) to a numbered regulation is to the regulation in these Regulations bearing that number;
(d) in a regulation or Schedule to a numbered paragraph is to the paragraph in that regulation or Schedule bearing that number;
(e) in a paragraph to a lettered or numbered sub-paragraph is to the sub-paragraph in that paragraph bearing that letter or number.

(4) The regulations in Part II and the provisions of the Schedules to these Regulations are subject to the regulations relating to special cases in Part III.

PART II
Calculation or estimation of child support maintenance

2. Calculation or estimation of amounts

(1) Where any amount falls to be taken into account for the purposes of these Regulations, it shall be calculated or estimated as a weekly amount and, except where the context otherwise requires, any reference to such an amount shall be construed accordingly.

(2) Subject to regulation 13(2), where any calculation made under these Regulations results in a fraction of a penny that fraction shall be treated as a penny if it is either one half or exceeds one half, otherwise it shall be disregarded.

(3) A child support officer shall calculate the amounts to be taken into account for the purposes of these Regulations by reference, as the case may be, to the dates, weeks, months or other periods specified herein provided that if he becomes aware of a material change of circumstances occurring after such date, week, month or other period but before the effective date, he shall take that change of circumstances into account.

3. Calculation of AG

(1) The amounts to be taken into account for the purposes of calculating AG in the formula set out in paragraph 1(2) of Schedule 1 to the Act are—

  (a) with respect to each qualifying child, an amount equal to the amount specified in column (2) of paragraph 2 of the relevant Schedule for a person of the same age (income support personal allowance for child or young person);
  (b) with respect to a person with care of a qualifying child aged less than 16, an amount equal to the amount specified in column (2) of paragraph 1(1)(e) of the relevant Schedule (income support personal allowance for a single claimant aged not less than 25);
  (c) an amount equal to the amount specified in paragraph 3 of the relevant Schedule (income support family premium);
  (d) where the person with care of the qualifying child or children has no partner, an amount equal to the amount specified in paragraph 15(1) of the relevant Schedule (income support lone parent premium).

(2) The amounts referred to in paragraph (1) shall be the amounts applicable at the effective date.

4. Basic rate of child benefit

For the purposes of paragraph 1(4) of Schedule 1 to the Act "basic rate" means the rate of child benefit which is specified in regulation 2(1) of the Child Benefit and Social Security (Fixing and Adjustment of Rates) Regulations 1976 (rates of child benefit) applicable to the child in question at the effective date.

5. The general rule

For the purposes of paragraph 2(1) of Schedule 1 to the Act—

(a) the value of C, otherwise than in a case where the other parent is the person with care, is nil; and
(b) the value of P is 0.5.

6. The additional element

(1) For the purposes of the formula in paragraph 4(1) of Schedule 1 to the Act, the value of R is 0.25.

(2) For the purposes of the alternative formula in paragraph 4(3) of Schedule 1 to the Act—

(a) the value of Z is 3;
(b) the amount for the purposes of paragraph (b) of the definition of Q is the same as the amount specified in regulation 3(1)(c) (income support family premium) in respect of each qualifying child.

7. Net income: calculation or estimation of N

(1) Subject to the following provisions of this regulation, for the purposes of the formula in paragraph 5(1) of Schedule 1 to the Act, the amount of N (net income of absent parent) shall be the aggregate of the following amounts—

(a) the amount, determined in accordance with Part I of Schedule 1, or any earnings of the absent parent;
(b) the amount, determined in accordance with Part II of Schedule 1, of any benefit payments under the Contributions and Benefits Act paid to or in respect of the absent parent;
(c) the amount, determined in accordance with Part III of Schedule 1, of any other income of the absent parent;
(d) the amount, determined in accordance with Part IV of Schedule 1, of any income of a relevant child which is treated as the income of the absent parent;
(e) any amount, determined in accordance with Part V of Schedule 1, which is treated as the income of the absent parent.

(2) Any amounts referred to in Schedule 2 shall be disregarded.

(3) Where an absent parent's income consists—

(a) only of a youth training allowance; or
(b) in the case of a student, only a grant, an amount paid in respect of grant contribution or student loan or any combination thereof; or
(c) only of prisoner's pay,

then for the purposes of determining N such income shall be disregarded.

(4) Where a parent and any other person are beneficially entitled to any income but the shares of their respective entitlements are not ascertainable the child support officer shall estimate their respective entitlements having regard to such information as is available but where sufficient information on which to base an estimate is not available the parent and that other person shall be treated as entitled to that income in equal shares.

(5) Where any income normally received at regular intervals has not been received it shall, if it is due to be paid and there are reasonable grounds for believing it will be received, be treated as if it had been received.

8. Net income: calculation or estimation of M

For the purposes of paragraph 5(2) of Schedule 1 to the Act, the amount of M (net income of the parent with care) shall be calculated in the same way as N is calculated under regulation 7 but as if references to the absent parent were references to the parent with care.

9. Exempt income: calculation or estimation of E

(1) For the purposes of paragraph 5(1) of Schedule 1 to the Act, the amount of E (exempt income of absent parent) shall, subject to paragraphs (3) and (4), be the aggregate of the following amounts—

    (a) an amount equal to the amount specified in column (2) of paragraph 1(1)(e) of the relevant Schedule (income support personal allowance for a single claimant aged not less than 25);

    (b) an amount in respect of housing costs determined in accordance with regulations 14 to 18;

    (c) where—

        (i) the absent parent of a relevant child; and

        (ii) if he were a claimant, the condition in paragraph 8 of the relevant Schedule (income support lone parent premium) would be satisfied but the conditions referred to in sub-paragraph (1)(d) would not be satisfied;

    an amount equal to the amount specified in column (2) of paragraph 15(1) of that Schedule (income support lone parent premium);

    (d) where, if the parent were a claimant aged less than 60, the conditions in paragraph 11 of the relevant Schedule (income support disability premium) would be satisfied in respect of him, an amount equal to the amount specified in column (2) of paragraph 15(4)(a) of that Schedule (income support disability premium);

    (e) where—

        (i) if the parent were a claimant, the conditions in paragraph 13 of the relevant Schedule (income support severe disability premium) would be satisfied, an amount equal to the amount specified in column (2) of paragraph 15(5)(a) of that Schedule (except that no such amount shall be taken into account in the case of an absent parent in respect of whom an invalid care allowance under section 70 of the Contributions and Benefits Act is payable to some other person);

        (ii) if the parent were a claimant, the conditions in paragraph 14ZA of the relevant Schedule (income support carer premium) would be satisfied in respect of him, an amount equal to the amount specified in column (2) of paragraph 15(7) of that Schedule;

    (f) where, if the parent were a claimant, the conditions in paragraph 3 of the relevant Schedule (income support family premium) would be satisfied in respect of a relevant child of that parent, the amount specified in that paragraph or, where those conditions would be satisfied only by virtue of the case being one to which paragraph (2) applies, half that amount;

    (g) in respect of each relevant child—

        (i) an amount equal to the amount of the personal allowance for that child, specified in column (2) of paragraph 2 of the relevant Schedule (income support personal allowance) or, where paragraph (2) applies, half that amount;

(ii) if the conditions set out in paragraph 14(b) and (c) of the relevant Schedule (income support disabled child premium) are satisfied in respect of that child, an amount equal to the amount specified in column (2) of paragraph 15(6) of the relevant Schedule or, where paragraph (2) applies, half that amount;

(h) where the absent parent in question or his partner is living in—

(i) accommodation provided under Part III of the National Assistance Act 1948;
(ii) accommodation provided under paragraphs 1 and 2 of Schedule 8 to the National Health Service Act 1977; or
(iii) a nursing home or residential care home,

the amount of the fees paid in respect of the occupation of that accommodation or, as the case may be, that home.

(2) This paragraph applies where—

(a) the absent parent has a partner;
(b) the absent parent and the partner are parents of the same relevant child; and
(c) the income of the partner, calculated under regulation 7(1) as if that partner were an absent parent to whom that regulation applied, exceeds the aggregate of—

(i) the amount specified in column 2 of paragraph 1(1)(e) of the relevant Schedule (income support personal allowance for a single claimant aged not less than 25);
(ii) half the amount of the personal allowance for that child specified in column (2) of paragraph 2 of the relevant Schedule (income support personal allowance);
(iii) half the amount of any income support disabled child premium specified in column (2) of paragraph 15(6) of that Schedule in respect of that child;
(iv) half the amount of any income support family premium specified in paragraph 3 of the Schedule except where such premium is payable irrespective of that child; and
(v) the amount by which the housing costs of the absent parent, calculated in accordance with these Regulations, have been reduced by an apportionment under regulation 17.

(3) Where an absent parent does not have day to day care of any relevant child for 7 nights each week but does have day to day care of one or more such children for fewer than 7 nights each week, any amounts to be taken into account under sub-paragraphs (1)(c) and (f) shall be reduced so that they bear the same proportion to the amounts referred to in those sub-paragraphs as the average number of nights each week in respect of which such care is provided has to 7.

(4) Where an absent parent has day to day care of a relevant child for fewer than 7 nights each week, any amounts to be taken into account under sub-paragraph (1)(g) in respect of such a child shall be reduced so that they bear the same proportion to the amounts referred to in that sub-paragraph as the average number of nights each week in respect of which such care is provided has to 7.

(5) The amounts referred to in paragraph (1) are the amounts applicable at the effective date.

10. Exempt income: calculation or estimation of F

For the purposes of paragraph 5(2) of Schedule 1 to the Act, the amount of F (exempt income of parent with care) shall be calculated in the same way as E is calculated under regulation 9 but as if references to the absent parent were references to the parent with care.

11. Protected income

(1) For the purposes of paragraph 6 of Schedule 1 to the Act the protected income level of an absent parent shall, subject to paragraphs (3) and (4), be the aggregate of the following amounts—

(a) where—

(i) the absent parent does not have a partner, an amount equal to the amount specified in column (2) of paragraph 1(1)(e) of the relevant Schedule (income support personal allowance for a single claimant aged not less than 25 years);

(ii) the absent parent has a partner, an amount equal to the amount specified in column (2) of paragraph 1(3)(c) of the relevant Schedule (income support personal allowance for a couple where both members are aged not less than 18 years);

(iii) the absent parent is a member of a polygamous marriage, an amount in respect of himself and one of his partners, equal to the amount specified in sub-paragraph (ii) and, in respect of each of his other partners, an amount equal to the difference between the amounts specified in sub-paragraph (ii) and sub-paragraph (i);

(b) an amount in respect of housing costs determined in accordance with regulations 14, 15, 16 and 18, or, in a case where the absent parent is a non-dependant member of a household who is treated as having no housing costs by regulation 15(10)(a), the non-dependant amount which would be calculated in respect of him under regulation 15(5);

(c) where, if the absent parent were a claimant, the condition in paragraph 8 of the relevant Schedule (income support lone parent premium) would be satisfied but the condition set out in paragraph 11 of that Schedule (income support disability premium) would not be satisfied, an amount equal to the amount specified in column (2) of paragraph 15(1) of that Schedule (income support lone parent premium);

(d) where, if the parent were a claimant, the conditions in paragraph 11 of the relevant Schedule (income support disability premium) would be satisfied, an amount equal to the amount specified in column (2) of paragraph 15(4) of that Schedule (income support disability premium);

(e) where, if the parent were a claimant, the conditions in paragraph 13 or 14ZA of the relevant Schedule (income support severe disability and carer premiums) would be satisfied in respect of either or both premiums, an amount equal to the amount or amounts specified in column (2) of paragraph 15(5) or, as the case may be, (7) of that Schedule in respect of that or those premiums (income support premiums);

(f) where, if the parent were a claimant, the conditions in paragraph 3 of the relevant Schedule (income support family premium) would be satisfied, the amount specified in that paragraph;

(g) in respect of each child who is a member of the family of the absent parent—

(i) an amount equal to the amount of the personal allowance for that child, specified in column (2) of paragraph 2 of the relevant Schedule (income support personal allowance);

(ii) if the conditions set out in paragraphs 14(b) and (c) of the relevant Schedule (income support disabled child premium) are satisfied in respect of that child, an amount equal to the amount specified in column (2) of paragraph 15(6) of the relevant Schedule;

(h) where, if the parent were a claimant, the conditions specified in Part III of the relevant Schedule would be satisfied by the absent parent in question or any member of his family in relation to any premium not otherwise included in this regulation, an amount equal to the amount specified in Part IV of that Schedule (income support premiums) in respect of that premium;

(i) where the absent parent in question or his partner is living in—

(i) accommodation provided under Part III of the National Assistance Act 1948;

(ii) accommodation provided under paragraphs 1 and 2 of Schedule 8 to the National Health Service Act 1977; or

(iii) a nursing home or residential care home,

the amount of the fees paid in respect of the occupation of that accommodation or, as the case may be, that home,

(j) the amount of council tax which the absent parent in question or his partner is liable to pay in respect of the home for which housing costs are included under sub-paragraph (b) less any council tax benefit;

(k) an amount of £80.00;

(l) where the income of—

(i) the absent parent in question;

(ii) any partner of his; and

(iii) any child or children for whom an amount is included under sub-paragraph (g)(i);

exceeds the sum of the amounts to which reference is made in sub-paragraphs (a) to (k), 10 per centum of the excess.

(2) For the purposes of sub-paragraph (1) of paragraph (1) "income" shall be calculated—

(a) in respect of the absent parent in question or any partner of his, in the same manner as N (net income of absent parent) is calculated under regulation 7 except—

(i) there shall be taken into account the basic rate of any child benefit for any maintenance which in either case is in payment in respect of any member of the family of the absent parent;

(ii) there shall be deducted the amount of any maintenance under a maintenance order which the absent parent or his partner is paying in respect of a child in circumstances where an application for a maintenance assessment could not be made in accordance with the Act in respect of that child; and

(b) in respect of any child in that family, as being the total of that child's income but only to the extent that such income does not exceed the amount included under sub-paragraph (g) of paragraph (1) (income support personal allowance for a child and income support disabled child premium) reduced, as the case may be, under paragraph (4).

(3) Where an absent parent does not have day to day care of any child (whether or not a relevant child) for 7 nights each week but does have day to day care of one or more such children for fewer than 7 nights each week, any amounts to be taken into account under

sub-paragraphs (c) and (f) of paragraph (1) (income support lone parent premium and income support family premium) shall be reduced so that they bear the same proportion to the amounts referred to in those sub-paragraphs as the average number of nights each week in respect of which such care is provided has to 7.

(4) Where an absent parent has day to day care of a child (whether or not a relevant child) for fewer than 7 nights each week any amounts in relation to that child to be taken into account under sub-paragraph (g) of paragraph (1) (income support personal allowance for child and income support disabled child premium) shall be reduced so that they bear the same proportion to the amounts referred to in that sub-paragraph as the average number of nights in respect of which such care is provided has to 7.

(5) The amounts referred to in paragraph (1) shall be the amounts applicable at the effective date.

12. Disposable income

(1) For the purposes of paragraph 6(4) of Schedule 1 to the Act (protected income), the disposable income of an absent parent shall be the aggregate of his income and any income of any member of his family calculated in like manner as under regulation 11(2).

(2) Subject to paragraph (3), where a maintenance assessment has been made with respect to the absent parent and payment of the amount of that assessment would reduce his disposable income below his protected income level the amount of the assessment shall be reduced by the minimum amount necessary to prevent his disposable income being reduced below his protected income level.

(3) Where the prescribed minimum amount fixed by regulations under paragraph 7 of Schedule 1 to the Act is applicable (such amount being specified in regulation 13) the amount payable under the assessment shall not be reduced to less than the prescribed minimum amount.

13. The minimum amount

(1) Subject to regulation 26, for the purposes of paragraph 7(1) of Schedule 1 to the Act the minimum amount shall be 5 per centum of the amount specified in paragraph 1(1)(e) of the relevant Schedule (income support personal allowance for single claimant aged not less than 25).

(2) Where an amount calculated under paragraph (1) results in a sum other than a multiple of 5 pence, it shall be treated as the sum which is the next higher multiple of 5 pence.

14. Eligible housing costs

Schedule 3 shall have effect for the purpose of determining the costs which are eligible to be taken into account as housing costs for the purposes of these Regulations.

15. Amount of housing costs

(1) Subject to the provisions of this regulation and regulations 16 to 18, a parent's housing costs shall be the aggregate of the eligible housing costs payable in respect of his home.

(2) Where a local authority has determined that a parent is entitled to housing benefit, the amount of his housing costs shall, subject to paragraphs (4) to (9), be the weekly amount treated as rent under regulations 10 and 69 of the Housing Benefit Regulations (rent and calculation of weekly amounts) less the amount of housing benefit.

(3) Where a parent has eligible housing costs and another person who is not a member of his family is also liable to make payments in respect of the home, the amount of the parent's housing costs shall be his share of those costs.

(4) Where one or more non-dependants are members of the parent's household, there shall be deducted from the amount of any housing costs determined under the preceding paragraphs of this regulation any non-dependant amount of amounts determined in accordance with the provisions of paragraphs (5) to (9).

(5) The non-dependant amount shall be an amount equal to the amount which would be calculated under paragraph 63 of the Housing Benefit Regulations (non-dependant deductions) for the non-dependant in question if he were a non-dependant in respect of whom a calculation were to be made under that regulation.

(6) For the purposes of paragraph (5)—

  (a) in the case of a couple or, as the case may be, the members of a polygamous marriage—

    (i) regard shall be had to their joint weekly income; and
    (ii) only one deduction shall be made at whichever is the higher rate.

(7) Where a person is a non-dependant in respect of more than one joint occupier of a dwelling (except where the joint occupiers are a couple of members of a polygamous marriage), the deduction in respect of that non-dependant shall be apportioned between the joint occupiers having regard to the number of joint occupiers and the proportion of the housing costs in respect of the home payable by each of them.

(8) No deduction shall be made in respect of any non-dependants occupying the home of the parent, if the parent or any partner of his is—

  (a) blind or treated as blind by virtue of paragraph 12 of the relevant Schedule (income support additional condition for the higher pensioner and disability premiums); or
  (b) receiving in respect of himself either—

    (i) attendance allowance under section 64 of the Contributions and Benefits Act; or
    (ii) the care component of disability living allowance.

(9) No deduction shall be made in respect of a non-dependant—

  (a) if, although he resides with the parent, it appears to the child support officer that his home is normally elsewhere; or
  (b) if he is in receipt of a training allowance paid in connection with a Youth Training Programme established under section 2 of the Employment and Training Act 1973 or section 2 of the Enterprise and New Towns (Scotland) Act 1990; or
  (c) if he is a student; or
  (d) if he is aged under 25 and in receipt of income support; or

(e) if he is not residing with the parent because he is a prisoner or because he has been a patient for a period, or two or more periods separated by not more than 28 days, exceeding 6 weeks.

(10) A parent shall be treated as having no housing costs where—

(a) he is a non-dependant member of a household and is not responsible for meeting housing costs except to another member, or other members, of that household; or

(b) but for this paragraph, his housing costs would be less than nil.

16. Weekly amount of housing costs

Where a parent pays housing costs—

(a) on a weekly basis, the amount of such housing costs shall be the weekly rate payable at the effective date;

(b) on a monthly basis, the amount of such housing costs shall be the monthly rate payable at the effective date, multiplied by 12 and divided by 52;

(c) on any other basis, the amount of such housing costs shall be the rate payable at the effective date, multiplied by the number of payment periods, or the nearest whole number of payment periods (any fraction of one half being rounded up), falling within a period of 365 days and divided by 52.

17. Apportionment of housing costs: exempt income

For the purposes of calculating or estimating exempt income the amount of the housing costs of a parent shall be—

(a) where the parent does not have a partner, the whole amount of the housing costs;

(b) where the parent has a partner, the proportion of the amount of the housing costs calculated by multiplying those costs by—

$$\frac{0.75 + (A \times 0.2)}{1.00 + (B \times 0.2)}$$

where—
A is the number of relevant (if any);
B is the number of children in that parent's family (if any);

(c) where the parent is a member of a polygamous marriage the proportion of the amount of the housing costs calculated by multiplying those costs by—

$$\frac{0.75 + (A \times 0.2)}{1.00 + (X \times 0.25) + (B \times 0.2)}$$

where—
A and B have the same meanings as in sub-paragraph (b); and
X is the number which is one less than the number of partners.

18. Excessive housing costs

(1) Subject to paragraph (2), the amount of the housing costs of an absent parent which are to be taken into account—

(a) under regulation 9(1)(b) shall not exceed the greater of £80.00 or half the amount of N as calculated or estimated under regulation 7;

(b) under regulation 11(1)(b) shall not exceed the greater of £80.00 or half of the amount calculated in accordance with regulation 11(2).

(2) The restriction imposed by paragraph (1) shall not apply where—

(a) the absent parent in question—

(i) has been awarded housing benefit (or is awaiting the outcome of a claim to that benefit);
(ii) has the day to day care of any child; or
(iii) is a person to whom a disability premium under paragraph 11 of the relevant Schedule applies in respect of himself or his partner or would so apply if he were entitled to income support and were aged less than 60;

(b) the absent parent in question, following a divorce from, or the breakdown of his relationship with, his former partner, remains in the home he occupied with his former partner;

(c) the absent parent in question has paid the housing costs under the mortgage, charge or agreement in question for a period in excess of 52 weeks before the date of the first application for child support maintenance in relation to a qualifying child of his and there has been no increase in those costs other than an increase in the interest payable under the mortgage or charge or, as the case may be, in the amount payable under the agreement under which the home is held;

(d) the housing costs in respect of the home in question would not exceed the amount set out in paragraph (1) but for an increase in the interest payable under a mortgage or charge secured on that home or, as the case may be, in the amount payable under any agreement under which it is held; or

(e) the absent parent is responsible for making payments in respect of housing costs which are higher than they would be otherwise by virtue of the unavailability of his share of the equity of the property formerly occupied with his partner and which remains occupied by that former partner.

PART III

Special cases

19. Both parents are absent

(1) Subject to regulation 27, where the circumstances of a case are that each parent of a qualifying child is an absent parent in relation to that child (neither being a person who is treated as an absent parent by regulation 20(2)) that case shall be treated as a special case for the purposes of the Act.

(2) For the purposes of this case—

(a) where the application is made in relation to both absent parents, separate assessments shall be made under Schedule 1 to the Act in respect of each so as to determine the amount of child support maintenance payable by each absent parent;

(b) subject to paragraph (3), where the application is made in relation to both absent parents, the value of C in each case shall be the assessable income of the other absent parent and where the application is made in relation to only one the value of C in the case of the other shall be nil;

(c) where the person with care is a body of persons corporate or unincorporate, the value of AG shall not include any amount mentioned in regulation 3(1)(d) (income support lone parent premium).

(3) Where, for the purposes of paragraph (2)(b), information regarding the income of the other absent parent has not been submitted to the Secretary of State or to a child support officer within the period specified in regulation 6(1) of the Maintenance Assessment Procedure Regulations then until such information is acquired the value of C shall be nil.

(4) When the information referred to in paragraph (3) is acquired the child support officer shall make a fresh assessment which shall have effect from the effective date in relation to that other absent parent.

20. Persons treated as absent parents

(1) Where the circumstances of a case are that—

  (a) two or more persons who do not live in the same household each provide day to day care for the same qualifying child; and
  (b) at least one of those persons is a parent of that child,

that case shall be treated as a special case for the purposes of the Act.

(2) For the purposes of this case a parent who provides day to day care for a child of his in the following circumstances is to be treated as an absent parent for the purposes of the Act and these Regulations—

  (a) a parent who provides such care to a lesser extent than the other parent, person or persons who provide such care for the child in question;
  (b) where the persons mentioned in paragraph (1)(a) include both parents and the circumstances are such that care is provided to the same extent by both but each provides care to a greater or equal extent than any other person who provides such care for that child—

    (i) the parent who is not in receipt of child benefit for the child in question; or
    (ii) if neither parent is in receipt of child benefit for that child, the parent who, in the opinion of the child support officer, will not be the principal provider of day to day care for that child.

(3) Subject to paragraphs (5) and (6), where a parent is treated as an absent parent under paragraph (2) child support maintenance shall be payable by that parent in respect of the child in question and the amount of the child support maintenance so payable shall be calculated in accordance with the formula set out in paragraph (4).

(4) The formula for the purposes of paragraph (3) is—

$$T = X - \left\{ (X + Y) \times \frac{J}{7 \times L} \right\}$$

  where—

    T is the amount of child support maintenance payable;
    X is the amount of child support maintenance which would be payable by the parent who is treated as an absent parent, assessed under Schedule 1 to the Act as if paragraphs 6 and 7 of that Schedule did not apply, and, where the other parent is an absent parent, as if the value of C was the assessable income of the other parent;
    Y is—

      (i) the amount of child support maintenance assessed under Schedule 1 to the Act payable by the other parent if he is an absent parent or which would be payable if he were an absent parent, and for the purposes of such calculation the value of C shall be the assessable income of the parent treated as an absent parent under paragraph (2); or,

(ii) if there is no such other parent, shall be nil;

J is the total of the weekly average number of nights for which day to day care is provided by the person who is treated as the absent parent in respect of each child included in the maintenance assessment and shall be calculated to 2 decimal places;

L is the number of children who are included in the maintenance assessment in question.

(5) Where the value of T calculated under the provisions of paragraph (4) is less than zero, no child support maintenance shall be payable.

(6) The liability to pay any amount calculated under paragraph (4) shall be subject to the provision made for protected income and minimum payments under paragraph 6 and 7 of Schedule 1 to the Act.

21. One parent is absent and the other is treated as absent

(1) Where the circumstances of a case are that one parent is an absent parent and the other parent is treated as an absent parent by regulation 20(2), that case shall be treated as a special case for the purposes of the Act.

(2) For the purpose of assessing the child support maintenance payable by an absent parent where this case applies, each reference in Schedule 1 to the Act to a parent who is a person with care shall be treated as a reference to a person who is treated as an absent parent by regulation 20(2).

22. Multiple applications relating to an absent parent

(1) Where the circumstances of a case are that—

(a) two or more applications for a maintenance assessment have been made which relate to the same absent parent (or to a person who is treated as an absent parent by regulation 20(2)); and

(b) those applications relate to different children,

that case shall be treated as a special case for the purposes of the Act.

(2) For the purposes of assessing the amount of child support maintenance payable in respect of each application where paragraph (1) applies, for references to the assessable income of an absent parent in the Act and in these Regulations there shall be substituted references to the amount calculated by the formula—

$$A \times \frac{B}{D}$$

where—

A is the assessable income of the absent parent;

B is the maintenance requirement calculated in respect of the application in question;

D is the sum of the maintenance requirements as calculated for the purposes of each application relating to the absent parent in question.

(3) Where more than one maintenance assessment has been made with respect to the absent parent and payment by him of the aggregate of the amounts of those assessments

would reduce his disposable income below his protected income level, the aggregate amount of those assessments shall be reduced (each being reduced by reference to the same proportion as those assessments bear to each other) by the minimum amount necessary to prevent his disposable income being reduced below his protected income level provided that the aggregate amount payable under those assessments shall not be reduced to less than the minimum amount prescribed in regulation 13(1).

(4) Where the aggregate of the child support maintenance payable by the absent parent is less than the minimum amount prescribed in regulation 13(1), the child support maintenance payable shall be that prescribed minimum amount apportioned between the two or more applications in the same ratio as the maintenance requirements in question bear to each other.

(5) Payment of each of the maintenance assessments calculated under this regulation shall satisfy the liability of the absent parent (or a person treated as such) to pay child support maintenance.

23. Person caring for children of more than one absent parent

(1) Where the circumstances of a case are that—

  (a) a person is a person with care in relation to two or more qualifying children; and
  (b) in relation to at least two of those children there are different persons who are absent parents or persons treated as absent parents by regulation 20(2);

that case shall be treated as a special case for the purposes of the Act.

(2) In calculating the maintenance requirements for the purposes of this case, for any amount which (but for this paragraph) would have been included under regulation 3(1)(b), (c) or (d) (amounts included in the calculation of AG) there shall be substituted an amount calculated by dividing the amount which would have been so included by the relevant number.

(3) In paragraph (2) "the relevant number" means the number equal to the total number of persons who, in relation to those children, are either absent parents or persons treated as absent parents by regulation 20(2) except that where in respect of the same child both parents are persons who are either absent parents or persons who are treated as absent parents under that regulation, they shall count as one person.

(4) Where the circumstances of a case fall within this regulation and the person with care is the parent of any of the children, for C in paragraph 2(1) of Schedule 1 to the Act (the assessable income of that person) there shall be substituted the amount which would be calculated under regulation 22(2) if the references therein to an absent parent were references to a parent with care.

24. Persons with part-time care—not including a person treated as an absent parent

(1) Where the circumstances of a case are that—

  (a) two or more persons who do not live in the same household each provide day to day care for the same qualifying child; and

    (b) those persons do not include any parent who is treated as an absent parent of that child by regulation 20(2),

that case shall be treated as a special case for the purposes of the Act.

(2) For the purposes of this case—

    (a) the person whose application for a maintenance assessment is being proceeded with shall, subject to paragraph (b), be entitled to receive all of the child support maintenance payable under the Act in respect of the child in question;

    (b) on request being made to the Secretary of State by—

        (i) that person; or
        (ii) any other person who is providing day to day care for that child and who intends to continue to provide that care,

        the Secretary of State may make arrangements for the payment of any child support maintenance payable under the Act to the persons who provide such care in the same ratio as that in which it appears to the Secretary of State, that each is to provide such care for the child in question;

    (c) before making an arrangement under sub-paragraph (b), the Secretary of State shall consider all of the circumstances of the case and in particular the interests of the child, the present arrangements for the day to day care of the child in question and any representations or proposals made by the persons who provide such care for that child.

25. Care provided in part by a local authority

(1) Where the circumstances of a case are that a local authority and a person each provide day to day care for the same qualifying child, that case shall be treated as a special case for the purposes of the Act.

(2) In a case where this regulation applies—

    (a) child support maintenance shall be calculated in respect of that child as if this regulation did not apply;

    (b) the amount so calculated shall be divided by 7 so as to produce a daily amount;

    (c) in respect of each night for which day to day care for that child is provided by a person other than the local authority, the daily amount relating to that period shall be payable by the absent parent (or, as the case may be, by the person treated as an absent parent under regulation 20(2));

    (d) child support maintenance shall not be payable in respect of any night for which the local authority provides day to day care for that qualifying child.

26. Cases where child support maintenance is not to be payable

(1) Where the circumstances of a case are that—

    (a) but for this regulation the minimum amount prescribed in regulation 13(1) would apply; and

    (b) any of the following conditions are satisfied—

        (i) the income of the absent parent includes one or more of the payments or awards specified in Schedule 4 or would include such a payment but for a provision preventing the receipt of that payment by reason of it over-lapping with some other benefit payment or would, in the case of the payments referred to in paragraph (a)(i) or (iv) of that Schedule, include such a payment if the relevant contribution conditions for entitlement had been satisfied;

      (ii) an amount to which regulation 11(1)(f) applies (protected income: income support family premium) is taken into account in calculating or estimating the protected income of the absent parent;

    (iii) the absent parent is a child within the meaning of section 55 of the Act;

    (iv) the absent parent is a prisoner; or

     (v) the absent parent is a person in respect of whom N (as calculated or estimated under regulation 7(1)) is less than the minimum amount prescribed by regulation 13(1),

the case shall be treated as a special case for the purposes of the Act.

(2) For the purposes of this case—

    (a) the requirement in paragraph 7(2) of Schedule 1 to the Act (minimum amount of child support maintenance fixed by an assessment to be the prescribed minimum amount) shall not apply;

    (b) the amount of the child support maintenance to be fixed by the assessment shall be nil.

27. Child who is a boarder or an in-patient

(1) Where the circumstances of a case are that—

    (a) a qualifying child is a boarder at a boarding school or is an in-patient in a hospital; and

    (b) by reason of those circumstances, the person who would otherwise provide day to day care is not doing so,

that case shall be treated as a special case for the purposes of the Act.

(2) For the purposes of this case, section 3(3)(b) of the Act shall be modified so for the reference to the person who usually provides day to day care for the child there shall be substituted a reference to the person who would usually be providing such care for that child but for the circumstances specified in paragraph (1).

28. Amount payable where absent parent is in receipt of income support or other prescribed benefit

(1) Where the condition specified in section 43(1)(a) of the Act is satisfied in relation to an absent parent (assessable income to be nil where income support or other prescribed benefit is paid), the prescribed conditions for the purposes of section 43(1)(b) of the Act are that—

    (a) the absent parent is aged 18 or over;

    (b) he does not satisfy the conditions in paragraph 3 of the relevant Schedule (income support family premium); and

    (c) he does not satisfy the conditions for entitlement to one or more of the payments or awards specified in Schedule 4 (other than by reason of a provision preventing receipt of overlapping benefits or by reason of a failure to satisfy the relevant contribution conditions).

(2) For the purposes of section 43(2)(a) of the Act, the prescribed amount shall be equal to the minimum amount prescribed in regulation 13(1) for the purposes of paragraph 7(1) of Schedule 1 to the Act.

SCHEDULE 1

Calculation of N and M

PART I

Earnings of an employed earner

1.—(1) Subject to sub-paragraphs (2) and (3), "earnings" means in the case of employment as an employed earner, any remuneration of profit derived from that employment and includes—

(a) any bonus, commission, royalty or fee;

(b) any holiday pay except any payable more than 4 weeks after termination of the employment;

(c) any payment by way of a retainer;

(d) any payment made by the parent's employer in respect of any expenses not wholly, exclusively and necessarily incurred in the performance of the duties of the employment;

(e) any award of compensation made under section 68(2) or 71(2)(a) of the Employment Protection (Consolidation) Act 1978 (remedies and compensation for unfair dismissal);

(f) any such sum as is referred to in section 112 of the Contributions and Benefits Act (certain sums to be earnings for social security purposes);

(g) any statutory sick pay under Part I of the Social Security and Housing Benefits Act 1982 or statutory maternity pay under Part V of the Social Security Act 1986;

(h) any payment in lieu of notice and any compensation in respect of the absence or inadequacy of any such notice but only insofar as such payment or compensation represents loss of income;

(i) any payment relating to a period of less than a year which is made in respect of the performance of duties as—

(i) an auxiliary coastguard in respect of coast rescue activities;

(ii) a part-time fireman in a fire brigade maintained in pursuance of the Fire Services Acts 1947 to 1959;

(iii) a person engaged part-time in the manning or launching of a lifeboat;

(iv) a member of any territorial or reserve force prescribed in Part I of Schedule 3 to the Social Security (Contributions) Regulations 1979;

(j) any payment made by a local authority to a member of that authority in respect of the performance of his duties as a member, other than any expenses wholly, exclusively and necessarily incurred in the performance of those duties.

(2) Earnings shall not include—

(a) any payment in respect of expenses wholly, exclusively and necessarily incurred in the performance of the duties of the employment;

(b) any occupational pension;

(c) any payment where—

(i) the employment in respect of which it was made has ceased; and

(ii) a period of the same length as the period by reference to which it was calculated has expired since that cessation but prior to the effective date;

(d) any advance of earnings or any loan made by an employer to an employee;

(e) any amount received from an employer during a period when the employee has withdrawn his services by reason of a trade dispute;

(f) any payment in kind;

(g) where, in any week or other period which falls within the period by reference to which earnings are calculated, earnings are received both in respect of a previous employment and in respect of a subsequent employment, the earnings in respect of the previous employment.

(3) The earnings to be taken into account for the purposes of calculating N and M shall be gross earnings less—

(a) any amount deducted from those earnings by way of—

(i) income tax;
(ii) primary Class 1 contributions under the Contributions and Benefits Act; and

(b) one half of any sums paid by the parent towards an occupational or personal pension scheme.

2. (1) Subject to sub-paragraphs (2) to (4)—

(a) where a person is paid weekly, the amount of those earnings shall be determined by aggregating the amounts received in the 5 weeks ending with the relevant week and dividing by 5;

(b) where a person is paid monthly, the amount of those earnings shall be determined by aggregating the amounts received in the 2 months ending with the relevant week, multiplying the aggregate by 6 and dividing by 52;

(c) where a person is paid by reference to some other period, the amount of those earnings shall be determined by aggregating the amounts received in the 3 months ending with the relevant week, multiplying the aggregate by 4 and dividing by 52.

(2) Where a person's earnings include a bonus or commission which is paid during the period of 52 weeks ending with the relevant week and is paid separately from, or, in relation to a longer period than, the other earnings with which it is paid, the amount of that bonus or commission shall be determined by aggregating such payments received in the 52 weeks ending with the relevant week and dividing by 52.

(3) Subject to sub-paragraph (4), the amount of any earnings of a student shall be determined by aggregating the amount received in the year ending with the relevant week and dividing by 52 or, where the person in question has been a student for less than a year, by aggregating the amount received in the period starting with his becoming a student and ending with the relevant week and dividing by the number of complete weeks in that period.

(4) Where a calculation would, but for this sub-paragraph, produce an amount which, in the opinion of the child support officer, does not accurately reflect the normal amount of the earnings of the person in question, such earnings, or any part of them, shall be calculated by reference to such other period as may, in the particular case, enable the normal weekly earnings of that person to be determined more accurately and for this purpose the child support officer shall have regard to—

(a) the earnings received, or due to be received, from any employment in which the person in question is engaged, has been engaged or is due to be engaged;

(b) the duration and pattern, or the expected duration and pattern, of any employment of that person.

Earnings of a self-employed earner

3.—(1) Subject to sub-paragraphs (2) and (3) and to paragraph 4, "earnings" in the case of employment as a self-employed earner means the gross receipts of the employment including, where an allowance in the form of periodic payments is paid under section 2 of the Employment and Training Act 1973 or section 2 of the Enterprise and New Towns (Scotland) Act 1990 in respect of the relevant week for the purpose of assisting him in carrying on his business, the total of those payments made during the period by reference to which his earnings are determined under paragraph 5.

(2) Earnings shall not include—

    (a) any allowance paid under either of those sections in respect of any part of the period by reference to which his earnings are determined under paragraph 5 if no part of that allowance is paid in respect of the relevant week;

    (b) any income consisting of payments received for the provision of board and lodging accommodation unless such payments form the largest element of the recipient's income.

(3) There shall be deducted from the gross receipts referred to in sub-paragraph (1)—

    (a) any expenses which are reasonably incurred and are wholly and exclusively defrayed for the purposes of the earner's business in the period by reference to which his earnings are determined under paragraph 5(1) or, where paragraph 5(2) applies, any such expenses relevant to the period there mentioned (whether or not defrayed in that period);

    (b) any value added tax paid in the period by reference to which earnings are determined in excess of value added tax received in that period;

    (c) any amount in respect of income tax determined in accordance with sub-paragraph (5);

    (d) any amount in respect of National Insurance contributions determined in accordance with sub-paragraph (6);

    (e) one half of any premium paid in respect of a retirement annuity contract or a personal pension scheme.

(4) For the purposes of sub-paragraph (3)(a)—

    (a) such expenses include—

        (i) repayment of capital on any loan used for the replacement, in the course of business, of equipment or machinery, or the repair of an existing business asset except to the extent that any sum is payable under an insurance policy for its repair;

        (ii) any income expended in the repair of an existing business asset except to the extent that any sum is payable under an insurance policy for its repair,

        (iii) any payment of interest on a loan taken out for the purposes of the business;

    (b) such expenses do not include—

        (i) repayment of capital on any other loan taken out for the purposes of the business;

        (ii) any capital expenditure;

        (iii) the depreciation of any capital asset;

        (iv) any sum employed, or intended to be employed, in the setting up or expansion of the business;

        (v) any loss incurred before the beginning of the period by reference to which earnings are determined;

        (vi) any expenses incurred in providing business entertainment;

(vii) any loss incurred in any other employment in which he is engaged as a self-employed earner.

(5) For the purposes of sub-paragraph (3)(c), the amount of income tax to be allowed against earnings shall be calculated as if those earnings, less any personal allowance applicable to the earner under Chapter 1 of Part VII of the Income and Corporation Taxes Act 1988 (Personal Relief) (or where the earnings are determined over a period of less than a year, a proportionate part of such relief), were assessable to income tax at the rates of tax applicable at the effective date.

(6) For the purposes of sub-paragraph (3)(d), the amount to be deducted in respect of National Insurance contributions shall be the total of—

(a) the amount of Class 2 contributions (if any) payable under section 11(1) or, as the case may be, (4) of the Contributions and Benefits Act; and
(b) the amount of Class 4 contributions (if any) payable under section 15(2) of that Act,

at the rates applicable at the effective date.

4. In a case where a person is self-employed as a childminder the amount of earnings referable to that employment shall be one-third of the gross receipts.

5. (1) Subject to sub-paragraphs (2) and (3)—

(a) where a person has been a self-employed earner for 52 weeks or more including the relevant week, the amount of his earnings shall be determined by reference to the average of the earnings which he has received in the 52 weeks ending with the relevant week;
(b) where the person has been a self-employed earner for a period of less than 52 weeks including the relevant week, the amount of his earnings shall be determined by reference to the average of the earnings which he has received during that period.

(2) Where a person who is a self-employed earner provides in respect of the employment a profit and loss account and, where appropriate, a trading account or a balance sheet or both, and the profit and loss account is in respect of a period of at least 6 months but not exceeding 15 months and that period terminates within the 12 months immediately preceding the effective date, the amount of his earnings shall be determined by reference to the average of the earnings over the period to which the profit and loss account relates and such earnings shall include receipts relevant to that period (whether or not received in that period).

(3) Where a calculation would, but for this sub-paragraph, produce an amount which, in the opinion of the child support officer, does not accurately reflect the normal amount of the earnings of the person in question, such earnings, or any part of them, shall be calculated by reference to such other period as may, in the particular case, enable the normal weekly earnings of that person to be determined more accurately and for this purpose the child support officer shall have regard to—

(a) the earnings received, or due to be received, from any employment in which the person in question is engaged, or has been engaged or is due to be engaged;
(b) the duration and pattern, or the expected duration and pattern, of any employment of that person.

(4) In sub-paragraph (2)—

   (a) "balance sheet" means a statement of the financial position of the employment disclosing its assets, liabilities and capital at the end of the period in question;
   (b) "profit and loss account" means a financial statement showing net profit or loss of the employment for the period in question; and
   (c) "trading account" means a financial statement showing the revenue from sales, the cost of those sales and the gross profit arising during the period in question.

PART II

Benefit Payments

6.—(1) The benefit payments to be taken into account in calculating or estimating N and M shall be determined in accordance with this Part.

(2) "Benefit payments" means any benefit payments under the Contributions and Benefits Act except amounts to be disregarded by virtue of Schedule 2.

(3) The amount of any benefit payment to be taken into account shall be determined by reference to the rate of that benefit applicable at the effective date.

7. (1) Where a benefit payment under the Contributions and Benefits Act includes an adult or child dependency increase—

   (a) if that benefit is payable to a parent, the income of that parent shall be calculated or estimated as if it did not include that amount;
   (b) if that benefit is payable to some other person but includes an amount in respect of the parent, the income of the parent shall be calculated or estimated as if it included that amount.

(2) Subject to sub-paragraph (3), payments to a person by way of family credit shall be treated as the income of the parent who has qualified for them by his engagement in, and normal engagement in, remunerative work.

(3) Subject to sub-paragraphs (4) and (5), where family credit is payable and the amount which is payable has been calculated by reference either to the weekly earnings of the absent parent and another person or the parent with care and another person—

   (a) if during the period which is used to calculate his earnings under paragraph 2 or, as the case may be, paragraph 5, the weekly earnings of that parent exceed those of the other person, the amount payable by way of family credit shall be treated as the income of that parent;
   (b) if during that period the normal weekly earnings of that parent equal those of the other person, half of the amount payable by way of family credit shall be treated as the income of that parent; and
   (c) if during that period the normal weekly earnings of that parent are less than those of that other person, the amount payable by way of family credit shall not be treated as the income of that parent.

(4) Where—

   (a) family credit (calculated, as the case may be, by reference to the weekly earnings of the absent parent and another person or the parent with care and another person) is in payment; and

(b) not later than the effective date either or both the persons by reference to whose engagement and normal engagement in remunerative work that payment has been calculated has ceased to be so employed,

half of the amount payable by way of family credit shall be treated as the income of the parent in question.

(5) Where—

(a) family credit is in payment; and
(b) not later than the effective date the person or, if more than one, each of the persons by reference to whose engagement, and normal engagement, in remunerative work that payment has been calculated is no longer the partner of the person to whom that payment is made,

the payment in question shall only be treated as the income of the parent in question where he is in receipt of it.

PART III

Other income

8. The amount of the other income to be taken into account in calculating or estimating N and M shall be the aggregate of the following amounts determined in accordance with this Part.

9. Any periodic payment of pension or other benefit under an occupational or personal pension scheme or a retirement annuity contract or other such scheme for the provision of income in retirement.

10. Any payment received on account of the provision of board and lodging which does not come within Part I of this Schedule.

11. Subject to regulation 7(3)(b) and paragraph 12, any payment to a student of—

(a) grant;
(b) an amount in respect of grant contribution;
(c) covenant income except to the extent that it has been taken into account under sub-paragraph (b);
(d) a student loan.

12. The income of a student shall not include any payment—

(a) intended to meet tuition fees or examination fees;
(b) intended to meet additional expenditure incurred by a disabled student in respect of his attendance on a course;
(c) intended to meet additional expenditure connected with term time residential study away from the student's educational establishment;
(d) on account of the student maintaining a home at a place other than that at which he resides during his course;
(e) intended to meet the cost of books, and equipment (other than special equipment) or, if not so intended, an amount equal to the amount allowed under regulation 38(2)(f) of the Family Credit (General) Regulations 1987 towards such costs;
(f) intended to meet travel expenses incurred as a result of his attendance on the course.

13. Any interest, dividend or other income derived from capital.

14. Any maintenance payments in respect of a parent.

15. Any other payments or other amounts received on a periodical basis which are not otherwise taken into account under Part I, II, IV or V of this Schedule.

16. (1) Subject to sub-paragraphs (2) to (6) the amount of any income to which this Part applies shall be calculated or estimated—

- (a) where it has been received in respect of the whole of the period of 26 weeks which ends at the end of the relevant week, by dividing such income received in that period by 26;
- (b) where it has been received in respect of part of the period of 26 weeks which ends at the end of the relevant week, by dividing such income received in that period by the number of complete weeks in respect of which such income is received and for this purpose income shall be treated as received in respect of a week if it is received in respect of any day in the week in question.

(2) The amount of maintenance payments made in respect of a parent—

- (a) where they are payable weekly and have been paid at the same amount in respect of each week in the period of 13 weeks which ends at the end of the relevant week, shall be the amount equal to one of those payments;
- (b) in any other case, shall be the amount calculated by aggregating the total amount of those payments received in the period of 13 weeks which ends at the end of the relevant week and dividing by the number of weeks in that period in respect of which maintenance was due.

(3) In the case of a student—

- (a) the amount of any grant and any amount paid in respect of grant contribution shall be calculated by apportioning it equally between the weeks in respect of which it is payable;
- (b) the amount of any covenant income shall be calculated by dividing the amount payable in respect of a year by 52 (or, where such amount is payable in respect of a lesser period, by the number of complete weeks in that period) and, subject to sub-paragraph (4), deducting £5.00;
- (c) the amount of any student loan shall be calculated by apportioning the loan equally between the weeks in respect of which it is payable and, subject to sub-paragraph (4), deducting £10.00.

(4) For the purposes of sub-paragraph (3)—

- (a) not more than £5.00 shall be deducted under sub-paragraph (3)(b);
- (b) not more than £10.00 in total shall be deducted under sub-paragraphs (3)(b) and (c).

(5) Where in respect of the period of 52 weeks which ends at the end of the relevant week a person is in receipt of interest, dividend or other income which has been produced by his capital, the amount of that income shall be calculated by dividing the aggregate of the income so received by 52.

(6) Where a calculation would, but for this sub-paragraph, produce an amount which, in the opinion of the child support officer, does not accurately reflect the normal amount of the other income of the person in question, such income, or any part of it, shall be calculated by reference to such other period as may, in the particular case, enable the

other income of that person to be determined more accurately and for this purpose the child support officer shall have regard to the nature and pattern of receipt of such income.

PART IV

Income of child treated as income of parent

17. The amount of any income of a child which is to be treated as the income of the parent in calculating or estimating N and M shall be the aggregate of the amounts determined in accordance with this Part.

18. Where a child has income which falls within the following paragraphs of this Part and that child is a member of the family of his parent (whether that child is a qualifying child in relation to that parent or not), the relevant income of that child shall be treated as that of his parent.

19. Where child support maintenance is being assessed for the support of only one qualifying child, the relevant income of that child shall be treated as that of the parent with care.

20. Where child support maintenance is being assessed to support more than one qualifying child, the relevant income of each of those children shall be treated as that of the parent with care to the extent that it does not exceed the aggregate of—

    (a) the amount determined under—

        (i) regulation 3(1)(a) (calculation of AG) in relation to the child in question; and

        (ii) the total of any other amounts determined under regulation 3(1)(b) to (d) which are applicable in the case in question divided by the number of children for whom child support maintenance is being calculated,

    less the basic rate of child benefit (within the meaning of regulation 4) for the child in question; and

    (b) three times the total of the amounts calculated under regulation 3(1)(a) (income support personal allowance for child or young person) in respect of that child and regulation 3(1)(c) (income support family premium).

21. Where child support maintenance is not being assessed for the support of the child whose income is being calculated or estimated, the relevant income of that child shall be treated as that of his parent to the extent that it does not exceed the amount determined under regulation 9(1)(g).

22. Where a benefit under the Contributions and Benefit Acts includes an adult or child dependency increase in respect of a relevant child, the relevant income of that child shall be calculated or estimated as if it included that amount.

23. For the purposes of this Part, "the relevant income of a child" does not include—

    (a) any earnings of the child in question,
    (b) payments by an absent parent in respect of the child for whom maintenance is being assessed;
    (c) where the class of persons who are capable of benefiting from a discretionary trust include the child in question, payments from that trust except in so far as

they are made to provide for food, ordinary clothing and footwear, gas, electricity or fuel charges or housing costs; or

(d) any interest payable on arrears of child support maintenance for that child.

24. The amount of the income of a child which is treated as the income of the parent shall be determined in the same way as if such income were the income of the parent.

PART V

Amounts treated as the income of a parent

25. The amounts which fall to be treated as income of the parent in calculating or estimating N and M shall include amounts to be determined in accordance with this Part.

26. Where a child support officer is satisfied—

(a) that a person has performed a service either—

(i) without receiving any remuneration in respect of it; or
(ii) for remuneration which is less than that normally paid for that service;

(b) that the service in question was for the benefit of—

(i) another person who is not a member of the same family as the person in question; or
(ii) a body which is neither a charity nor a voluntary organisation;

(c) that the service in question was performed for a person who, or as the case may be, a body which was able to pay remuneration at the normal rate for the service in question;

(d) that the principal purpose of the person undertaking the service without receiving any or adequate remuneration is to reduce his assessable income for the purposes of the Act; and

(e) that any remuneration forgone would have fallen to be taken into account as earnings,

the value of the remuneration forgone shall be estimated by a child support officer and an amount equal to the value so estimated shall be treated as income of the person who performed those services.

27. Subject to paragraphs 28 to 30, where the child support officer is satisfied that, otherwise than in the circumstances set out in paragraph 26, a person has intentionally deprived himself of—

(a) any income or capital which would otherwise be a source of income;

(b) any income or capital which it would be reasonable to expect would be secured by him,

with a view to reducing the amount of his assessable income, his net income shall include the amount estimated by a child support officer as representing the income which that person would have had if he had not deprived himself of or failed to secure that income, or as the case may be, that capital.

28. No amount shall be treated as income by virtue of paragraph 27 in relation to—

(a) one parent benefit;

(b) if the parent is a person to, or in respect of, whom income support is payable, unemployment benefit;

(c) a payment from a discretionary trust or a trust derived from a payment made in consequence of a personal inquiry.

29. Where an amount is included in the income of a person under paragraph 27 in respect of income which would become available to him on application, the amount included under that paragraph shall be included from the date on which it could be expected to be acquired.

30. Where a child support officer determines under paragraph 27 that a person has deprived himself of capital which would otherwise be a source of income, the amount of that capital shall be reduced at intervals of 52 weeks, starting with the week which falls 52 weeks after the first week in respect of which income from it is included in the calculation of the assessment in question, by an amount equal to the amount which the child support officer estimates would represent the income from that source in the immediately preceding period of 52 weeks.

31. Where a payment is made on behalf of a parent or a relevant child in respect of food, ordinary clothing or footwear, gas, electricity or fuel charges, housing costs or council tax, an amount equal to the amount which the child support officer estimates represents the value of that payment shall be treated as the income of the parent in question except to the extent that such amount is—

(a) disregarded under paragraph 38 of Schedule 2;
(b) a payment of school fees paid by or on behalf of someone other than the absent parent.

32. Where paragraph 26 applies the amount to be treated as the income of the parent shall be determined as if it were earnings from employment as an employed earner and in a case to which paragraph 27 or 31 applies the amount shall be determined as if it were other income to which Part III of this Schedule applies.

SCHEDULE 2

Amounts to be disregarded when calculating or estimating N and M

1. The amounts referred to in this Schedule are to be disregarded when calculating or estimating N and M (parent's net income).

2. An amount in respect of income tax applicable to the income in question where not otherwise allowed for under these Regulations.

3. Where a payment is made in a currency other than sterling, an amount equal to any banking charge or commission payable in converting that payment to sterling.

4. Any amount payable in a country outside the United Kingdom where there is a prohibition against the transfer to the United Kingdom of that amount.

5. Any compensation for personal injury and any payments from a trust fund set up for that purpose.

6. Any advance of earnings or any loan made by an employer to an employee.

7. Any payment by way of, or any reduction or discharge of liability resulting from entitlement to, housing benefit or council tax benefit.

8. Any disability living allowance, mobility supplement or any payment intended to compensate for the non-payment of any such allowance or supplement.

9. Any payment which is—

   (a) an attendance allowance under section 64 of the Contributions and Benefits Act;
   (b) an increase of disablement pension under section 104 or 105 of that Act (increases where constant attendance needed or for exceptionally severe disablement);
   (c) a payment made under regulations made in exercise of the power conferred by Schedule 8 to that Act (payments for pre-1948 cases);
   (d) an increase of an allowance payable in respect of constant attendance under that Schedule;
   (e) payable by virtue of articles 14, 15, 16, 43 or 44 of the Personal Injuries (Civilians) Scheme 1983 (allowances for constant attendance and exceptionally severe disablement and severe disablement occupational allowance) or any analogous payment; or
   (f) a payment based on the need for attendance which is paid as part of a war disablement pension.

10. Any payment under section 148 of the Contributions and Benefits Act (pensioners' Christmas bonus).

11. Any social fund payment within the meaning of Part VIII of the Contributions and Benefits Act.

12. Any payment made by the Secretary of State to compensate for the loss (in whole or in part) of entitlement to housing benefit.

13. Any payment made by the Secretary of State to compensate for loss of housing benefit supplement under regulation 19 of the Supplementary Benefit (Requirements) Regulations 1983.

14. Any payment made by the Secretary of State to compensate a person who was entitled to supplementary benefit in respect of a period ending immediately before 11th April 1988 but who did not become entitled to income support in respect of a period beginning with that day.

15. Any concessionary payment made to compensate for the non-payment of income support, disability living allowance, or any payment to which paragraph 9 applies.

16. Any payments of child benefit to the extent that they do not exceed the basic rate of that benefit as defined in regulation 4.

17. Any payment made under regulations 9 to 11 or 13 of the Welfare Food Regulations 1988 (payments made in place of milk tokens or the supply of vitamins).

18. Subject to paragraph 20 and to the extent that it does not exceed £10.00—

   (a) war disablement pension or war widow's pension or a payment made to compensate for non-payment of such a pension;
   (b) a pension paid by the government of a country outside Great Britain and which either—

      (i) is analogous to a war disablement pension; or
      (ii) is analogous to a war widow's pension.

19. (1) Except where sub-paragraph (2) applies and subject to sub-paragraph (3) and paragraphs 20, 38 and 47, £10.00 of any charitable or voluntary payment made, or due to be made, at regular intervals.

(2) Subject to sub-paragraph (3) and paragraphs 38 and 47, any charitable or voluntary payment made or due to be made at regular intervals which is intended and used for an item other than food, ordinary clothing or footwear, gas, electricity or fuel charges, housing costs of any member of the family or the payment of council tax.

(3) Sub-paragraphs (1) and (2) shall not apply to a payment which is made by a person for the maintenance of any member of his family or of his former partner or of his children.

(4) For the purposes of sub-paragraph (1) where a number of charitable or voluntary payments fall to be taken into account they shall be treated as though they were one such payment.

20. (1) Where, but for this paragraph, more than £10.00 would be disregarded under paragraphs 18 and 19(1) in respect of the same week, only £10.00 in aggregate shall be disregarded and where an amount falls to be deducted from the income of a student under paragraph 16(3)(b) or (c) of Schedule 1, that amount shall count as part of the £10.00 disregard allowed under this paragraph.

(2) Where any payment which is due to be paid in one week is paid in another week, sub-paragraph (1) and paragraphs 18 and 19(1) shall have effect as if that payment were received in the week in which it was due.

21. In the case of a person participating in arrangements for training made under section 2 of the Employment and Training Act 1973 or section 2 of the Enterprise and New Towns (Scotland) Act 1990 (functions in relation to training for employment etc.) or attending a course at an employment rehabilitation centre established under section 2 of the 1973 Act—

   (a) any travelling expenses reimbursed to the person;
   (b) any living away from home allowance under section 2(2)(d) of the 1973 Act or section 2(4)(c) of the 1990 Act;
   (c) any training premium,

but this paragraph, except in so far as it relates to a payment mentioned in sub-paragraph (a), (b) or (c), does not apply to any part of any allowance under section 2(2)(d) of the 1973 Act or section 2(4)(c) of the 1990 Act.

22. Where a parent occupies a dwelling as his home and that dwelling is also occupied by a person, other than a non-dependant or a person who is provided with board and lodging accommodation, and that person is contractually liable to make payments in respect of his occupation of the dwelling to the parent, the amount or, as the case may be, the amounts specified in paragraph 19 of Schedule 2 to the Family Credit (General) Regulations 1987 which apply in his case, or, if he is not in receipt of family credit, the amounts which would have applied if he had been in receipt of that benefit.

23. Where a parent, who is not a self-employed earner, is in receipt of rent or any other money in respect of the use and occupation of property other than his home, that rent or other payment to the extent of any sums which that parent is liable to pay by way of—

   (a) payments which would be treated as housing costs by paragraph 3 of Schedule 3 if that property were his home (except income: additional provisions relating to housing costs);

(b) council tax payable in respect of that property;

(c) water and sewerage charges payable in respect of that property.

24. Where a parent provides board and lodging accommodation in his home otherwise than as a self-employed earner—

(a) £20.00 of any payment for that accommodation made by the person to whom that accommodation is provided; and

(b) where any such payment exceeds £20.00, 50 per centum of the excess.

25. Any payment made to a person in respect of an adopted child who is a member of his family that is made in accordance with any regulations made under section 57A or pursuant to section 57A(6) of the Adoption Act 1976 (permitted allowances) or, as the case may be, section 51 of the Adoption (Scotland) Act 1978 (schemes for the payment of allowances to adopters)—

(a) where the child is not a child in respect of whom child support maintenance is being assessed, to the extent that it exceeds the amount referred to in regulation 9(1)(g)(i), reduced, as the case may be, under regulation 9(4);

(b) in any other case, to the extent that it does not exceed the amount of the income of a child which is treated as that of his parent by virtue of Part IV.

26. Where a local authority makes a payment in respect of the accommodation and maintenance of a child in pursuance of paragraph 15 of Schedule 1 to the Children Act 1989 (local authority contribution to child's maintenance) to the extent that it exceeds the amount referred to in regulation 9(1)(g)(i) (reduced, as the case may be, under regulation 9(4)).

27. Any payment received under a policy of insurance taken out to insure against the risk of being unable to maintain repayments on a loan taken out to acquire an interest in, or to meet the cost of repairs or improvements to, the parent's home and used to meet such repayments, to the extent that the payment received under that policy does not in any period exceed the total of—

(a) any interest payable on that loan;

(b) any capital repayable on that loan; and

(c) any premiums payable on that policy.

28. In the calculation of the income of the parent with care, any maintenance payments made by the absent parent in respect of his qualifying child.

29. Any payment made by a local authority to a person who is caring for a child under section 23(2)(a) of the Children Act 1989 (provision of accommodation and maintenance by a local authority for children whom the authority is looking after) or, as the case may be, section 21 of the Social Work (Scotland) Act 1968 or by a voluntary organisation under section 59(1)(a) of the Children Act 1989 (provision of accommodation by voluntary organisations) or by a care authority under regulation 9 of the Boarding Out and Fostering of Children (Scotland) Regulations 1985 (provision of accommodation and maintenance for children in care).

30. Any payment made by a health authority, local authority or voluntary organisation in respect of a person who is not normally a member of the household but is temporarily in the care of a member of it.

31. Any payment made by a local authority under section 17 or 24 of the Children Act 1989 or, as the case may be, section 12, 24 or 26 of the Social Work (Scotland) Act 1968 (local authorities' duty to promote welfare of children and powers to grant financial assistance to persons looked after, or in, or formerly in, their care).

32. Any resettlement benefit which is paid to the parent by virtue of regulation 3 of the Social Security (Hospital In-Patients) Amendment (No.2) Regulations 1987 (transitional provisions).

33. (1) Any payment or repayment made—

- (a) as respects England and Wales, under regulation 3, 5 or 8 of the National Health Service (Travelling Expenses and Remission of Charges) Regulations 1988 (travelling expenses and health service supplies);
- (b) as respects Scotland, under regulation 3, 5 or 8 of the National Health Service (Travelling Expenses and Remission of Charges) (Scotland) Regulations 1988 (travelling expenses and health service supplies).

(2) Any payment or repayment made by the Secretary of State for Health, the Secretary of State for Scotland or the Secretary of State for Wales which is analogous to a payment or repayment mentioned in sub-paragraph (1).

34. Any payment made (other than a training allowance), whether by the Secretary of State or any other person, under the Disabled Persons Employment Act 1944 or in accordance with arrangements made under section 2 of the Employment and Training Act 1973 to assist disabled persons to obtain or retain employment despite their disability.

35. Any contribution to the expenses of maintaining a household which is made by a non-dependant member of that household.

36. Any sum in respect of a course of study attended by a child payable by virtue of regulations made under section 81 of the Education Act 1944 (assistance by means of scholarship or otherwise), or by virtue of section 2(1) of the Education Act 1962 (awards for courses of further education) or section 49 of the Education (Scotland) Act 1980 (power to assist persons to take advantage of educational facilities).

37. Where a person receives income under an annuity purchased with a loan which satisfies the following conditions—

- (a) that loan was made as part of a scheme under which not less than 90 per centum of the proceeds of the loan were applied to the purchase by the person to whom it was made of an annuity ending with his life or with the life of the survivor of two or more persons (in this paragraph referred to as "the annuitants") who include the person to whom the loan was made;
- (b) that the interest on the loan is payable by the person to whom it was made or by one of the annuitants;
- (c) that at the time the loan was made the person to whom it was made or each of the annuitants had attained the age of 65;
- (d) that the loan was secured on a dwelling in Great Britain and the person to whom the loan was made or one of the annuitants owns an estate or interest in that dwelling; and
- (e) that the person to whom the loan was made or one of the annuitants occupies the dwelling on which it was secured as his home at the time the interest is paid,

the amount, calculated on a weekly basis equal to—

(i) where, or insofar as, section 26 of the Finance Act 1982 (deduction of tax from certain loan interest) applies to the payments of interest on the loan, the interest which is payable after the deduction of a sum equal to income tax on such payments at the basic rate for the year of assessment in which the payment of interest becomes due;

(ii) in any other case the interest which is payable on the loan without deduction of such a sum.

38. Any payment of the description specified in paragraph 39 of Schedule 9 to the Income Support Regulations (disregard of payments made under certain trusts and disregard of certain other payments) and any income derived from the investment of such payments.

39. Any payment made to a juror or witness in respect of attendance at court other than compensation for loss of earnings or for loss of a benefit payable under the Contributions and Benefits Act.

40. Any special war widows' payment made under—

(a) the Naval and Marine Pay and Pensions (Special War Widows Payment) Order 1990 made under section 3 of the Naval and Marine Pay and Pensions Act 1865;

(b) the Royal Warrant dated 19th February 1990 amending the Schedule to the Army Pensions Warrant 1977;

(c) the Queen's Order dated 26th February 1990 made under section 2 of the Air Force (Constitution) Act 1917;

(d) the Home Guard War Widows Special Payments Regulations 1990 made under section 151 of the Reserve Forces Act 1980;

(e) the Orders dated 19th February 1990 amending Orders made on 12th December 1980 concerning the Ulster Defence Regiment made in each case under section 140 of the Reserve Forces Act 1980,

and any analogous payment by the Secretary of State for Defence to any person who is not a person entitled under the provisions mentioned in sub-paragraphs (a) to (e).

41. Any payment to a person as holder of the Victoria Cross or the George Cross or any analogous payment.

42. Any payment made either by the Secretary of State for the Home Department or by the Secretary of State for Scotland under a scheme established to assist relatives and other persons to visit persons in custody.

43. Any amount by way of a refund of income tax deducted from profits or emoluments chargeable to income tax under Schedule D or Schedule E.

44. Maintenance payments (whether paid under the Act or otherwise) insofar as they are not treated as income under Part III or IV.

45. Where following a divorce or separation—

(a) capital is divided between the parent and the person who was his partner before the divorce or separation; and

(b) that capital is intended to be used to acquire a new home for that parent or to acquire furnishings for a home of his,

income derived from the investment of that capital for one year following the date on which that capital became available to the parent.

46. Payments in kind.

47. Any payment made by the Joseph Rowntree Memorial Trust from money provided to it by the Secretary of State for Health for the purpose of maintaining a family fund for the benefit of severely handicapped children.

48. Any payment of expenses to a person who is—

(a) engaged by a charitable or voluntary body; or
(b) a volunteer,

if he otherwise derives no remuneration or profit from the body or person paying those expenses.

49. In this Schedule—

"concessionary payment" means a payment made under arrangements made by the Secretary of State with the consent of the Treasury which is charged either to the National Insurance Fund or to a Departmental Expenditure Vote to which payments of benefit under the Contributions and Benefits Act are charged;
"health authority" means a health authority established under the National Health Service Act 1977 or the National Health Service (Scotland) Act 1978;
"mobility supplement" has the same meaning as in regulation 2(1) of the Income Support Regulations;
"war disablement pension" and "war widow" have the same meanings as in section 150(2) of the Contributions and Benefits Act.

SCHEDULE 3

Eligible housing costs

1. Eligible housing costs for the purposes of determining exempt income and protected income

Subject to the following provisions of this Schedule, the following payments in respect of the provision of a home shall be eligible to be taken into account as housing costs for the purposes of these Regulations—

(a) payments of, or by way of, rent;
(b) mortgage interest payments;
(c) interest payments under a hire purchase agreement to buy a home;
(d) interest payments on loans for repairs and improvements to the home;
(e) payments by way of ground rent or in Scotland, payments by way of feu duty;
(f) payments under a co-ownership scheme;
(g) payments in respect of, or in consequence of, the use and occupation of the home;
(h) where the home is a tent, payments in respect of the tent and the site on which it stands;
(i) payments in respect of a licence or permission to occupy the home (whether or not board is provided);
(j) payments by way of mesne profits or, in Scotland, violent profits;
(k) payments of, or by way of, service charges, the payment of which is a condition on which the right to occupy the home depends;
(l) payments under or relating to a tenancy or licence of a Crown tenant;
(m) mooring charges payable for a houseboat;

(n) where the home is a caravan or a mobile home, payments in respect of the site on which it stands;

(o) any contribution payable by a parent resident in an almshouse provided by a housing association which is either a charity of which particulars are entered in the register of charities established under section 4 of the Charities Act 1960 (register of charities) or an exempt charity within the meaning of that Act, which is a contribution towards the cost of maintaining that association's almshouses and essential services in them;

(p) payments under a rental purchase agreement, that is to say an agreement for the purchase of a home under which the whole or part of the purchase price is to be paid in more than one instalment and the completion of the purchase is deferred until the whole or a specified part of the purchase price has been paid;

(q) where, in Scotland, the home is situated on or pertains to a croft within the meaning of section 3(1) of the Crofters (Scotland) Act 1955, the payment in respect of the croft land;

(r) where the home is provided by an employer (whether under a condition or term in a contract of service or otherwise), payments to that employer in respect of the home, including payments made by the employer deducting the payment in question from the remuneration of the parent in question;

(s) payments analogous to those mentioned in this paragraph;

(t) payments in respect of a loan taken out to pay off another loan but only to the extent that it was incurred for that purpose and only to the extent to which the interest on that other loan would have been met under this paragraph.

2. Loans for repairs and improvements to the home

For the purposes of paragraph 1(d) "repairs and improvements" means major repairs necessary to maintain the fabric of the home and any of the following measures undertaken with a view to improving its fitness and occupation—

(a) installation of a fixed bath, shower, wash basin or lavatory, and necessary associated plumbing;

(b) damp proofing measures;

(c) provision or improvement of ventilation and natural lighting;

(d) provision of electric lighting and sockets;

(e) provision or improvement of drainage facilities;

(f) improvement of the structural condition of the home;

(g) improvements to the facilities for the storing, preparation and cooking of food;

(h) provision of heating, including central heating;

(i) provision of storage facilities for fuel and refuse;

(j) improvements to the insulation of the home;

(k) other improvements which the child support officer considers reasonable in the circumstances.

3. Exempt income: additional provisions relating to eligible housing costs

(1) The additional provisions made by this paragraph shall have effect only for the purpose of calculating or estimating exempt income.

(2) Subject to sub-paragraph (6), where the home of an absent parent or, as the case may be, a parent with care, is subject to a mortgage or charge and that parent makes periodical payments to reduce the capital secured by that mortgage or charge of an amount provided for in accordance with the terms thereof, the amount of those payments shall be eligible to be taken into account as the housing costs of that parent.

(3) Subject to sub-paragraph (6), where the home of an absent parent or, as the case may be, a parent with care, is held under an agreement and certain payments made under that agreement are included as housing costs by virtue of paragraph 1 of this Schedule, the weekly amount of any other payments which are made in accordance with that agreement by the parent in order either—

(a) to reduce his liability under that agreement; or
(b) to acquire the home to which it relates,

shall also be eligible to be taken into account as housing costs.

(4) Where a policy of insurance has been obtained and retained for the purpose of discharging a mortgage or charge on the home of the parent in question, the amount of the premiums paid under that policy shall be eligible to be taken into account as a housing cost.

(5) Where a policy of insurance has been obtained and retained for the purpose of discharging a mortgage or charge on the home of the parent in question and also for the purpose of accruing profits on the maturity of the policy, the part of the premiums paid under that policy which are necessarily incurred for the purpose of discharging the mortgage or charge shall be eligible to be taken into account as a housing cost; and, where that part cannot be ascertained, 0.0277 per centum of the amount secured by the mortgage or charge shall be deemed to be the part which is eligible to be taken into account as a housing cost.

(6) For the purposes of sub-paragraphs (2) and (3), housing costs shall not include—

(a) any payment of arrears or payments in excess of those which are required to be made under or in respect of a mortgage, charge or agreement to which either of those sub-paragraphs relate;
(b) payments under any second or subsequent mortgage on the home to the extent that they are attributable to arrears or would otherwise not be eligible to be taken into account as housing costs;
(c) premiums payable in respect of any policy of insurance against loss caused by the destruction of or damage to any building or land.

4. Conditions relating to eligible housing costs

(1) Subject to the following provisions of this paragraph the housing costs referred to in this Schedule shall be included as housing costs only where—

(a) they are incurred in relation to the parent's home;
(b) the parent or, if he is one of a family, he or a member of his family, is responsible for those costs; and
(c) the liability to meet those costs is to a person other than a member of the same household.

(2) For the purposes of sub-paragraph (1)(b) a parent shall be treated as responsible for housing costs where—

(a) because the person liable to meet those costs is not doing so, he has to meet those costs in order to continue to live in the home and either he was formerly the partner of the person liable, or he is some other person whom it is reasonable to treat as liable to meet those costs; or
(b) he pays a share of those costs in a case where—

    (i)   he is living in a household with other persons;

    (ii) those other persons include persons who are not close relatives of his or his partner;

    (iii) a person who is not such a close relative is responsible for those costs under the preceding provisions of this paragraph or has an equivalent responsibility for housing expenditure; and

    (iv) it is reasonable in the circumstances to treat him as sharing that responsibility.

5. Accommodation also used for other purposes

Where amounts are payable in respect of accommodation which consists partly of residential accommodation and partly of other accommodation, only such proportion thereof as is attributable to residential accommodation shall be eligible to be taken into account as housing costs.

6. Ineligible service and fuel charges

Housing costs shall not include—

(a) where the costs are inclusive of ineligible service charges within the meaning of paragraph 1 of Schedule 1 to the Housing Benefit (General) Regulations 1987 (ineligible service charges), the amounts attributable to those ineligible service charges or, where that amount is not separated from or separately identified within the housing costs to be met under this paragraph, such part of the payments made in respect of those housing costs which are fairly attributable to the provision of those ineligible services having regard to the costs of comparable services;

(b) where the costs are inclusive of any of the items mentioned in paragraph 5(2) of Schedule 1 to the Housing Benefit (General) Regulations 1987 (payment in respect of fuel charges), the deductions prescribed in that paragraph unless the parent provides evidence on which the actual or approximate amount of the service charge for fuel may be estimated, in which case the estimated amount; and

(c) charges for water, sewerage or allied environmental services and where the amount of such charges is not separately identified, such part of the charges in question as is attributable to those services.

7. Interpretation

In this Schedule except where the context otherwise requires—

"close relative" means a parent, parent-in-law, son, son-in-law, daughter, daughter-in-law, step-parent, step-son, step-daughter, brother, sister, or the spouse of any of the preceding persons or, if that person is one of an unmarried couple, the other member of that couple;

"co-ownership scheme" means a scheme under which the dwelling is let by a housing association and the tenant, or his personal representative, will, under the terms of the tenancy agreement or of the agreement under which he became a member of the association, be entitled, on his ceasing to be a member and subject to any conditions stated in either agreement, to a sum calculated by reference directly or indirectly to the value of the dwelling;

"housing association" has the meaning assigned to it by section 1(1) of the Housing Association Act 1985.

SCHEDULE 4

Cases where child support maintenance is not to be payable

The payments and awards specified for the purposes of regulation 26(1)(b)(i) are—

    (a) the following payments under the Contributions and Benefits Act—

          (i) sickness benefit under section 31;
          (ii) invalidity pension under section 33;
          (iii) invalidity pension for widowers under section 34;
          (iv) maternity allowance under section 35;
          (v) invalidity pension for widows under section 40;
          (vi) attendance allowance under section 64;
          (vii) severe disablement allowance under section 68;
          (viii) invalid care allowance under section 70;
          (ix) disability living allowance under section 71;
          (x) disablement benefit under section 103;
          (xi) disability working allowance under section 129;
          (xii) statutory sick pay within the meaning of section 151;
          (xiii) statutory maternity pay within the meaning of section 164;

    (b) awards in respect of disablement made under (or under provisions analogous to)—

          (i) the War Pensions (Coastguards) Scheme 1944;
          (ii) the War Pensions (Naval Auxiliary Personnel) Scheme 1964;
          (iii) the Pensions (Polish Forces) Scheme 1964;
          (iv) the War Pensions (Mercantile Marine) Scheme 1964;
          (v) the Royal Warrant of 21st December 1964 (service in the Home Guard before 1945);
          (vi) the Order by Her Majesty of 22nd December 1964 concerning pensions and other grants in respect of disablement or death due to service in the Home Guard after 27th April 1952;
          (vii) the Order by Her Majesty (Ulster Defence Regiment) of 4th January 1971;
          (viii) the Personal Injuries (Civilians) Scheme 1983;
          (ix) the Naval, Military and Air Forces Etc. (Disablement and Death) Service Pensions Order 1983; and

    (c) payments from the Independent Living Fund.

CHILD SUPPORT (ARREARS, INTEREST AND ADJUSTMENT OF MAINTENANCE ASSESSMENTS) REGULATIONS 1992
(SI 1992/1816)

ARRANGEMENT OF REGULATIONS

PART I

General

1. Citation, commencement and interpretation

(1) These Regulations may be cited as the Child Support (Arrears, Interest and Adjustment of Maintenance Assessments) Regulations 1992 and shall come into force on 5th April 1993.

(2) In these Regulations, unless the context otherwise requires—

"absent parent" includes a person treated as an absent parent by virtue of regulation 20 of the Maintenance Assessments and Special Cases Regulations;
"the Act" means the Child Support Act 1991;
"arrears" means arrears of child support maintenance;
"arrears of child support maintenance" is to be construed in accordance with section 41(1) and (2) of the Act;
"arrears notice" has the meaning prescribed in regulation 2;
"due date" has the meaning prescribed in regulation 3;
"Maintenance Assessments and Special Cases Regulations" means the Child Support (Maintenance Assessments and Special Cases) Regulations 1992;
"Maintenance Assessment Procedure Regulations" means the Child Support (Maintenance Assessment Procedure) Regulations 1992;
"parent with care' means a person who, in respect of the same child or children, is both a parent and a person with care;
"relevant person" has the same meaning as in the Maintenance Assessment Procedure Regulations.

(3) In these Regulations, unless the context otherwise requires, a reference—

(a) to a numbered regulation is to the regulation in these Regulations bearing that number;
(b) in a regulation to a numbered paragraph is to the paragraph in that regulation bearing that number;
(c) in a paragraph to a lettered or numbered sub-paragraph is to the sub-paragraph in that paragraph bearing that letter or number.

PART II

Arrears of child support maintenance and interest on arrears

2. Applicability of provisions as to arrears and interest and arrears notices

(1) The provisions of paragraphs (2) to (4) and regulations 3 to 9 shall apply where—

(a) a case falls within section 41(1) of the Act; and
(b) the Secretary of State is arranging for the collection of child support maintenance under section 29 of the Act.

(2) Where the Secretary of State is considering taking action with regard to a case falling within paragraph (1), he shall serve a notice (an "arrears notice") on the absent parent.

(3) An arrears notice shall—

(a) itemize the payments of child support maintenance due and not paid;
(b) set out in general terms the provisions as to arrears and interest contained in this regulation and regulations 3 to 9; and

(c) request the absent parent to make payment of all outstanding arrears.

(4) Where an arrears notice has been served under paragraph (2), no duty to serve a further notice under that paragraph shall arise in relation to further arrears unless those further arrears have arisen after an intervening continuous period of not less than 12 weeks during the course of which all payments of child support maintenance due from the absent parent have been paid on time in accordance with regulations made under section 29 of the Act.

3. Liability to make payments of interest with respect to arrears

(1) Subject to paragraph (2) and regulations 4 and 5, interest shall be payable with respect to any amount of child support maintenance due in accordance with a maintenance assessment and not paid by the date specified by the Secretary of State in accordance with regulations made under section 29 of the Act (the "due date"), and shall be payable in respect of the period commencing on that day and terminating on the date that amount is paid.

(2) Subject to paragraph (3), interest with respect to arrears shall only be payable if the Secretary of State has served an arrears notice in relation to those arrears, and shall not be payable in respect of any period terminating on a date earlier than 14 days prior to the date the arrears notice is served on the absent parent.

(3) Where the Secretary of State has served an arrears notice, the provisions of paragraph (2) shall not apply in relation to further arrears unless the conditions mentioned in regulation 2(4) are satisfied.

(4) Subject to paragraph (6), where, following a review under section 18 or 19 of the Act or an appeal under section 20 of the Act, a fresh maintenance assessment is made with retrospective effect, interest in respect of the relevant retrospective period shall be payable with respect to the arrears calculated by reference to that fresh assessment.

(5) The provisions of paragraph (4) shall apply to a fresh assessment following a review under section 18 or 19 of the Act or an appeal under section 20 of the Act prior to any adjustment of that assessment under the provisions of regulation 10.

(6) For the purposes of paragraph (4), where the review under section 18 or 19 of the Act or an appeal under section 20 of the Act results in an increased assessment, and arrears in relation to that assessment arise, no interest shall be payable with respect to the arrears relating to the additional maintenance payable under that assessment in respect of any period prior to that date the absent parent is notified of the increased assessment.

4. Circumstances in which no liability to pay interest arises

(1) An absent parent shall not be liable to make payments of interest with respect to arrears in respect of any period if the conditions set out in paragraph (2) are satisfied in relation to that period.

(2) The conditions referred to in paragraph (1) are—
  (a) the absent parent did not know, and could not reasonably have been expected to know, of the existence of the arrears; or
  (b) the arrears have arisen solely in consequence of an operational or administrative error on the part of the Secretary of State or a child support officer.

5. Payment of arrears by agreement

(1) The Secretary of State may at any time enter into an agreement in writing with an absent parent (an "arrears agreement") for the absent parent to pay all outstanding arrears.

(2) An arrears agreement shall specify the dates on which the payments of arrears shall be made and the amount to be paid on each such date.

(3) If an arrears agreement is entered into within 28 days of the due date, and the terms of that agreement are adhered to by the absent parent, there shall be no liability to make payments of interest under the provisions of regulation 3 with respect to the arrears in relation to which the arrears agreement was entered into.

(4) If an arrears agreement is entered into later than 28 days after the due date and the terms of that agreement are adhered to by the absent parent, there shall, with respect to the arrears in relation to which that agreement was entered into, be no liability to make payments of interest in respect of any period commencing on the date that agreement was entered into.

(5) The Secretary of State may at any time enter into a further arrears agreement with the absent parent in relation to all arrears then outstanding.

(6) Where the terms of any arrears agreement are not adhered to by an absent parent, interest shall be payable with respect to arrears in accordance with the provisions of regulation 3.

(7) It shall be an implied term of any arrears agreement that any payment of child support maintenance that becomes due whilst that agreement is in force shall be made by the due date.

6. Rate of interest and calculation of interest

(1) The rate of interest payable where liability to pay interest under regulation 3 arises shall be one per centum per annum above the median base rate prevailing from time to time calculated on a daily basis.

(2) Interest shall be payable only with respect to arrears of child support maintenance and shall not be payable with respect to any interest that has already become due.

(3) For the purposes of paragraph (1)—

    (a) the median base rate, in relation to a year or part of a year, is the base rate quoted by the reference banks; or, if different base rates are quoted, the rate which, when the base rate quoted by each bank is ranked in a descending sequence of seven, is fourth in the sequence;

    (b) the reference banks are the seven largest institutions—

        (i) authorised by the Bank of England under the Banking Act 1987, and

        (ii) incorporated in and carrying on a deposit-taking business within the United Kingdom,

    which quote a base rate in sterling; and

    (c) the size of an institution is to be determined by reference to its total consolidated gross assets in sterling, as shown in its audited end-year accounts last published.

(4) In paragraph (3)(c), the reference to the consolidated gross assets of an institution is a reference to the consolidated gross assets of that institution together with any subsidiary (within the meaning of section 736 of the Companies Act 1985).

7. Receipt and retention of interest paid

(1) Payments of interest with respect to arrears shall be made in accordance with regulations under section 29 of the Act as though they were payments of child support maintenance payable in accordance with a maintenance assessment, and shall be made within 14 days of being demanded by the Secretary of State.

(2) Subject to paragraph (3), where the Secretary of State has been authorised to recover child support maintenance under section 6 of the Act and income support is paid to or in respect of the parent with care, interest with respect to arrears relating to the period during which income support is paid shall be payable to the Secretary of State and may be retained by him.

(3) Where a case falls within paragraph (2), but the Secretary of State considers that, if the absent parent had made payments of child support maintenance due from him in accordance with that assessment, the parent with care would not have been entitled to income support, any interest shall be payable to the parent with care.

(4) Where the child support maintenance payable under a maintenance assessment is payable to more than one person, any interest in respect of arrears under that assessment shall be apportioned in the same ratio as the child support maintenance that is payable, and the provisions of paragraphs (1) to (3) shall apply to each amount of interest so apportioned.

8. Retention of recovered arrears of child support maintenance by the Secretary of State

Where the Secretary of State recovers arrears from an absent parent and income support is paid to or in respect of the person with care, the Secretary of State may retain such amount of those arrears as is equal to the difference between the amount of income support that was paid to or in respect of the person with care and the amount of income support that he is satisfied would have been paid had the absent parent paid the child support maintenance due in accordance with the maintenance assessment in force by the due dates.

PART III

Attribution of payments and adjustment of the amount payable under a maintenance assessment

9. Attribution of payments

Where a maintenance assessment is or has been in force and there are arrears of child support maintenance, the Secretary of State may attribute any payment of child support maintenance made by an absent parent to child support maintenance due as he thinks fit.

10. Adjustment of the amount payable under a maintenance assessment

(1) Where a new or a fresh maintenance assessment has retrospective effect, the amount payable under that assessment may be adjusted by a child support officer for the

purpose of taking account of the retrospective effect of the assessment by such amount as, subject to the provisions of paragraph (4), he considers appropriate in the circumstances of the case.

(2) Subject to paragraph (3), where the payments of child support maintenance have been over-payments or under-payments, the amount payable under a maintenance assessment may be adjusted by a child support officer for the purpose of taking account of such over-payments or under-payments by such amount as, subject to the provisions of paragraph (5), he considers appropriate in the circumstances of the case.

(3) The provisions of paragraph (2) shall not apply to any case falling within section 41 of the Act.

(4) Where a case falls within paragraph (1), the child support officer shall—

(a) in the case of a new assessment, not increase the amount payable under that assessment by an amount greater than 1.5 multiplied by that assessment;
(b) in the case of a fresh assessment, not adjust the amount payable under that assessment by an amount greater than 1.5 multiplied by the difference between the amount payable under the earlier assessment and the amount payable under the fresh assessment.

(5) Where a case falls within paragraph (2), the child support officer shall not adjust the amount payable under a maintenance assessment by an amount greater than 1.5 multiplied by the mean over-payment or the mean under-payment, as the case may be.

(6) For the purposes of paragraph (5), the mean over-payment or the mean under-payment shall be the total net over-payment or the total net under-payment divided by the number of occasions on which, in respect of the period being taken into account for the purposes of paragraph (2), there have been over-payments or, as the case may be, under-payments of child support maintenance.

PART IV

Miscellaneous

11. Notifications following an adjustment under the provisions of regulation 10

(1) Where a child support officer has, under the provisions of regulation 10, adjusted the amount payable under a maintenance assessment, he shall immediately notify the relevant persons, so far as that is reasonably practicable, of the amount and period of the adjustment, and the amount payable during the period of the adjustment.

(2) A notification under paragraph (1) shall include information as to the provisions of regulation 12(1) and regulation 13(1) in so far as it relates to time limits for an application for a review under regulation 12(1).

12. Review of adjustments under regulation 10 or of the calculation of arrears or interest

(1) Where the amount payable under a maintenance assessment has been adjusted under the provisions of regulation 10, a relevant person may apply to the Secretary of State for a review of that adjustment as if it were a case falling within section 18 of the Act and, subject to the modifications set out in paragraph (2), section 18(5) to (9) and (11) of the Act shall apply to such a review.

(2) The modifications referred to in paragraph (1) are—

(a) section 18(6) of the Act shall have effect as if for "the refusal, assessment or cancellation in question" there is substituted "the adjustment of the amount payable under regulation 10 of the Child Support (Arrears, Interest and Adjustment of Maintenance Assessments) Regulations 1992";

(b) section 18(9) of the Act shall have effect as if for "a maintenance assessment or (as the case may be) a fresh maintenance assessment" there is substituted "a revised adjustment of the amount payable under regulation 10 of the Child Support (Arrears, Interest and Adjustment of Maintenance Assessments) Regulations 1992".

(3) Where there has been a calculation of arrears due under a maintenance assessment or a calculation of the interest payable with respect to arrears, a relevant person may apply to the Secretary of State for a review of that calculation as if it were a case falling within section 18 of the Act and, subject to the modifications set out in paragraph (4), section 18(5) to (9) and (11) and the Act shall apply to such a review.

(4) The modifications referred to in paragraph (3) are—

(a) section 18(6) of the Act shall have effect as if—

(i) for "the refusal, assessment or cancellation in question" there is substituted "the calculation of arrears due under a maintenance assessment or the calculation of the interest payable with respect to arrears";

(ii) after "law" in paragraph (c) there is inserted—
" or
(d) involved an arithmetical error";

(b) section 18(9) of the Act shall have effect as if for "a maintenance assessment or (as the case may be) a fresh maintenance assessment" there is substituted "a fresh calculation of the arrears due under a maintenance assessment or a fresh calculation of the interest payable with respect to arrears".

(5) Where the amount payable under a maintenance assessment has been adjusted under the provisions of regulation 10 a child support officer may revise that adjustment if he is satisfied that one or more of the circumstances set out in paragraphs (a) to (c) of section 19(1) of the Act apply to that adjustment.

(6) Where there has been a calculation of the arrears due under a maintenance assessment or a calculation of interest payable with a respect to arrears, a child support officer may re-calculate the arrears or the interest if he is satisfied that one or more of the circumstances set out in paragraphs (a) to (c) of section 19(1) of the Act apply or that there has been an arithmetical error in the calculation.

13. Procedure and notifications on applications and reviews under regulation 12

(1) The provisions of regulations 24 to 26 of the Maintenance Assessment Procedure Regulations shall apply to an application for a review under regulation 12(1) or (3).

(2) Where a child support officer refuses an application for a review under regulation 12(1) or (3) on the grounds set out in section 18(6) of the Act (as applied by regulation 12), he shall immediately notify the applicant, so far as that is reasonably practicable, and shall give the reasons for his refusal in writing.

(3) Where a child support officer adjusts the amount payable under a maintenance assessment following a review under regulation 12(1) or (5), he shall immediately notify

the relevant persons, so far as that is reasonably practicable, of the amount and period of the adjustment, and the amount payable during the period of adjustment.

(4) Where a child support officer refuses to adjust the amount payable under a maintenance assessment following a review under regulation 12(1) he shall immediately notify the relevant persons, so far as that is reasonably practicable, of the refusal, and shall give the reasons for his refusal in writing.

(5) Where a child support officer has conducted a review under regulation 12(3), or has revised the calculation of the arrears due or the interest payable with respect to arrears following a review under regulation 12(6), he shall immediately notify the relevant persons, so far as that is reasonably practicable, of his decision.

(6) A notification under paragraphs (2) to (5) shall include information as to the provisions of section 20 of the Act.

14. Non-disclosure of information to third parties

The provisions of regulation 10(3) of the Maintenance Assessment Procedure Regulations shall apply to any document given or sent under the provisions of regulation 11 or 13.

15. Applicability of regulations 1(6) and 53 to 56 of the Maintenance Assessment Procedure Regulations

Regulations 1(6) and 53 to 56 of the Maintenance Assessment Procedure Regulations shall apply to the provisions of these Regulations.

CHILD SUPPORT (COLLECTION AND ENFORCEMENT) REGULATIONS 1992
(SI 1992/1989)

ARRANGEMENT OF REGULATIONS

SCHEDULES

PART I

General

1. Citation, commencement and interpretation

(1) These Regulations may be cited as the Child Support (Collection and Enforcement) Regulations 1992 and shall come into force on 5th April 1993.

(2) In these Regulations "the Act" means the Child Support Act 1991.

(3) Where under any provision of the Act or of these Regulations—

   (a) any document or notice is given or sent to the Secretary of State, it shall be treated as having been given or sent on the day it is received by the Secretary of State; and
   (b) any document or notice is given or sent to any other person, it shall, if sent by post to that person's last known or notified address, be treated as having been given or sent on the second day after the day of posting, excluding any Sunday or any day which is a bank holiday under the Banking and Financial Dealings Act 1971.

(4) In these Regulations, unless the context otherwise requires, a reference—

   (a) to a numbered Part is to the Part of these Regulations bearing that number;
   (b) to a numbered regulation is to the regulation in these Regulations bearing that number;
   (c) in a regulation to a numbered or lettered paragraph or sub-paragraph is to the paragraph or sub-paragraph in that regulation bearing that number or letter;
   (d) in a paragraph to a lettered or numbered sub-paragraph is to the sub-paragraph in that paragraph bearing that letter or number;
   (e) to a numbered Schedule is to the Schedule to these Regulations bearing that number.

PART II

Collection of child support maintenance

2. Payment of child support maintenance

(1) Where a maintenance assessment has been made under the Act and the case is one to which section 29 of the Act applies, the Secretary of State may specify that payments of child support maintenance shall be made by the liable person—

(a) to the person caring for the child or children in question or, where an application has been made under section 7 of the Act, to the child who made the application;
(b) to, or through, the Secretary of State; or
(c) to, or through, such other person as the Secretary of State may, from time to time, specify.

(2) In paragraph (1) and in the rest of this Part, "liable person" means a person liable to make payments of child support maintenance.

3. Method of payment

(1) Payments of child support maintenance shall be made by the liable person by whichever of the following methods the Secretary of State specifies as being appropriate in the circumstances—

(a) by standing order;
(b) by any other method which requires one person to give his authority for payments to be made from an account of his to an account of another's on specific dates during the period for which the authority is in force and without the need for any further authority from him;
(c) by an arrangement whereby one person gives his authority for payments to be made from an account of his, or on his behalf, to another person or to an account of that other person;
(d) by cheque or postal order;
(e) in cash.

(2) The Secretary of State may direct a liable person to take all reasonable steps to open an account from which payments under the maintenance assessment may be made in accordance with the method of payment specified under paragraph (1).

4. Interval of payment

(1) The Secretary of State shall specify the day and interval by reference to which payments of child support maintenance are to be made by the liable person and may from time to time vary such day or interval.

(2) In specifying the day and interval of payment the Secretary of State shall have regard to all the circumstances and in particular to—

(a) the needs of the person entitled to receive payment and the day and interval by reference to which any other income is normally received by that person;
(b) the day and interval by reference to which the liable person's income is normally received; and
(c) any period necessary to enable the clearance of cheques or otherwise necessary to enable the transmission of payments to the person entitled to receive them.

5. Transmission of payments

(1) Payments of child support maintenance made through the Secretary of State or other specified person shall be transmitted to the person entitled to receive them in whichever of the following ways the Secretary of State specifies as being appropriate in the circumstances—

(a) by a transfer of credit to an account nominated by the person entitled to receive the payments;

(b) by cheque, girocheque or other payable order;
(c) in cash.

(2) The Secretary of State shall specify the interval by reference to which the payments referred to in paragraph (1) are to be transmitted to the person entitled to receive them.

(3) The interval referred to in paragraph (2) may differ from the interval referred to in regulation 4 and may from time to time be varied by the Secretary of State.

(4) In specifying the interval for transmission of payments the Secretary of State shall have regard to all the circumstances and in particular to—

(a) the needs of the person entitled to receive payment and the interval by reference to which any other income is normally received by that person;
(b) any period necessary to enable the clearance of cheques or otherwise necessary to enable the transmission of payments to the person entitled to receive them.

6. Representations about payment arrangements

The Secretary of State shall, insofar as is reasonably practicable, provide the liable person and the person entitled to receive the payments of child support maintenance with an opportunity to make representations with regard to the matters referred to in regulations 2 to 5 and the Secretary of State shall have regard to those representations in exercising his powers under those regulations.

7. Notice to liable person as to requirements about payment

(1) The Secretary of State shall send the liable person a notice stating—

(a) the amount of child support maintenance payable;
(b) to whom it is to be paid;
(c) the method of payment; and
(d) the day and interval by reference to which payments are to be made.

(2) A notice under paragraph (1) shall be sent to the liable person as soon as is reasonably practicable after—

(a) the making of a maintenance assessment, and
(b) after any change in the requirements referred to in any previous such notice.

PART III

Deduction from earnings orders

8. Interpretation of this Part

(1) For the purposes of this Part—

"disposable income" means the amount determined under regulation 12(1) of the Child Support (Maintenance Assessments and Special Cases) Regulations 1992;
"earnings" shall be construed in accordance with paragraphs (3) and (4);
"exempt income" means the amount determined under regulation 9 of the Child Support (Maintenance Assessments and Special Cases) Regulations 1992;
"net earnings" shall be construed in accordance with paragraph (5);

"normal deduction rate" means the rate specified in a deduction from earnings order (expressed as a sum of money per week, month or other period) at which deductions are to be made from the liable person's net earnings;

"pay-day" in relation to a liable person means an occasion on which earnings are paid to him or the day on which such earnings would normally fall to be paid;

"prescribed minimum amount" means the minimum amount prescribed in regulation 13 of the Child Support (Maintenance Assessments and Special Cases) Regulations 1992;

"protected earnings rate" means the level of earnings specified in a deduction from earnings order (expressed as a sum of money per week, month or other period) below which deductions of child support maintenance shall not be made for the purposes of this Part;

"protected income level" means the level of protected income determined in accordance with regulation 11 of the Child Support (Maintenance Assessments and Special Cases) Regulations 1992.

(2) For the purposes of this Part the relationship of employer and employee shall be treated as subsisting between two persons if one of them, as a principal and not as a servant or agent, pays to the other any sum defined as earnings under paragraph (1) and "employment", "employer" and "employee" shall be construed accordingly.

(3) Subject to paragraph (4), "earnings" are any sums payable to a person—

   (a) by way of wages or salary (including any fees, bonus, commission, overtime pay or other emoluments payable in addition to wages or salary or payable under a contract of service);
   (b) by way of pension (including an annuity in respect of past service, whether or not rendered to the person paying the annuity, and including periodical payments by way of compensation for the loss, abolition of relinquishment, or diminution in the emoluments, of any office or employment);
   (c) by way of statutory sick pay.

(4) "Earnings" shall not include—

   (a) sums payable by any public department of the Government of Northern Ireland or of a territory outside the United Kingdom;
   (b) pay or allowances payable to the liable person as a member of Her Majesty's forces;
   (c) pension, allowances or benefit payable under any enactment relating to social security;
   (d) pension or allowances payable in respect of disablement or disability;
   (e) guaranteed minimum pension within the meaning of the Social Security Pensions Act 1975.

(5) "Net earnings" means the residue of earnings after deduction of—

   (a) income tax;
   (b) primary class I contributions under Part I of the Contributions and Benefits Act 1992;
   (c) amounts deductible by way of contributions to a superannuation scheme which provides for the payment of annuities or lump sums—
      (i) to the employee on his retirement at a specified age or on becoming incapacitated at some earlier age; or
      (ii) on his death or otherwise, to his personal representative, widow, relatives or dependants.

9. Deduction from earnings orders

A deduction from earnings order shall specify—

    (a) the name and address of the liable person;
    (b) the name of the employer at whom it is directed;
    (c) where known, the liable person's place of work, the nature of his work and any works or pay number;
    (d) the normal deduction rate;
    (e) the protected earnings rate;
    (f) the address to which amounts deducted from earnings are to be sent.

10. Normal deduction rate

(1) The period by reference to which the normal deduction rate is set shall be the period by reference to which the liable person's earnings are normally paid or, if none, such other period as the Secretary of State may specify.

(2) The Secretary of State, in specifying the normal deduction rate, shall not include any amount in respect of arrears or interest if, at the date of making of the current assessment—

    (a) the liable person's disposable income was below the level specified in paragraph (3); or
    (b) the deduction of such an amount from the liable person's disposable income would have reduced his disposable income below the level specified in paragraph (3).

(3) The level referred to in paragraph (2) is the liable person's protected income level less the prescribed minimum amount.

11. Protected earnings rate

(1) The period by reference to which the protected earnings rate is set shall be the same as the period by reference to which the normal deduction rate is set under regulation 10(1).

(2) The amount to be specified as the protected earnings rate in respect of any period shall be an amount equal to the liable person's exempt income in respect of that period as calculated at the date of the current assessment.

12. Amount to be deducted by employer

(1) Subject to the provisions of this regulation, an employer who has been served with a copy of a deduction from earnings order in respect of a liable person in his employment shall, each pay-day, make a deduction from the net earnings of that liable person of an amount equal to the normal deduction rate.

(2) Where the deduction of the normal deduction rate would reduce the liable person's net earnings below the protected earnings rate and employer shall deduct only such amount as will leave the liable person with net earnings equal to the protected earnings rate.

(3) Where the liable person receives a payment of earnings at an interval greater or lesser than the interval specified in relation to the normal deduction rate and the protected earnings rate ("the specified interval") the employer shall, for the purpose of

such payments, take as the normal deduction rate and the protected earnings rate such amounts (to the nearest whole penny) as are in the same proportion to the interval since the last pay-day as the normal deduction rate and the protected earnings rate bear to the specified interval.

(4) Where, on any pay-day, the employer fails to deduct an amount due under the deduction from earnings order or deducts an amount less than the amount of the normal deduction rate the shortfall shall, subject to the operation of paragraph (2), be deducted in addition to the normal deduction rate at the next available pay-day or days.

(5) Where, on any pay-day, the liable person's net earnings are less than his protected earnings rate the amount of the difference shall be carried forward to his next pay-day and treated as part of his protected earnings in respect of that pay-day.

(6) Where, on any pay-day, an employer makes a deduction from the earnings of a liable person in accordance with the deduction from earnings order he may also deduct an amount not exceeding £1 in respect of his administrative costs and such deduction for administrative costs may be made notwithstanding that it may reduce the liable person's net earnings below the protected earnings rate.

13. Employer to notify liable person of deduction

(1) An employer making a deduction from earnings for the purposes of this Part shall notify the liable person in writing of the amount of the deduction, including any amount deducted for administrative costs under regulation 12(6).

(2) Such notification shall be given not later than the pay-day on which the deduction is made or, where that is impracticable, not later than the following pay-day.

14. Payment by employer to Secretary of State

(1) Amounts deducted by an employer under a deduction from earnings order (other than any administrative costs deducted under regulation 12(6)) shall be paid to the Secretary of State by the 19th day of the month following the month in which the deduction is made.

(2) Such payment may be made—

    (a) by cheque;
    (b) by automated credit transfer; or
    (c) by such other method as the Secretary of State may specify.

15. Information to be provided by liable person

(1) The Secretary of State may, in relation to the making or operation of a deduction from earnings order, require the liable person to provide the following details—

    (a) the name and address of his employer;
    (b) the amount of his earnings and anticipated earnings;
    (c) his place of work, the nature of his work and any works or pay number;

and it shall be the duty of the liable person to comply with any such requirement within 7 days of being given written notice to that effect.

(2) A liable person in respect of whom a deduction from earnings order is in force shall notify the Secretary of State in writing within 7 days of every occasion on which he leaves employment or becomes employed or re-employed.

16. Duty of employers and others to notify Secretary of State

(1) Where a deduction from earnings order is served on a person on the assumption that he is the employer of a liable person but the liable person to whom the order relates is not in his employment, the person on whom the order was served shall notify the Secretary of State of that fact in writing, at the address specified in the order, within 10 days of the date of service on him of the order.

(2) Where an employer is required to operate a deduction from earnings order and the liable person to whom the order relates ceases to be in his employment the employer shall notify the Secretary of State of that fact in writing, at the address specified in the order, within 10 days of the liable person ceasing to be in his employment.

(3) Where an employer becomes aware that a deduction from earnings order is in force in relation to a person who is an employee of his he shall, within 7 days of the date on which he becomes aware, notify the Secretary of State of that fact in writing at the address specified in the order.

17. Requirement to review deduction from earnings orders

The Secretary of State shall review a deduction from earnings order in the following circumstances—

  (a) where there is a change in the amount of the maintenance assessment;
  (b) where any arrears and interest on arrears payable under the order are paid off.

18. Power to vary deduction from earnings orders

(1) The Secretary of State may (whether on a review under regulation 17 or otherwise) vary a deduction from earnings order so as to—

  (a) include any amount which may be included in such an order or exclude or decrease any such amount;
  (b) substitute a subsequent employer for the employer at whom the order was previously directed.

(2) The Secretary of State shall serve a copy of any deduction from earnings order, as varied, on the liable person's employer and on the liable person.

19. Compliance with deduction from earnings order as varied

(1) Where a deduction from earnings order has been varied and a copy of the order as varied has been served on the liable person's employer it shall, subject to paragraph (2), be the duty of the employer to comply with the order as varied.

(2) The employer shall not be under any liability for non-compliance with the order, as varied, before the end of the period of 7 days beginning with the date on which a copy of the order, as varied, was served on him.

20. Discharge of deduction from earnings orders

(1) The Secretary of State may discharge a deduction from earnings order where—

  (a) no further payments under it are due; or
  (b) it appears to him that the order is ineffective or that some other way of securing that payments are made would be more effective.

(2) The Secretary of State shall give written notice of the discharge of the deduction from earnings order to the liable person and to the liable person's employer.

21. Lapse of deduction from earnings orders

(1) A deduction from earnings order shall lapse (except in relation to any deductions made or to be made in respect of the employment not yet paid to the Secretary of State) where the employer at whom it is directed ceases to have the liable person in his employment.

(2) The order shall lapse from the pay-day coinciding with, or, if none, the pay-day following, the termination of the employment.

(3) A deduction from earnings order which has lapsed under this regulation shall nonetheless be treated as remaining in force for the purposes of regulations 15 and 24.

(4) Where a deduction from earnings order has lapsed under paragraph (1) and the liable person recommences employment (whether with the same or another employer), the order may be revived from such date as may be specified by the Secretary of State.

(5) Where a deduction from earnings order is revived under paragraph (4), the Secretary of State shall give written notice of that fact to, and serve a copy of the notice on, the liable person and the liable person's employer.

(6) Where an order is revived under paragraph (4), no amount shall be carried forward under regulation 12(4) or (5) from a time prior to the revival of the order.

22. Appeals against deduction from earnings orders

(1) A liable person in respect of whom a deduction from earnings order has been made may appeal to the magistrates' court, or in Scotland the sheriff, having jurisdiction in the area in which he resides.

(2) Any appeal shall—

(a) be by way of complaint for an order or, in Scotland, by way of application;
(b) be made within 28 days of the date on which the matter appealed against arose.

(3) An appeal may be made only on one or both of the following grounds—

(a) that the deduction from earnings order is defective;
(b) that the payments in question do not constitute earnings.

(4) Where the court or, as the case may be, the sheriff is satisfied that the appeal should be allowed the court, or sheriff, may—

(a) quash the deduction from earnings order; or
(b) specify which, if any, of the payments in question do not constitute earnings.

23. Crown employment

Where a liable person is in the employment of the Crown and a deduction from earnings order is made in respect of him then for the purposes of this Part—

(a) the chief officer for the time being of the Department, office or other body in which the liable person is employed shall be treated as having the liable person in his employment (any transfer of the liable person from one Department, office or body to another being treated as a change of employment); and

(b) any earnings paid by the Crown or a minister of the Crown, or out of the public revenue of the United Kingdom, shall be treated as paid by that chief officer.

24. Priority as between orders

(1) Where an employer would, but for this paragraph, be obliged, on any pay-day, to make deductions under two or more deduction from earnings orders he shall—

(a) deal with the orders according to the respective dates on which they were made, disregarding any later order until an earlier one has been dealt with;

(b) deal with any later order as if the earnings to which it relates were the residue of the liable person's earnings after the making of any deduction to comply with any earlier order.

(2) Where an employer would, but for this paragraph, be obliged to comply with one or more deduction from earnings orders and one or more attachment of earnings orders he shall—

(a) in the case of an attachment of earnings order which was made either wholly or in part in respect of the payment of a judgment debt or payments under an administration order, deal first with the deduction from earnings order or orders and thereafter with the attachment of earnings order as if the earnings to which it relates were the residue of the liable person's earnings after the making of deductions to comply with the deduction from earnings order or orders;

(b) in the case of any other attachment of earnings order, deal with the orders according to the respective dates on which they were made in like manner as under paragraph (1).

"Attachment of earnings order" in this paragraph means an order made under the Attachment of Earnings Act 1971 or under regulation 32 of the Community Charge (Administration and Enforcement) Regulations 1989.

(3) Paragraph (2) does not apply to Scotland.

(4) In Scotland, where an employer would, but for this paragraph, be obliged to comply with one or more deduction from earnings orders and one or more diligences against earnings he shall deal first with the deduction from earnings order or orders and thereafter with the diligence against earnings as if the earnings to which the diligence relates were the residue of the liable person's earnings after the making of deductions to comply with the deduction from earnings order or orders.

25. Offences

The following regulations are designated for the purposes of section 32(8) of the Act (offences relating to deduction from earnings orders)—

(a) regulation 15(1) and (2);

(b) regulation 16(1), (2) and (3);

(c) regulation 19(1).

PART IV

Liability orders

26. Extent of this Part

This Part, except regulation 29(2), does not apply to Scotland.

27. Notice of intention to apply for a liability order

(1) The Secretary of State shall give the liable person at least 7 days' notice of his intention to apply for a liability order under section 33(2) of the Act.

(2) Such notice shall set out the amount of child support maintenance which it is claimed has become payable by the liable person and has not been paid and the amount of any interest in respect of arrears payable under section 41(3) of the Act.

(3) Payment by the liable person of any part of the amounts referred to in paragraph (2) shall not require the giving of a further notice under paragraph (1) prior to the making of the application.

28. Application for a liability order

(1) An application for a liability order shall be by way of complaint for an order to the magistrates' court having jurisdiction in the area in which the liable person resides.

(2) An application under paragraph (1) may not be instituted more than 6 years after the day on which payment of the amount in question became due.

(3) A warrant shall not be issued under section 55(2) of the Magistrates' Courts Act 1980 in any proceedings under this regulation.

29. Liability orders

(1) A liability order shall be made in the form prescribed in Schedule 1.

(2) A liability order made by a court in England or Wales or any corresponding order made by a court in Northern Ireland may be enforced in Scotland as if it had been made by the sheriff.

(3) A liability order made by the sheriff in Scotland or any corresponding order made by a court in Northern Ireland may, subject to paragraph (4), be enforced in England and Wales as if it had been made by a magistrates' court in England and Wales.

(4) A liability order made by the sheriff in Scotland or a corresponding order made by a court in Northern Ireland shall not be enforced in England or Wales unless registered in accordance with the provisions of Part I of the Maintenance Orders Act 1950 and for this purpose—

  (a) a liability order made by the sheriff in Scotland shall be treated as if it were a decree to which section 16(2)(b) of that Act applies (decree for payment of aliment);
  (b) a corresponding order made by a court in Northern Ireland shall be treated as if it were an order to which section 16(2)(c) of that Act applies (order for alimony, maintenance or other payments).

30. Enforcement of liability orders by distress

(1) A distress made pursuant to section 35(1) of the Act may be made anywhere in England and Wales.

(2) The person levying distress on behalf of the Secretary of State shall carry with him the written authorisation of the Secretary of State, which he shall show to the liable person if so requested, and he shall hand to the liable person or leave at the premises where the distress is levied—

- (a) copies of this regulation, regulation 31 and Schedule 2;
- (b) a memorandum setting out the amount which is the appropriate amount for the purposes of section 35(2) of the Act;
- (c) a memorandum setting out details of any arrangement entered into regarding the taking of possession of the goods distrained; and
- (d) a notice setting out the liable person's rights of appeal under regulation 31 giving the Secretary of State's address for the purposes of any appeal.

(3) A distress shall not be deemed unlawful on account of any defect or want of form in the liability order.

(4) If, before any goods are seized, the appropriate amount (including charges arising up to the time of the payment or tender) is paid or tendered to the Secretary of State, the Secretary of State shall accept the amount and the levy shall not be proceeded with.

(5) Where the Secretary of State has seized goods of the liable person in pursuance of the distress, but before sale of those goods the appropriate amount (including charges arising up to the time of the payment or tender) is paid or tendered to the Secretary of State, the Secretary of State shall accept the amount, the sale shall not be proceeded with and the goods shall be made available for collection by the liable person.

31. Appeals in connection with distress

(1) A person aggrieved by the levy of, or an attempt to levy, a distress may appeal to the magistrates' court having jurisdiction in the area in which he resides.

(2) The appeal shall be by way of complaint for an order.

(3) If the court is satisfied that the levy was irregular, it may—

- (a) order the goods distrained to be discharged if they are in the possession of the Secretary of State;
- (b) order an award of compensation in respect of any goods distrained and sold of an amount equal to the amount which, in the opinion of the court, would be awarded by way of special damages in respect of the goods if proceedings under section 35(6) of the Act were brought in trespass or otherwise in connection with the irregularity.

(4) If the court is satisfied that an attempted levy was irregular, it may by order require the Secretary of State to desist from levying in the manner giving rise to the irregularity.

32. Charges connected with distress

Schedule 2 shall have effect for the purpose of determining the amounts in respect of charges in connection with the distress for the purposes of section 35(2)(b) of the Act.

33. Application for warrant of commitment

(1) For the purposes of enabling an inquiry to be made under section 40 of the Act as to the liable person's conduct and means, a justice of the peace having jurisdiction for the area in which the liable person resides may—

(a) issue a summons to him to appear before a magistrates' court and (if he does not obey the summons) issue a warrant for his arrest; or
(b) issue a warrant for his arrest without issuing a summons.

(2) In any proceedings under section 40 of the Act, a statement in writing to the effect that wages of any amount have been paid to the liable person during any period, purporting to be signed by or on behalf of his employer, shall be evidence of the facts there stated.

(3) Where an application under section 40 of the Act has been made but no warrant of commitment is issued or term of imprisonment fixed, the application may be renewed on the ground that the circumstances of the liable person have changed.

34. Warrant of commitment

(1) A warrant of commitment shall be in the form specified in Schedule 3, or in a form to the like effect.

(2) The amount to be included in the warrant under section 40(4)(a)(ii) of the Act in respect of costs shall be such amount as in the view of the court is equal to the costs reasonably incurred by the Secretary of State in respect of the costs of commitment.

(3) A warrant issued under section 40 of the Act may be executed anywhere in England and Wales by any person to whom it is directed or by any constable acting within his police area.

(4) A warrant may be executed by a constable notwithstanding that it is not in his possession at the time but such warrant shall, on the demand of the person arrested, be shown to him as soon as possible.

(5) Where, after the issue of a warrant, part-payment of the amount stated in it is made, the period of imprisonment shall be reduced proportionately so that for the period of imprisonment specified in the warrant there shall be substituted a period of imprisonment of such number of days as bears the same proportion to the number of days specified in the warrant as the amount remaining unpaid under the warrant bears to the amount specified in the warrant.

(6) Where the part-payment is of such an amount as would, under paragraph (5), reduce the period of imprisonment to such number of days as have already been served (or would be so served in the course of the day of payment), the period of imprisonment shall be reduced to the period already served plus one day.

SCHEDULE 1
Liability order prescribed form

Section 33 of the Child Support Act 1991 and regulation 29(1) of the Child Support (Collection and Enforcement) Regulations 1992

.... Magistrates' Court

Date:

Defendant:

Address:

On the complaint of the Secretary of State for Social Security that the sums specified below are due from the defendant under the Child Support Act 1991 and Part IV of the Child Support (Collection and Enforcement) Regulations 1992 and are outstanding, it is adjudged that the defendant is liable to pay the aggregate amount specified below.

Sum payable and outstanding — child support maintenance
— interest
— other periodical payments
collected by virtue of
section 30 of the Child
Support Act 1991

Aggregate amount in respect of which the liability order is made:

Justice of the Peace

[*or* by order of the Court
Clerk of the Court]

SCHEDULE 2

Charges connected with distress

1. The sum in respect of charges connected with the distress which may be aggregated under section 35(2)(b) of the Act shall be set out in the following table —

(1) *Matter connected with distress*	(2) *Charge*
A For making a visit to premises with a view to levying distress (whether the levy is made or not):	Reasonable costs and fees incurred, but not exceeding an amount which, when aggregated with charges under this head for any previous visits made with a view to levying distress in relation to an amount in respect of which the liability order concerned was made, is not greater than the relevant amount calculated under paragraph 2(1) with respect to the visit.
B For levying distress:	An amount (if any) which, when aggregated with charges under head A for any visits made with a view to levying distress in relation to an amount in respect of which the liability order concerned was made, is equal to the relevant amount calculated under paragraph 2(1) with respect to the levy.
C For the removal and storage of goods for the purposes of sale:	Reasonable costs and fees incurred.
D For the possession of goods as described in paragraph 2(3)—	
(i) for close possession (the person in possession on behalf of the Secretary of State to provide his own board):	£4.50 per day.
(ii) for walking possession:	45p per day.
E For appraisement of an item distrained, at the request in writing of the liable person:	Reasonable fees and expenses of the broker appraising.
F For other expenses of, and commission on, a sale by auction—	
(i) where the sale is held on the auctioneer's premises:	The auctioneer's commission fee and out-of-pocket expenses (but not exceeding in aggregate 15 per cent. of the sum realised), together with reasonable costs and fees incurred in respect of advertising.

(ii) where the sale is held on the liable person's premises:	The auctioneer's commission fee (but not exceeding 7½ per cent. of the sum realised), together with the auctioneer's out-of-pocket expenses and reasonable costs and fees incurred in respect of advertising.
G For other expenses incurred in connection with a proposed sale where there is no buyer in relation to it:	Reasonable costs and fees incurred.

2. (1) In heads A and B of the Table to paragraph 1, "the relevant month" with respect to a visit or a levy means—

   (a) where the sum due at the time of the visit or of the levy (as the case may be) does not exceed £100, £12.50;
   (b) where the sum due at the time of the visit or of the levy (as the case may be) exceeds £100, 12½ per cent. on the first £100 of the sum due, 4 per cent. on the next £400, 2½ per cent. on the next £1,500, 1 per cent. on the next £8,000 and ¼ per cent. on any additional sum;

and the sum due at any time for these purposes means so much of the amount in respect of which the liability order concerned was made as is outstanding at the time.

(2) Where a charge has arisen under head B with respect to an amount, no further charge may be aggregated under heads A or B in respect of that amount.

(3) The Secretary of State takes close or walking possession of goods for the purposes of head D of the Table to paragraph 1 if he takes such possession in pursuance of an agreement which is made at the time that the distress is levied and which (without prejudice to such other terms as may be agreed) is expressed to the effect that, in consideration of the Secretary of State not immediately removing the goods distrained upon from the premises occupied by the liable person and delaying the sale of the goods, the Secretary of State may remove and sell the goods after a later specified date if the liable person has not by then paid the amount distrained for (including charges under this Schedule); and the Secretary of State is in close possession of goods on any day for these purposes if during the greater part of the day a person is left on the premises in physical possession of the goods on behalf of the Secretary of State under such an agreement.

3. (1) Where the calculation under this Schedule of a percentage of a sum results in an amount containing a fraction of a pound, that fraction shall be reckoned as a whole pound.

(2) In the case of dispute as to any charge under this Schedule, the amount of the charge shall be taxed.

(3) Such a taxation shall be carried out by the district judge of the county court for the district in which the distress is or is intended to be levied, and he may give such directions as to the costs of the taxation as he thinks fit; and any such costs directed to be paid by the liable person to the Secretary of State shall be added to the sum which may be aggregated under section 35(2) of the Act.

(4) References in the Table in paragraph 1 to costs, fees and expenses include references to amounts payable by way of value added tax with respect to the supply of goods or services to which the costs, fees and expenses relate.

SCHEDULE 3

Form of warrant of commitment

Section 40 of the Child Support Act 1991 and regulation 34(1) of the Child Support (Collection and Enforcement) Regulations 1992

.... Magistrates' Court

Date:

Liable Person:

Address:

A liability order ("the order") was made against the liable person by the [   ] Magistrates' Court on [   ] under section 33 of the Child Support Act 1991 ("the Act") in respect of an amount of [   ].

The court is satisfied—

    (i) that the Secretary of State sought under section 35 of the Act to levy by distress the amount then outstanding in respect of which the order was made;

[and/or]

that the Secretary of State sought under section 36 of the Act to recover through the [   ] County Court, by means of [garnishee proceedings] or [a charging order], the amount then outstanding in respect of which the order was made;

    (ii) that such amount, or any portion of it, remains unpaid; and

    (iii) having inquired in the liable person's presence as to his means and as to whether there has been [wilful refusal] or [culpable neglect] on his part, the court is of the opinion that there has been [wilful refusal] or [culpable neglect] on his part.

The decision of the court is that the liable person be [committed to prison] [detained] for [   ] unless the aggregate amount mentioned below in respect of which this warrant is made is sooner paid.*

This warrant is made in respect of—
Amount outstanding (including any interest, costs and charges):
Costs of commitment of the Secretary of State:

Aggregate amount:

And you *[name of person or persons to whom warrant is directed]* are hereby required to take the liable person and convey him to *[name of prison or place of detention]* and there deliver him to the [governor] [officer in charge] thereof; and you, the [governor] [officer in charge], to receive the liable person into your custody and keep him for *[period of imprisonment]* from the date of his arrest under this warrant or until he be sooner discharged in due course of law.

Justice of the Peace

[*or* by order of the Court
Clerk of the Court].

Note: The period of imprisonment will be reduced as provided by regulation 34(5) and (6) of the Child Support (Collection and Enforcement) Regulations 1992 if part-payment is made of the aggregate amount.

CHILD SUPPORT COMMISSIONERS (PROCEDURE) REGULATIONS 1992
(SI 1992/2640)

ARRANGEMENT OF REGULATIONS

PART I

Introduction

1. Citation, commencement and interpretation

(1) These Regulations may be cited as the Child Support Commissioners (Procedure) Regulations 1992 and shall come into force on 5th April 1993.

(2) In these Regulations, unless the context otherwise requires—

"the Act" means the Child Support Act 1991;
"appeal tribunal" means a child support appeal tribunal;
"the chairman", for the purposes of regulations 2 and 3, means—

  (i) the person who was the chairman of the appeal tribunal which gave the decision against which leave to appeal is being sought; or
  (ii) where the application for leave to appeal to a Commissioner was dealt with under regulation 2(2), the chairman who dealt with the application;

"Chief Commissioner" means the Chief Child Support Commissioner appointed under section 22(1) of the Act;
"Commissioner" means the Chief or any other Child Support Commissioner appointed under section 22(1) of the Act and includes a Tribunal of Commissioners constituted under paragraph 5 of Schedule 4 to the Act;
"proceedings" means any proceedings before a Commissioner, whether by way of an application for leave to appeal to, or from, a Commissioner, or by way of an appeal or otherwise;
"respondent" means any person, other than the applicant or appellant, who participated as a party to the proceedings before the appeal tribunal, and any other person who, pursuant to a direction given under regulation 7(1)(a), is served with notice of the appeal; and
"summons" in relation to Scotland, means "citation" and regulation 14 shall be construed accordingly.

(3) In these Regulations, unless the context otherwise requires, a reference—

  (a) to a numbered regulation is to the regulation in these Regulations bearing that number;
  (b) in a regulation to a numbered paragraph is to the paragraph in that regulation bearing that number;
  (c) in a paragraph to a lettered sub-paragraph is to the sub-paragraph in that paragraph bearing that letter.

PART II

Applications for leave to appeal and appeals to a commissioner

2. Application to the chairman of an appeal tribunal or to a Commissioner for leave to appeal to a Commissioner

(1) An application for leave to appeal to a Commissioner from the decision of an appeal tribunal shall be made—

- (a) in the case of an application to the chairman of an appeal tribunal, within the period of 3 months beginning with the date on which notice of the decision of the tribunal was given or sent to the applicant; or
- (b) in the case of an application to a Commissioner, within the period of 42 days beginning with the date on which notice of the refusal of leave to appeal by the chairman of the appeal tribunal was given or sent to the applicant.

(2) Where in any case it is impracticable, or it would be likely to cause undue delay for an application for leave to appeal against a decision of an appeal tribunal to be determined by the person who was the chairman of that tribunal, that application shall be determined by any other person qualified under paragraph 3 of Schedule 3 to the Act to act as a chairman of appeal tribunals.

(3) Subject to paragraph (4), an application may be made to a Commissioner for leave to appeal against a decision of an appeal tribunal only where the applicant has been refused leave to appeal by the chairman of the appeal tribunal.

(4) Where there has been a failure to apply to the chairman of the tribunal, either within the time specified in paragraph (1)(a) or at all, an application for leave to appeal may be made to a Commissioner who may, if for special reasons he thinks fit, accept and proceed to consider and determine the application.

(5) A Commissioner may accept and proceed to consider and determine an application for leave to appeal under paragraph (3) notwithstanding that the period specified for making the application has expired if for special reasons he thinks fit.

3. Notice of application for leave to appeal to a Commissioner

(1) An application for leave to appeal shall be brought by a notice in writing to the clerk to the tribunal at the Central Office of Child Support Appeal Tribunals at Anchorage Two, Anchorage Quay, Salford Quays, Manchester, M5 2YN or, as the case may be, to a Commissioner, and shall contain—

- (a) the name and address of the applicant;
- (b) the grounds on which the applicant intends to rely;
- (c) an address for service of notices and other documents on the applicant; and
- (d) where the applicant is to be represented by a person who is not a barrister, advocate or solicitor, the written authority of the applicant for that person to represent him,

and the notice shall have annexed to it a copy of the decision against which leave to appeal is being sought.

(2) In the case of an application for leave to appeal to a Commissioner made to a Commissioner where the applicant has been refused leave to appeal by the chairman of an appeal tribunal the notice shall also have annexed to it a copy of the decision refusing

leave to appeal, and shall state the date on which the applicant was given notice of the refusal of leave.

(3) Where the applicant has failed to apply within the time specified in regulation 2(1)(a) or, as the case may be, 2(1)(b) for leave to appeal, the notice of application for leave to appeal shall, in addition to complying with paragraph (1), state the grounds relied upon for seeking acceptance of the application notwithstanding that the relevant period has expired.

(4) In a case where the application for leave to appeal is made by a child support officer he shall send a copy of the application to each person who was a party to the proceedings before the appeal tribunal, and in any other case the clerk to the tribunal or, as the case may be, the Office of the Commissioner shall send a copy of the application to each person, other than the applicant, who was such a party.

(5) An applicant for leave to appeal to a Commissioner may at any time before the application is determined withdraw it by giving written notice of withdrawal to the clerk to the tribunal or, as the case may be, to the Commissioner.

4. Determination of applications for leave to appeal

(1) The determination of an application for leave to appeal to a Commissioner made to the chairman of an appeal tribunal shall be recorded in writing by the chairman and a copy of the determination shall be sent by the clerk to the tribunal to the applicant and every other person to whom notice of the application was given under regulation 3(4).

(2) Unless a Commissioner directs to the contrary, where a Commissioner grants leave to appeal on a application made in accordance with regulation 3, notice of appeal shall be deemed to have been duly given on the date when notice of the determination was given to the applicant and the notice of application shall be deemed to be a notice of appeal duly served under regulation 5.

(3) If on consideration of an application for leave to appeal to him from the decision of an appeal tribunal the Commissioner grants leave he may, with the consent of the applicant and each respondent, treat the application as an appeal and determine any question arising on the application as though it were a question arising on an appeal.

5. Notice of appeal

(1) Subject to regulation 4(2), an appeal shall be brought by a notice to a Commissioner containing—

   (a) the name and address of the appellant;
   (b) the date on which leave to appeal was granted;
   (c) the grounds on which the appellant intends to rely;
   (d) an address for service of notices and other documents on the appellant,

and the notice shall have annexed to it a copy of the determination granting leave to appeal and a copy of the decision against which leave to appeal has been granted.

6. Time limit for appealing

(1) Subject to paragraph (2), a notice of appeal shall not be valid unless it is served on a Commissioner within 42 days of the date on which the applicant was given notice in writing that leave to appeal had been granted.

(2) A Commissioner may accept a notice of appeal served after the expiry of the period prescribed by paragraph (1) if for special reasons he thinks fit.

7. Directions on notice of appeal

(1) As soon as practicable after the receipt of a notice of appeal a Commissioner shall give such directions as appear to him to be necessary, specifying—

    (a) the parties who are to be respondents to the appeal; and
    (b) the order in which and the time within which any party is to be allowed to make written observations on the appeal or on the observations made by any other party.

(2) If in any case two or more persons who were parties to the proceedings before the appeal tribunal give notice of appeal to a Commissioner, a Commissioner shall direct which one of them is to be treated as the appellant, and thereafter, but without prejudice to any rights of powers conferred on appellants by the Act or these Regulations, any other person who has given notice of appeal shall be treated as a respondent.

(3) Subject to regulation 23(2)(b), the time specified in directions given under paragraph (1)(b) as being the time within which written observations are to be made shall be not less than 30 days beginning with the day on which the notice of the appeal or, as the case may be, the observations were sent to the party concerned.

8. Acknowledgement of a notice of appeal and notification to each respondent

There shall be sent by the office of the Child Support Commissioners—

    (a) to the appellant, an acknowledgement of the receipt of the notice of appeal; and
    (b) to each respondent, a copy of the notice of appeal.

9. Secretary of State as respondent to an appeal

The Secretary of State may at any time apply to a Commissioner for leave to intervene in an appeal pending before a Commissioner, and if such leave is granted the Secretary of State shall thereafter be treated as a respondent to that appeal.

PART III
General procedure

10. Other directions

(1) Where it appears to a Commissioner that an application or appeal which is made to him gives insufficient particulars to enable the question at issue to be determined, he may direct the party making the application or appeal or any respondent to furnish such further particulars as may reasonably be required.

(2) At any stage of the proceedings a Commissioner may, either of his own motion or on application, give such directions or further directions as he may consider necessary or desirable for the efficient and effective despatch of the proceedings.

(3) Without prejudice to the provisions of paragraph (2), a Commissioner may direct any party to any proceedings before him to make such written observations as may seem to him necessary to enable the question at issue to be determined.

(4) An application under paragraph (2) shall be made in writing to a Commissioner and shall set out the direction which the applicant is seeking to have made and the grounds for the application.

(5) Unless a Commissioner otherwise determines, an application made pursuant to paragraph (2) shall be copied by the office of the Child Support Commissioners to the other parties.

(6) The powers to give directions conferred by paragraphs (2) and (3) include power to revoke or vary any such direction.

11. Requests for oral hearings

(1) Subject to paragraphs (2) and (3), a Commissioner may determine an application for leave to appeal or an appeal without an oral hearing.

(2) Where in any proceedings before a Commissioner a request is made by any party for an oral hearing the Commissioner shall grant the request unless, after considering all the circumstances of the case and the reasons put forward in the request for the hearing, he is satisfied that the application or appeal can properly be determined without a hearing, in which event he may proceed to determine the case without a hearing and he shall in writing either before giving his determination or decision, or in it, inform the person making the request that it has been refused.

(3) A Commissioner may of his own motion at any stage, if he is satisfied that an oral hearing is desirable, direct such a hearing.

12. Representation at an oral hearing

At any oral hearing a party may conduct his case himself (with assistance from any person if he wishes) or be represented by any person whom he may appoint for the purpose.

13. Oral hearings

(1) This regulation applies to any oral hearing to which these Regulations apply.

(2) Reasonable notice (being not less than 10 days beginning with the day on which notice is given and ending on the day before the hearing of the case is to take place) of the time and place of any oral hearing before a Commissioner shall be given to the parties by the office of the Child Support Commissioners.

(3) If any party to whom notice of an oral hearing has been given in accordance with these Regulations should fail to appear at the hearing, the Commissioner may, having regard to all the circumstances including any explanation offered for the absence, proceed with the case notwithstanding that party's absence, or may give such directions with a view to the determination of the case as he thinks fit.

(4) Any oral hearing before a Commissioner shall be in public except where the Commissioner for special reasons directs otherwise, in which case the hearing or any part thereof shall be in private.

(5) Where a Commissioner holds an oral hearing the applicant or appellant and every respondent shall be entitled to be present and be heard.

(6) Any person entitled to be heard at an oral hearing may—

    (a) address the Commissioner;

    (b) with the leave of the Commissioner but not otherwise, give evidence, call witnesses and put questions directly to any other person called as a witness.

(7) Nothing in these Regulations shall prevent a member of the Council on Tribunals or of the Scottish Committee of the Council in his capacity as such from being present at an oral hearing before a Commissioner notwithstanding that the hearing is not in public.

14. Summoning of witnesses

(1) Subject to paragraph (2), a Commissioner may summon any person to attend as a witness at an oral hearing, at such time and place as may be specified in the summons, to answer any questions or produce any documents in his custody or under his control which relate to any matter in question in the proceedings.

(2) No person shall be required to attend in obedience to a summons under paragraph (1) unless he has been given at least 7 days' notice of the hearing or, if less than 7 days, has informed the Commissioner that he accepts such notice as he has been given.

(3) A Commissioner may upon the application of a person summoned under this regulation set the summons aside.

(4) A Commissioner may require any witness to give evidence on oath and for that purpose there may be administered an oath in due form.

15. Postponement and adjournment

(1) A Commissioner may, either of his own motion or on an application by any party to the proceedings, postpone an oral hearing.

(2) An oral hearing, once commenced, may be adjourned by the Commissioner at any time either on the application of any party to the proceedings or of his own motion.

16. Withdrawal of applications for leave to appeal and appeals

(1) At any time before it is determined, an application to a Commissioner for leave to appeal against a decision of an appeal tribunal may be withdrawn by the applicant by giving written notice to a Commissioner of his intention to do so.

(2) At any time before the decision is made, an appeal to a Commissioner may, with the leave of a Commissioner, be withdrawn by the appellant.

(3) A Commissioner may, on application by the party concerned, give leave to reinstate any application or appeal which has been withdrawn in accordance with paragraphs (1) and (2) and, on giving leave, he may make such directions as to the future conduct of the proceedings as he thinks fit.

17. Irregularities

Any irregularity resulting from failure to comply with the requirements of these Regulations before a Commissioner has determined the application or appeal shall not by itself invalidate any proceedings, and the Commissioner, before reaching his decision, may waive the irregularity or take such steps as he thinks fit to remedy the irregularity whether by amendment of any document, or the giving of any notice or directions or otherwise.

PART IV

Decisions

18. Determinations and decisions of a Commissioner

(1) The determination of a Commissioner on an application for leave to appeal shall be in writing and signed by him.

(2) The decision of a Commissioner on an appeal shall be in writing and signed by him and, except in respect of a decision made with the consent of the parties, he shall record the reasons.

(3) A copy of the determination or decision and any reasons shall be sent to the parties by the office of the Child Support Commissioners.

(4) Without prejudice to paragraphs (2) and (3), a Commissioner may announce his determination or decision at the conclusion of an oral hearing.

(5) When giving his decision on an application or appeal, whether in writing or orally, a Commissioner shall omit any reference to the surname of any child to whom the appeal relates and any other information which would be likely, whether directly or indirectly, to identify that child.

19. Correction of accidental errors in decisions

(1) Subject to regulation 21, accidental errors in any decision or record of a decision may at any time be corrected by the Commissioner who gave the decision.

(2) A correction made to, or to the record of, a decision shall become part of the decision or record thereof and written notice thereof shall be given by the office of the Child Support Commissioners to any party to whom notice of the decision had previously been given.

20. Setting aside of decisions on certain grounds

(1) Subject to the following provisions of this regulation and regulation 21, on an application made by any party a decision may be set aside by the Commissioner who gave the decision in a case where it appears just to do so on the ground that—

   (a) a document relating to the proceedings was not sent to, or was not received at an appropriate time by, a party or his representative, or was not received at an appropriate time by the Commissioner, or
   (b) a party or his representative had not been present at an oral hearing which had been held in the course of the proceedings; or
   (c) there has been some other procedural irregularity or mishap.

(2) An application under this regulation shall be made in writing to a Commissioner within 30 days from the date on which notice in writing of the decision was given by the office of the Child Support Commissioners to the party making the application.

(3) Where an application to set aside a decision is made under paragraph (1), each party shall be sent by the office of the Child Support Commissioners a copy of the application and shall be afforded a reasonable opportunity of making representations on it before the application is determined.

(4) Notice in writing of a determination of an application to set aside a decision shall be given by the office of the Child Support Commissioners to each party and shall contain a statement giving the reasons for the determination.

21. Provisions common to regulations 19 and 20

(1) In regulations 19 and 20 the word "decision" shall include determinations of applications for leave to appeal as well as decisions on appeals.

(2) Subject to a direction by a Commissioner to the contrary, in calculating any time for applying for leave to appeal against a Commissioner's decision there shall be disregarded any day falling before the day on which notice was given of a correction of a decision or the record thereof pursuant to regulation 19 or on which notice was given of a determination that a decision shall not be set aside under regulation 20, as the case may be.

(3) There shall be no appeal against a correction or a refusal to correct under regulation 19 or a determination given under regulation 20.

(4) If it is impracticable or likely to cause undue delay for a decision or record of a decision to be dealt with pursuant to regulation 19 or 20 by the Commissioner who gave the decision, the Chief Commissioner or another Commissioner may deal with the matter.

PART V
Miscellaneous and supplementary

22. Confidentiality

(1) No information such as is mentioned in paragraph (2), and which has been furnished for the purposes of any proceedings to which these Regulations apply, shall be disclosed except with the written consent of the person to whom the information relates.

(2) The information mentioned in paragraph (1) is—

   (a) the address, other than the address of the office of the Commissioner concerned and the place where the oral hearing (if any) is to be held; and
   (b) any other information the use of which could reasonably be expected to lead to a person being located.

23. General powers of a Commissioner

(1) Subject to the provisions of these Regulations, and without prejudice to regulations 7 and 10, a Commissioner may adopt such procedure in relation to any proceedings before him as he sees fit.

(2) A Commissioner may, if he thinks fit—

   (a) subject to regulations 2(5) and 6(2), extend the time specified by or under these Regulations for doing any act, notwithstanding that the time specified may have expired;
   (b) abridge the time so specified; or
   (c) expedite the proceedings in such manner as he thinks fit.

(3) Subject to paragraph (4), a Commissioner may, if he thinks fit, either on the application of a party or of his own motion, strike out for want of prosecution any application for leave to appeal or any appeal.

(4) Before making an order under paragraph (3), the Commissioner shall send notice to the party against whom it is proposed that it shall be made giving him an opportunity to show cause why it should not be made.

(5) A Commissioner may, on application by the party concerned, give leave to reinstate any application or appeal which has been struck out in accordance with paragraph (3) and, on giving leave, he may make such directions as to the future conduct of the proceedings as he thinks fit.

(6) Nothing in these Regulations shall be construed as derogating from any other power which is exercisable apart from these Regulations.

24. Manner of and time for service of notices, etc

(1) Any notice or other document required or authorised to be given or sent to any party under the provisions of these Regulations shall be deemed to have been given or sent if it was sent by post properly addressed and pre-paid to that party at his ordinary or last notified address.

(2) Any notice or other document given, sent or served by post shall be deemed to have been given on the day on which it was posted.

(3) Any notice or other document required to be given, sent or submitted to or served on a Commissioner—

(a) shall be given, sent or submitted to an office of the Child Support Commissioners;
(b) shall be deemed to have been given, sent or submitted if it was sent by post properly addressed and pre-paid to an office of the Child Support Commissioners.

25. Application to a Commissioner for leave to appeal to the Courts

(1) A person who was a party to the proceedings in which the original decision or appeal decision was given (both of those expressions having the meaning assigned to them by section 25 of the Act) may appoint any person for the purpose of making an application for leave to appeal under section 25 of the Act.

(2) An application to a Commissioner under section 25 of the Act for leave to appeal against a decision of a Commissioner shall be made in writing and shall be made within 3 months from the date on which the applicant was given written notice of the decision.

(3) In a case where the Chief Commissioner considers that it is impracticable, or would be likely to cause undue delay, for such an application to be determined by the Commissioner who decided the case, that application shall be determined—

(a) where the decision was a decision of an individual Commissioner, by the Chief Commissioner or a Commissioner selected by the Chief Commissioner; and
(b) where the decision was a decision of a Tribunal of Commissioners, by a differently constituted Tribunal of Commissioners selected by the Chief Commissioner.

(4) If the office of Chief Commissioner is vacant, or if the Chief Commissioner is unable to act, paragraph (3) shall have effect as if the expression "the Chief Commissioner" referred to such other of the Commissioners as may have been nominated to act for the purpose either by the Chief Commissioner or, if he has not made such a nomination, by the Lord Chancellor.

(5) Regulations 16(1) and 16(3) shall apply to applications to a Commissioner for leave to appeal from a Commissioner as they do to the proceedings therein set out.

CHILD SUPPORT APPEAL TRIBUNALS (PROCEDURE) REGULATIONS 1992
(SI 1992/2641)

ARRANGEMENT OF REGULATIONS

1. Citation, commencement and interpretation

(1) These Regulations may be cited as the Child Support Appeal Tribunals (Procedure) Regulations 1992 and shall come into force on 5th April 1993.

(2) In these Regulations, unless the context otherwise requires—

"absent parent" has the meaning assigned to it in section 3(2) of the Act;
"the Act" means the Child Support Act 1991;
"Central Office" means the Central Office of Child Support Appeal Tribunals at Anchorage Two, Anchorage Quay, Salford Quays, Manchester, M5 2YN;
"chairman", subject to paragraph (3), means a person nominated under paragraph 3 of Schedule 3 to the Act and includes the President and any full-time chairman;
"clerk to the tribunal" means a person appointed under paragraph 6 of Schedule 3 to the Act;
"Commissioner" means the Chief or any other Child Support Commissioner appointed under section 22 of the Act;
"full-time chairman" means a regional or other full-time chairman of a child support appeal tribunal appointed under paragraph 4 of Schedule 3 to the Act;
"party to the proceedings" means—

(a) the person with care;
(b) the absent parent;
(c) any child who has made an application for a maintenance assessment under section 7 of the Act;
(d) the child support officer;
(e) any other person, who on an application made by him, appears to the chairman of the tribunal to be interested in the proceedings;

"person with care" has the meaning assigned to it by section 3(3) of the Act;

"President" has the meaning assigned to it in paragraph 1(1) of Schedule 3 to the Act;

"proceedings" means proceedings on an appeal or application to which these Regulations apply; and

"tribunal" means a child support appeal tribunal constituted in accordance with section 21 of the Act.

(3) Unless otherwise provided, where by these Regulations anything is required to be done by, or any power is conferred on, a chairman, then—

(a) if that thing is to be done or the power is to be exercised at the hearing of an appeal or application, it shall be done or exercised by the chairman of the tribunal hearing the appeal or application; and

(b) otherwise, shall be done or exercised by a person who is eligible to be nominated to act as a chairman of a child support appeal tribunal under paragraph 3(2) of Schedule 3 to the Act.

(4) In these Regulations, unless the context otherwise requires, a reference—

(a) to a numbered regulation is to the regulation in these Regulations bearing that number; and

(b) in a regulation to a numbered paragraph is to the paragraph in that regulation bearing that number.

2. Service of notices or documents

(1) Where by any provision of the Act or of these Regulations any notice or other document is required to be given or sent to the clerk to the tribunal that notice or document shall be treated as having been so given or sent on the day that it is received by the clerk to the tribunal.

(2) Where by any provision of the Act or of these Regulations any notice or other document is required to be given or sent to any person other than the clerk to the tribunal that notice or document shall, if sent by post to that person's last known address, be treated as having been given or sent on the day that it was posted.

3. Making an appeal or application and time limits

(1) An appeal to a tribunal under section 20(1) of the Act or an application to a tribunal to set aside its decision under regulation 15 shall be by notice in writing signed by the person making it or by his representative where it appears to a chairman that he was unable to sign personally, or by a barrister, advocate or solicitor on his behalf.

(2) The notice shall be made or given by sending or delivering it to the clerk to the tribunal at the Central Office.

(3) An appeal under section 20(1) of the Act shall be brought within the period of 28 days beginning with the date on which notification of the decision in question was given or sent to the appellant.

(4) An application under regulation 15 shall be made within the period of 3 months beginning with the date when a copy of the record of the decision was given or sent to the applicant.

(5) In paragraphs (6) and (7) "the specified time" means the time specified in paragraph (3) or, as the case may be, paragraph (4).

(6) When an appeal or application is made after the specified time has expired, that time may for special reasons be extended by the chairman to the date of the making of the appeal or application.

(7) Any appeal or application made after the specified time has expired which does not include an application for an extension of time shall be deemed to include such an application, and if it appears to a chairman that an application for an extension of time does not state reasons for the appeal or application being made after the specified time the chairman may before determining it give the person making the application for an extension of time a reasonable opportunity to provide reasons.

(8) An application for an extension of time which has been refused may not be renewed, but any chairman may set aside a refusal if it appears to him just to do so on any of the grounds set out in regulation 15(1).

(9) In the case of an appeal the notice shall contain sufficient particulars of the decision under appeal to enable that decision to be identified.

(10) Any notice of appeal or application other than an application for an extension of time shall state the grounds on which it is made.

(11) If it appears to a chairman that the notice of appeal does not enable the decision under appeal to be identified or that the notice of appeal or application does not state the grounds on which it is made the chairman may direct the person making it to provide such particulars as the chairman may reasonably require.

4. Lack of jurisdiction

When a chairman is satisfied that the tribunal does not have jurisdiction to entertain a purported appeal he may make a declaration to that effect and such declaration shall dispose of the purported appeal.

5. Directions

At any stage of the proceedings a chairman may either of his own motion or on a written application made to the clerk to the tribunal by any party to the proceedings give such directions as he may consider necessary or desirable for the just, effective and efficient conduct of the proceedings and may direct any party to provide such further particulars or to produce such documents as may reasonably be required.

6. Striking out of proceedings

(1) Subject to paragraph (2), a chairman may, either of his own motion or on the application of any party to the proceedings, order that the appeal or application be struck out because of the failure of the appellant or applicant to comply with a direction under regulation 3(11) or 5 or to reply to an enquiry from the clerk to the tribunal about his availability to attend a hearing.

(2) Before making an order under paragraph (1) the chairman shall send notice to the person against whom it is proposed that any such order should be made and any other party to the proceedings giving each of them a reasonable opportunity to show cause why such an order should not be made.

(3) The chairman may, on application by any party to the proceedings made not later than one year beginning with the date of the order made under paragraph (1), give leave to reinstate any appeal or application which has been struck out in accordance with that order.

7. Withdrawal of appeals and applications

(1) Any appeal to a tribunal may be withdrawn by the person making the appeal—

   (a) at a hearing with the leave of the chairman; or
   (b) at any other time, by giving written notice of intention to withdraw to the clerk to the tribunal and either—

      (i) with the consent in writing of every other party to the proceedings; or
      (ii) with the leave of the chairman after every other party to the proceedings has had a reasonable opportunity to make representations.

(2) A person who has made an application to a tribunal to set aside their decision under regulation 15 may withdraw it at any time before the application is determined by giving written notice of withdrawal to the clerk to the tribunal.

8. Postponement

(1) Where a person to whom notice of a hearing has been given wishes to request a postponement of that hearing he shall give notice in writing to the clerk to the tribunal stating his reasons for the request and a chairman may grant or refuse the request as he thinks fit.

(2) A chairman may of his own motion at any time before the beginning of the hearing postpone the hearing.

9. Representation of parties to the proceedings

Any party to the proceedings may be accompanied and (whether or not the party himself attends) may be represented by another person whether having a professional qualification or not, and for the purposes of any proceedings any such representative shall have all the rights and powers to which the person represented is entitled under these Regulations, except that a representative who is not a barrister, advocate or solicitor shall not have the power to sign the notice of appeal or application.

10. Summoning of witnesses

(1) A chairman may by summons or, in Scotland, citation require any person in Great Britain to attend as a witness at a hearing of an appeal or application at such time and place as shall be specified in the summons or citation and, subject to paragraph (2), at the hearing to answer any question or produce any documents in his custody or under his control which relate to any matter in question in the appeal or application, but—

   (a) no person shall be required to attend in obedience to such a summons or citation unless he has been given at least 10 days' notice of the hearing or, if less than 10 days' notice is given, he has informed the tribunal that he accepts that notice as sufficient; and
   (b) no person shall be required to attend and give evidence or to produce any document in obedience to such a summons or citation unless the necessary expenses of attendance are paid or tendered to him.

(2) No person shall be compelled to give any evidence or produce any document or other material that he could not be compelled to give or produce on a trial of an action in a court of law in that part of Great Britain where the hearing takes place.

(3) In exercising the powers conferred by this regulation, the chairman shall take into account the need to protect any matter that relates to intimate personal or financial circumstances, is commercially sensitive, consists of information communicated or obtained in confidence or concerns national security.

(4) Every summons or citation issued under this regulation shall contain a statement to the effect that the person in question may apply in writing to a chairman to vary or set aside the summons or citation.

11. Hearings

(1) A tribunal shall hold an oral hearing of every appeal, and may hold an oral hearing of an application, and subject to the provisions of the Act and of these Regulations the procedure in connection with the hearing shall be such as the chairman shall determine.

(2) Not less than 10 days' notice (beginning with the day on which it is given and ending on the day before the hearing) of the time and place of any hearing shall be given to every party to the proceedings, and if such notice has not been given to a person to whom it should have been given under the provisions of this paragraph the hearing may proceed only with the consent of that person.

(3) At any hearing any party to the proceedings shall be entitled to be present and be heard.

(4) Any person entitled to be heard at a hearing may address the tribunal, give evidence, call witnesses and put questions directly to any other party to the proceedings, to any representative of the child support officer or to any other person called as a witness.

(5) A tribunal may require any witness to give evidence on oath or affirmation and for that purpose there may be administered an oath or affirmation in due form.

(6) If a party to the proceedings to whom notice has been given under paragraph (2) fails to appear at the hearing the tribunal may, having regard to all the circumstances including any explanation offered for the absence, proceed with the appeal notwithstanding his absence or give such directions with a view to the determination of the appeal as it may think proper.

(7) Any hearing before the tribunal shall be in private unless the chairman directs that the hearing, or part of it, shall be in public.

(8) The following persons shall also be entitled to be present at a hearing even though it is in private—

    (a) the President, any full-time chairman and the clerk to the tribunal;
    (b) any person undergoing training as a chairman or other member of the tribunal or as a clerk to the tribunal;
    (c) any person acting on behalf of the President in the training or supervision of clerks to tribunals;
    (d) a member of the Council on Tribunals or of the Scottish Committee of the Council;

(e) any person undergoing training as a child support officer or as the representative of a child support officer and any person acting on behalf of the Chief Child Support Officer or the Secretary of State in the training or supervision of child support officers or representatives of child support officers or in the monitoring of standards of adjudication by child support officers;

(f) with leave of the chairman and the consent of every party to the proceedings actually present, any other person.

(9) For the purposes of arriving at its decision a tribunal shall, and for the purposes of discussing any question of procedure may, notwithstanding anything contained in these Regulations, order all persons to withdraw from the sitting of the tribunal other than the members of the tribunal, any of the persons mentioned in sub-paragraphs (a), (b) and (d) of paragraph (8) and, with the leave of the chairman and if no party to the proceedings actually present objects, any of the persons mentioned in sub-paragraphs (c) and (f) of that paragraph.

(10) None of the persons mentioned in paragraph (8) shall take any part in the hearing or (where entitled or permitted to remain) in the deliberations of the tribunal.

12. Adjournments

(1) A hearing may be adjourned by the tribunal at any time on the application of any party to the proceedings or of its own motion.

(2) Where a hearing has been adjourned and it is not practicable, or would cause undue delay, for it to be resumed before a tribunal consisting of the same members, the appeal or application shall be heard by a tribunal none of the members of which was a member of the original tribunal and the proceedings shall be by way of a complete re-hearing of the case.

13. Decisions

(1) A decision of the tribunal may be taken by a majority.

(2) The chairman shall—

(a) record in writing the decision of the tribunal;
(b) include in the record of every decision a statement of the reasons for it, the findings of the tribunal on questions of fact material to the decision and the terms of any direction given under section 20(4) of the Act; and
(c) if a decision is not unanimous, record a statement that one of the members dissented and the reasons given by him for so dissenting.

(3) As soon as may be practicable after the decision of the tribunal a copy of the record of the decision made in accordance with this regulation shall be sent to every party to the proceedings who shall also be informed of the conditions governing appeals to a Commissioner.

(4) If a child support officer to whom a case is referred by the Secretary of State under section 20(3) of the Act (procedure following a successful appeal) is uncertain, having regard to the terms of the decision and of any directions contained in it, how he should deal with the case, he may apply to the tribunal or another tribunal for directions or further directions, and the tribunal may give such directions or further directions as it thinks fit.

(5) Upon receiving an application from a child support officer under paragraph (4) the clerk to the tribunal shall send a copy of it to all the other parties to the case, and the tribunal shall not give any directions or further directions on the application until those other parties have had a reasonable opportunity of making representations on it.

14. Corrections

(1) Subject to regulation 16 (provisions common to regulations 14 and 15) accidental errors (whether of omission or commission) in any decision or record of any decision may at any time be corrected by the tribunal who gave the decision or by another tribunal.

(2) A correction made to a decision or to the record of a decision shall be deemed to be part of the decision or of the record thereof and written notice of it shall be given as soon as practicable to every party to the proceedings.

15. Setting aside

(1) Subject to regulation 16 (provisions common to regulations 14 and 15) on an application made by a party to the proceedings a decision may be set aside by the tribunal who gave the decision or by another tribunal in a case where it appears just to do so on the grounds that—

(a) a document relating to the proceedings in which the decision was given was not sent to, or was not received at an appropriate time by, a party to the proceedings or the party's representative or was not received at an appropriate time by the tribunal who gave the decision;

(b) a party to the proceedings in which the decision was given or the party's representative was not present at the hearing notice of which had been given under regulation 11(2); or

(c) there has been some other procedural irregularity or mishap.

(2) An application under this regulation shall be made in accordance with regulation 3.

(3) Where an application to set aside a decision is made under paragraph (1) every party to the proceedings shall be sent a copy of the application and shall be afforded a reasonable opportunity of making representations on it before the application is decided.

(4) Notice in writing of a decision on an application to set aside a decision shall be given to every party to the proceedings as soon as may be practicable and the notice shall contain a statement giving the reasons for the decision.

(5) For the purpose of deciding an application to set aside a decision under these Regulations there shall be disregarded regulation 2 and any provision in any enactment or instrument to the effect that any notice or other document required or authorised to be given or sent to any person shall be deemed to have been given or sent if it was sent by post to the person's last known address.

16. Provisions common to regulations 14 and 15

(1) In calculating time under regulation 2(1) of the Child Support Commissioners (Procedure) Regulations 1992 (applications for leave to appeal to a Commissioner) there shall be disregarded any day falling before the day on which notice was given of a correction of a decision or record thereof pursuant to regulation 14 or on which notice is

given of a decision that a prior decision shall not be set aside following an application made under regulation 15, as the case may be.

(2) Notwithstanding anything contained in these Regulations, there shall be no appeal against a correction made under regulation 14, or a refusal to make such a correction, or against a decision given under regulation 15.

(3) Nothing in these Regulations shall be construed as derogating from any power to correct errors or set aside decisions which is exercisable apart from these Regulations.

17. Confidentiality

(1) No information such as is mentioned in paragraph (2), and which has been provided for the purposes of any proceedings to which these Regulations apply, shall be disclosed except with the written consent of the person to whom the information relates.

(2) The information referred to in paragraph (1) is—

    (a) any address, other than the address of the Central Office and the place where the oral hearing is to be held; and

    (b) any other information the use of which could reasonably be expected to lead to a person being located.

CHILD SUPPORT (COLLECTION AND ENFORCEMENT OF OTHER FORMS OF MAINTENANCE) REGULATIONS 1992
(SI 1992/2643)

1. Citation, commencement and interpretation

(1) These Regulations may be cited as the Child Support (Collection and Enforcement of Other Forms of Maintenance) Regulations 1992 and shall come into force on 5th April 1993.

(2) In these Regulations—

"the Act" means the Child Support Act 1991;
"child of the family" has the same meaning as in the Matrimonial Causes Act 1973 or, in Scotland, the Family Law (Scotland) Act 1985; and
"periodical payments" includes secured periodical payments.

2. Periodical payments and categories of person prescribed for the purposes of section 30 of the Act

The following periodical payments and categories of persons are prescribed for the purposes of section 30(1) of the Act—

  (a) payments under a maintenance order made in relation to a child in accordance with the provisions of section 8(6) (periodical payments in addition to child support maintenance), 8(7) (periodical payments to meet expenses incurred in connection with the provision of instruction or training) or 8(8) of the Act (periodical payments to meet expenses attributable to disability);
  (b) any periodical payments under a maintenance order which are payable to or for the benefit of a spouse or former spouse who is the person with care of a child who is a qualifying child in respect of whom a child support maintenance assessment is in force in accordance with which the Secretary of State has arranged for the collection of child support maintenance under section 29 of the Act; and
  (c) any periodical payments under a maintenance order payable to or for the benefit of a former child of the family of the person against whom the order is made, that child having his home with the person with care.

3. Collection and enforcement—England and Wales

In relation to England and Wales, sections 29(2) and (3) and 31 to 40 of the Act, and any regulations made under those sections, shall apply for the purpose of enabling the Secretary of State to enforce any obligation to pay any amount which he is authorised to collect under section 30 of the Act, with the modification that any reference in those sections or regulations to child support maintenance shall be read as a reference to any of the periodical payments mentioned in regulation 2 above, and any reference to a maintenance assessment shall be read as a reference to any of the maintenance orders mentioned in that regulation.

4. Collection and enforcement—Scotland

In relation to Scotland, for the purpose of enforcing any obligation to pay any amount which the Secretary of State is authorised to collect under section 30 of the Act—

(a) the Secretary of State may bring any proceedings and take any other steps (other than diligence against earnings) which could have been brought or taken by or on behalf of the person to whom the periodical payments are payable; and

(b) sections 29(2) and (3), 31 and 32 of the Act, and any regulations made under those sections, shall apply, with the modification that any reference in those sections or regulations to child support maintenance shall be read as a reference to any of the periodical payments mentioned in regulation 2 above, and any reference to a maintenance assessment shall be read as a reference to any of the maintenance orders mentioned in that regulation.

5. Collection and enforcement—supplementary

Nothing in Regulations 3 or 4 applies to any periodical payment which falls due before the date specified by the Secretary of State by a notice in writing to the absent parent that he is arranging for those payments to be collected, and that date shall be not earlier than the date the notice is given.

CHILD SUPPORT (MAINTENANCE ARRANGEMENTS AND JURISDICTION) REGULATIONS 1992
(SI 1992/2645)

1. Citation, commencement and interpretation

(1) These Regulations may be cited as the Child Support (Maintenance Arrangements and Jurisdiction) Regulations 1992 and shall come into force on 5th April 1993.

(2) In these Regulations—

"the Act" means the Child Support Act 1991;
"Maintenance Assessments and Special Cases Regulations" means the Child Support (Maintenance Assessments and Special Cases) Regulations 1992;
"effective date" means the date on which a maintenance assessment takes effect for the purposes of the Act;
"maintenance order" has the meaning given in section 8(11) of the Act.

(3) In these Regulations, unless the context otherwise requires, a reference—

(a) to a numbered regulation is to the regulation in these Regulations bearing that number;
(b) in a regulation to a numbered paragraph is to the paragraph in that regulation bearing that number;
(c) in a paragraph to a lettered or numbered sub-paragraph is to the sub-paragraph in that paragraph bearing that letter or number.

2. Prescription of enactment for the purposes of section 8(11) of the Act

The Affiliation Proceedings Act 1957 is prescribed for the purposes of section 8(11) of the Act.

3. Relationship between maintenance assessments and certain court orders

(1) Orders made under the following enactments are of a kind prescribed for the purposes of section 10(1) of the Act—

(a) the Affiliation Proceedings Act 1957;
(b) Part II of the Matrimonial Causes Act 1973;
(c) the Domestic Proceedings and Magistrates' Courts Act 1978;
(d) Part III of the Matrimonial and Family Proceedings Act 1984;
(e) the Family Law (Scotland) Act 1985;
(f) Schedule 1 to the Children Act 1989.

(2) Subject to paragraphs (3) and (4), where a maintenance assessment is made with respect to—

(a) all of the children with respect to whom an order falling within paragraph (1) is in force; or
(b) one or more but not all of the children with respect to whom an order falling within paragraph (1) is in force and where the amount payable under the order to or for the benefit of each child is separately specified,

that order shall, so far as it relates to the making or securing of periodical payments to or for the benefit of the children with respect to whom the maintenance assessment has been made, cease to have effect.

(3) The provisions of paragraph (2) shall not apply where a maintenance order has been made in accordance with section 8(7) or (8) of the Act.

(4) In Scotland, where—

> (a) an order has ceased to have effect by virtue of the provisions of paragraph (2) to the extent specified in that paragraph; and
> (b) a child support officer no longer has jurisdiction to make a maintenance assessment with respect to a child with respect to whom the order ceased to have effect,

that order shall, so far as it relates to that child, again have effect from the date a child support officer no longer has jurisdiction to make a maintenance assessment with respect to that child.

(5) Where a maintenance assessment is made with respect to children with respect to whom an order falling within paragraph (1) is in force, the effective date of that assessment shall be two days after the assessment is made.

(6) Where the provisions of paragraph (2) apply to an order, that part of the order to which those provisions apply shall cease to have effect from the effective date of the maintenance assessment.

4. Relationship between maintenance assessments and certain agreements

(1) Maintenance agreements within the meaning of section 9(1) of the Act are agreements of a kind prescribed for the purposes of section 10(2) of the Act.

(2) Where a maintenance assessment is made with respect to—

> (a) all of the children with respect to whom an agreement falling within paragraph (1) is in force; or
> (b) one or more but not all of the children with respect to whom an agreement falling within paragraph (1) is in force and where the amount payable under the agreement to or for the benefit of each child is separately specified,

that agreement shall, so far as it relates to the making or securing of periodical payments to or for the benefit of the children with respect to whom the maintenance assessment has been made, become unenforceable from the effective date of the assessment.

(3) Where an agreement becomes unenforceable under the provisions of paragraph (2) to the extent specified in that paragraph, it shall remain unenforceable in relation to a particular child until such date as a child support officer no longer has jurisdiction to make a maintenance assessment with respect to that child.

5. Notifications by child support officers

(1) Where a child support officer is aware that an order of a kind prescribed in paragraph (2) is in force and considers that the making of a maintenance assessment has affected, or is likely to affect, that order, he shall notify the persons prescribed in paragraph (3) in respect of whom that maintenance assessment is in force, and the persons prescribed in paragraph (4) holding office in the court where the order in question was made or subsequently registered, of the assessment and its effective date.

(2) The prescribed orders are those made under an enactment mentioned in regulation 3(1).

(3) The prescribed persons in respect of whom the maintenance assessment is in force are—

    (a) a person with care;

    (b) an absent parent;

    (c) a person who is treated as an absent parent under regulation 20 of the Maintenance Assessments and Special Cases Regulations;

    (d) a child who has made an application for a maintenance assessment under section 7 of the Act.

(4) The prescribed person holding office in the court where the order in question was made or subsequently registered is—

    (a) in England and Wales—

        (i) in relation to the High Court, the senior district judge of the principal registry of the Family Division or, where proceedings were instituted in a district registry, the district judge;

        (ii) in relation to a county court, the proper officer of that court within the meaning of Order 1, Rule 3 of the County Court Rules 1981;

        (iii) in relation to a magistrates' court, the clerk to the justices of that court;

    (b) in Scotland—

        (i) in relation to the Court of Session, the Deputy Principal Clerk of Session;

        (ii) in relation to a sheriff court, the sheriff clerk.

6. Notification by the court

(1) Where a court is aware that a maintenance assessment is in force and makes an order mentioned in regulation 3(1) which it considers has affected, or is likely to affect, that assessment, the person prescribed in paragraph (2) shall notify the Secretary of State to that effect.

(2) The prescribed person is the person holding the office specified below in the court where the order in question was made or subsequently registered—

    (a) In England and Wales—

        (i) in relation to the High Court, the senior district judge of the principal registry of the Family Division or, where proceedings were instituted in a district registry, the district judge;

        (ii) in relation to a county court, the proper officer of that court within the meaning of Order 1, Rule 3 of the County Court Rules 1981;

        (iii) in relation to a magistrates' court, the clerk to the justices of that court;

    (b) in Scotland—

        (i) in relation to the Court of Session, the Deputy Principal Clerk of Session;

        (ii) in relation to a sheriff court, the sheriff clerk.

7. Cancellation of a maintenance assessment on grounds of lack of jurisdiction

(1) Where—

    (a) a person with care;

    (b) an absent parent; or

(c) a qualifying child

with respect to whom a maintenance assessment is in force ceases to be habitually resident in the United Kingdom, a child support officer shall cancel that assessment.

(2) Where the person with care is not an individual, paragraph (1) shall apply as if sub-paragraph (a) were omitted.

(3) Where a child support officer cancels a maintenance assessment under paragraph (1) or by virtue of paragraph (2), the assessment shall cease to have effect from the date that the child support officer determines is the date on which—

   (a) where paragraph (1) applies, the person with care, absent parent or qualifying child; or
   (b) where paragraph (2) applies, the absent parent or qualifying child

with respect to whom the assessment was made ceases to be habitually resident in the United Kingdom.

8. Maintenance assessments and maintenance orders made in error

(1) Where—

   (a) at the time that a maintenance assessment with respect to a qualifying child was made a maintenance order was in force with respect to that child;
   (b) the absent parent has made payments of child support maintenance due under that assessment; and
   (c) the child support officer cancels that assessment on the grounds that it was made in error,

the payments of child support maintenance shall be treated as payments under the maintenance order and that order shall be treated as having continued in force.

(2) Where—

   (a) at the time that a maintenance order with respect to a qualifying child was made a maintenance assessment was in force with respect to that child;
   (b) the absent parent has made payments of maintenance due under that order; and
   (c) the maintenance order is revoked by the court on the grounds that it was made in error,

the payments under the maintenance order shall be treated as payments of child support maintenance and the maintenance assessment shall be treated as not having been cancelled.

CHILD SUPPORT FEES REGULATIONS 1992
(SI 1992/3094)

1. Citation, commencement and interpretation

(1) These Regulations may be cited as the Child Support Fees Regulations 1992 and shall come into force on 5th April 1993.

(2) In these Regulations, unless the context otherwise requires—

"the Act" means the Child Support Act 1991;
"assessable income" has the meaning given in paragraph 5 of Schedule 1 to the Act;
"Maintenance Assessment Procedure Regulations" means the Child Support (Maintenance Assessment Procedure) Regulations 1992;
"parent with care" means a person who, in respect of the same child or children, is both a parent and a person with care.

(3) In these Regulations, unless the context otherwise requires, a reference—

(a) to a numbered regulation is to the regulation in these Regulations bearing that number;
(b) in a regulation to a numbered paragraph is to the paragraph in that regulation bearing that number;
(c) in a paragraph to a lettered or numbered sub-paragraph is to the sub-paragraph in that paragraph bearing that letter or number.

2. Circumstances when fees are payable

Where a maintenance assessment is made following an application under section 4, 6 or 7 of the Act fees shall be payable to the Secretary of State in accordance with regulations 3 and 4.

3. Persons liable to pay fees

(1) Subject to the provisions of paragraph (2), where a maintenance assessment is in force the following persons shall be liable to pay fees, in accordance with the provisions of regulation 4—

(a) the parent with care; and
(b) the absent parent

with respect to whom the assessment was made.

(2) No fees shall be payable by the following categories of person—

(a) any person to or in respect of whom income support, family credit or disability working allowance under Part VII of the Social Security Contributions and Benefits Act 1992 is paid;
(b) any person under the age of 16 or under the age of 19 and receiving full-time education which is not advanced education;
(c) any person whose assessable income is nil;
(d) an absent parent to whom the provisions of paragraph 6 of Schedule 1 to the Act (protected income) apply.

(3) The provisions of paragraph (2) shall—

  (a) be applied in relation to any occasion when a liability to pay fees under the provisions of regulation 4 would otherwise arise; and
  (b) have no effect on the fees payable by any other person.

(4) For the purposes of paragraph (2)(b), "advanced education" has the same meaning as in paragraph 2 of Schedule 1 to the Maintenance Assessment Procedure Regulations (meaning of "child" for the purposes of the Act), and education is to be treated as full-time education if it satisfies the conditions set out in paragraph 3 of that Schedule.

4. Services in respect of which fees are payable

(1) There shall be two categories of fee—

  (a) a fee in respect of the assessment of child support maintenance (an "assessment fee");
  (b) a fee in respect of the Secretary of State arranging for the collection of child support maintenance payable in accordance with an assessment and, if necessary, arranging for the enforcement of the obligation to pay child support maintenance in accordance with that assessment (a "collection fee").

(2) The first assessment fee shall become payable on the date a maintenance assessment is made following an application under section 4, 6 or 7 of the Act and an assessment fee shall thereafter become payable on each anniversary of that date.

(3) The first collection fee shall become payable on the date the Secretary of State arranges for the collection of child support maintenance payable in accordance with an assessment and a collection fee shall thereafter become payable on the date the assessment fee becomes payable.

(4) Subject to paragraphs (5) and (6)—

  (a) the assessment fee shall be £44;
  (b) the collection fee shall be £34,

(5) Where the first collection fee becomes payable on a date other than a date on which an assessment fee becomes payable, the amount of that fee shall be an amount equal to the collection fee specified in paragraph (4) above, multiplied by the number of complete weeks between that date and the date the assessment fee next becomes payable, and divided by 52.

(6) No additional assessment or collection fee shall be payable by a person with respect to whom more than one maintenance assessment is in force.

(7) Where a liability to pay an assessment fee or a collection fee under these Regulations arises, the fee shall become due on the fourteenth day after the date the fee invoice is given or sent by the Secretary of State.

(8) If a fee invoice is sent by post to a person's last known or notified address, it shall be treated as having been given or sent on the second day after the day of posting, excluding any Sunday or any day which is a bank holiday in England, Wales, Scotland or Northern Ireland under the Banking and Financial Dealings Act 1971.

APPENDIX 3
MAINTENANCE APPLICATION FORM

your details

CSA 1

child support agency
an executive agency of the Department of Social Security

Your details see help notes page 4

Read pages 2 and 3 of the Help Notes before filling in this form.
Where you see a ⓗ next to a question see the help notes for guidance.

You	Your partner who lives with you now

ⓗ Surname — Mr / Mrs / Miss / Ms — Mr / Mrs / Miss / Ms

Other names

ⓗ Any other name you or your partner are known by

Sex — Male ☐ Female ☐ — Male ☐ Female ☐

Date of birth — / / — / /

ⓗ What is your marital status now ?

ⓗ National Insurance (NI) number — Letters Numbers Letter — Letters Numbers Letter

Address — Postcode

ⓗ Postal address if different — Postcode

ⓗ Daytime telephone number — ( )

Evening telephone number — ( )

Your details - continued see help notes page 5

page 2

You / **Your partner who lives with you now**

h Are you or your partner registered blind ?

You — No / Yes

Your partner — No / Yes

Is anyone getting Invalid Care Allowance for you or your partner ?

You — No / Yes

Your partner — No / Yes

h Do you or your partner get Disability Living Allowance ?

You — No / Yes

Your partner — No / Yes

Which rate of care component is included ?

You — Higher / Middle / Lower / None

Which rate of care component is included ?

Your partner — Higher / Middle / Lower / None

Do you or your partner get Attendance Allowance ?

No / Yes

Are there any other people, other than your partner, living in your household who are aged 18 or over ?

No / Yes

Have you applied to the courts for maintenance and been told to apply to the Child Support Agency ?

No / Yes

h Do you and your partner, who lives with you now, have any children of this relationship ?

No / Yes

Do any of these children live with you and your partner ?

No / Yes

Children who live with you - child 1 see help notes pages 6 and 7

page 3

- Give details of all children under 19 years of age who live with you, not just the children you are applying to get child support maintenance for.

This child's full name
Please put their surname last.

National Insurance number if the child is over 16

Mother's full name

Date of birth / /

Sex Male ☐ Female ☐

Father's full name

Are you applying for child support maintenance for this child?
No ☐
Yes ☐

Has any other person received child support maintenance for this child in the last 8 weeks?
No ☐
Yes ☐ Who was this paid to?

Is Child Benefit paid for this child?
No ☐
Yes ☐ If this is paid at the higher amount, please tick this box ☐

Is this child in full-time education?
No ☐
Yes ☐

Is or has this child ever been married?
No ☐
Yes ☐

Is this child registered blind?
No ☐
Yes ☐

Is Disability Living Allowance or Attendance Allowance paid for this child?
No ☐
Yes ☐

Does this child stay with someone else for part of the time?
No ☐
Yes ☐ Who do they stay with? How often do they stay with them?

Is this child in Local Authority care for part of the time?
No ☐
Yes ☐ We will contact you about this.

Children who stay with you continued - child 2 see help notes pages 6 and 7   page 4

h This child's full name
Please put their surname last.

Date of birth   /   /

h National Insurance number
If the child is over 16

Sex   Male ☐   Female ☐

h Mother's full name

Father's
full name

h Are you applying for
child support maintenance
for this child ?

No ☐
Yes ☐

Has any other person received child
support maintenance for this child in
the last 8 weeks ?

No ☐
Yes ☐   Who was this
         paid to ?

h Is Child Benefit paid for this child ?

No ☐
Yes ☐   If this is paid at the higher amount, please tick this box ☐

Is this child in full-time education ?

No ☐
Yes ☐

Is or has this child ever been married ?

No ☐
Yes ☐

h Is this child registered blind ?

No ☐
Yes ☐

h Is Disability Living Allowance or
Attendance Allowance paid for this
child ?

No ☐
Yes ☐

h Does this child stay with someone
else for part of the time ?

No ☐
Yes ☐   Who do they
         stay with ?

How often do they stay
with them ?

h Is this child in Local Authority care for
part of the time ?

No ☐
Yes ☐   We will contact you about this.

Children who live with you continued - child 3 see help notes pages 6 and 7

page 5

This child's full name
Please put their surname last.

National Insurance number
if the child is over 16

Mother's full name

Date of birth   /   /

Sex   Male ☐   Female ☐

Father's
full name

Are you applying for
child support maintenance
for this child ?

No ☐
Yes ☐

Has any other person received child
support maintenance for this child in
the last 8 weeks ?

No ☐
Yes ☐   Who was this
        paid to ?

Is Child Benefit paid for this child ?

No ☐
Yes ☐   If this is paid at the higher amount, please tick this box ☐

Is this child in full-time education ?

No ☐
Yes ☐

Is or has this child ever been married ?

No ☐
Yes ☐

Is this child registered blind ?

No ☐
Yes ☐

Is Disability Living Allowance or
Attendance Allowance paid for this
child ?

No ☐
Yes ☐

Does this child stay with someone
else for part of the time ?

No ☐
Yes ☐   Who do they
        stay with ?

        How often do they stay
        with them ?

Is this child in Local Authority care for
part of the time ?

No ☐
Yes ☐   We will contact you about this.

Children who live with you continued – child 4   see help notes pages 6 and 7   page 6

This child's full name
Please put their surname last.

Date of birth   / /

National Insurance number
if the child is over 16

Sex   Male ☐   Female ☐

Mother's full name

Father's full name

Are you applying for child support maintenance for this child ?
☐ No
☐ Yes

Has any other person received child support maintenance for this child in the last 8 weeks ?
☐ No
☐ Yes   Who was this paid to ?

Is Child Benefit paid for this child ?
☐ No
☐ Yes   If this is paid at the higher amount, please tick this box ☐

Is this child in full-time education ?
☐ No
☐ Yes

Is or has this child ever been married ?
☐ No
☐ Yes

Is this child registered blind ?
☐ No
☐ Yes

Is Disability Living Allowance or Attendance Allowance paid for this child ?
☐ No
☐ Yes

Does this child stay with someone else for part of the time ?
☐ No
☐ Yes   Who do they stay with ?   How often do they stay with them ?

Is this child in Local Authority care for part of the time ?
☐ No
☐ Yes   We will contact you about this

Do you have any other children under 19 years of age who normally live with you?
☐ No
☐ Yes   We will send you a form to give details of the other children

Absent parent's details see help notes pages 8 and 9

page 7

- For a full explanation of **Absent parent** and **Other absent parent** please read the Help Notes.
  If you are unable or unwilling to give us **Absent parent** details, please see Help Notes **page 8.**

h Are you applying to get child support maintenance from more than 2 absent parents ?

No ☐
Yes ☐ Give details of 2 of the absent parents below. We will contact you for the other absent parent's details.

	▶ Absent parent	Other absent parent - if there is one

h Full name
Please put their surname last.

Any other names they are known by or have been known by

Sex

Male ☐ Female ☐   Male ☐ Female ☐

Date of birth or age

/ / years   / / years

National Insurance (NI) number
if you know it

Letters ☐ Numbers ☐☐☐☐☐☐ Letter ☐

Letters ☐ Numbers ☐☐☐☐☐☐ Letter ☐

Address
This could be the present or last known address.

Postcode ☐

Postcode ☐

Please tick if this is their

present address ☐ last known address ☐

present address ☐ last known address ☐

Telephone number

( )

( )

Please tell us the first names of all the children you are applying to get child support maintenance for from this absent parent, even if you have not been able to tell us about all of them on **pages 3 to 6**

Is the absent parent aware of the existence of all these children ?

No ☐
Yes ☐

Absent parent's details see help notes page 8 and 9

page 8

	Absent parent	Other absent parent - if there is one
h Does the absent parent work for an employer ?	No ☐ Yes ☐	No ☐ Yes ☐
What is their employer's name and address ?		
	Postcode	Postcode
Employer's telephone number	( )	( )
Work number, department or job title		
h Is the absent parent self-employed ?	No ☐ Yes ☐	No ☐ Yes ☐
What is the name and address of their business ?		
	Postcode	Postcode
Their business telephone number	( )	( )
What type of business is this ?		
h Is the absent parent unemployed ?	No ☐ Yes ☐	No ☐ Yes ☐
h Is the absent parent claiming any Social Security benefits ? If you are not sure, please tell us which benefit you think they may be getting.	No ☐ Yes ☐ Which benefits are they getting ?	No ☐ Yes ☐ Which benefits are they getting ?

● Please give us any other information that may help us to get in touch with the absent parent on **page 31**.

page 9

Existing maintenance payments see help notes page 10

	Absent parent	Other absent parent - if there is one
Do you have a court order for the payment of maintenance by the absent parent for the children ?	No ☐ Yes ☐	No ☐ Yes ☐
ⓗ Does this court order cover all of the children you are applying to get child support maintenance for ?	No ☐ Yes ☐ Please send us the court order or a certified copy.	No ☐ Yes ☐ Please send us the court order or a certified copy.
Do you have any other existing arrangement with the absent parent to pay you maintenance for the children ? This could be a voluntary or informal arrangement.	No ☐ Yes ☐	No ☐ Yes ☐
ⓗ Does this arrangement cover all the children you are applying to get child support maintenance for ?	No ☐ Yes ☐	No ☐ Yes ☐
When was this arrangement made ?	/ /	/ /
Total amount	£ every	£ every
	Please send us the agreement or confirmation of this arrangement.	Please send us the agreement or confirmation of this arrangement.

Child Support Agency services see help notes page 11

ⓗ **Do you wish to use the Child Support Agency collection service ?**

Fees are chargeable for both the assessment service and the collection service.

Please see the Help Notes **page 11** for further details about these services, fees which will be charged and details about those people who may not have to pay the fees.

No ☐ Yes ☐

Payment of child support maintenance   see help notes pages 12 and 13   page 10

h Please give details of your bank or building society account, if you have one, into which automated credit transfers can be made.

Bank/building society

Branch address

Postcode

Type of account

Account number

Sort code number

Absent parent

h Do you have any objections to payment being sent direct to you by the absent parent?

No ☐

Yes ☐   Please tell us why

h How would you prefer to be paid?

Direct from the absent parent by

☐ standing order to your bank or building society account

☐ or cheque - sent to your address

☐ or postal order - sent to your address

Payment through the Child Support Agency by

☐ automated credit transfers to a suitable bank account

☐ or girocheque - sent to your home address

How often would you prefer to be paid?

Weekly ☐   Monthly ☐

Other ☐   Please say how often

Name and address of post office you would use if payment was made by a girocheque

Postcode

h For postal security reasons, please tick the box that applies to you

own letter box ☐   shared letter box ☐

Other absent parent - if there is one

No ☐

Yes ☐   Please tell us why

Direct from the absent parent by

☐ standing order to your bank or building society account

☐ or cheque - sent to your address

☐ or postal order - sent to your address

Payment through the Child Support Agency by

☐ automated credit transfers to a suitable bank account

☐ or girocheque - sent to your home address

income details

Income details

Are you, or your partner who lives with you now, getting Income Support ?

No ☐   **Please continue to fill in the rest of this form.**

Yes ☐   **Please go to Further Information on page 31. Remember to sign the Declaration on page 33.**

Are you the natural or adoptive parent of any of the children you are applying to get child support maintenance for ?

No ☐   **Please go to Further Information on page 31. Remember to sign the Declaration on page 33.**

Yes ☐   **Please continue to fill in the rest of this form.**

Student income   see help notes page 14

Are you a student ?

No ☐
Yes ☐   Please go to **page 12**.

Do you get a grant from an education authority ?

No ☐
Yes ☐   Please send us the award notice.

Do you get any parental contribution towards a grant ?

No ☐
Yes ☐   Please send us the award notice.

Do you have a student loan ?

No ☐
Yes ☐   Please send us details.

Do you get any other income in addition to your grant ?

No ☐
Yes ☐

Employment details see help notes pages 14 and 15

page 12

Are you self-employed ?

No ☐
Yes ☐

What is your status as a self-employed person ?

childminder ☐ sole trader ☐ sub-contractor ☐ partner in a business ☐

other ☐ Please specify _____

We will contact you for further information about your self-employment.

Do you work for an employer ?
Tick **Yes**, if you are on Youth Training.

No ☐
Yes ☐

Do you work for more than one employer ?

No ☐
Yes ☐ Please tell us about your main job below.
We will contact you about your other job.

Employer's name and address

Postcode

Employer's telephone number ( )

Work number, department or job title

How often are you paid ? every

How much is your gross pay before any deductions are made for things like Income Tax and National Insurance ? Do not include any expenses, bonuses or commission.

£

We need to see your wage slips. Please see the Help Notes for the number of wage slips you should send with this form.

Is the gross amount shown on the wage slips you are sending us different from your normal gross pay ?

No ☐
Yes ☐ Please send us some extra wage slips which show your normal gross pay.

Employment details continued see help notes pages 15 and 16 page 13

h Did you get any bonus or commission paid in the last 52 weeks?

No ☐
Yes ☐

When was this paid? / /

How much did you get? £ _____ every _____

Was this included on the wage slips you are sending us?

No ☐ Please send us confirmation of the amount you got.
Yes ☐

h Do you get any expenses?

No ☐
Yes ☐

What are these expenses for?

Are these expenses included on the wage slips you are sending us?

No ☐ Please send us confirmation of the amount you get.
Yes ☐

Pensions see help notes page 16

h Do you pay into or contribute to a
- personal pension scheme
- company pension scheme
- occupational pension scheme?

No ☐ Please go to page 14.
Yes ☐

Scheme 1	Scheme 2	Scheme 3

Name of scheme

Total amount paid £ _____ every _____ | £ _____ every _____ | £ _____ every _____

Is this deducted from your wages?

Scheme 1: No ☐ Please send us confirmation of the amount you pay. / Yes ☐

Scheme 2: No ☐ Please send us confirmation of the amount you pay. / Yes ☐

Scheme 3: No ☐ Please send us confirmation of the amount you pay. / Yes ☐

Income from benefits see help notes pages 16 and 17

h **Do you, or any of the children who live with you, get any benefits ?**
Please tell us about all the benefits you get except for Child Benefit, Housing Benefit and Council Tax Benefit.

No ☐   Please go to **page 15**.

Yes ☐

Benefit 1

Name of benefit

Name of person benefit is paid to

h Name of person benefit is paid for

Amount paid   £   every

h Name of office which pays the benefit

Benefit 2

£   every

Benefit 3

£   every

Benefit 4

Name of benefit

Name of person benefit is paid to

h Name of person benefit is paid for

Amount paid   £   every

h Name of office which pays the benefit

Benefit 5

£   every

Benefit 6

£   every

Do you, or any of the children who live with you, have any other benefits ?

No ☐

Yes ☐   We will contact you about this.

Income from maintenance or capital – for you see help notes pages 17 and 18   page 15

● **Do you get any income from maintenance, savings, capital or investments for yourself ?**

No ☐   Please go to **page 16**.

Yes ☐

● **Do you get any maintenance for yourself as a result of a court order ?**

No ☐

Yes ☐

Name of the person paying maintenance ☐

Name of court and reference number ☐

Date of court order ☐ / / ☐

Total amount you got in the last 13 weeks £ ☐

● If you have started to get this maintenance within the last 13 weeks, what date was it paid from ? ☐ / / ☐

● **Do you get any other payments from a maintenance arrangement for yourself ?**
This could be a voluntary or informal arrangement.

No ☐

Yes ☐

Name of the person who is making the payment ☐

Total amount you got in the last 13 weeks £ ☐

● If you have started to get this money within the last 13 weeks, what date was it paid from ? ☐ / / ☐

Did you get any income from your savings, capital or investments in the last 52 weeks ?

No ☐

Yes ☐

Total amount you got in the last 52 weeks ? £ ☐

● Did any part of this income come from money you got as a result of a divorce or separation ?

No ☐

Yes ☐

How much of this income came from the lump sum settlement ? £ ☐

When was the settlement made ? ☐ / / ☐

If the settlement money is set aside for a special use, please tell us what this is. ☐

Income from maintenance or capital for child 1   see help notes pages 19 and 20   page 16

- Please give details of any income from maintenance, savings, capital or investments for all the children who live with you.

Do any of the children who live with you get any income from maintenance, savings, capital or investments for themselves?

No ☐   Please go to **page 20**.
Yes ☐

This child's full name

Is there any maintenance in payment as a result of a court order for this child?

No ☐
Yes ☐

Name of court and reference number

Date of court order   /   /

Total amount paid in the last 13 weeks   £

If payment of this maintenance started within the last 13 weeks, what date was it paid from?   /   /

Are there any other payments from a maintenance arrangement for this child?
This could be a voluntary or informal arrangement.

No ☐
Yes ☐

Total amount paid in the last 13 weeks   £

If payment started within the last 13 weeks, what date was it paid from?   /   /

Has there been any income from savings, capital or investments in the last 52 weeks for this child?

No ☐
Yes ☐

Total amount paid in the last 52 weeks   £

Income from maintenance or capital for child 2 see help notes pages 19 and 20 page 17

This child's full name

Is there any maintenance in payment as a result of a court order for this child ?

No ☐
Yes ☐

Name of court and reference number

Date of court order   /   /

Total amount paid in the last 13 weeks   £

If payment of this maintenance started within the last 13 weeks, what date was it paid from ?   /   /

Are there any other payments from a maintenance arrangement for this child ?
This could be a voluntary or informal arrangement.

No ☐
Yes ☐

Total amount paid in the last 13 weeks   £

If payment started within the last 13 weeks, what date was it paid from ?   /   /

Has there been any income from savings, capital or investments in the last 52 weeks for this child ?

No ☐
Yes ☐

Total amount paid in the last 52 weeks   £

Income from maintenance or capital for child 3   see help notes pages 19 and 20   page 18

This child's full name

h **Is there any maintenance in payment as a result of a court order for this child ?**

- [ ] No
- [ ] Yes

Name of court and reference number

Date of court order   /   /

Total amount paid in the last 13 weeks   £

h If payment of this maintenance started within the last 13 weeks, what date was it paid from ?   /   /

h **Are there any other payments from a maintenance arrangement for this child ?**
This could be a voluntary or informal arrangement.

- [ ] No
- [ ] Yes

Total amount paid in the last 13 weeks   £

h If payment started within the last 13 weeks, what date was it paid from ?   /   /

Has there been any income from savings, capital or investments in the last 52 weeks for this child ?

- [ ] No
- [ ] Yes

Total amount paid in the last 52 weeks   £

Income from maintenance or capital for child 4 see help notes pages 19 and 20 page 19

This child's full name

h Is there any maintenance in payment as a result of a court order for this child ?

No ☐
Yes ☐

Name of court and reference number

Date of court order   /   /

Total amount paid in the last 13 weeks   £

h If payment of this maintenance started within the last 13 weeks, what date was it paid from ?   /   /

h Are there any other payments from a maintenance arrangement for this child ?
This could be a voluntary or informal arrangement.

No ☐
Yes ☐

Total amount paid in the last 13 weeks   £

h If payment started within the last 13 weeks, what date was it paid from ?   /   /

Has there been any income from savings, capital or investments in the last 52 weeks for this child ?

No ☐
Yes ☐

Total amount paid in the last 52 weeks   £

Income from rent see help notes page 20

page 20

h Do you get any income from renting out accommodation in your home or another property that you own ?

No ☐   Please go to **page 21**.

Yes ☐

	Tenant 1	Tenant 2	Tenant 3
Tenant's name			

h Do they pay the same amount of rent each week ?

	Tenant 1	Tenant 2	Tenant 3
	No ☐ We will contact you about this.	No ☐ We will contact you about this.	No ☐ We will contact you about this.
	Yes ☐ How much do they pay you ?	Yes ☐ How much do they pay you ?	Yes ☐ How much do they pay you ?
	£	£	£

Does the rent include the cost of heating ?

	Tenant 1	Tenant 2	Tenant 3
	No ☐	No ☐	No ☐
	Yes ☐	Yes ☐	Yes ☐

Do you provide this accommodation in your own home ?

	Tenant 1	Tenant 2	Tenant 3
	No ☐	No ☐	No ☐
	Yes ☐	Yes ☐	Yes ☐

h Do you provide this accommodation in another property that you own ?

	Tenant 1	Tenant 2	Tenant 3
	No ☐	No ☐	No ☐
	Yes ☐ We will contact you about this.	Yes ☐ We will contact you about this.	Yes ☐ We will contact you about this.

Do you have any other tenants ?

No ☐

Yes ☐   We will contact you about this.

Income from board and lodging see help notes pages 20 and 21

page 21

h Do you get any income from providing board and lodging in your own home or another property that you own ?

No ☐ Please go to **page 22**.
Yes ☐

Lodger's name

	Lodger 1	Lodger 2	Lodger 3
	[_____]	[_____]	[_____]

h Do they pay the same amount for board and lodging each week ?

	Lodger 1	Lodger 2	Lodger 3
No	☐ We will contact you about this.	☐ We will contact you about this.	☐ We will contact you about this.
Yes	☐ How much do they pay you ?	☐ How much do they pay you ?	☐ How much do they pay you ?
	£ [_____]	£ [_____]	£ [_____]

Do you provide board and lodging in your own home ?

No	☐	☐	☐
Yes	☐	☐	☐

h Do you provide board and lodging in another property that you own ?

No	☐	☐	☐
Yes	☐ We will contact you about this.	☐ We will contact you about this.	☐ We will contact you about this.

Do you have any other lodgers ?

No ☐
Yes ☐ We will contact you about this.

page 22

Other income see help notes page 21

h **Did you, or any of the children who live with you, get any other income in the last 26 weeks ?**

No ☐ Please go to **page 23**.

Yes ☐

Other income 1

Total amount paid in the last 26 weeks £ ☐

Name of the person this was paid to ☐

Name of the person this was paid for ☐

What was this income ? ☐

If this income started to be paid in the last 26 weeks, what date was it paid from ? ☐ / /

Other income 2

Total amount paid in the last 26 weeks £ ☐

Name of the person this was paid to ☐

Name of the person this was paid for ☐

What was this income ? ☐

If this income started to be paid in the last 26 weeks, what date was it paid from ? ☐ / /

Other income 3

Total amount paid in the last 26 weeks £ ☐

Name of the person this was paid to ☐

Name of the person this was paid for ☐

What was this income ? ☐

If this income started to be paid in the last 26 weeks, what date was it paid from ? ☐ / /

Other income 4

Total amount paid in the last 26 weeks £ ☐

Name of the person this was paid to ☐

Name of the person this was paid for ☐

What was this income ? ☐

If this income started to be paid in the last 26 weeks, what date was it paid from ? ☐ / /

housing details

Housing details

Do you and your partner who lives with you now, live with relatives or friends as part of their family ?

No ☐
Yes ☐ Please go to **page 31**.

Paying rent see help notes page 22

h Do you, or your partner who lives with you now, rent the property you live in ?

No ☐ Please go to **page 24**.
Yes ☐

h Do you or your partner get any Housing Benefit ?

No ☐
Yes ☐

Have you or your partner applied for Housing Benefit but have not been told the result of the claim ?

No ☐
Yes ☐

How much is the rent before deducting any Housing Benefit ?

£ ☐ Please send us the rent book or rent agreement.

h How much eligible rent has been allowed by the Local Authority when they worked out the Housing Benefit ?

£ ☐ Please send us the Housing Benefit award notice, if you have one.

How much is the rent after deducting any Housing Benefit ?

£ ☐ every ☐

h Does the rent include an amount for services ?

No ☐
Yes ☐ How much is included ?

£ ☐

What services are included ?

☐

Please send us the rent agreement which shows the amount of charges included for services.

Do you and your partner share the tenancy with someone else ?

No ☐
Yes ☐ Please send us the agreement.

Paying for board and lodging see help notes page 23

h **Do you, or your partner who lives with you now, pay for board and lodging where you live ?**

No ☐ Please go to **page 25**.

Yes ☐

h Do you or your partner get any Housing Benefit ?

No ☐

Yes ☐

Have you or your partner applied for Housing Benefit but have not been told the result of your claim ?

No ☐

Yes ☐

How much is the board and lodging charge before deducting any Housing Benefit ?

£ [ ] Please send us some confirmation of this charge.

h How much eligible board and lodging charge has been allowed by the Local Authority when they worked out the Housing Benefit ?

£ [ ] Please send us the Housing Benefit award notice, if you have one.

How much is the board and lodging charge after deducting any Housing Benefit ?

£ [ ] every [ ]

Does the board and lodging charge include the cost of meals ?

No ☐

Yes ☐ How many meals does it include per week ?

Breakfasts [ ]

Lunches [ ]

Evening meals [ ]

h Does the board and lodging charge include an amount for services ?

No ☐

Yes ☐ How much is included ?

£ [3]

What services are included ?

[ ]

Please send us the agreement which shows the amount of charges included for services.

Paying for your own home see help notes page 24

h Do you, or your partner who lives with you now, own the property you live in ?

No ☐
Yes ☐ Please go to **page 26.**

h Do you or your partner have a mortgage or home loan on the property you live in ?

No ☐
Yes ☐

h Do you or your partner have a shared mortgage or home loan with someone else for the property you live in ?

No ☐
Yes ☐ Who is it shared with ?

_____

What proportion do you or your partner pay ?

_____

h Is any part of the property you and your partner live in used for non-residential or business purposes ?

No ☐
Yes ☐ We will contact you about this.

Do you or your partner pay any ground rent, or in Scotland feu duty ?

No ☐
Yes ☐ How much is the charge ?

£ _____ every _____

Please send us confirmation of this amount.

h Do you or your partner pay any service charges for the property ?

No ☐
Yes ☐ How much are the charges ?

£ _____ every _____

What services are included ?

_____

Please send us the agreement which shows the amount of charges for these services.

Mortgage or home loan details see help notes pages 25 to 27

h **Do you, or your partner who lives with you now, have a mortgage or home loan exclusively for the purchase of the property you are living in ?**

No ☐　Please go to **page 27.**

Yes ☐

- We will need to see confirmation of the information we ask for below. We will require the original mortgage offer, and the latest statement from the lender.

- If you or your partner are unable to answer the questions below or provide confirmation of the information we ask for, you can send **page 35** at the back of this form to the lender for them to fill in. They may charge you for this service. For joint or shared mortgages the lender may require authority from all the mortgagees.

- If you or your partner have an endowment mortgage the lender may not be able to give details of the endowment premium. You may have to go to the assurance company for this information.

- If you or your partner are asking the lender to provide details of the mortgage or home loan, please tick this box ☐

Name of lender that you or your partner have the mortgage or home loan with

[ ]

Original amount of mortgage or home loan when the property was bought

£ [ ]

What date was the original mortgage or home loan taken out ?

[ ] / [ ] / [ ]

h **How much is shown as outstanding on the last statement, excluding arrears ?**

£ [ ]

How much is the monthly interest, excluding property insurance ?

£ [ ]

h **Do you or your partner have a**
- **repayment mortgage**
- **or repayment home loan ?**

No ☐
Yes ☐

Total monthly capital repayments, excluding arrears

£ [ ]

h **Do you or your partner have an**
- **endowment mortgage**
- **or endowment home loan ?**

No ☐
Yes ☐

Total monthly endowment premium, excluding arrears

£ [ ]

Please send us the annual statement.

What type of endowment policy do you or your partner have ?

Term assurance ☐　　Low cost endowment ☐

Full cost (with profit) endowment ☐　　Other ☐ Please specify

[ ]

What is the name of the assurance company ?

[ ]

Second mortgage or loan details see help notes pages 27 to 29

h **Do you, or your partner who lives with you now, have a second mortgage or loan for major repairs or improvements to the property you are living in ?**

No ☐ Please go to **page 28**.

Yes ☐

- We will need to see confirmation of the information we ask for below. We will require the second mortgage or loan offer, and the latest statement from the lender.
- If you or your partner are unable to answer the questions below or provide confirmation of the information we ask for, you can send **page 35** at the back of this form to the lender for them to fill in. They may charge you for this service. For joint or shared mortgages the lender may require authority from all the mortgagees.

- If you or your partner have an endowment mortgage or endowment loan, the lender may not be able to give details of the endowment premium. You may have to go to the assurance company for this information.
- If the second mortgage or loan is with a different lender, and you want them to provide confirmation of the information we ask below, get in touch with the office that sent you this form. They will send you a form for each lender.
- If you or your partner are asking the lender to provide details of the second mortgage or home loan, please tick this box ☐

Name of lender that you or your partner have the second mortgage or loan with

_____

What was the second mortgage or loan for ?

_____

Original amount of second mortgage or loan

£ _____

What date was the second mortgage or loan taken out ?

_____ / _____ / _____

How much is the monthly interest, excluding property insurance ?

£ _____

h Do you or your partner have a
- repayment mortgage
- or repayment loan ?

No ☐

Yes ☐

Total monthly capital repayments, excluding arrears

£ _____

h Do you or your partner have an
- endowment mortgage
- or endowment loan ?

No ☐

Yes ☐

Total monthly endowment premium, excluding arrears

£ _____

Please send us the annual statement.

What type of endowment policy do you or your partner have ?

Term assurance ☐   Low cost endowment ☐

Full cost (with profit) endowment ☐   Other ☐ Please specify

_____

What is the name of the assurance company ?

_____

Do you or your partner have any other mortgages or loans on the property you are living in?

No ☐

Yes ☐   We will contact you about this

page 28

Living in residential accommodation see help notes page 29

h Do you, or your partner who lives with you now, live in residential accommodation, a residential care home or nursing home at present ?

No ☐ Please go to **page 29**.

Yes ☐ We will contact you about this.

page 29

Other people in your household see help notes pages 29 to 31

h Are there any other people aged 18 or over who normally live in your household that you have not already mentioned in this form?

No ☐ Please go to Further Information on **page 31**.

Yes ☐ Please tell us about them. You do not have to give their full name.

	Person 1	Person 2
This person's name		
h Are they on Youth Training?	No ☐ Yes ☐	No ☐ Yes ☐
h Are they a student?	No ☐ Yes ☐	No ☐ Yes ☐
Are they under 25 years of age and getting Income Support?	No ☐ Yes ☐	No ☐ Yes ☐
Are they in prison at present?	No ☐ Yes ☐	No ☐ Yes ☐
h Are they in hospital at present?	No ☐ Yes ☐	No ☐ Yes ☐
Have they been there for more than 6 weeks?	No ☐ Yes ☐	No ☐ Yes ☐
h Do they work for more than 16 hours a week?	No ☐ Yes ☐	No ☐ Yes ☐
What is their average gross weekly wage?	£ ☐	£ ☐
h Do they get any other type of income?	No ☐ Yes ☐	No ☐ Yes ☐
What is this income?		
What is their average gross weekly income?	£ ☐	£ ☐

Other people in your household continued   see help notes pages 29 to 31

	Person 3	Person 4
This person's name		
Are they on Youth Training ?	No ☐ Yes ☐	No ☐ Yes ☐
h Are they a student ?	No ☐ Yes ☐	No ☐ Yes ☐
Are they under 25 years of age and getting Income Support ?	No ☐ Yes ☐	No ☐ Yes ☐
Are they in prison at present ?	No ☐ Yes ☐	No ☐ Yes ☐
h Are they in hospital at present ?	No ☐ Yes ☐	No ☐ Yes ☐
	Have they been there for more than 6 weeks ? No ☐ Yes ☐	Have they been there for more than 6 weeks ? No ☐ Yes ☐
h Do they work for more than 16 hours a week ?	No ☐ Yes ☐	No ☐ Yes ☐
	What is their average gross weekly wage ? £ [ ]	What is their average gross weekly wage ? £ [ ]
h Do they get any other type of income ?	No ☐ Yes ☐	No ☐ Yes ☐
	What is this income ?	What is this income ?
	What is their average gross weekly income ? £ [ ]	What is their average gross weekly income ? £ [ ]

Are any of the people you have told us about married to each other or living together as if they are married ?   No ☐   Yes ☐

[ ] is the partner of [ ]

Are there any other people aged 18 or over who normally live in your household ?   No ☐   Yes ☐   We will contact you about this

other details

Further information see help notes page 32

page 31

h Please use this part of the form to give us any
other information which you think might be useful

page 32

Checklist see help notes page 32

h **Please tick the relevant boxes to show which documents you are sending with this form**

You should send the original documents.
They will be returned to you.

Document		Reference
Court order or certified copy	☐	page 9
Existing maintenance arrangement or confirmation of arrangement	☐	page 9
Student grant notice of award	☐	page 11
Wage slips	☐	page 12
Confirmation of bonus or commission	☐	page 13
Confirmation of expenses	☐	page 13
Confirmation of pension contributions	☐	page 13
Rent book or agreement	☐	page 23
Housing Benefit award notice	☐	pages 23 and 24
Confirmation of rent service charges	☐	page 23
Shared tenancy agreement	☐	page 23
Confirmation of board and lodging charge	☐	page 24
Confirmation of board and lodging service charge	☐	page 24
Confirmation of ground rent or feu duty	☐	page 25
Confirmation of service charges	☐	page 25
Confirmation of mortgage or home loan details - original mortgage offer - latest mortgage statement - endowment policy annual statement	☐	page 26 and 27
Other Please tell us what else you are sending	☐	

Declaration see help notes page 33

- I declare that the information I have given on this form is correct and complete.
- I authorise the Secretary of State to act on my behalf, if I am required to give this authorisation, in accordance with the Child Support Act.
- I have read the introductory leaflet and I understand that fees may be chargeable for Child Support Agency services.

Client's signature

Date / /

- **Any information given by you will not be disclosed to any unauthorised persons.**
- **Send this form and anything else we have asked for back to us. Use the envelope we sent you. It does not need a stamp.**

Representative details see help notes page 34

- Only complete this part of the form if you are acting as a representative for the client.

What is your status ?

Acting under a power of attorney ☐   Receiver under Section 99 of the Mental Health Act 1983 ☐

Scottish Mental Health Custodian ☐   Mental Health appointee ☐

Please fill in your details below. Please note that all correspondence and any payments will be sent to you instead of the client. The client does not need to sign the client's authority below. Please send us confirmation of your authority to act for the client.

Solicitor ☐   Lawyer ☐   Other representative - CAB, Welfare rights etc. ☐

Please fill in your details below. Payments will be sent to the client.
Please note that if you want all other correspondence to be sent to you instead of the client, the client should sign the client's authority below.

Surname

Mr / Mrs / Miss / Ms   Other names

Address

Postcode

Daytime telephone number ( )   Evening telephone number ( )

Client's authority

I agree to my representative filling in this form for me and for all correspondence to be sent to them instead of me.

Client's signature

page 34

For Child Support Agency use

● I have read back to the client the entries I made on this form, based on the information supplied by the client. The client has agreed that they are correct.

Interviewing officer's signature

Client's signature

Date   /   /

Local office name and number

Routeing reference number

AU / RFA number

NI number

mortgage details

child support agency
an executive agency of the Department of Social Security

Mortgage or home loan details

What you should do

- Please fill in **Part A** if you want the lender to provide confirmation or original information about your mortgage or home loan.

- Use one form for each lender. If you get a mortgage or home loan from more than one lender, get in touch with the office that sent you this form. They will send you a form for each lender.

- Then detach this page and send it to the lender.

- For joint or shared mortgages, the lender may require authority from all the mortgagees.

To the lender

- Can you please fill in **Part B** with details of the the mortgage or home loan, for the person named in **Part A**.

- If the mortgagee has more than two mortgages or home loans with your company, please copy this form.

- Please return the form in the envelope provided. If no envelope is provided please return this to the Child Support Agency. The address is given below.

Part A Your details

Full name

Date of birth

/ /

National Insurance (NI) number

Letters   Numbers   Letter

Address this form should be returned to
You will find this on the letter that came with this form.

Child Support Agency

Postcode

Mortgagee's full name
If the mortgage or home loan is in joint names, give both names.

Roll or account number

Address of the property on which the money was borrowed

Postcode

- I agree to the information requested in Part B being given to the Child Support Agency.

Mortgagee's signature

Date

/ /

Part B to be filled in by the lender

	main mortgage or home loan	additional mortgage or loan

Loan reference number

Type of mortgage or loan

What was it for?
eg home purchase or home improvements.

What date was the original mortgage
or home loan taken out ?

Original amount borrowed

Amount outstanding, excluding arrears

Monthly interest payment
excluding property insurance

Monthly capital repayments

Endowment mortgage only
Type of endowment policy, if known

Name of assurance company, if known

Monthly endowment premium, if known

● I certify that the information in **Part B** of this form is correct and
complete to the best of my knowledge and belief.

Signature

Date

Name

Position

Telephone number ( )

Business stamp

● Please send this form to the Child Support Agency office shown in **Part A.**

Index

References are to paragraph numbers